MODERN
WOMEN
A DOCUMENTARY HISTORY

MODERN AMERICAN WOMEN

A DOCUMENTARY HISTORY

Susan Ware
Radcliffe College

THE MCGRAW-HILL COMPANIES, INC.

New York   St. Louis   San Francisco   Auckland   Bogotá
Caracas   Lisbon   London   Madrid   Mexico City   Milan
Montreal   New Delhi   San Juan   Singapore   Sydney   Tokyo   Toronto

McGraw-Hill

A Division of The McGraw·Hill Companies

This book was set in Times Roman by ComCom, Inc.
The editors were Lyn Uhl, Monica Freedman, and Elaine Rosenberg;
the production supervisor was Richard A. Ausburn.
The cover was designed by Christopher Brady.
The photo editor was Anne Manning.
Project supervision was done by Hockett Editorial Service.
R. R. Donnelley & Sons Company was printer and binder.

MODERN AMERICAN WOMEN

A Documentary History

This book was printed on acid-free paper.

1 2 3 4 5 6 7 8 9 0   DOC DOC   909876

ISBN 0-07-071527-0

Library of Congress Cataloging-in-Publication Data

Modern American women : a documentary history / [compiled by] Susan
  Ware. — [2nd ed.]
     p.   cm.
  Includes bibliographical references.
  ISBN 0-07-071527-0
  1. Women—United States—History—20th century—Sources.
  2. Feminism—United States—History—20th century—Sources.
  3. Women reformers—United States—History—Sources.   I. Ware,
  Susan (date)
  HQ1410.M63   1997
  305.4'0973—dc20   96-22486

CONTENTS

ACKNOWLEDGMENTS

Preparing a second edition of this anthology has given me the chance to renew old acquaintances and make new friends as I decided which selections to keep and which to add. Just reviewing the new scholarship that has appeared since the first edition in 1989 confirms the vitality of women's history, a field of which I am proud to be a part.

Nancy Woloch has demonstrated unwavering belief in our linked anthologies, and I would like to thank her for her friendship, support, and good humor. Working together on our respective revisions prefigures what I hope will be more collaborative projects in the future. It is also a treat to be able to thank Amy Richter and Debra Michals of New York University for sharing suggestions of selections based on their own research. And I would like to acknowledge with gratitude the ongoing support of Joyce Antler, who has always been a big fan of this book and whose friendship means a great deal to me.

I am delighted that McGraw-Hill will be publishing this new edition, and I look forward to a long association with the College Division. Thanks to Lyn Uhl and Monica Freedman for their editorial support, and to Elaine Rosenberg for her cheerful help in the production process. Thanks especially to Wesley Hall, who handled the complicated permissions for the book with persistence and good humor. The final manuscript was also strengthened by the comments of the following reviewers: Sara Alpern, Texas A&M; Patricia Cohen, University of California, Santa Barbara; and Mary Hill, Bucknell University.

Finally, I would like to thank Radcliffe College, and especially the staff of the Schlesinger Library, for providing such a congenial setting for the study of women's history.

Susan Ware

INTRODUCTION

How does the world look through women's eyes? How have different women viewed that world? How does our perception of history change when women are placed at its center rather than on the margins? This anthology provides a woman-centered view of modern America. With only two exceptions (Supreme Court decisions on protective legislation and abortion), every document was written by women about women. Alas, there were no women on the Supreme Court until 1981, or perhaps those documents too would have been a woman's work. In this book, history unfolds through the perspectives of the participants—women themselves—rather than through prescriptive literature designed to tell women what they ought to do and who they ought to be. When women tell their own stories, they emerge as actors and participants in a host of activities beyond home and family, providing strong evidence for the pioneer feminist historian Mary Beard's characterization of women as *force in history.*

In keeping with feminist scholarship and women's history methodology, no single female voice emerges from these documents, but rather a multiplicity of voices. There are intellectuals and housewives, seasoned political veterans and teenagers, radicals and antifeminists. Stories describe the despair of the unemployed in the 1930s and the anger of women on welfare in the 1960s, the exhilaration of learning to ride a bicycle in the 1890s and the thrill of experimenting with new feminist lifestyles in the 1920s. There are many women of courage in this anthology—settlement house leaders, civil rights activists, pioneer doctors, labor organizers, writers, and radicals, all of whom helped to shape the course of modern American history. There are also women whose courage was more private: women trying to feed their families during hard times, an anxious rural mother worrying that the doctor would not get there when her labor pains began, Japanese-American women coping with forced relocation during World War II, women living with disease or disabilities. The experiences of both the extraordinary women who shape public events and the ordinary women whose lives comprise the social history of the times find their places here.

This anthology is dedicated to documenting the diversity of American women's lives. There is much more to the story of American women in the twentieth century than the perspectives of the white, middle-class, urban, heterosexual women who have been its most visible actors. For every experience of a white woman, it is necessary to think how the lives of black women or Latinas or Native Americans might have been different, while also remembering the significant differences among minority women themselves. For every example from urban America, we need to recall the experiences of rural women, who were after all a majority until the 1920s and a significant minority every since. And it is vitally important to contrast the lives of married women with their unmarried sisters, especially those who chose to remain single as an expression of a different sexual or affectional preference.

Two methodological tools are useful for highlighting and interpreting an even further diversity in women's lives. The first is the *life cycle:* that is, looking at women's experiences over the entire course of their lives. Women who choose to marry and have children can still spend a majority of their adult years working outside the home—in other words, once a homemaker, not necessarily always a homemaker. Women born and raised on farms might move *el rancho al barrio*—from rural area to the city—only to return late in life to the rural communities where they grew up. This life-cycle approach has the potential to capture the cumulative effects of small changes over time. It also can demonstrate how women's lives are shaped by outside events at the same time they are changing from within.

The other useful tool for understanding twentieth-century women's history is a *generational approach.* At any given historical moment, several generations of women are participating in events and interacting among themselves. A generational approach is especially well suited to understanding the 1920s and the 1980s and 1990s, two periods in which younger women inherited the victories of earlier feminist activism without having to fight for the gains themselves. A generational approach dramatically increases the complexity of the story historians are trying to tell, because at any given moment women of different age groups may be undergoing very different experiences. In conjunction with attention to the life cycle and minority perspectives, a generational approach reminds us that a host of factors simultaneously shape women's lives—ranging from class, ethnic, or racial identification to sexual preference, age, and geographical location. There can be no such thing as a "typical American woman"; instead there are stories of a multitude of American women.

This anthology is divided into three parts, with its periodization designed to help structure and organize the past century of American women's history. Part One covers the period between 1890 and 1920, when women literally and figuratively left the nineteenth century behind and stepped into the modern era and into a period of reform that historians refer to as the Progressive era. Part Two traces women's lives in the postsuffrage era, situating their individual stories within periods of prosperity alternating with depression, world wars and their aftermaths, periods of conservatism and incipient political activism. Part Three focuses on the revival of feminism and its aftershocks, with 1963 chosen as a symbolic starting date because that year marked the publication of Betty Friedan's *The Feminine Mystique*. The new realities in women's lives are here to stay, although they continue to be the subject of ongoing public debate about their meaning and future.

The portrait that emerges from this collection of women's voices confirms the resourcefulness of American women and demonstrates their contributions to the shaping of the society at large. It captures women's hopes and aspirations for themselves, their families, and their communities, as well as their inevitable disappointments and setbacks. The history of the twentieth century, both its politics and everyday life, looks richer, fuller, and certainly more representative when the diverse stories of the nation's women occupy center stage. Here, then, is modern women's America.

MODERN AMERICAN WOMEN

A DOCUMENTARY HISTORY

PART ONE

Modern Women in the Making

1890–1920

CHAPTER 1

Visions of the New Woman

By the 1890s, a new woman had appeared on the American scene in education, athletics, reform, and the job market. One way to capture what was "new" about the new woman is to examine how she was dressed. Rather than encumbered in yards of material, heavy corsets, and petticoats like her mother and grandmother wore, the new woman was dressed comfortably in tailored suits or long dark skirts worn with simple blouses. Artist Charles Dana Gibson popularized this image of women with his magazine illustrations of "Gibson Girls." The new styles were more than just a change in fashion. Not only did these women look self-reliant, but they acted that way. Style changes allowed more freedom of movement, increased athleticism, and more physicality on the part of women who were no longer confined by corsets and hoopskirts. As such, the new style symbolized the freedom and opportunity available to the new woman of the 1890s.

The new woman was one product of the vast changes under way in American society due to the maturation of the American economy and the growing urban orientation of the country. The increase in opportunity for higher education for women in the late nineteenth century and the corresponding growth in professional careers provided avenues for gainful employment and a viable alternative to marriage. In many ways, the late nineteenth century was a golden age for single women: such women as settlement pioneer Jane Addams were widely revered for their contributions to public life. Approximately 10 percent of the cohort of women born between 1860 and 1880 remained single—one of the highest rates recorded. Choosing not to marry did not mean, however, giving up a fulfilling emotional life, for many of these new professional women chose to share their lives with other women in lifelong relationships.

In addition to these changes for single women, there were also important changes in the lives of married women, especially the white, middle-class homemakers who lived in urban areas. Technological changes began to free women from some of the hardest toil associated with housekeeping. Such improvements as central heating, electricity, indoor plumbing, and kitchen appliances lightened their chores; so too did the availability of store-bought goods and food, such as commercially baked bread or men's ready-to-wear clothing. The family was completing a long-term shift from a unit of production to one of consumption. In a related trend, as more families settled in urban areas rather than rural, the economic rewards of large families diminished. The birth rate had declined steadily throughout the nineteenth century, and by 1900, women were having an average of 3.5 children, half the level in 1800.

The lessened time that middle-class women devoted to housekeeping and child rearing helped pave the way for women's increased activism beyond the four walls of their homes. One of the most striking characteristics of American society by the 1890s was the proliferation of women's organizations. The key to understanding this development lies in the way that women extended the values they prized in their families and domestic sphere to the broader body politic. Historian Mary Beard described how this progression worked in a 1915 study of women's work in municipalities:

> Woman's historic function having been along the line of cleanliness, her instinct when she looks forth from her own clean windows is toward public cleanliness. Her indoor battle has been against the dirt that blew in from outside, against the dust and ashes of the streets, and the particles of germ-laden matter carried in from neglected refuse piles. Ultimately she begins to take an interest in that portion of municipal dusting and sweeping assigned to men: namely street cleaning.

This ideology is often called *municipal housekeeping.*

Historians usually refer to the period between 1890 and 1920 as the Progressive era. During this cycle of reform and activism, the United States began to confront the problems raised by its recent industrialization, the massive immigration under way, and the increasing concentration of population in urban areas. Although no one strand unifies Progressive era historiography, the period certainly looks different when women are included. Instead of just hearing about efficiency, regulation, scientific management, and experts (the dominant interpretations of men's participation), the women's perspective directs attention toward humanitarian and social reform: concern for child labor, unhealthy conditions in city neighborhoods, and long hours and low pay in factories or sweatshops. What had long been women's province through voluntary associations and charitable benevolence was increasingly defined as a proper scope for public policy.

Middle-class women, black and white, did not lack institutional or organizational bodies with which to influence public policy. Starting with the women's club movement in the post-Civil War period, women strove to fuse politics with their domestic ideals. Such an ideology also helped the final push for suffrage. The responsibilities that instruments of government increasingly took on for improving the social welfare of citizens testifies to women's impact. Women's activities also show how fluid and porous the supposed separation of the public and private spheres had become by the early twentieth century.

Many of these developments were limited to the members of the middle and upper classes who had the option of taking advantage of these new opportunities. Very few recent immigrants from Italy or Poland were sending their daughters off to Wellesley in the 1890s, nor were immigrant families who were crowded in the nation's cities able to enjoy the advantages of the new housekeeping technologies. But the nation's working-class women were far from passive, downtrodden victims. They, especially the younger women, were actors in shaping a new destiny for themselves in the urban environment of factory, shop, department store, and dance hall. Women of different classes and racial and ethnic backgrounds did feel a stirring, an awakening to the new possibilities that the "new woman" represented.

As women claimed these new roles, they played a major role in shaping the course of the Progressive era and women's history. Their lives were, tentatively, beginning to prefigure patterns that resemble women's lives today. And yet, alongside the excitement about new opportunities for women went a continuation of old attitudes and ideas that still relegated women to an unequal status. While visions of the new woman held out the promise for a fuller life, her freedom remained incomplete.

"Girl Reporter Derring-Do"

Nellie Bly

Perhaps there is no better image of the open-ended possibilities for American women at the end of the nineteenth century than that of the plucky journalist Nellie Bly setting off to travel around the world on her own in 1889. Her inspiration, as she pitched the idea to her editor at *The World*, was to beat the record of the fictional Phileas Fogg in Jules Verne's *Around the World in Eighty Days* (1873) and share the story of her travel adventures with readers back home. As this selection from her book chronicling her journey describes, her editor was reluctant to send a young woman off alone (she was then twenty-five years old, although she cut three years off her age to heighten her youthfulness). He was also worried that a female traveler would insist on taking dozens of trunks. Nellie Bly proved him wrong on both counts, safely traveling the world by commercial transportation in 72 days, 6 hours, and 11 minutes. Her luggage? The traveling dress and cape she wore, plus the contents of a small gripsack. So much for female vanity!

Nellie Bly was the name Elizabeth Cochrane adopted when she became a reporter—it came from a popular Stephen Foster song. Born in 1864 in a small Pennsylvania town, she entered journalism at age twenty when her spirited response to an anti-feminist article in a Pittsburgh paper so captured an editor's attention that he offered her a by-line. Much of her journalistic output, including her trip around the world, was what has been called detective or stunt journalism—she would conceal her identity (she once feigned insanity to write about conditions within an asylum) or put herself in an unusual situation and then write about it for audiences. The often crusading nature of these pieces foreshadowed the muckraking journalism of the early twentieth century.

Nellie Bly's around the world trip was a commercial and financial success. *The World* saw its circulation soar, and more than 300,000 readers participated in a contest to guess the exact time of her return. (The winner, who got a free trip to Europe, was only off by two-fifths of a second.) Bly found herself in great demand as a lecturer and author, and her image was commercialized on games, cards, and other collectors' items. However, she left *The World,* and the public eye, soon after. In 1895 she married a 72-year-old New York businessperson named Robert L. Seaman and lived quietly in New York until his death in 1910. Bly tried to revive her journalism career but never regained her former celebrity. She died in 1922.

What gave me the idea?

It is sometimes difficult to tell exactly what gives birth to an idea. Ideas are the chief stock in trade of newspaper writers and generally they are the scarcest stock in market, but they do come occasionally.

This idea came to me one Sunday. I had spent a greater part of the day and half the night vainly trying to fasten on some idea for a newspaper article. It was my custom to think up ideas on Sunday and lay them before my editor for his approval or disapproval on Monday. But ideas did not come that day and three o'clock in the morning found me weary and with an aching head tossing about in my bed. At last tired and provoked at my slowness in finding a subject, something for the week's work, I thought fretfully.

"I wish I was at the other end of the earth!"

"And why not?" the thought came: "I need a vacation; why not take a trip around the world?"

It is easy to see how one thought followed another. The idea of a trip around the world pleased me and I added: "If I could do it as quickly as Phileas Fogg did, I should go."

Then I wondered if it were possible to do the trip in eighty days and afterwards I went easily off to sleep with the determination to know before I saw my bed again if Phileas Fogg's record could be broken. . . .

I approached my editor rather timidly on the subject. I was afraid that he would think the idea too wild and visionary. . . .

To my dismay he told me that in the office they had thought of this same idea before, and the intention was to send a man. However he offered me the

Source: Nellie Bly, *Around the World in Seventy-Two Days* (New York: The Pictorial Weeklies Company, 1890), pp. 3–4, 5–6, 8–9, 10–11, 11–13, 14.

consolation that he would favor my going, and then we went to talk with the business manager about it.

"It is impossible for you to do it," was the terrible verdict. "In the first place you are a woman and would need a protector, and even if it were possible for you to travel alone you would need to carry so much baggage that it would detain you in making rapid changes. Besides you speak nothing but English, so there is no use talking about it; no one but a man can do this."

"Very well," I said angrily, "Start the man and I'll start the same day for some other newspaper and beat him."

"I believe you would," he said slowly. I would not say that this had any influence on their decision, but I do know that before we parted I was made happy by the promise that if any one was commissioned to make the trip, I should be that one. . . .

I bought one hand-bag with the determination to confine my baggage to its limit.

That night there was nothing to do but write to my few friends a line of farewell and to pack the hand-bag.

Packing that bag was the most difficult undertaking of my life; there was so much to go into such little space.

I got everything in at last except the extra dress. Then the question resolved itself into this: I must either add a parcel to my baggage or go around the world in and with one dress. I always hated parcels so I sacrificed the dress, but I brought out a last summer's silk bodice and after considerable squeezing managed to crush it into the hand-bag. . . .

The evening before I started I went to the office and was given £200 in English gold and Bank of England notes. The gold I carried in my pocket. The Bank of England notes were placed in a chamois-skin bag which I tied around my neck. Besides this I took some American gold and paper money to use at different ports as a test to see if American money was known outside of America.

Down in the bottom of my hand-bag was a special passport, number 247, signed by James G. Blaine, Secretary of State. Someone suggested that a revolver would be a good companion piece for the passport, but I had such a strong belief in the world's greeting me as I greeted it, that I refused to arm myself. I knew if my conduct was proper I should always find men ready to protect me, let them be Americans, English, French, German or anything else. . . .

I have been asked very often since my return how many changes of clothing I took in my solitary hand-bag. Some have thought I took but one; others think I carried silk which occupies but little space, and others have asked if I did not buy what I needed at the different ports.

One never knows the capacity of an ordinary hand-satchel until dire necessity compels the exercise of all one's ingenuity to reduce every thing to the smallest possible compass. In mine I was able to pack two traveling caps, three veils, a pair of slippers, a complete outfit of toilet articles, ink-stand, pens, pencils, and copy-paper, pins, needles and thread, a dressing gown, a tennis blazer, a small flask and a drinking cup, several complete changes of underwear, a liberal supply of handkerchiefs and fresh ruchings and most bulky and uncompromising of all, a jar of cold cream to keep my face from chapping in the varied climates I should encounter.

That jar of cold cream was the bane of my existence. It seemed to take up more room than everything else in the bag and was always getting into just the place that would keep me from closing the satchel. Over my arm I carried a silk waterproof, the only provision I made against rainy weather. After-experience showed me that I had taken too much rather than too little baggage. At every port where I stopped at I could have bought anything from a ready-made dress down, except possibly at Aden, and as I did not visit the shops there I cannot speak from knowledge. . . .

So much for my preparations. It will be seen that if one is traveling simply for the sake of traveling and not for the purpose of impressing one's fellow passengers, the problem of baggage becomes a very simple one. On one occasion—in Hong Kong, where I was asked to an official dinner—I regretted not having an evening dress with me, but the loss of that dinner was a very small matter when compared with the responsibilities and worries I escaped by not having a lot of trunks and boxes to look after.

The Fair Women, Chicago, 1893

Bertha Palmer

When the World's Columbian Exhibition opened in Chicago in May 1893, one of its most popular exhibits was the Woman's Building. Visitors had a chance to see women's art, sculpture, and handicrafts; visit a room devoted to women's organizations; and leave their children in a supervised childcare facility. Many women were somewhat ambivalent about separating women's contributions in a separate building; why not compete on an equal basis with men throughout the fair? The participants reasoned that the success of this pavilion (which consciously drew on the Women's Pavilion at the Philadelphia Centennial of 1876) would encourage women to be seen as human beings, and thus, the organizers argued, "women's buildings, women's exhibits, may safely become things of the past."

The Woman's Building was planned and executed by a Board of Lady Managers, headed by Bertha Honoré Palmer (1849–1918). This board confirmed the influence that women were wielding in urban life, especially in the expanding city of Chicago. The wife of Chicago financial leader Potter Palmer, Bertha Palmer had long been active both as an arts patron and as a participant in social-reform causes through such groups as the Chicago Woman's Club. Palmer presided over the opening ceremonies for the Woman's Building on May 1, 1893. This speech, whose rhetoric and style is symptomatic of women's public speaking at the time, conveys women's pride in female accomplishments around the world; at the same time, it suggests a tentative feminism critical of men for excluding women from activities in the public sphere. The speech demonstrates especially well the connection women saw between the advancement for their sex and the general uplift of humanity.

Like all major exhibitions at the time, the temporary structures of the 1893 Columbian Exhibition were torn down later that year. Once again, Bertha Palmer reigned over the ceremonies. Her remarks reflected what she, and many other public-spirited women, hoped they had accomplished: "When our palace in the White City shall have vanished like a dream, when grass and flowers cover the spot where it now stands, may its memory and influence still remain as a benediction to those who have wrought within its walls."

Members of the Board of Lady Managers and Friends:—The moment of fruition has arrived. Hopes which for more than two years have gradually been gaining strength and definiteness now become realities. Today the Exposition opens its gates. On this occasion of the formal opening of the Woman's Building, the Board of Lady Managers is singularly fortunate in having the honor to welcome distinguished official representatives of many of the able foreign committees and of the state boards, which have so effectively co-operated with it in accomplishing the results now to be disclosed to the world.

We have traveled together a hitherto untrodden path, have been subjected to tedious delays and overshadowed by dark clouds, which threatened disaster to our enterprise. We have been obliged to march with peace offerings in our hands, lest hostile motives be ascribed to us. Our burdens have been greatly lightened, however, by the spontaneous sympathy and aid which have reached us from women in every part of the world, and which have proved an added incentive and inspiration. Experience has brought many surprises, not the least of which is an impressive realization of the unity of human interests, notwithstanding differences of race, government, language, temperament and external conditions. The people of all civilized lands are studying the same problems. Each success and each failure in testing and developing new theories is valuable to the whole world. Social and industrial questions are paramount, and are receiving the thoughtful consideration of statesmen, students, political economists, humanitarians, employers and employed. . . .

The theory which exists among the conservative people, that the sphere of woman is her home—that it is unfeminine, even monstrous, for her to wish to take a place beside or to compete with men in the various lucrative industries—tells heavily against her, for manufacturers and producers take advantage of it to disparage her work and obtain her services for a nominal price, thus profiting largely by the necessities and helplessness of their victim. That so many should cling to respectable occupations while starving in following them, and

Source: Address by Mrs. Potter Palmer, in *The Congress of Women,* ed. Mary Kavanaugh Oldham Eagle (Chicago: American Publishing House, 1894). Reprinted by Arno Press, New York, 1974, pp. 25, 26, 28–29.

should refuse to yield to discouragement and despair, shows a high quality of steadfastness and principle. These are the real heroines of life, whose handiwork we are proud to install in the Exposition, because it has been produced in factories, workshops and studios under the most adverse conditions and with the most sublime patience and endurance.

Men of the finest and most chivalric type, who have poetic theories about the sanctity of the home and the refining, elevating influence of woman in it, theories inherited from the days of romance and chivalry, which we wish might prevail forever—these men have asked many times whether the Board of Lady Managers thinks it well to promote a sentiment which may tend to destroy the home by encouraging occupations for women which take them out of it. We feel, therefore, obliged to state our belief that every woman, who is presiding over a happy home, is fulfilling her highest and truest function, and could not be lured from it by temptations offered by factories or studios. Would that the eyes of these idealists could be thoroughly opened, that they might see, not the fortunate few of a favored class, with whom they possibly are in daily contact, but the general status of the labor market throughout the world and the relation to it of women. They might be astonished to learn that the conditions under which the vast majority of the "gentler sex" are living, are not so ideal as they assume; that each is not "dwelling in a home of which she is the queen, with a manly and loving arm to shield her from rough contact with life." Because of the impossibility of reconciling their theories with the stern facts, they might possibly consent to forgive the offense of widows with dependent children and those wives of drunkards and criminals who so far forget the high standard established for them as to attempt to earn for themselves daily bread, lacking which they must perish. The necessity for their work under present conditions is too evident and too urgent to be questioned. They must work or they must starve.

We are forced, therefore, to turn from the realm of fancy to meet and deal with existing facts. The absence of a just and general appreciation of the truth concerning the position and status of women has caused us to call special attention to it and to make a point of attempting to create, by means of the Exposition, a well defined public sentiment in regard to their rights and duties, and the propriety of their becoming not only self-supporting, but able to assist in maintaining their families when necessary. We hope that the statistics which the Board of Lady Managers has been so earnestly attempting to secure may give a correct idea of the number of women—not only those without natural protectors, or those thrown suddenly upon their own resources, but the number of wives of mechanics, laborers, artists, artisans and workmen of every degree—who are forced to work shoulder to shoulder with their husbands in order to maintain the family. . . .

The board does not wish to be understood as placing an extravagant or sentimental value upon the work of any woman because of her sex. It willingly acknowledges that the industries, arts and commerce of the world have been for centuries in the hands of men who have carefully trained themselves for the responsibilities devolving upon them, and who have, consequently, without question, contributed vastly more than women to the valuable thought, research, invention, science, art and literature, which have become the rich heritage of the human race. Notwithstanding their disadvantages, however, a few gifted women have made their value felt, and have rendered exceptional service to the cause of humanity.

Realizing that woman can never hope to receive the proper recompense for her services until her usefulness and success are not only demonstrated but fully understood and acknowledged, we have taken advantage of the opportunity presented by the Exposition to bring together such evidences of her skill in the various industries, arts and professions, as may convince the world that ability is not a matter of sex. Urged by necessity, she has shown that her powers are the same as her brothers', and that like encouragement and fostering care may develop her to an equal point of usefulness.

The fact that the Woman's Building is so small that it can hold only a tithe of the beautiful objects offered, has been a great disadvantage. The character of the exhibits and the high standard attained by most of them serve, therefore, only as an index of the quality and range of the material from which we have drawn. When our invitation asking co-operation was sent to foreign lands, the commissioners already appointed generally smiled doubtfully and explained that their women were doing nothing; that they would not feel inclined to help us, and, in many cases, stated that it was not the custom of their country for women to take part in any public effort, that they only attended to social duties. But as soon as these ladies received our message, sent in a brief and formal letter, the free masonry among women proved to be such that they needed no explanation; they understood at once the possibilities. Strong committees were immediately formed of women having large hearts and brains, women who cannot selfishly enjoy the ease of their own lives without giving a thought to their helpless and wretched sisters.

Our unbounded thanks are due to the exalted and influential personages who became, in their respective countries, patronesses and leaders of the movement inaugurated by us to represent what women are doing. They entered with appreciation into our work for the Exposition because they saw an opportunity, which they gracefully and delicately veiled behind the magnificent laces forming the central objects in their superb collections, to aid their women by opening new markets for their industries.

The Exposition will thus benefit women, not alone by means of the material objects brought together, but there will be a more lasting and permanent result through the interchange of thought and sympathy among influential and leading women of all countries now for the first time working together with a common purpose and an established means of communication. Government recognition and sanction give to these committees of women official character and dignity. Their work has been magnificently successful, and the reports which will be made of the conditions found to exist will be placed on record as public documents among the archives of every country. Realizing the needs and responsibilities of the hour, and that this will be the first official utterance of women on behalf of women, we shall weigh well our words, words which should be so judicious and convincing that hereafter they may be treasured among the happy influences which made possible new and better conditions.

We rejoice in the possession of this beautiful building, in which we meet today, in its delicacy, symmetry and strength. We honor our architect and the artists who have given not only their hands but their hearts and their genius to its decoration. For it[s] women in every part of the world have been exerting their efforts and talents, for it[s] looms have wrought their most delicate fabrics, the needle has flashed in the hands of maidens under tropical suns, the lacemaker has bent over her cushion weaving her most artful web, the brush and chisel have sought to give form and reality to the visions haunting the brain of the artist—all have wrought with the thought of making our building worthy to serve its great end. We thank them all for their successful efforts.

The eloquent President of the Commission last October dedicated the great Exposition buildings to humanity. We now dedicate the Woman's Building to an elevated womanhood—knowing that by so doing we shall best serve the cause of humanity.

Black Women Plan to Lead Their Race

Anna J. Cooper

Black women matched white women in organizational talent in the late nineteenth and early twentieth centuries. Like their white sisters, they set an ambitious agenda that included not only larger roles for women but also general uplift for the race. The two were integrally related. As Anna J. Cooper said in 1892, "only the BLACK WOMAN can say 'when and where I enter in the quiet, undisputed dignity of my womanhood, without violence and without suing or special patronage, then and there the whole NEGRO RACE ENTERS WITH ME.' "

Much of the organizational energy of black women occurred within the club movement, which owing to the prevailing racism of the times ran on a separate but parallel track to the white women's club movement. Often groups came into existence to work for educational or social welfare goals in local communities; this commitment necessarily engendered a strong emphasis on race pride and racial advancement. By the 1890s, black women's clubs and organizations had coalesced into a national movement. When the National Association of Colored Women was founded in 1896 (Mary Church Terrell served as its first president), it counted one hundred member organizations; by 1914, the NACW represented fifty thousand women in one thousand clubs.

Source: Anna J. Cooper, *A Voice from the South, By a Black Woman of the South* (Xenia, Ohio: The Aldine Printing House, 1892), pp. 134–137, 142–145.

Anna J. Cooper (1858–1964) represents the values and consciousness of these black organizational women at the turn of the century.
Her book, *A Voice from the South* (1892), recognizes the unique situation of black women to reflect on both the woman question and the
race problem. This excerpt from her chapter on the status of women
in America calls on black women to take on wider social responsibilities in their communities as a way of uplifting both themselves and
the entire black population. Such a dual consciousness has often characterized African-American women from the nineteenth century
through the present.

The colored woman of to-day occupies, one may say, a unique position in this
country. In a period of itself transitional and unsettled, her status seems one of
the least ascertainable and definitive of all the forces which make for our civilization. She is confronted by both a woman question and a race problem, and
is as yet an unknown or an unacknowledged factor in both. While the women
of the white race can with calm assurance enter upon the work they feel by nature appointed to do, while their men give loyal support and appreciative coun-
tenance to their efforts, recognizing in most avenues of usefulness the propriety and the need of woman's distinctive co-operation, the colored woman too
often finds herself hampered and shamed by a less liberal sentiment and a more
conservative attitude on the part of those for whose opinion she cares most.
That this is not universally true I am glad to admit. There are to be found both
intensely conservative white men and exceedingly liberal colored men. But as
far as my experience goes the average man of our race is less frequently ready
to admit the actual need among the sturdier forces of the world for woman's
help or influence. That great social and economic questions await her interference, that she could throw any light on problems of national import, that her
intermeddling could improve the management of school systems, or elevate the
tone of public institutions, or humanize and sanctify the far reaching influence
of prisons and reformatories and improve the treatment of lunatics and imbe-
ciles,—that she has a word worth hearing on mooted questions in political economy, that she could contribute a suggestion on the relations of labor and capital, or offer a thought on honest money and honorable trade, I fear the majority
of "Americans of the colored variety" are not yet prepared to concede. It may
be that they do not yet see these questions in their right perspective, being absorbed in the immediate needs of their own political complications. A good deal
depends on where we put the emphasis in this world; and our men are not perhaps to blame if they see everything colored by the light of those agitations in
the midst of which they live and move and have their being. The part they have
had to play in American history during the last twenty-five or thirty years has
tended rather to exaggerate the importance of mere political advantage, as well
as to set a fictitious valuation on those able to secure such advantage. It is the
astute politician, the manager who can gain preferment for himself and his fa-
vorites, the demagogue known to stand in with the powers at the White House
and consulted on the bestowal of government plums, whom we set in high

places and denominate great. It is they who receive the hosannas of the multitude and are regarded as leaders of the people. The thinker and the doer, the man who solves the problem by enriching his country with an invention worth thousands or by a thought inestimable and precious is given neither bread nor a stone. He is too often left to die in obscurity and neglect even if spared in his life the bitterness of fanatical jealousies and detraction.

And yet politics, and surely American politics, is hardly a school for great minds. Sharpening rather than deepening, it develops the faculty of taking advantage of present emergencies rather than the insight to distinguish between the true and the false, the lasting and the ephemeral advantage. Highly cultivated selfishness rather than consecrated benevolence is its passport to success. Its votaries are never seers. At best they are but manipulators—often only jugglers. It is conducive neither to profound statesmanship nor to the higher type of manhood. Altruism is its *mauvais succes,* and naturally enough it is indifferent to any factor which cannot be worked into its own immediate aims and purposes. As woman's influence as a political element is as yet nil in most of the commonwealths of our republic, it is not surprising that with those who place the emphasis on mere political capital she may yet seem almost a nonentity so far as it concerns the solution of great national or even racial perplexities. . . .

Fifty years ago woman's activity according to orthodox definitions was on a pretty clearly cut "sphere," including primarily the kitchen and the nursery, and rescued from the barrenness of prison bars by the womanly mania for adorning every discoverable bit of china or canvass with forlorn looking cranes balanced idiotically on one foot. The woman of to-day finds herself in the presence of responsibilities which ramify through the profoundest and most varied interests of her country and race. Not one of the issues of this plodding, toiling, sinning, repenting, falling, aspiring humanity can afford to shut her out, or can deny the reality of her influence. No plan for renovating society, no scheme for purifying politics, no reform in church or in state, no moral, social, or economic question, no movement upward or downward in the human plane is lost on her. A man once said when told his house was afire: "Go tell my wife; I never meddle with household affairs." But no woman can possibly put herself or her sex outside any of the interests that affect humanity. All departments in the new era are to be hers, in the sense that her interests are in all and through all; and it is incumbent on her to keep intelligently and sympathetically *en rapport* with all the great movements of her time, that she may know on which side to throw the weight of her influence. She stands now at the gateway of this new era of American civilization. In her hands must be moulded the strength, the wit, the statesmanship, the morality, all the psychic force, the social and economic intercourse of that era. To be alive at such an epoch is a privilege, to be a woman then is sublime.

In this last decade of our century, changes of such moment are in progress, such new and alluring vistas are opening out before us, such original and radical suggestions for the adjustment of labor and capital, of government and the governed, of the family, the church and the state, that to be a possible factor though an infinitesimal one in such a movement is pregnant with hope and weighty with responsibility. To be a woman in such an age carries with it a privilege and an opportunity never implied before. But to be a woman of the Negro race in America, and to be able to grasp the deep significance of the possibilities of the crisis, is to have a heritage, it seems to me, unique in the ages. In the first place, the race is young and full of the elasticity and hopefulness of youth. All its achievements are before it. It does not look on the masterly triumphs of nineteenth century civilization with that *blasé* world-weary look which characterizes the old washed out and worn out races which have already, so to speak, seen their best days.

Said a European writer recently: "Except the Sclavonic, the Negro is the only original and distinctive genius which has yet to come to growth—and the feeling is to cherish and develop it."

Everything to this race is new and strange and inspiring. There is a quickening of its pulses and a glowing of its self-consciousness. Aha, I can rival that! I can aspire to that! I can honor my name and vindicate my race! Something like this, it strikes me, is the enthusiasm which stirs the genius of young Africa in America; and the memory of past oppression and the fact of present attempted repression only serve to gather momentum for its irrepressible powers. Then again, a race in such a stage of growth is peculiarly sensitive to impressions. Not the photographer's sensitized plate is more delicately impressionable to outer influences than is this high strung people here on the threshold of a career.

What a responsibility then to have the sole management of the primal lights and shadows! Such is the colored woman's office. She must stamp weal or woe on the coming history of this people. May she see her opportunity and vindicate her high prerogative.

Frances Willard Equates Learning to Ride a Bicycle with Opening New Frontiers for Women

Frances Willard (1839–1898) was the indefatigable leader of the Women's Christian Temperance Union (WCTU). After serving as head of the Methodist-run Evanston College for Ladies in the 1870s, Willard shifted her attention to the temperance issue then gaining force in the United States, especially among Protestant women. Her rise to national

Source: Frances Willard, *A Wheel within a Wheel; How I Learned to Ride the Bicycle,* 1895. Found in Stephanie Twin, *Out of the Bleachers* (Old Westbury, N.Y.: Feminist Press, 1979), pp. 104–105, 112–114.

prominence was swift: in 1879, she was elected the national president of the WCTU, a position she held for the next twenty years. Although the WCTU made prohibition of the use of liquor its top priority (Willard coined the "home protection" rallying cry, and promoted the white ribbon as a symbol of the purity of the home), under Willard's leadership the WCTU embraced a wide host of reforms, including woman suffrage, social hygiene, labor unions, and even participation in politics. Willard's motto was succinct: "Do Everything!"

A tomboy as a youth, Frances Willard called herself Frank and bemoaned the day she had to put on long skirts and pin up her hair. Not until she was in her fifties did she learn to ride a bicycle. In the 1890s, approximately thirty thousand women were experiencing the freedom of mobility and exercise bicycles provided. Willard methodically set out to master the physical skill of riding the bike in the same way that she proposed women make contributions to the wider world. So enamored was Willard of the experience (she gave her bicycle the name of Gladys!) that she wrote an entire book about it, *A Wheel within a Wheel; How I Learned to Ride the Bicycle* (1895), from which these selections are drawn.

From my earliest recollections, and up to the ripe age of fifty-three, I had been an active and diligent worker in the world. This sounds absurd; but having almost no toys except such as I could manufacture, my first plays were but the outdoor work of active men and women on a small scale. Born with an inveterate opposition to staying in the house, I very early learned to use a carpenter's kit and a gardener's tools, and followed in my mimic way the occupations of the poulterer and the farmer, working my little field with a wooden plow of my own making, and felling saplings with an ax rigged up from the old iron of the wagon-shop. Living in the country, far from the artificial restraints and conventions by which most girls are hedged from the activities that would develop a good physique, and endowed with the companionship of a mother who let me have my own sweet will, I "ran wild" until my sixteenth birthday, when the hampering long skirts were brought, with their accompanying corset and high heels; my hair was clubbed up with pins, and I remember writing in my journal, in the first heartbreak of a young human colt taken from its pleasant pasture, "Altogether, I recognize that my occupation is gone."

From that time on I always realized and was obedient to the limitations thus imposed, though in my heart of hearts I felt their unwisdom even more than their injustice. My work then changed from my beloved and breezy outdoor world to the indoor realm of study, teaching, writing, speaking, and went on almost without a break or pain until my fifty-third year, when the loss of my mother accentuated the strain of this long period in which mental and physical life were out of balance, and I fell into a mild form of what is called nervewear by the patient and nervous prostration by the lookers-on. Thus ruthlessly thrown out of the usual lines of reaction on my environment, and sighing for new worlds to conquer, I determined that I would learn the bicycle. . . .

Let me remark to any young woman who reads this page that for her to tumble off her bike is inexcusable. The lightsome elasticity of every muscle, the quickness of the eye, the agility of motion, ought to preserve her from such a catastrophe. I have had [only one] fall. . . . I have proceeded on a basis of the utmost caution, and aside from . . . one pitiful performance the bicycle has cost me hardly a single bruise.

They that know nothing fear nothing. Away back in 1886 my alert young friend, Miss Anna Gordon, and my ingenious young niece, Miss Katherine Willard, took to the tricycle as naturally as ducks take to water. . . . Remembering my country bringing-up and various exploits in running, climbing, horseback-riding, to say nothing of my tame heifer that I trained for a Bucephalus, I said to myself, "If those girls can ride without learning so can I!" Taking out my watch I timed them as they, at my suggestion, set out to make a record in going round the square. Two and a half minutes was the result. I then started with all my forces well in hand, and flew around in two and a quarter minutes. Not contented with this, but puffed up with foolish vanity, I declared that I would go around in two minutes; and, encouraged by their cheers, away I went without a fear till the third turning-post was reached, when the left hand played me false, and turning at an acute angle, away I went sidelong, machine and all, into the gutter, falling on my right elbow, which felt like a glassful of chopped ice, and I knew that for the first time in a life full of vicissitudes I had been really hurt. Anna Gordon's white face as she ran toward me caused me to wave my uninjured hand and call out, "Never mind!" and with her help I rose and walked into the house, wishing above all things to go straight to my own room and lie on my own bed, and thinking as I did so how pathetic is that instinct that makes "the stricken deer go weep," the harmed hare seek the covert.

Two physicians were soon at my side, and my mother, then over eighty years of age, came in with much controlled agitation and seated herself beside my bed, taking my hand and saying, "O Frank! you were always too adventurous."

If I am asked to explain why I learned the bicycle I should say I did it as an act of grace, if not of actual religion. The cardinal doctrine laid down by my physician was, "Live out of doors and take congenial exercise"; but from the day when, at sixteen years of age, I was enwrapped in the long skirts that impeded every footstep, I have detested walking and felt with a certain noble disdain that the conventions of life had cut me off from what in the freedom of my prairie home had been one of life's sweetest joys. Driving is not real exercise; it does not renovate the river of blood that flows so sluggishly in the veins of those who from any cause have lost the natural adjustment of brain to brawn. Horseback-riding, which does promise vigorous exercise, is expensive. The bicycle meets all the conditions and will ere long come within the reach of all. Therefore, in obedience to the laws of health, I learned to ride. I also wanted to help women to a wider world, for I hold that the more interests women and men can have in common, in thought, word, and deed, the happier will it be for the home. Besides, there was a special value to women in the conquest of the bicycle by a woman in her fifty-third year, and one who had so many comrades in the white-ribbon army[1] that her action would be widely influential. . . .

It is needless to say that a bicycling costume was a prerequisite. This consisted of a skirt and blouse of tweed, with belt, rolling collar, and loose cravat, the skirt three inches from the ground; a round straw hat; and walking-shoes with gaiters. It was a simple, modest suit, to which no person of common sense could take exception.

As nearly as I can make out, reducing the problem to actual figures, it took me about three months, with an average of fifteen minutes' practice daily, to learn, first, to pedal; second, to turn; third, to dismount; and fourth, to mount independently this most mysterious animal. January 20th will always be a red-letter bicycle day, because although I had already mounted several times with no hand on the rudder, some good friend had always stood by to lend moral support; but summoning all my force, and, most forcible of all, what Sir Benjamin Ward Richardson declares to be the two essential elements—decision and precision—I mounted and started off alone. From that hour the spell was broken; Gladys was no more a mystery: I had learned all her kinks, had put a bridle in her teeth, and touched her smartly with the whip of victory. Consider, ye who are of a considerable chronology: in about thirteen hundred minutes, or, to put it more mildly, in twenty-two hours, or, to put it most mildly of all, in less than a single day as the almanac reckons time—but practically in two days of actual practice—amid the delightful surroundings of the great outdoors, and inspired by the bird-songs, the color and fragrance of an English posy-garden, in the company of devoted and pleasant comrades, I had made myself master of the most remarkable, ingenious, and inspiring motor ever yet devised upon this planet.

Moral: *Go thou and do likewise!*

An Immigrant Daughter Awakens to the Possibilities of the New World

Anzia Yezierska

Anzia Yezierska (1880?–1970) is best known for her chronicles of Jewish immigrant life on New York's Lower East Side. Her writings were often autobiographical, drawing on her family's experience of emigrating from Poland to New York City at the turn of the century. A

[1]Women who belonged to the Women's Christian Temperance Union.
Source: Excerpt from "The Hard Heart," included in *Bread Givers* by Anzia Yezierska, pp. 134–138, copyright © 1925 by Doubleday, renewed 1952 by Anzia Yezierska, transferred to Louise Levitas Henriksen 1970. Reprinted by permission of Persea Books.

collection of her short stories called *Hungry Hearts* (1920) caught the attention of Hollywood producer Samuel Goldwyn, who offered her $10,000 to write a screenplay of the stories. But Yezierska found it impossible to write the kind of stories she knew best in the conspicuous and flamboyant Hollywood atmosphere, and she returned to New York soon after. By the 1930s she (like much of the rest of the country) had fallen on hard times. A short stint on the Federal Writers' Project, about which she wrote engagingly in her last autobiographical novel, *Red Ribbon on a White Horse* (1950), restored her spirits.

Yezierska's stories often featured strong-willed and independent female characters who took advantage of the possibilities that turn-of-the-century America could offer to such immigrant daughters: education, satisfying work, and the option to choose one's own marriage partner rather than being forced to submit to an arranged match. *Bread Givers* (1925) is one of Yezierska's most powerful books. Its subtitle, "A struggle between a father of the Old World and a daughter of the New," anticipates its major theme of the conflict between heroine Sara Smolinsky (modeled on Yezierska) and her father, a Talmudic scholar who dominates his family's destiny once they are in America. In Reb Smolinsky's view, women are to be the servants of men, and that applies to daughters as well as wives. Sara's three sisters let their father rule their lives with disastrous results, especially in matrimonial choices, but Sara refuses to go along. In this scene, the seventeen-year-old protagonist decides to leave home after an argument with her father in a small grocery store the family has opened. She consciously equates America with independence and autonomy for women, a stark contrast to the restrictions of the Old World.

In the rest of the novel, Yezierska follows Sara Smolinsky through a variety of jobs and finally to school, confirming the importance of education for immigrant girls as well as boys. After college, she becomes a teacher, an inspiring feat of upward mobility for a young woman on her own. At the end of the novel, however, Sara realizes that she too has roots in the Old World, and she reconciles with her family and with many of their customs and values. Such an ending reflects the ambivalence with which immigrant daughters found themselves "between two worlds."

While Father was preaching Mother back into her place, a girl came in for a pound of rice. When she went to pay, she had only ten cents.

"The rice is twelve cents," I told her.

"Can I have it now? I just live next door and I'll bring back the two cents later."

I handed Father the ten cents, saying it was for a pound of rice.

"Crazy! Where was your head? Don't you know yet, rice is twelve cents?"

"I trusted her the two cents—"

"Without asking me? I'm the one to decide who is to be trusted."

"But you're never here. You're away praying most of the time."

"Hold your mouth! You're talking too much."

"Why do you make such a holler on me over two cents, when you, yourself, gave away four hundred dollars to a crook for empty shelves?"

"Blood-and-iron! How dare you question your father his business? What's the world coming to in this wild America? No respect for fathers. No fear of God." His eyes flamed as he shook his fist at me. "Only dare open your mouth to me again! Here I struggle to work up a business and she gives away all the profits of my goods. No heart. No conscience. Two cents here and two cents there. That's how all my hard-earned dollars bleed away."

Oh, God! *Two cents!* My gall burst in me! For seventeen years I had stood his preaching and his bullying. But now all the hammering hell that I had to listen to since I was born cracked my brain. His heartlessness to Mother, his pitiless driving away Bessie's only chance to love, bargaining away Fania to a gambler and Mashah to a diamond-faker—when they each had the luck to win lovers of their own—all these tyrannies crashed over me. Should I let him crush me as he crushed them? No. This is America, where children are people.

"I can't stand it! I can't!" I cried, rushing to the back of the store. "Two cents! Two cents! All that cursing and thundering over two cents!"

Blindly, I grabbed my things together into a bundle. I didn't care where I was going or what would become of me. Only to break away from my black life. Only not to hear Father's preaching voice again.

As I put on my hat and coat, I saw Mother, clutching at her heart in helplessness, her sorrowful eyes gazing at me. All the suffering of her years was in the dumb look she turned on me. Bending over, she took out from her stocking the red handkerchief with the knot that held her saved-up rent money. And without a word, she pushed it into my hand.

As I came through the door with my bundle, Father caught sight of me. "What's this?" he asked. "Where are you going?"

"I'm going back to work, in New York."

"What? Wild-head! Without asking, without consulting your father, you get yourself ready to go? Do you yet know that I want you to work in New York? Let's first count out your carfare to come home every night. Maybe it will cost so much there wouldn't be anything left from your wages."

"But I'm not coming home!"

"What? A daughter of mine, only seventeen years old, not home at night?"

"I'll go to Bessie or Mashah."

"Mashah is starving poor, and you know how crowded it is by Bessie."

"If there's no place for me by my sisters, I'll find a place by strangers."

"A young girl, alone, among strangers? Do you know what's going on in the world? No girl can live without a father or a husband to look out for her. It says in the Torah, only through a man has a woman an existence. Only through a man can a woman enter Heaven."

"I'm smart enough to look out for myself. It's a new life now. In America, women don't need men to boss them."

"*Blut-und-Eisen!* They ought to put you in a madhouse till you're cured of your crazy nonsense!"

Always before, when Father began the drum, drum of his preaching on me, my will was squelched. But now he saw the stony hardness of my eyes. And suddenly his whole face saddened with the hurt of a wounded martyr, suffering for his righteousness.

"Is this your thanks for all your father did for you?" he pleaded, with the gentle patience of a holy one. "Where do you find a poor father who has done for his children as much as I? I didn't cripple you. I didn't give you consumption. I didn't send you to work at the age of six like some poor fathers do. You didn't start work till you were over ten. Now, when I begin to have a little use from you, you want to run away and live for yourself?"

"I've got to live my own life. It's enough that Mother and the others lived for you."

"*Chzufeh!* You brazen one! The crime of crimes against God—daring your will against your father's will. In olden times the whole city would have stoned you!"

"Thank God, I'm not living in olden times. Thank God, I'm living in America! You made the lives of the other children! I'm going to make my own life!"

"You hard heart! You soul of stone! You're the curse from all my children. They all honoured and obeyed their father."

"And what's their end? Look at them now! You think I'll slave for you till my braids grow gray—wait till you find me another fish-peddler to sell me out in marriage! You think I'm a fool like Bessie! No! No!"

Wild with all that was choked in me since I was born, my eyes burned into my father's eyes. "My will is as strong as yours. I'm going to live my own life. Nobody can stop me. I'm not from the old country. I'm American!"

"You blasphemer!" His hand flung out and struck my cheek. "Denier of God! I'll teach you respect for the law!"

I leaped back and dashed for the door. The Old World had struck its last on me.

Dance Hall Madness

Belle Lindner Israels

One working-class variant of the new woman was the young urban worker who chose to spend her leisure time sampling the dance halls, amusement parks, and movie theaters that dotted city life by the turn of the century. After a hard day at work, working women could seek

Source: Belle Lindner Israels, "The Way of the Girl," *The Survey* XXII, no. 4 (July 3, 1909), pp. 486–488, 496–497.

out the glamour and attraction of commercialized amusements where they could mix with men in a setting that symbolized the increasingly heterosexual orientation of leisure time. "My mother doesn't know I go out here," said one, "but I want some fun, and it only costs ten cents."

By far the most popular form of amusement for working-class women was the dance hall. By the 1920s, the greater New York area boasted over five hundred such dance halls where young women (usually under twenty) could meet men, dance, and get "treated" to drinks and other entertainment. The owners of such establishments realized how important it was to attract women, so they charged unescorted females only a dime to enter, while men paid twenty-five cents.

While young working women in turn-of-the-century cities saw such public amusements as part of their quest for personal autonomy as well as a break from the rigors of their jobs, middle-class reformers were not so sympathetic. While recognizing the need for leisure and activities off the job, reformers often saw the mixed-sex atmospheres of such cheap amusements as promiscuous and dangerous, a place where men could prey on weak girls through the temptations of the high life. Belle Lindner Israels's 1909 article, "The Way of the Girl," suggests the ambivalence with which middle-class women watched working-class women aggressively and self-confidently take over public space. The caption of a photograph accompanying the article stated ominously: "The whole story—the dance, the drink, the man, the girl."

Social activist Belle Lindner Israels Moskowitz (1877–1933) was involved in a variety of educational and recreational reforms in New York during the Progressive era; after the publication of this article, she was instrumental in the passage of a 1911 state law to licence dance halls. In the 1920s, she served as a close adviser to Governor Alfred E. Smith of New York, thus becoming one of America's first female politicians.

The girls say that "carfare" is all it costs for a summer day at North Beach, admission fees the only "price" for a winter evening at a dancing academy. "With the voice of joy—with a multitude that kept holiday," they come and go at both places. In the summer the problem is what to do during enforced idleness; in the winter it focuses on where to go for relaxation. The beaches are summer types of amusement. The dancing academy of the winter months is at one end of a slide, with stops *en route,* to the saloon where dancing is allowed as a thirst accelerator—where girls are an asset only in proportion to the amount of liquid refreshment that they can induce the men to buy.

The amusement resources of the working girl run the gamut from innocent and innocuous vacation homes and settlement dancing schools, sparsely furnished for those "well recommended," to the plentiful allurements of the day boat, with its easily rented rooms, the beach, the picnic ground, with its ill-lighted grove and "hotel," to numberless places where one may dance and find partners, with none too scrupulous a supervision.

Having made accusations, let us proceed to substantiate them.

It is an industrial fact that the summer months find thousands of working girls either in the position of compulsory idleness through slack season in the trades with which they are familiar, or attempting "to kill time" through one or two weeks of a vacation, unwelcome because it bears no definite recreative fruit. The general aspects of the amusement problem of the working girl bear certain undetermined relation to the undercurrents besetting society in a large city, in proportion as opportunities for healthful outlet for social desire are adequate or inadequate. Industrial activity demands diversion. Industrial idleness cries out for rational recreation. As these are provided wisely and freely, the population of the underworld decreases. As they are neglected, the tide rises. Like Janus, the problem looks two ways—towards an escape from enforced idleness and relaxation from necessary labor. Active participation in athletics gives a natural outlet for the boy. The recreative desire of the young girl leads not to Sunday baseball—except as "he" may be playing—nor is it able to content itself with a comparatively expensive and therefore infrequent visit to the theater. Her aspirations demand attention from the other sex. No amusement is complete in which "he" is not a factor. The distinction between the working woman and her more carefully guarded sister of the less driven class is one of standards, opportunities, and a chaperon. Three rooms in a tenement, overcrowded with the younger children, make the street a private apartment. The public resort similarly overcrowded, but with those who are not inquisitive, answers as her reception room.

There is no need to dwell on what have come to be almost axiomatic statements of the uncomfortable home surroundings of the average working girl in a large city. It is perhaps equally ineffectual to harp on her natural desire for amusement. These things taken for granted, we must survey the field which spreads itself before her, first for the summer months and then for the indoor season.

The range of summer amusements around New York city covers first, beach resorts; second, amusement parks; third, the picnic park utilized for the outing, the chowder and the summer night's festival; fourth, the excursion boat; fifth, the vacation home or camp provided by settlements, churches, and girls' clubs.

Of the beach resorts, Coney Island and Rockaway are naturally in the van of public thought. Rockaway is expensive to reach. Its *clientèle* is of the upper class of saleswomen and office workers. They enjoy the ocean bath and spend a comparatively simple day at the beach; and, being better provided with the world's goods than the average girl whom we wish to consider, are not seeking the same kinds of excitement.

Coney Island—the people's playground—where each year "everything is new but the ocean" is the most gigantic of the efforts to amuse.

A dancing master said: "If you haven't got the girls, you can't do business! Keep attracting 'em. The fellows will come if the girls are there."

Coney Island does attract them. It only costs fare down and back, and for the rest of it the boys you "pick up," "treat."

When the girl is both lucky and clever, she frees herself from her self-selected escort before home-going time, and finds a feminine companion in his place for the midnight ride in the trolley. When she is not clever, some one of her partners of the evening may exact tribute for "standing treat." Then the day's outing costs more than carfare. With due recognition of the simpler amusement places on the island—such as Steeplechase Park, where no liquor is sold, and also of the innocent pleasure along the beach front, not even belittling the fact that "nice" people dance in the Dreamland ball room, the fact remains that the average girl has small powers of discrimination. So many hundred places abound on the island to counter-balance the few safe ones, that "careers" without number find their initial stage in a Raines law hotel at this resort.

The danger is not in the big places on the island, where orderly shows and dance halls are run, and where young persons may go unattended. But the greatest number of music halls and dance resorts are along the side streets of the Bowery, and, with the exception of one or two semi-respectable places, are thoroughly disreputable. On Saturday and Sunday nights many young working girls are attracted to these places. They know the bad reputation of some of them, but the dancing floor is good, there are always plenty of men, and there are laughter and liberty galore. . . .

Girls do not of intention select bad places to go to. The girl whose temperament and disposition crave unnatural forms of excitement is nearly beyond the bounds of salvation; but ninety out of one hundred girls want only what they are entitled to—innocent relaxation. The moving picture show is on the wane. The skating rink had its day long ago. The dance is destined to be the next feature in popular amusement.

Let us provide it plentifully, safely, and inexpensively. . . .

We must recover from the idea that the public is intrinsically bad. It needs instruction in the fine art of using, not abusing its privileges, and a little faith in the great American proletariat will develop a marvelous return.

Let us frankly recognize that youth demands amusement. When the cities begin to see their duties to the little ones, playgrounds come. Youth plays too. Instead of sand-piles give them dance platforms; instead of slides and seesaws, theaters; instead of teachers of manual occupations, give them the socializing force of contact with good supervising men and women. Replace the playground, or more properly, progress from the playground to the rational amusement park.

Denial of these privileges peoples the underworld; furnishing them is modern preventive work and should be an integral part of any social program.

A Woman Homesteader

Edith Eudora Ammons

The New Woman who traveled the globe, rode a bicycle, or flirted in a dance hall had a Western "sister"—the female homesteader. While many of our images of the West are male, women were always part of the westward migration and settlement. A surprising number went as homesteaders, taking advantage of the Homestead Act of 1862 promising 160 acres of land to anyone who kept up residence and made improvements for five years. The law did not discriminate against women: all a settler had to be was the head of a household and over twenty-one. According to figures cited by historian Glenda Riley, women made up 11.9 percent of homestead entrants in Lamar, Colorado, and Douglas, Wyoming, in 1887, 1891, 1907, and 1908. And women were more tenacious at sticking with their claims, with 43 percent of women "proving up" their claims as against 37 percent of men.

Like men who staked claims, there was no single reason why women decided to homestead. For an unmarried woman, it could be a good investment, a way to look for a husband, or a statement of independence; for a widowed or divorced woman, it could be a way to make a living for her family. But all homesteaders had to have some sense of adventure and courage, because staking a claim was hard, hard work, not something to be undertaken lightly.

This is the story of two unmarried sisters, Edith Eudora Ammons and Ida Mary Ammons, who bought a semi-improved claim in South Dakota in 1907. Since their initial costs for land, a shack, supplies, and fuel were probably only around $300, the sisters saw this as a good investment, but they also were lured by what Edith called the "wild adventure" of homesteading. This selection describes their disillusioning first view of the piece of land they had just bought. The next year they tried another piece, but just as they were able to finalize the claim, a fire caused by a severe drought raged over the prairie and burned them out.

Edith and Ida Ammons exemplify the independence that is often associated with women in the West. Although their lives were tough and physical, Edith concluded that a woman "had more independence here than in any other part of the world," noting that the hardships "were more than compensated for by its unshackled freedom. . . . The opportunities for a full and active life were infinitely greater here." And, yes, even though this was not their original intention, both sisters did marry.

Source: Edith Eudora Kohl, *Land of the Burnt Thigh* (St. Paul: Minnesota Historical Press, 1986; first published by Funk and Wagnalls, 1938), pp. 5–6, 7–9, 10–13.

Oddly enough, we had never questioned the impulse which led two young city girls to go alone into unsettled land, homesteading. Our people had been pioneers, always among those who pushed back the frontier. The Ammonses had come up from Tennessee into Illinois in the early days and cleared the timberland along the Mississippi Valley some forty miles out of St. Louis. They built their houses of the hand-hewn logs and became land and stock owners. They were not sturdy pioneers, but they were tenacious.

Some of them went on into what Grandma Ammons called the Santa Fe Bottoms, a low marshy country along the river, where they became wealthy—or well-to-do, at least—by fattening droves of hogs on acorns. Generally speaking, my mother's family ran to professions, and my father's family to land. Though there was father's cousin, Jack Hunter, who had been west and when he came to visit us now and then told wild tales about the frontier to which my sister and I as little children listened wide-eyed. He wove glowing accounts of the range country where he was going to make a million dollars raising cattle. Cousin Jack always talked big.

It was from his highly colored yarns that we had learned all we knew of the West—and from the western magazines which pictured it as an exciting place where people were mostly engaged in shooting one another.

While Ida Mary and I were still very young our mother died, and after that we divided our time between our father's home—he had married again and had a second family to take care of—and the home of his sister. As a result my sister and I came to depend on ourselves and on each other more than two girls of our age usually do.

By the time we were old enough to see that things were not going well financially at home, we knew we must make our own way. Some of the girls we knew talked about "going homesteading" as a wild adventure. They boasted of friends or relatives who had gone to live on a claim as though they had gone lion-hunting in Africa or gold-hunting in Alaska. A homestead. At first thought the idea was absurd. We were both very young; both unusually slight, anything but hardy pioneers; and neither of us had the slightest knowledge of homesteading conditions, or experience extending beyond the conventional, sheltered life of the normal city girl in the first decade of the century.

We were wholly unfitted for the frontier. We had neither training nor physical stamina for roughing it. When I tried to explain to an uncle of mine that I wanted to go west, to make something of myself, he retorted that "it was a hell of a place to do it." In spite of the discussion which our decision occasioned, we made our plans, deciding to risk the hazards of a raw country alone, cutting ourselves off from the world of everyone and everything we had ever known. And with little money to provide against hardships and emergencies. . . .

How did one go about homesteading? we asked. Well, all you had to do to get a deed to a quarter-section—160 acres of land—was to file on it at the nearest Land Office, live on it eight months, pay the government $1.25 an acre—and the land was yours. Easy as falling off a log!

The only improvement required by the government was some sort of abode as proof that one had made the land his bona-fide residence for the full eight months.

What would that cost? And the whole undertaking? It depended partly on what kind of shack one built and whether he did it himself or hired it done. A shack cost all the way from $25 to $100 or more. Some of those who had families and intended to stay, built cheap two- and three-room houses.

Of course, it cost women who had to hire things done more to homestead. But with grub, fuel and other necessities we figured it would cost not more than $500 all told.

Then we learned of this quarter-section with a shack already built, bunk and all. It had been filed on and the owner had left before proving-up time so that the claim, shack and all, had reverted to the government. We had about $300 saved up, and this was enough, we decided, to cover homesteading expenses, inasmuch as the shack was provided. So we had all but the final payment of $200 to the government, which would be due when we had "made proof."

We decided to let the money for that final payment take care of itself. The thing to do was to get hold of a piece of land before it was all gone. To hear people talk, it was the last day of grace to apply for a claim. They talked like that for ten years. We did not know there were several million acres lying out there between the Missouri and the Pacific waiting to be settled. We would have all winter to figure out how to prove up. And we found that one could get $1000 to $1500 for a raw claim after getting a deed to it.

The claim with the shack on it was in South Dakota; thirty miles from a town called Pierre. We looked that up in the geography to make sure it really existed. But when we tried to get detailed information, facts and figures to help us prepare for what was to come, we got only printed pamphlets of rules and regulations which were of no real help at all. Land Offices were so busy in those days that all they could do was to send out a package of printed information that no one could understand.

Armed with our meager array of facts, we talked to our father—as though the information we gave him so glibly had any real bearing on this precarious undertaking of his two young daughters. Whatever his doubts and hesitations, he let us decide for ourselves; it was only when we boarded the old Bald Eagle at St. Louis one summer day in 1907, bound up the river, that he clung to our hands as though unable to let us go, saying, "I'm afraid you are making a mistake. Take care of yourselves."

"It will be all right," Ida Mary told him cheerfully. "It is only for eight months. Nothing can happen in eight months. . . ."

Section 18, Range 77W—about thirty miles from Pierre. It seemed more real now. The hotel proprietor promised to find us a claim locator to whom that cryptic number made sense.

The next morning at sun-up we were on our way. At that hour the little homestead town of Ft. Pierre lay quiet. Other homesteaders were ready to start out: a farmer and his wife from Wisconsin, who were busy sandwiching their four children into a wagon already filled with immigrant goods, a cow and horse tied on behind.

At a long table in the fly-specked hotel dining room we ate flapjacks and fried potatoes and drank strong coffee in big heavy cups. Then, at long last, perched on the seat of the claim locator's high spring wagon, we jolted out of town, swerving to let a stagecoach loaded with passengers whip past us, waiting while a team of buffalo ambled past, and finally jogged along the beaten road through the bad lands outside of town.

Beyond the rough bad lands we came upon the prairie. We traveled for miles along a narrow, rutted road crossed now and then by dim trails leading nowhere, it seemed. Our own road dwindled to a rough trail, and the spring wagon lurched over it while we clung to the sides to ease the constant jolting, letting go to pull our hats over our eyes which ached with the glare, or over the back of our necks which were blistered from the sun.

Our frantic haste to arrive while the land lasted seemed absurd now. There was land enough for all who wanted it, and few enough to claim it. All that weary day we saw no people save in the distance a few homesteaders mowing strips of the short dry grass for hay. Now and then we passed a few head of horses and a cow grazing. Here and there over the hot, dusty plain we saw shacks and makeshift houses surrounded by patches of corn or flax or dried-up garden. Why were the houses so scattered, looking as though they had been thrown down at random? "They had to be set on the claims," our locator said dryly.

About noon we stopped at a deserted ranch house, surrounded by corrals—a camp, our driver explained, where some stockman held his cattle overnight in driving them to market. Here we ate a lunch and the locator fed and watered the team, refilling the jars from an old well with its long wooden water troughs.

There the trail ended. Now we struck out over a trackless land that grew rougher the farther we went. To look for a quarter-section here was like looking for a needle in a haystack. It was late summer and the sun beat down on the hot prairie grass and upon our heads. We had driven all day without sign of shade—and save for that brief interval at noon, without sight of water. Our faces and hands were blistered, our throats parched from the hot wind.

This was not the West as I had dreamed of it, not the West even of banditry and violent action. It was a desolate, forgotten land, without vegetation save for the dry, crackling grass, without visible tokens of fertility. Drab and gray and empty. Stubborn, resisting land. Heroics wouldn't count for much here. It would take slow, back-breaking labor, and time, and the action of the seasons to make the prairie bloom. People had said this was no place for two girls. It began to seem that they were right.

And this was the goal of our long journey—the tar-paper shack. We pushed the trunk over in front of the door which had no lock, piled the chairs and suitcases on top of the trunk; spread a comfort over the criss-cross rope bed and threw ourselves across it without undressing. We had no gun or other weapon for protection and were not brave enough to use one had we possessed it.

The little cellar windows which stood halfway between the low ceiling and the floor were nailed shut. But we needed neither window nor door, so far as air was concerned. It poured through the wide cracks like water through a sieve.

While we tossed, too tired and sick at heart to sleep, I asked: "What became of the young man who built this shack?"

"He lived here only a few weeks and abandoned it," Ida Mary explained. "The claim reverted to the government, shack, bunk and all. He couldn't stick it out."

CHAPTER 2

Expanding Horizons for Educated Women

One of the most far-reaching changes in the post-Civil War period was the expansion of higher education for women. In the late nineteenth century, educating daughters still remained controversial. In 1873, a Harvard physician named Edward Clarke published a book called *Sex in Education,* which argued that if women used their "limited energy" on studying, it would harm the "female apparatus." Doctors such as Mary Putnam Jacobi soon produced scientific studies demonstrating that women college students could think and menstruate at the same time, but Clarke's impact lingered. Not until several generations of college women had shown that higher education did not in fact unsex them did such fears disappear.

The expansion of women's education took several routes. The most widely known experiments were the Eastern women's colleges such as Vassar (1865), Wellesley and Smith (1875), and Bryn Mawr (1884). But as early as the 1870s, a majority of women were enrolled in coeducational schools rather than single-sex institutions. Some private universities in the East, such as Boston University and Cornell, opened their doors to women in the 1870s, but much of the progress came in the large state universities of the Midwest and West, such as Wisconsin (1867), Michigan, and California (1870). A third route was the establishment of coordinate colleges, such as Radcliffe (1884) to Harvard, and Barnard (1889) to Columbia. In almost all cases, it took the determined efforts of women, and a few male allies, to win these breakthroughs in higher education.

While still limited to a tiny minority of American women, the numbers of college women grew steadily after 1870, as did their proportion of total students. By 1900, there were eighty-five thousand women enrolled in colleges and universities, comprising almost 37 percent of all students; just twenty years later, 283,000 women made up 47.3 percent of enrollments. In fact, some schools such as Stanford and the University of Chicago became alarmed at what they perceived as the feminization of higher education and took steps (unsuccessfully) to limit women's enrollment. This response suggests a certain uneasiness about how far American society should go in providing a college education for its women.

Female students enjoyed the stimulation of intellectual work, strenuous physical education (to counter Dr. Clarke), and a myriad of extracurricular activities. But on graduation came the difficult question of "after college, what?" Many women, especially the first generation of college graduates from the 1870s and 1880s, felt in limbo; they had been educated to be useful and productive, but there were few outlets to put their education to use. More options for professional work, stimulating reform or volunteer activities, or graduate study greeted the next generation, those graduating in the 1890s and early 1900s, but the transition from college student to educated, adult woman was rarely easy.

The question of marriage was always uppermost. Parents had been reassured that a college education would not cause daughters to be unfit for marriage. Despite popular fears that unmarried college women were causing "race suicide," they did marry, but at a somewhat lower rate than non-college women and at a later age. Most of the women who married did not intend to combine marriage with career: for women of these early generations, this decision operated as an either/or choice. By the early twentieth century, some professional women were beginning to juggle the two, but such pioneers were still unusual. One group that did consistently combine professional work with marriage was African-American women teachers, reflecting the much higher wage-force participation rate of African-American women than their white counterparts.

One of the greatest benefits of a college education was that it provided a way for women who chose not to marry to support themselves, rather than remaining a superfluous unmarried daughter at home. By the 1890s, middle-class women could find paid employment that allowed them to establish households of their own. Often, they chose to share their lives with other like-minded professional women. Such long-term relationships won approval from family and society alike as an alternative to what was perceived as lonely spinsterhood.

Educated women took advantage of expanding opportunities when they entered the professions, but they never enjoyed anywhere near as wide options as did men with comparable education and training. Men were applauded for ambition, decisiveness, and drive for success (the very personality traits necessary for professional achievement); such traits in women were viewed as unfeminine, undesirable, and highly suspect. As a result, women were often marginalized in professional life, segregated to fields dominated by women (like teaching, social work, and librarianship) or consigned to lesser ranks with no hopes of advancement in others (like science). Women were always paid less than men. A further characteristic of women's professional activity was that it was often interpreted as an extension of women's traditional responsibilities in the home, hence the term *helping professions.*

Some figures help to illustrate the range of options open to professional women in the early twentieth century. In 1910, women made up 1 percent of lawyers and 6 percent of physicians, but 52 percent of social workers and 79 percent of librarians. Teaching was always open to college women; an 1898 survey by the Association of Collegiate Alumnae found that 72.4 percent of college graduates had taught at some point in their lives. Some women went on to do graduate work, at first in Europe and then in the United States, but these academics found that the women's colleges were often the only places that would hire a woman Ph.D.

Despite such a discouraging outlook for professional advancement, women college graduates in the early twentieth century felt like pioneers, as indeed they were. The ability to contemplate useful, interesting work outside the home (which could apply to volunteer work on the part of married women as well) was a definite expansion of options over earlier times. These college-educated women provided many of the recruits who fueled Progressive reform.

M. Carey Thomas at Cornell

It was an exciting, if somewhat daunting, prospect for young women to attend college in the 1870s and 1880s. Educator and feminist Martha Carey Thomas (1857–1935) had to battle her father for permission to enroll at the recently opened Cornell University, where she received her B.A. in 1877. Thomas's journals convey the life of a female undergraduate. Her work occupies center stage, and she approaches her studies with a seriousness that reflects her desire to bring credit to the cause of higher education for women. Yet college was not all work and no play, as her descriptions of undergraduate social life suggest.

One interesting aspect of M. Carey Thomas's journals (she dropped the Martha at Cornell) was her description of the intense emotional attachment she formed to another Cornell undergraduate during her senior year. This phenomenon, known as *smashing*, occurred when two young women fell violently in love and formed intense bonds expressed in explicitly passionate language. One description of smashing comes from Vassar in the 1870s: "When a Vassar girl takes a shine to another, she straightway enters upon a regular course of bouquet sending, interspersed with tinted notes, mysterious packages of 'Ridley's Mixed Candies,' locks of hair perhaps, and many other tended tokens, until at last the object of her attentions is captured, the two become inseparable, and the aggressor is considered by her circle of acquaintances as—SMASHED." Such relationships were a recognized and accepted part of women's emotional lives in the late nineteenth century.

M. Carey Thomas never married. After her graduation from Cornell, she found the opportunities for graduate work for women in the United States so limited that she enrolled at the University of Zurich. In 1882, she received her Ph.D. summa cum laude, the first foreigner and the first woman to achieve that distinction. In 1885, she became dean and professor of English at the recently founded Bryn Mawr, outside Philadelphia; in 1894, this strong-willed woman became its president. For the rest of her career, M. Carey Thomas was intimately associated with the college. Besides serving as an advocate for the expansion of higher education for women, Thomas strongly supported professional careers for women, woman suffrage, and other feminist causes.

July 16, 1875

Well, it is *done:* on the 13, 14, 15 of last June I passed the entrance examinations at Cornell University for the Admission into the Classical Course. This last summer it seemed impossible. But the whole of this year with a steady, unalterable determination that surprised myself even—I have been working for it. Father was terribly opposed and last Christmas when Miss Slocum was at our house, said he never while he lived would give his consent. Many and dreadful are the talks we have had upon this subject, but Mother, my own splendid mother, helped me in this as she always has in everything and sympathized with me. Again and again last winter did the old difficulty of deciding between "duty to ourselves and others" come up— for it was not a religious duty of course to go to Cornell and sometimes it seemed as it ought to be given up. I know all the Grove people thought so— but I *could* not. Then too the difficulty of preparing without knowing how they examined and of getting teachers, but, above all, Father's feeling so about it. For I love him dearly and cannot bear to disappoint him. How it was done I do not know but if it had not been for Mother I am sure he would not have consented. But about three weeks before, he gave up and I began to prepare for the examinations.

I never did such terrible studying every moment for those three weeks. . . . However, it is over with—Professor Peck said I passed a splendid examination in Latin, ditto Professor Oliver in Algebra and Geometry. . . . Almost all the professors complimented Father and Mother upon my passing so well. Mr. Howland when he saw me said he was proud that a *Howland* graduate, etc., etc. The strain was terrible because I could not have endured failure. And it was an inexpressible satisfaction to pass well. Father and Mother were up there and explored the university while I was getting examined. Mother was delighted with it and I think Father was pleased. The

Source: M. Carey Thomas journal entries, July 16, 1875, and June 12, 1877, in *The Making of a Feminist,* ed. Marjorie Dobkin (Kent, Ohio: Kent State University Press, 1979), pp. 100–101, 116–119.

last night he said to me, "Well Minnie, I'm proud of thee, but this university is an awful place to swallow thee up."

If I can help it he and Mother shall never regret having yielded to me in this thing.

June 12, 1877

Sage College, Cornell University. It is almost two years since I have made an entry. I have now finished all my senior examinations and have nothing to do for the next nine days except wait for my degree. . . .

At last the object of my ambition—the one purpose that runs through my journals has been attained. I have graduated at a university. I have a degree that represents more than a Vassar one.

I wish I had kept a slight, at least, record of my experience here and now it is too late to recall it. The first two years I had a difficult time to get into the new methods of study and especially in Latin I entered behind.

Altogether I have learned a great deal and it has been thoroughly profitable to be here—it has given me a new outlook. Though I feel very far from a good Latin and Greek scholar, yet I do see light somewhat. My life here has been very hermit like, except seven girls. I have seen very few people, half the men here are uncultivated and Cornell misses all that glorious culture that one reads of in college books. The girls are for the most part of a different social station and I have seen very little of them as they have nothing to counterbalance that fact.

I want to write about my fifth friendship, for in spite of myself I have one. When I came here I made up my mind that at Howland I had wasted a great deal of time with friends and that it amounted to very little except pleasure and that especially away from home the pain of being separated more than overbalanced the other.

The first girl I saw was a young lady in Algebra examination—lace-dressed, in gray with a brown hat with a wing in it. She was up at Pres. White's to tea and we had a little talk. I thought she was smart and well prepared in the examinations next day. I "rather hoped" I should see her again next fall. Next fall came—she was the first person I saw as I drove up to the Sage College. Her mother was with her and together we chose our rooms on the same corridor third hall. Miss Mills was to room with Miss Hicks and would not unpack until she had heard from her examinations. Miss Putnam whom I had met at Prof. Russel's chose a room on the same floor. It was lonely at first—my only consolation was going down to Howland every other Friday and seeing Carrie [Ladd]. At first I rather looked down on the girls in our hall. Miss Hicks, Miss Putnam, Miss Mills, Miss Head and Miss Mitchell—they seemed more interested in fun than anything else. And not one of them was smart except Miss Hicks; the other girls in the Sage were good enough students but not ladies, and the gentlemen, except Prof. Boyesen, were second rate, "half cut" Bessie would say.

Well, I began to see more and more of Miss Hicks. She got in the habit of coming and reading me her mother's letters and of bidding me good night. We used to go and study some time in Casquadilla woods and when it would get dark we would sit under her blue shawl and talk. Then we came across Swinburne's "Atalanta in Calydon" and Miss Hicks would come in her wrapper after I was in bed and we would read it out loud and we learned several of the choruses. One night we had stopped reading later than usual and obeying a sudden impulse I turned to her and asked, "Do you love me?" She threw her arms around me and whispered, "I love you passionately." She did not go home that night and we talked and talked. She told me she had been praying that I might care for her.

That was the beginning and from that time, it was the fall of '75, till June '77 we have been inseparable. I put this all down because I cannot understand it. I am sure it is not best for people to care about each other so much. In the first place it wasted my time—it was a pleasure to be with Miss Hicks and as I cared to be with no one else, I would have spent all that time in reading. It was different with her—as she likes a great many people and liked the other girls and would have wasted her time anyway. In the second place it was almost more pain than pleasure because we quarreled so. All our ideas were opposite. Miss Hicks' mother I think is rising in society and there is not the least bit of fastidiousness in Miss Hicks' nature. She likes everyone. She cares for everyone's opinion. She would do a great many things I did not think suitable. I would object and say more than I ought to and Miss Hicks would fling herself on the lounge in a passion of tears and sometimes we would both cry—although it was dreadful—yet all the time we cared about each other so much that we could not give up our friendship. Again and again we gave up in despair and then we would care and have such lovely times that we began again and the whole thing was over again. Often I prayed that I might stop loving her.

This high tragedy seems ridiculous written but I know I shall forget the possibility of such things unless I do. It seems rather too bad when one goes to college to study to be distracted by such things. It was not Miss Hicks' fault but I know I did not study as well because of her, but I could not help it. I was mastered by it—one thing that made our friendship as unpleasant as it sometimes was was my feeling that I ought not to give way to it. Miss Hicks has no generous abandon in study—her companionship did not help me, I think, in an intellectual way. I tell her she ought to be obliged to me. I taught her to love passionately and to be passionately angry. Neither of which she had experienced before.

She is lovely in many ways. She has a sweet simplicity and straightforwardness about her, an utter faithfulness—I would trust her absolutely with any secret—she is naturally very smart but I think, at least until she came to Cornell, she studies because she had nothing else to do and because of her love of approbation. She wants to be an architect and seems very fond of it

but I do not feel as if she would make a success. She seems to me to be easily turned aside by people. It is hard to talk to her—I never feel except when
she is angry as if she were really saying what she feels with all her heart. In
her manners she wants a certain quiet self assurance. I think she will probably get married. These are almost all unfavorable things but I leave out all
her prettiness and her traits of character that attract me—in fact I just fell in
love with her and I did it gradually too (not that adoring worship I had for
Libbie [Conkey], nor the equal fun and earnest loving devoted friendship
Carrie and I have) but, that Atalanta night I knew I did not care as much as
she did and so it went on, I getting fonder and fonder of her until it was as I
say—all the time against my better judgment and yet I cannot tell why it was.
She is lovely, in many many ways much better than I am.

Jane Addams Struggles with the Problem of "After College, What?"

Jane Addams (1860–1935) had a harder time finding her professional
niche than did M. Carey Thomas. Addams graduated from Rockford
Seminary in 1881, but spent the next seven years aimlessly drifting as
she tried to balance the "social claim" (her interest in broader societal
and economic questions raised by her education) with the "family
claim" (the tendency of families to regard daughters as dependent possessions, rather than full individuals in their own right). The solution
to her dilemma came on an extended European trip with her step-
mother, as Addams later recounted it: "I gradually became convinced
that it would be a good thing to rent a house in a part of the city where
many primitive and actual needs are found, in which young women
who had been given over too exclusively to study might restore a balance of activity along traditional lines and learn of life from life itself.
. . ." Thus did the settlement house movement come to the United
States, with Jane Addams and Hull House (founded in 1889) quickly
its most famous practitioners.

The settlement house offered compensations both to its residents
and the surrounding neighborhood. The Nineteenth ward in which
Hull House was located was one of Chicago's poorest, containing fifty
thousand people, seven churches, no public schools, and 255 saloons.
Hull House developed an extensive range of social services and recreational programs including day care, health and hygiene, language
classes, crafts, poetry readings, and the like. This selection from Addams's autobiography, *Twenty Years at Hull-House* (1910), describes the
first days at Hull House and introduces some of the neighbors who
visited the settlement house.

Source: Jane Addams, *Twenty Years at Hull-House* (New York: Macmillan, 1910; Signet Classic
reprint, New American Library, 1960), pp. 75, 77–79, 87–89.

Settlement house residents, primarily college-educated women from the middle classes, also reaped rewards. They found useful roles that allowed them to move beyond charity work in the "Lady Bountiful" tradition to the scientific investigation that characterized Progressive era reform. They lived together in an atmosphere that resembled a college dorm, an especially congenial setting for women who chose not to marry. Hull House residents included Julia Lathrop, Alice Hamilton, and Grace and Edith Abbott, all noted Progressive era reformers. In addition, the institution drew on the support of women's groups in Chicago, including the Chicago Woman's Club, which had been influential in building support for the Woman's Building at the 1893 Columbian Exhibition.

At age thirty-three, in 1893, Jane Addams remarked, "I find that I am considered quite the grandmother of American settlements." During the Progressive era, she was the most admired woman in America, a symbol of women's new roles in public life.

The next January found Miss Starr[1] and myself in Chicago, searching for a neighborhood in which we might put our plans into execution. . . . We decided upon a location somewhere near the junction of Blue Island Avenue, Halsted Street, and Harrison Street. I was surprised and overjoyed on the very first day of our search for quarters to come upon the hospitable old house, the quest for which I had so recently abandoned. The house was of course rented, the lower part of it used for offices and storerooms in connection with a factory that stood back of it. However, after some difficulties were overcome, it proved to be possible to sublet the second floor and what had been the large drawing-room on the first floor. . . .

The fine old house responded kindly to repairs, its wide hall and open fireplaces always insuring it a gracious aspect. Its generous owner, Miss Helen Culver, in the following spring gave us a free leasehold of the entire house. Her kindness has continued through the years until the group of thirteen buildings, which at present comprises our equipment, is built largely upon land which Miss Culver has put at the service of the Settlement which bears Mr. Hull's name. In those days the house stood between an undertaking establishment and a saloon. "Knight, Death, and the Devil," the three were called by a Chicago wit, and yet any mock heroics which might be implied by comparing the Settlement to a knight quickly dropped away under the genuine kindness and hearty welcome extended to us by the families living up and down the street.

We furnished the house as we would have furnished it were it in another part of the city, with the photographs and other impedimenta we had collected in Europe, and with a few bits of family mahogany. While all the new furniture which was bought was enduring in quality, we were careful to keep it in character with the fine old residence. Probably no young matron ever placed

[1]Ellen Gates Starr (1859–1940), a classmate of Jane Addams at Rockford Seminary, was a cofounder of Hull House. However, the venture was always publicly identified with the more famous Jane Addams.

her own things in her own house with more pleasure than that with which we first furnished Hull-House. We believed that the Settlement may logically bring to its aid all those adjuncts which the cultivated man regards as good and suggestive of the best life of the past.

On the 18th of September, 1889, Miss Starr and I moved into it, with Miss Mary Keyser, who began by performing the housework, but who quickly developed into a very important factor in the life of the vicinity as well as in that of the household, and whose death five years later was most sincerely mourned by hundreds of our neighbors. In our enthusiasm over "settling," the first night we forgot not only to lock but to close a side door opening on Polk Street, and were much pleased in the morning to find that we possessed a fine illustration of the honesty and kindliness of our new neighbors. . . .

On our first New Year's Day at Hull-House we invited the older people in the vicinity, sending a carriage for the most feeble and announcing to all of them that we were going to organize an Old Settlers' Party.

Every New Year's Day since, older people in varying numbers have come together at Hull-House to relate early hardships and to take for the moment the place in the community to which their pioneer life entitles them. Many people who were formerly residents of the vicinity, but whom prosperity has carried into more desirable neighborhoods, come back to these meetings and often confess to each other that they have never since found such kindness as in early Chicago when all its citizens came together in mutual enterprises. Many of these pioneers, so like the men and women of my earliest childhood that I always felt comforted by their presence in the house, were very much opposed to "foreigners," whom they held responsible for a depreciation of property and a general lowering of the tone of the neighborhood. Sometimes we had a chance for championship; I recall one old man, fiercely American, who had reproached me because we had so many "foreign views" on our walls, to whom I endeavored to set forth our hope that the pictures might afford a familiar island to the immigrants in a sea of new and strange impressions. The old settler guest, taken off his guard, replied, "I see; they feel as we did when we saw a Yankee notion from down East"—thereby formulating the dim kinship between the pioneer and the immigrant, both "buffeting the waves of a new development." The older settlers as well as their children throughout the years have given genuine help to our various enterprises for neighborhood improvement, and from their own memories of earlier hardships have made many shrewd suggestions for alleviating the difficulties of that first sharp struggle with untoward conditions.

In those early days we were often asked why we had come to live on Halsted Street when we could afford to live somewhere else. I remember one man who used to shake his head and say it was "the strangest thing he had met in his experience," but who was finally convinced that it was "not strange but natural." In time it came to seem natural to all of us that the Settlement should be there. If it is natural to feed the hungry and care for the sick, it is certainly natural to give pleasure to the young, comfort to the aged, and to minister to the deep-seated craving for social intercourse that all men feel. Whoever does it is rewarded by something which, if not gratitude, is at least spontaneous and vital and lacks that irksome sense of obligation with which a substantial benefit is too often acknowledged.

In addition to the neighbors who responded to the receptions and classes, we found those who were too battered and oppressed to care for them. To these, however, was left that susceptibility to the bare offices of humanity which raises such offices into a bond of fellowship.

From the first it seemed understood that we were ready to perform the humblest neighborhood services. We were asked to wash the newborn babies, and to prepare the dead for burial, to nurse the sick, and to "mind the children."

Occasionally these neighborly offices unexpectedly uncovered ugly human traits. For six weeks after an operation we kept in one of our three bedrooms a forlorn little baby who, because he was born with a cleft palate, was most unwelcome even to his mother, and we were horrified when he died of neglect a week after he was returned to his home; a little Italian bride of fifteen sought shelter with us one November evening, to escape her husband who had beaten her every night for a week when he returned home from work, because she had lost her wedding ring; two of us officiated quite alone at the birth of an illegitimate child because the doctor was late in arriving, and none of the honest Irish matrons would "touch the likes of her"; we ministered at the deathbed of a young man, who during a long illness of tuberculosis had received so many bottles of whisky through the mistaken kindness of his friends, that the cumulative effect produced wild periods of exultation, in one of which he died.

We were also early impressed with the curious isolation of many of the immigrants; an Italian woman once expressed her pleasure in the red roses that she saw at one of our receptions in surprise that they had been "brought so fresh all the way from Italy." She would not believe for an instant that they had been grown in America. She said that she had lived in Chicago for six years and had never seen any roses, whereas in Italy she had seen them every summer in great profusion. During all that time, of course, the woman had lived within ten blocks of a florist's window; she had not been more than a five-cent car ride away from the public parks; but she had never dreamed of faring forth for herself, and no one had taken her. Her conception of America had been the untidy street in which she lived and had made her long struggle to adapt herself to American ways.

But in spite of some untoward experiences, we were constantly impressed with the uniform kindness and courtesy we received. Perhaps these first days laid the simple human foundations which are certainly essential for continuous living among the poor: first, genuine preference for residence in an industrial quarter to any other part of the city, because it is interesting and makes the human appeal; and second, the conviction, in the words of Canon Barnett, that the things which make men alike are finer and better than the things that keep them apart, and that these basic likenesses, if they are properly accentuated, easily transcend the less essential differences of race, language, creed, and tradition.

Perhaps even in those first days we made a beginning toward that object which was afterward stated in our charter: "To provide a center for a higher civic and social life; to institute and maintain educational and philanthropic enterprises, and to investigate and improve the conditions in the industrial districts of Chicago."

Alice Hamilton Explores the Dangerous Trades

One of the most appealing careers for educated women in the late nineteenth century was that of physician. Around 1900, as many as one in five doctors were women, a percentage that would not be reached again until the 1970s. One such physician was Hull House resident Alice Hamilton (1869–1970), an 1893 graduate of the University of Michigan medical school. In her autobiography *Exploring the Dangerous Trades* (1943), she explained why she had settled on that career: "I chose medicine, not because I was scientifically minded, for I was deeply ignorant of science. I chose it because as a doctor I could go anywhere I pleased—to far-off lands or to city slums—and be quite sure that I could be of use anywhere. I should meet all sorts and conditions of men, I should not be tied down to a school or college as a teacher is, or have to work under a superior, as a nurse must do." Hamilton became a pioneer in the field of industrial medicine, that is, the investigation of the workplace effects of poisons and chemicals on employees. She was especially well known for her pioneering studies of lead.

Alice Hamilton was no narrow-minded scientific investigator; this selection from her autobiography describes her methods of investigation and her sympathy and sensitivity for the victims. Hamilton's almost single-handed development of the field of industrial medicine led to her appointment to the Harvard Medical School faculty in 1919, the first woman appointed. (It would be World War II before Harvard would admit women students to its medical school.) She limited her teaching to one semester a year in order to spend the rest of her time traveling or at Hull House. Thus did she blend professional achievement with personal satisfaction in a way characteristic of the early generations of college graduates and professional women.

It was pioneering, exploration of an unknown field. No young doctor nowadays can hope for work as exciting and rewarding. Everything I discovered was new and most of it was really valuable. I knew nothing of manufacturing

Source: Alice Hamilton, *Exploring the Dangerous Trades* (Boston: Little, Brown, 1943; reprinted by Northeastern University Press, 1985), pp. 121–122, 123–124, 125–126.

processes, but I learned them on the spot, and before long every detail of the Old Dutch Process and the Carter Process of white-lead production was familiar to me, also the roasting of red lead and litharge and the smelting of lead ore and refining of lead scrap. From the first I became convinced that what I must look for was lead dust and lead fumes, that men were poisoned by breathing poisoned air; not by handling their food with unwashed hands. Nowadays that fact has been so strongly established by experimental proof that nobody would think of disputing it. But in 1910 and for many years after, the firm (and comforting) belief of foremen and employers was that if a man was poisoned by lead it was because he did not wash his hands and scrub his nails, although a little intelligent observation would have been enough to show its absurdity. . . .

Here are four histories, picked at random, from my notes of 1910.

A Bohemian, an enameler of bathtubs, had worked eighteen months at his trade, without apparently becoming poisoned, though his health had suffered. One day, while at the furnace, he fainted away and for four days he lay in coma, then passed into delirium during which it was found that both forearms and both ankles were palsied. He made a partial recovery during the following six months but when he left for his home in Bohemia he was still partly paralyzed.

A Hungarian, thirty-six years old, worked for seven years grinding lead paint. During this time he had three attacks of colic, with vomiting and headache. I saw him in the hospital, a skeleton of a man, looking almost twice his age, his limbs soft and flabby, his muscles wasted. He was extremely emaciated, his color was a dirty grayish yellow, his eyes dull and expressionless. He lay in an apathetic condition, rousing when spoken to and answering rationally but slowly, with often an appreciable delay, then sinking back into apathy.

A Polish laborer worked only three weeks in a very dusty white-lead plant at an unusually dusty emergency job, at the end of which he was sent to the hospital with severe lead colic and palsy of both wrists.

A young Italian, who spoke no English, worked for a month in a white-lead plant but without any idea that the harmless-looking stuff was poisonous. There was a great deal of dust in his work. One day he was seized with an agonizing pain in his head which came on him so suddenly that he fell to the ground. He was sent to the hospital, semiconscious, with convulsive attacks, and was there for two weeks; when he came home, he had a relapse and had to go back to the hospital. Three months later he was still in poor health and could not do a full day's work. . . .

Life at Hull-House had accustomed me to going straight to the homes of people about whom I wished to learn something and talking to them in their own surroundings, where they have courage to speak out what is in their minds. They were almost always foreigners, Bulgarians, Serbs, Poles, Italians, Hungarians, who had come to this country in the search for a better life for themselves and their children. Sometimes they thought they had found it, then when sickness struck down the father things grew very black and there were no old friends and neighbors and cousins to fall back on as there had been in the old country. Often it was an agent of a steamship company who had coaxed them over with promises of a land flowing with jobs and high wages. Six hundred Bulgarians had been induced to leave their villages by these super-salesmen, and to come to Chicago. Of course they took the first job they could find and if it proved to be one that weakened and crippled them—well, that was their bad luck!

It sometimes seemed to me that industry was exploiting the finest and best in these men—their love of their children, their sense of family responsibility. I think of an enameler of bathtubs whom I traced to his squalid little cottage. He was a young Slav who used to be so strong he could run up the hill on which his cottage stood and spend all the evening digging in his garden. Now, he told me, he climbed up like an old man and sank exhausted in a chair, he was so weary, and if he tried to hoe or rake he had to give it up. His digestion had failed, he had a foul mouth, he couldn't eat, he had lost much weight. He had had many attacks of colic and the doctor told him if he did not quit he would soon be a wreck. "Why did you keep on," I asked, "when you knew the lead was getting you?" "Well, there were the payments on the house," he said, "and the two kids." The house was a bare, ugly, frame shack, the children were little, underfed things, badly in need of a handkerchief, but for them a man had sacrificed his health and his joy in life. When employers tell me they prefer married men, and encourage their men to have homes of their own, because it makes them so much steadier, I wonder if they have any idea of all that that implies.

African-American Women Enter the Teaching Profession

Mamie Garvin Fields

Teaching has always been a profession dominated by women. For black women, the choice of a teaching career often involved an element of racial self-consciousness, because teaching future generations was seen as a concrete way to improve conditions in the black community. It is no coincidence that many African-American leaders, among them Fannie Jackson Coppin, Charlotte Hawkins Brown, and Mary McLeod Bethune, all taught at some point during their lives.

The segregated school systems of the South and the northern cities created a steady demand for black teachers, a by-product of the publicly supported system of segregation in force in the United States until the 1950s. In 1910, there were 17,266 black women teaching in the South, comprising 1 percent of all the black women workers. Like white teachers, blacks tended to be young and single, although black teachers were far more likely to be married than whites. Yet black teachers faced special handicaps: their contracts and budgets were at the mercy of white administrators; their pay, averaging $25 to $30 a month, was less than half their white counterparts, while their classes were twice as large; and they often could not count on full-time or year-round employment because black schools sometimes ran for as little as three months a year.

The career of Mamie Garvin Fields shows the importance black women attached to teaching as well as the handicaps under which they labored. Born in 1888 in Charleston, South Carolina, Fields's commitment to uplifting the black community through teaching comes through clearly in this excerpt from her 1983 memoir, *Lemon Swamp and Other Places*. A graduate of Claflin University, Fields's first jobs were in poor rural areas of South Carolina, where two teachers could have upwards of one hundred students in a single room. After her marriage, Mamie Garvin Fields alternated teaching with volunteer and civic contributions in Charleston.

The first school I ever taught in was the Pine Wood School, Pine Wood, South Carolina, in what we call the "Sand Hills." The Sand Hills of Sumter County is a belt of sandy land that crosses the state in the south central portion. It's the poorest part of the state. The women there did two types of work. They would "muddy" for eels or mullet, and they would fish for cats in the Pee Dee River and its creeks. ("Muddying" meant that they would hike their dresses up and wade in, taking up the fish in baskets or nets.) The men went to nearby mills or into the forest to cut crossties for the railroad. My sister Hattie and I taught there in 1908–1909.

The people of Pine Wood were the poorest people I had ever seen. The whites there were poor too, but at least they had a six-month school for their children, and the building was on the main street in town. There was no school building for Negro children. But some of the Negro people had a lodge hall, a queer building designed like a train coach, long and narrow. When they found out that they would be given a teacher, they decided to use this building. They made benches and a table for the teacher, and they painted blackboards.

Over a hundred children came in November, when Hattie was to start teaching, so she asked for an assistant. The trustee said that if they divided the hall through the center, they would be given another teacher, which is how Sister sent for me in December. We were to have a three-month school that year, and I would teach for one month. (However, parents in the School House Meeting raised the money so that I could stay another month.) By the time they got the hall divided, we had 5 feet apiece, half the width of the hall. When we finished putting the benches end to end for about 30 feet length, very little space was left to pass in front of the children. If you were on one end, you couldn't see the children on the other, so you had to move up and down this narrow space. They put a door in the partition so that my principal and I could communicate. Believe me, we really had to work together, because you could hear the children on the other side. If Sister was doing something noisy and I wasn't, it would ruin my lesson, and so forth. Now I wonder how we did it. . . .

In 1909 I landed a school on John's Island, a coveted venture, because very few of the black graduates were getting jobs. All the schools were taught by white women, mainly the wives of trustees. But even the old rebel Department of Education became convinced that the Negro graduates should be given a chance. But since white people taught in the city schools, you had to try to go in the county. The way to get in Charleston County was to know a cook or maid or butler who came in touch with the powers that be. You had to get your job through the kitchen, through any of those who worked for the "aristocrats" below Broad Street. However, I said to myself, "You mean to tell me I got my education and still have to go through the kitchen? Never!" That was one of my words, "never!" My old aunts and uncles of the early days had race pride. Although slaves, they stood up. It must have been those ancestors, working through me, when I chose not to go to the kitchen for an appointment, after spending all my life so far in school and graduating with honors.

I went down to the superintendent's office and knocked. He said, "Come in," but when he saw I was a Negro, he bent back over his work as though I wasn't there. After ten minutes passed, he looked up and said, "Well?" I answered, "Mr. Waring, I brought my diploma to show you, as I want to teach in Charleston County." He said, "I have 100 ahead of you." I answered, "Please put me down 101. I have prepared to teach at home and have nowhere else to go." He took my diploma and copied my name and my degree, "Licentiate of Instruction," given to those who took special work in pedagogy. He reached for a red pencil and marked an "X" by my name. I thought then that I was doomed. On my way out, I met Reverend John Green, who taught on James Island and was one of our Methodist preachers. When Reverend Green got in, the superintendent asked if the reverend knew me. Reverend Green said he did and paid quite a tribute to me. The superintendent: "Do you know where she lives? Go by and tell her she will teach at our Humbert Wood Elementary on John's Island, with another Claflinite, Miss Rosalee Brown."

Well! When I began teaching on John's Island, eyebrows were raised by the Sam Fabers and by people who wanted to teach. "How did *she* get it?" they wanted to know. "Who gave it to her?" I opened many a person's eyes to the possibility of using their own brain. Then, strange to say, everybody came to me to see if I could get them a job. I told them to go down to the powers that be, as I did: don't wait for a go-between. In fact, even the go-betweens came to see how I did it: they wanted to know who helped me. But that system of going to go-betweens didn't break up for a long time. It gave some colored people power over the rest. . . .

John's Island was wild then, with great, thick woods of pine and live oak, with Spanish moss hanging from the branches, black all around you. You could hear forest noises and the wagon wheels. You could hear the horse. But that was all. You couldn't see anything. Our host didn't do much talking. Rosalee and I about held our breath. On the way we came to a gully that separated us from the people we were to stay with, our future home. They had a log across the divide to walk on. Rosalee, who lived all her life on James Island, crossed this log with success, but I slipped and fell down in the gully, in the big old deep gully with the frogs and everything. Lord, I almost died! I went screaming, for I knew I was visiting the realm of snakes, lizards, spiders, and what-have-you. Although I could see none of them, the pitch black made me "see" all of them! Fortunately, though, no water was in the gully. My host pulled me out, dirty and frightened to death. . . .

You couldn't find the school for the weeds growing around it. It just looked God-forsaken. I must have had a look on my face, because the children said, "Well, you know, we going to clean the ya'd." I know for sure that I had a look when we got in the door. Lord have mercy, everything was inside! I thought about snakes, and the children told me, "You know, last year when the teacher sit over there, snake come right down on the teacher!" Telling stories to scare me! But it looked so bad I thought it might be true, so we all looked, and we found several snakes, here and there. The children killed them—as I looked on from afar. By the time we got through killing snakes, I was worried about Rosalee. In the time she took, nowadays she could have gone to New York. She finally returned from the trustee's house about noon. Why so late? She said the ox decided to stop pulling and lie down in the road. They had to wait until he could be coaxed to get up.

The school was just an old wooden house with two rooms. The benches inside had no backs. Next day we told the children not to put on their school clothes, to come on down and let's rake out the yard and clean up the house. Bring your hoe and rake. The children even had to bring brooms, because the county didn't give you a thing. I said, "No blackboard?" "No, don't have no blackboard." "You have crayon?" "Crayon! Ee ain't got no crayon." The county gave you a big old brass bell with a black handle, the only pretty thing they had. Our school equipment was the bell and the rollbook.

We started with about sixty or seventy children between the two of us, and before long we got to a hundred and some. Before us, they had been taught by a white teacher, the trustee's wife. She let us know that we needn't bother much: the children didn't come to school. Well, the white folks didn't much care if our children came to school or didn't, but we tried hard to get them to come. But goodness, they had every type of reason for not coming. Some had no pants, no shoes, or no sweater to wear when it was cold. If it rained, they would say the road was too muddy to pass, or else they couldn't get the school clothes dry. Some children told me they had nobody to come with; and if they came alone, the bigger children would "fight me in the road, and no kin to take up for me." Certain mothers would say, "Mr. so-and-so [a white farmer] want us to work, so nobody to dress 'em, nobody to comb the hair." Many of the reasons for absence had to do with poverty, one way or the other. But some had to do with custom. If the mother and dad went to a funeral, the children would stay home "out of respect." But the biggest reason was that the parents weren't trained to send their children to school regularly. The teacher could have a lot to do with that. Rosalee and I couldn't just stand in the school and wait for the children to come. We had to help the parents to get the clothes or whatever was needed. And of course, we wanted to work with the children. The teacher before Rosalee and me hardly cared if they came or not. We tried to bring in all the children of school age.

A Pioneering Dean of Women

Lucy Sprague Mitchell

The life choices of Lucy Sprague Mitchell (1878–1967) tell us much about the modern woman in the making. The product of an economically privileged but emotionally unsupportive family in Chicago, she began to glimpse new worlds as a student at Radcliffe, from which she graduated in 1900 with honors in philosophy. In 1906, she became dean of women at the University of California at Berkeley, where she worked diligently to expand educational and social opportunities for her women students.

It was in order to explore the possibility of training women for professions other than teaching that she took the four-month leave described here to observe firsthand professional opportunities for women in New York City in 1911. She apprenticed in a settlement house, a charity organization, a foundation, the Salvation Army, and public school administration—all areas where recent college graduates might find employment. The women she mentions—Lillian Wald, Florence Kelley, Pauline Goldmark, and Julia Richman—were all leading figures in the Progressive era.

The fact-finding trip to New York had monumental personal and professional results for this young woman. She resigned as dean and decided to devote herself to early childhood education. Even more importantly, she decided to marry economist Wesley Clair Mitchell (the "Robin" in the selection), finally overcoming her own doubts that marriage would put an end to her professional aspirations. Both decisions were successful. The Mitchells moved to New York City, where Wesley joined the Columbia faculty and Lucy founded the Bureau of Educational Experiments, which she guided for the next four decades. Their personal life flourished as well with four children. Lucy Sprague Mitchell's ability to find unity between her personal needs and her professional goals marks her as a pioneer in women's attempts to combine marriage and career in their twentieth-century lives.

Source: Lucy Sprague Mitchell, *Two Lives: The Story of Wesley Clair Mitchell and Myself* (New York: Simon & Schuster, 1953), pp. 207–211. Copyright © 1953 by Lucy Sprague Mitchell. Reprinted by permission of McIntosh and Otis, Inc.

When I returned to Berkeley for two more years, Lucy Ward Stebbins, whom I had known at Radcliffe, was appointed as my assistant with the hope that she would be my successor. She was. Before my resignation should take place, I wanted to do something more definite, more constructive about the kind of opportunities the University offered its women students. My early protest against the narrowness of professional training offered had increased rather than decreased. The more I saw of these vigorous western girls, the more preposterous it seemed that they should have no choice except to become teachers—preposterous for them and certainly not desirable for children. For what other professions could the University prepare them? To find an answer to that question became an obsession. Once I had an answer, I might be able to give some impulse to new offerings within the University, but it was no use complaining until I had something constructive to suggest. My plan was to take a four months' leave in New York to find the answer. It was certainly a naïve plan. But I put it through.

John Graham Brooks was visiting me when I evolved this plan. It seemed to him an inspiration. He outfitted me with a suitcaseful of letters of introductions ranging from Anne Morgan to Lillian Wald. And as soon as it could be arranged, off I went to New York. I felt I could not understand much as a mere observer. So I asked six different organizations to let me work for them for a few weeks each, not for any result that could benefit them—I was not as naïve as that!—but to help me understand their problems, how they were tackling them and what kind of qualities each job demanded. I made my request in the high cause of broadening women's education! And in every case, I was accepted. They not only gave me a small practical job to do, but they explained the relation of my small job to their total work. They let me sit in on committees and staff meetings. I learned more in those few months than in any comparable period in my life. They were months of turmoil in more ways than what was happening to me in New York. For I was then receiving long letters from Robin every few days and writing him as many in return. I was trying to decide whether I should marry him.

I went first to Lillian Wald at the Henry Street Settlement. I became her big-eyed shadow for several weeks, listening in at discussions of social, economic and particularly labor problems in real, not theoretical, situations. I took over a class of boys a few times. Not knowing what to do with them, I took them on a trip to near-by Brooklyn Bridge, and we became absorbed in the shipping we could see as we peered down at the East River and docks. I went for awhile as an assistant to one of the Henry Street nurses. I found that my German made it possible for me to understand Yiddish, which most of the patients talked. Henry Moskovitch, then a young man living at Henry Street, took me to the Yiddish theater. He took me often to a restaurant where I met newspaper men from Yiddish papers. They talked about the "gentile press" and the "gentile theater." I realized with a start that I was a "gentile" to them. I had never thought of myself or my many Jewish friends as anything except Americans with different religious backgrounds. It was my first genuine realization of the cleavage in our culture between Jews and gentiles.

One supplemental experience at Henry Street gave me a jolt. I arrived during the garbage strike, and for days no one mentioned that the great heaps of uncollected garbage were not the usual place for the children on the East Side to play. Another jolting experience at the settlement was rooming with Florence Kelley, whom I had known only by name as a great figure in labor problems. Never before or since have I met such a single-minded human dynamo. She was then living in a huge room, the parlor floor of one of the Henry Street houses; she retired to one end, and I was put in at the other. She had two dresses, made alike. Each had a kind of dickey which could be yanked out, and suddenly her work dress was transformed into her evening dress. All her possessions were equally pruned. Her life was concentrated on current labor legislation, and she budgeted her time and her interests to further this drive. She took me on for a time. I followed her around, worked on a text in her office and listened to labor discussions and tirades against capitalists and politicians. I can still feel my terror at crossing through the traffic of New York streets with her. She behaved like Moses crossing the Red Sea. And the traffic behaved like the Red Sea. It simply dammed up on both sides while Florence Kelley and I walked through an empty lane.

Then I went to Mary Richmond at the Charity Organization, where I investigated cases and reported to her. Mrs. Kelley was so indignant at my wasting my time on mawkish charity that she scarcely spoke to me during that time. I soon found that living at the Henry Street Settlement and rooming with Florence Kelley was more than I could take, physically and emotionally. I decided that I must move to a hotel if I were to get through the rest of these intense months with more shifts of work. In a small hotel in the West Forties I felt like a pampered darling but I began to sleep again.

My next job was with Pauline Goldmark, then a beautiful young research worker with eyes like moonstones. She was in charge of a survey of a district in the West Fifties made by the Russell Sage Foundation under the Glenns. Here I met a new kind of intensity—the passion to gather accurate social facts and interpret them by logical, impersonal reasoning. I was out of the turmoil of dealing with practical emergencies and into the turmoil of thinking scientifically. It was blessed relief, and I fell to work eagerly with materials new to me.

Then I thought I'd like to see these same people whom I knew on paper in a detached, scientific way, through completely different lenses. So I signed up as a Salvation Army worker in this district. Again, as with the Henry Street nurse, I began climbing tenement stairs. But now the help I was supposed to bring along with food and old clothes was spiritual. There was great human kindness mingled with the religious fervor of the Salvation Army workers but not the constructive attack on family needs such as I found at Henry Street. I learned much about city institutions, for I took people to Bellevue Hospital and other clinics. One old lady I took to Randalls Island. The poor old soul knew she would never leave that ghastly poorhouse. She begged me to tell them I was her cousin. "It makes a difference, you know, Dearie!"

My last ten days I spent with Julia Richman, who was attacking the problem of education within the public schools with freshness and intelligence. During this last period I was only an observer. I did not use this time to investigate teaching as a profession for our women students, but to help me solve my own personal problems about the work I wanted to do. For me, this brief time in a New York public school was of tremendous significance. This is the work for me, I thought. Public education is the most constructive attack on social problems, for it deals with children and the future. It requires endless research concerning children and what they need to make them grow wholesomely. It requires experimentation in curriculum for children and in teacher education. It requires an understanding of our culture. It is the synthesis of all my interests, all my hopes for humanity. I returned to Berkeley with a clear focus in my own life from which I have never since deviated. My whole later work life in New York had public education as its aim. But it took over thirty years in New York before I could get into actual working relations with the public schools.

I wrote like mad in the peace of the long lonely trip across the continent. In Berkeley, I soon submitted a report to President Wheeler with suggestions for new courses and field work to be given at the University. On the train, I made outlines for two articles which I wrote at once. I don't remember if I gave a title to the first article. Nowadays I should probably call it "Social Studies for Grownups." It bore the imprint of Robin and the thinking he had stimulated in me in his course on Economic Origins. It was my attempt to show the contributions of psychology, sociology, economics and anthropology in understanding human beings and our culture in the United States—all applied to teacher education. I remember that I worked out the interrelations on a big chart. The name Human Geography had not yet been invented, but much of my later work in geography was a follow-up of this first fumbling effort of mine to show the interdependence of people and the earth and how social institutions and attitudes grow out of the work that people do which is economically important to them.

The title of my second article was "The Whole Child." This phrase is now stale and stereotyped but then it represented a new and independent conception in me. It was my first formulation of an educational credo which I have been trying to clarify ever since. I showed my articles to Robin and also to Sadie Gregory, whose genius for friendship made it easy to share even half-thoughts with her. Then I put them away for the time being. But I did not put their contents out of my mind.

My New York experiences intensified my desire to resign as Dean and go into work with children, if possible in New York. I was thoroughly dissatisfied with the education that my college students had had before coming to college. I was equally dissatisfied with the smug satisfaction of the faculty with their off-the-earth courses. I was tired of working in an academic ivory tower, with golden domes but no firm foundations. I wanted to mix cement and sharp stones and build an educational foundation which would develop people with live thinking and live feelings.

Women and Progressive Politics

Mary Ritter Beard

One of the most striking aspects of American life in the Progressive era is the prominent role played by women reformers. Undaunted by the lack of the vote, women reformers moved far beyond their earlier charitable and philanthropic work to boldly enter the public arena, often participating in local and state politics to achieve their goals.

Mary Ritter Beard (1876–1958) was both a participant in and chronicler of women's urban activism. Active in both the woman suffrage and trade union movements, her path-breaking 1915 book, *Women's Work in Municipalities*, chronicled the scope and variety of women's activities in cities and towns across the country. Her goal was to show that women were participating equally with men in confronting the great social forces of the day. As she documented women's contributions, Beard discovered "in the making, before our very eyes, a conscious national womanhood."

This selection, about the campaign for pure milk stations, is typical of the tactics that Progressive women employed to force municipalities to deal with issues that they felt strongly about as women and mothers. They consciously linked the issue of contaminated milk with broader social issues such as infant mortality, conditions of women's industrial employment, and political corruption; the result, as Mary Beard forcefully demonstrates, is that "babies' milk thus becomes essentially a social-economic problem." The crusade for pure milk occurred in most major cities across the country, primarily spearheaded by women.

As far back as 1915, Mary Beard recognized women's contributions to the Progressive era, an insight historians are now mining for its implications both for women's history and the history of Progressive reform. In her later years, Beard turned more to writing than activism; she achieved her widest recognition as the coauthor (with her historian husband Charles Beard) of *The Rise of American Civilization* (1927). Beard's *Woman As Force in History* (1946), arguably her most original book, demonstrates her ongoing commitment to feminist scholarship.

Source: Mary Ritter Beard, *Women's Work in Municipalities* (New York: D. Appleton-Century-Crofts, 1915), pp. 59–63.

In the education of public opinion on the question of reducing infant mortality, it is inevitable that great attention should be given to the matter of pure milk. One cannot think of a baby without thinking of milk, so that the effort to provide pure milk is directly associated with every effort to reduce infant mortality and make children strong. The problem of milk is twofold: to supply the best possible grade for bottle-fed babies, on the one hand, and on the other to provide the mother of the breast-fed baby with necessary conditions for nursing her infant properly. There is no dispute as to the greater importance of the latter phase of the problem.

The milk station to supply pure milk to the poor at low cost is an outgrowth of the knowledge that the greater part of infant mortality comes in summer months from the feeding of babies upon unsatisfactory milk. The risk of death among such babies is far greater than it is among breast-fed babies so that emphasis has perhaps naturally been placed there to an undue degree. Knowing that bottle babies were subject to such danger, the first thought was to minimize the peril for such babies. As Miss Lathrop[1] points out, however, in harmony with the best scientific teaching: "There may be and in some places there have been certain attending dangers where the furnishing of milk has been the only thing attempted. On this account in many, if not most, milk stations, positive proof is required that the mother either cannot or ought not to nurse her baby before she can get the pure milk, and this precaution has been found necessary in order to prevent an increase in bottle feeding in the community as a result of the feeling of greater safety which the pure-milk station gives to mothers who, while perfectly able to nurse their children, would prefer, for insufficient reasons, not to do so. It is never intended that there should be less insistence upon the duty of breast feeding because of the milk station, for while the death rate among the bottle-fed is reduced by pure milk, the death rate among the bottle-fed from the purest milk possible is still much higher than the death rate among the breast-fed, and if there is any perceptible increase in bottle feeding as against breast feeding because of the milk station the latter might thus become an agency to increase rather than decrease infant mortality."

Dr. S. Josephine Baker of the Bureau of Child Hygiene of the New York Health Department also has a large perspective in dealing with this problem. She says: "The evolution of the infants' milk station is essential. Pure milk, however desirable, will never alone solve the infant-mortality problem. Under our system of home visiting to instruct mothers in the care of babies we have demonstrated that babies may be kept under continuous supervision at the cost of 60 cents per month per baby, and the death rate among babies so cared for by us has been 1.4 per cent. The death rate among babies under the care of milk

---

[1] Julia Lathrop (1858–1932) was head of the Children's Bureau within the federal Department of Commerce and Labor from 1912 to 1921.

stations has been 2.5 per cent, and the cost $2 per month per baby. Without overlooking the value of pure milk, I believe this problem must primarily be solved by educational measures. In other words, the solution of the problem of infant mortality is 20 per cent pure milk and 80 per cent training of the mothers. The infants' milk stations will serve their wider usefulness when they become educational centers for prenatal instruction and the encouragement of breast feeding and teaching better hygiene, with the mother instructed to buy the proper grade of milk at a place most convenient to her home."

Here, as in medical prescriptions, it is futile to insist that a mother who is physically able shall nurse her baby if she is so poor that she must work under conditions that weaken her and thus reduce the grade and quality of her milk or that preclude leisure in which to nourish the infant. The question of poverty, that skeleton in every social closet, looms up here with an insistency that nothing will banish. No kind of philanthropy will solve the requirements of infant welfare when poverty or labor conditions are the root of the problem.

Babies' milk thus becomes essentially a social-economic problem. It is so recognized by many women and is becoming more and more recognized as such by those who work along baby-saving lines. No one sees this fact more clearly perhaps than Miss Lathrop who joins in the ever-growing cry for a "war on poverty." Mothers' pensions, and every attempt to increase the wage of the husband or of the wife before the child-bearing experience has entered into her life, that she may lay by a sum for that function, reaches infant mortality more fundamentally and directly than do milk stations. In spite of this truth, milk stations are a useful supplementary social service and the value of pure milk where mothers cannot nurse their offspring or secure a competent wet-nurse must not be underestimated. The milk station, too, for one thing, affords an acceptable avenue through which to reach mothers and instruct them in the care of infants, to assist them with a nurse in times of trouble or crisis, and to prepare them for the hour when milk from the stations becomes a necessity.

In most cases women now recognize the milk station not as a private but as a public responsibility. They first demonstrated the wisdom and practicability of the enterprise as direct health activity, then urged the municipalities to incorporate the plans into their regular health department program. Cities have accepted the lesson readily, although there are still places like our national capital, where the death rate among infants is disgracefully high and where no provision is made by the commissioners, during even the hot summer months, to care for babies in this way.

The superiority of breast feeding is so well known that the provision of wet-nurses is recognized as a social advantage. The examination, registration, pay and care of wet-nurses are matters of increasing interest to women health workers and the Women's Municipal League of Boston is attempting to deal seriously with this social mother.

No more interesting story of women's help on the problem of general milk supply is to be found than comes from the Oranges, although it is fairly typical of the way women have viewed their responsibility elsewhere. In the spring of 1913, the Civic Committee of the Woman's Club of Orange, New Jersey, offered, for the summer, the services of its secretary to the Orange Board of Health in order that a more thorough study of the milk supply might be made than was possible with the limited official staff alone. "Through the courtesy of the Board, Miss Hall was made a temporary special milk inspector in June, 1913, and has enjoyed the use of the department's laboratory in assisting in the test of over 600 samples on which conclusions are based as to the quality of the milk furnished in the Oranges." Those conclusions are published in a report by the aforesaid club in order to give the consumer a better knowledge of the production and supply of milk "in the hope of arousing citizen interest in a union of effort among the four municipalities, toward a more efficient control."

The joint effort of the Woman's Club and of the Department of Health led to their common support of certain proposals dealing with the milk situation in the four Oranges. In this case, after a careful and detailed study of all the elements that enter into the provision of milk for these communities, the women determined upon a citizen support of the health officers that, among other proposals, they might obtain better appropriations for the work of inspection. Their publications and general agitation have been marked by exact information.

From New York on the eastern seaboard to Portland on the western come countless reports of the activities of organized groups of women in behalf of pure milk. The "Portland Pure Milk War" was graphically described by Stella Walker Durham in a recent number of *Good Housekeeping*. The struggle to secure the kind of milk they wanted meant a year's fight for the women who knew and proved that they knew the true conditions of their city's milk supply.

CHAPTER 3

Women at Work

The post-Civil War period saw a dramatic expansion of women at work; by 1910, women comprised 20 percent of the work force, up from 14 percent in 1870. The numbers of working women increased from 1.7 million to 7 million during that forty-year timespan. The typical woman worker was young (aged fourteen to twenty-four), single, and usually the daughter of immigrants. She was unskilled and concentrated in a low-paying "women's job." She lived in an urban environment and usually saw her work as temporary until she married and established her own household.

The kinds of jobs that women held were shaped by the structural needs of the economy as well as by deeply ingrained patterns that divided the workplace into men's and women's jobs. Women worked primarily in jobs alongside other women; rarely did they work directly with men. It was also rare for women to displace men from jobs; many of the job opportunities that caused the spurt in women's employment in the late nineteenth century were created by industrialization, rather than being taken over from men. Although the largest employment category for women remained domestic service (which employed one quarter of the urban female work force in 1900), the proportion of working women in service had by the twentieth century entered a permanent decline in response to other, more desirable occupations. (To most working women, anything was preferable to domestic service.) Other areas where women were concentrated included the sewing trades, clerical work, teaching, laundry work, nursing, retail sales, and textile manufacturing.

Which jobs were taken by which women also varied in relation to class, racial, and ethnic patterns. The highest status jobs were usually reserved for the daughters of native-born Americans: clerical work (an expanding field that quickly came to be dominated by women), retail sales in the new department stores, and teaching. Although hours were long, working conditions tough (especially for saleswomen, who had to endure long stretches standing up), women would take these jobs over better-paying factory work precisely because of the status involved. Winning such a job was a measure of definite upward mobility for a woman from an immigrant background.

Other women could only aspire to such jobs. Young immigrant women were most likely concentrated in the expanding factory and sweatshop work, especially in such sectors as textiles and sewing, which were highly dependent on women's work. These workers were overwhelmingly single. It was quite rare for married women to work for wages outside the home, although many took in boarders in order to stretch the family income. Such work was not counted as employment in census tabulations, nor were women's contributions to farm labor, suggesting that statistics consistently underrepresent women's contributions to family income.

Black women faced the most restricted economic opportunities of all. Barred from industrial work, black women were heavily represented in domestic service, laundry work, and, in the rural areas where the vast majority of blacks still lived at the turn of the century, as agricultural workers. Because black women's income was crucial to family survival, they showed a wage force participation rate twice as high as white women in 1900. The number of married black women who worked was especially high (25 percent) compared to white and immigrant groups (3 percent).

The conditions of life and work for the growing urban class of self-supporting women were harsh. A woman could expect to work at least sixty hours a week over six days, with only Sundays and Saturday afternoons off. Her wages would barely cover her expenses of lodging, food, and the most minimal clothing needs, even if she was working full time; seasonal layoffs and periodic unemployment increased the difficulties of her existence. A further hazard was industrial accidents. No wonder some urban women turned to prostitution, where wages were five times higher than what a working girl could make on the job.

These conditions were a cause of concern to reformers, especially during the Progressive era. Two possible routes to improve working conditions were available—through labor unions, or through legislation to regulate hours, wages, and safety conditions. Although dramatic examples such as the Shirtwaist strike in New York in 1909–1910 (the so-called "uprising of twenty thousand") demonstrated that women could be successfully organized, unions were typically uninterested or hostile to women's interests. Union leaders, almost all men, saw working women as hard to organize because they planned to leave the work force when they married; such leaders also believed that women really belonged at home, not on the job, and that the goal of the labor movement was to win a decent family wage for the male breadwinner so that female family members did not need to work. Consequently, women made up only 2.2 percent of union members in 1900.

The other solution, protective labor legislation, was the one favored by many Progressive era reformers. Although attempts to regulate the working conditions of men had been ruled unconstitutional by the courts, middle-class reformers were able to win passage of state laws that limited working hours for women, regulated night work, set minimum wages, and imposed minimal safety conditions. Such legislation, sold in part on the premise that women were weaker than men and thus needed special protection, confirmed women's unequal status in the work force at the same time it gave them improvements in hours and wages.

By 1920, the self-supporting working girl was a totally accepted part of the urban economic landscape. No longer credible were the dire predictions of the 1870s and 1880s about urban women being swallowed up in prostitution rings or becoming unfit for future motherhood by their work. Women workers had proven themselves a crucial part of the economic structure, and such work was seen as a normal stage in women's lives before marriage.

There was a shift under way in the kinds of women working, however. The young, single, poor immigrant girl was being joined by a new woman worker: an older, often married woman, who was no longer desperately poor but working to improve her family's economic situation. With the declining birthrate and improvements in household technology, it was somewhat easier for married women to take on employment outside the home. An especially important factor was the decline in child labor after 1900, in large part because of legislation mandating school attendance and outlawing child labor. Attitudes about family roles were changing too. Increasingly, the supplemental family wage earner would be the mother rather than the child under fourteen. By 1920, therefore, the era of the working girl was beginning to give way to the era of the working mother, one of the most far-reaching changes of twentieth-century women's lives.

The Burdens of Rural Women's Lives

In 1901, when this autobiographical piece was published in *The American Kitchen Magazine,* the majority of Americans still lived in rural areas. Not until 1920, according to the United States Census Bureau, would urbanites outnumber rural dwellers. Life in rural farm communities was rough no matter how you sliced it: sunrise to sundown labor, the vagaries of the weather, debt, crop failure, and isolation. Farm households worked longer hours than the nation's overworked industrial workers. Rural women had it especially hard. Not only did they have the full responsibility for bearing and raising children and maintaining their households, as did their urban counterparts, but they also actively participated in farm labor.

Farm women undertook these chores with precious little help from the conveniences increasingly available in urban areas. The lack of electricity was the most obvious deficit; as late as the 1930s, only one farm in ten was electrified. Lack of electricity meant that all water had to be pumped by hand and then hauled to the household or barn. Since the average family used two hundred gallons a day, that was a lot of hauling. If it was washday (and Monday was always washday on the farm), the farm wife had to fetch and heat large tubs of water for the washing, bleaching, and rinsing of a week's worth of farm clothes. Only rarely did a farm wife have the help of a hired girl; usually daughters were pressed into service, their own apprenticeship for their later lives on the farm. And yet farm women, such as this anonymous chronicler who took part in Cornell University's Reading Course for Farm Wives, rarely complained.

Two things I have been taught in my long farm life: one is, that work never kills, and the other is, that we must calculate work beforehand in order to save steps and do a great amount of work. I am fifty-eight years old. Have been on a farm all my life until a year ago, when we built a new house on one end of our farm which opens on a public road and is retired from farm labor. My father was a farmer and a minister of the old school, who believed in no salary, but believed in working for a living. I learned to milk when seven years old, and always did my share while at home. I was sent to school, but at fourteen commenced to teach a district school on a third grade license. I soon received a second and then the first grade. I boarded around. I was married at nineteen, and then my farm life began in earnest. We always kept a dairy, from twelve to fourteen head. When we were married we did not own a foot of land. My husband and I bought thirty acres the day after we were married, joining the old homestead of his people with whom we lived. They owned fifty acres, but there was a mortgage of three hundred and fifty dollars on that. We took care of them until they died, paid the mortgage, bought enough more to make us two hundred acres. We had a sugar orchard and made from three to five hundred pounds of sugar and a great deal of sirup every year. We kept sheep and always worked up the wool, spun, wove, and made full cloth for men's wear and for flannel sheets. We knit our own socks and stockings. I would always rise in the morning at four or half past, winter and summer, and have built my own fires, milked from four to eight cows, prepared the breakfast and had it at six. Until about ten years ago we made butter, and since then have sent it to a factory. I always did my own churning, and many are the books of poems, histories, stories, and newspapers I have read through while churning. I am the mother of eight children, five of whom are living. The others died when small. The oldest living is thirty-six and the youngest is twelve. Three of them have graduated from high school and been a number of terms at an academy. One has been for five years at Cornell University. I have always done my own wash-

Source: Cornell Reading Course for Farmers' Wives, *The American Kitchen Magazine* XIV (October 1900–March 1901), quoted in *So Sweet to Labor: Rural Women in America, 1865–1895,* Norton Juster, ed. (New York: Viking Press, 1979), pp. 101–102.

ing and weaving of carpets, as I have a large house and it is furnished with rag carpets. I make my own garden and have helped rake hay and husk corn. One fall, alone, I husked between five and six hundred bushels. I had one daughter and she was at home at that time; so I did no housework while husking, although I attended to the milk and butter, milked, and got breakfast. One summer I piled up one hundred cords of wood and did my own housework. You will say there was no call for this. We were married the first year of the Civil War. In '63 my husband was drafted, paid his three hundred dollars, and stayed at home. That had to be met in hard times for the farmer. Not many modern wives would think they could pull flax, cut corn, dig potatoes, and do all things on a farm that we used to do. All this time I had a hired girl only a year and a half. We made our own table linen and toweling, spinning and weaving it, and our flannel dresses. I have been with the sick a great deal, and always went to church and Sunday school, and attended societies which belonged to the church. To-day I can walk a mile or more as quickly as any one. At the present time I have two old people to care for; one of them is eighty-six and the other is eighty-three. There are five in our family, and I am doing all the work myself, and am going to take the teacher to board next year. So you see, work does not kill and there must have been some calculation to save steps. My husband says, "You helped earn and saved more than I did." The boys many times say, "If it had not been for your pushing and helping us to school, we never could have done so well." All this time I have kept up with the general reading of the day.

I never counted my steps but once and that was when I spun a skein of woolen yarn. I went a little over a mile.

Buffalobird Woman's Story

The agricultural practices of Indian women add another perspective on rural life at the turn of the century. In many tribes women owned the land and did most of the agricultural work using traditional farming methods passed down through mothers and grandmothers. By the late nineteenth century, however, the United States government had forced many Indian tribes onto reservations, where federal officials introduced changes in how agriculture was practiced. As this selection demonstrates, Native Americans were often reluctant to give up traditional food practices and tribal organization, with good reason.

The story of these changes is told by Maxi'diwiac, or Buffalobird Woman, a Hidatsa Indian who lived near the Missouri River in what is now North Dakota. The name Hidatsa is said to mean "willows" in the Sioux language, deriving from the promise of the god Itsikama'hidic that villagers would be as numerous as the willows that line the Missouri River. Buffalobird Woman was born around 1839, the daughter of Small Ankle, who was a leader of Hidatsas at the time they were being removed from their traditional land to the Fort Berthold reservation. According to her son Tsaka'kasakic, or Goodbird, his mother "knows more about old ways of raising corn and squashes than any one else on this reservation." Goodbird, who was educated at mission schools and became a congregational minister, served as interpreter for his mother, who did not speak English.

Buffalobird Woman's story was sought by Gilbert Livingston Wilson, a graduate student in anthropology at the University of Minnesota, who in 1911 wanted to study traditional agriculture, preferably from a woman's perspective. Buffalobird Woman's descriptions formed the basis for his doctoral thesis, and he collaborated on a book with Goodbird as well. Wilson offered Buffalobird Woman to readers in this spirit: "May the Indian woman's story of her toil be a plea for our better appreciation of her race." Or to put it in a slightly different way, may it be a plea for a better appreciation of the contributions that Indian women made to their race and to Western history.

The government has changed our old way of cultivating corn and our other vegetables, and has brought us seeds of many new vegetables and grains, and taught us their use. We Hidatsas and our friends, the Mandans, have also been removed from our village at Like-a-fishhook bend, and made to take our land in allotments; so that our old agriculture has in a measure fallen into disuse.

I was thirty-three years old when the government first plowed up fields for us; two big fields were broken, one between the village and the agency, and another on the farther side of the agency.

New kinds of seeds were issued to us, oats and wheat; and we were made to plant them in these newly plowed fields. Another field was plowed for us down in the bottom land along the Missouri; and here we were taught to plant potatoes. Each family was given a certain number of rows to plant and cultivate.

At first we Hidatsas did not like potatoes, because they smelled so strongly! Then we sometimes dug up our potatoes and took them into our earth lodges; and when cold weather came, the potatoes were frozen, and spoiled. For these reasons we did not take much interest in our potatoes, and often left them in the ground, not bothering to dig them.

Other seeds were issued to us, of watermelons, big squashes, onions, turnips, and other vegetables. Some of these we tried to eat, but did not like them very well; even the turnips and big squashes, we thought not so good as our own squashes and our wild prairie turnips. Moreover, we did not know how to dry these new vegetables for winter; so we often did not trouble even to harvest them.

The government was eager to teach the Indians to raise potatoes; and to get us women to cultivate them, paid as much as two dollars and a half a day for planting them in the plowed field. I remember I was paid that sum for plant-

Source: Gilbert Livingston Wilson, "Agriculture of the Hidatsa Indians: An Indian Interpretation," *University of Minnesota Studies in the Social Sciences,* 9 (November 1917), pp. 119–120.

ing them. After three or four years, finding the Indians did not have much taste for potatoes and rather seldom ate them, our agent made a big cache pit—a root cellar you say it was—and bought our potato crop of us. After this he would issue seed potatoes to us in the spring, and in the fall we would sell our crop to him. Thus, handling potatoes each year, we learned little by little to eat them.

The government also broke up big fields of prairie ground, and had us plant corn in them; but these fields on the prairie near the hills I do not think are so good as our old fields down in the timber lands along the Missouri. The prairie fields get dry easily and the soil is harder and more difficult to work.

Then I think our old way of raising corn is better than the new way taught us by white men. Last year, 1911, our agent held an agricultural fair on this reservation; and we Indians competed for prizes for the best corn. The corn which I sent to the fair took the first prize. I raised it on new ground; the ground had been plowed, but aside from that, I cultivated the corn exactly as in old times, with a hoe.

The Harsh Conditions of Domestic Service

Domestic service has always been a woman's job. As late as 1870, seven out of ten working women were employed as servants in other women's homes. Of the country's approximately one million domestic workers in 1900, 26 percent were native born, 19 percent were the daughters of immigrants, 28 percent were foreign born, and 27 percent were black. As the twentieth century progressed, white women increasingly found jobs other than domestic service, especially in the expanding manufacturing, clerical, and sales sectors. Black women rarely had such options. Excluded from industrial and service jobs by discrimination, black women formed a steady pool of domestic servants, especially in the South. According to the 1890 census, 31 percent of employed black women were servants; the two other largest categories of occupations for them were agriculture (38 percent) and laundry work (15 percent).

This anonymous 1912 article entitled "More Slavery at the South" confirms through one woman's eyes the intolerable conditions under which black women toiled. In many ways, such work was a continuation of slavery patterns, where blacks were expected to be servants first and allowed to lead their own lives only after hours. The surplus of potential black servants robbed any hope of improving working conditions or pay, which averaged twelve to fourteen hours a day at wages of $4 to $8 a month. One key to getting by was the "service pan" of leftover food that southern servants took home every day, a custom that if stretched creatively could augment a meager income.

One final note. This anonymous black woman identifies herself as a nurse, but that label does not reflect a higher occupational status. In fact, there was little value placed on labor specialization within the home, and a nurse's chores would go beyond helping the sick and taking care of children to other tasks such as cleaning and gardening.

I am a negro woman, and I was born and reared in the South. I am now past forty years of age and am the mother of three children. My husband died nearly fifteen years ago, after we had been married about five years. For more than thirty years—or since I was ten years old—I have been a servant in one capacity or another in white families in a thriving Southern city, which has at present a population of more than 50,000. In my early years I was at first what might be called a "house-girl," or better, a "house-boy." I used to answer the doorbell, sweep the yard, go on errands, and do odd jobs. Later on I became a chambermaid and performed the usual duties of such a servant in a home. Still later I was graduated into a cook, in which position I served at different times for nearly eight years in all. During the last ten years I have been a nurse. I have worked for only four different families during all these thirty years. But, belonging to the servant class, which is the majority class among my race at the South, and associating only with servants, I have been able to become intimately acquainted not only with the lives of hundreds of household servants, but also with the lives of their employers. I can, therefore, speak with authority on the so-called servant question; and what I say is said out of an experience which covers many years.

To begin with, then, I should say that more than two-thirds of the negroes of the town where I live are menial servants of one kind or another, and besides that more than two-thirds of the negro women here, whether married or single, are compelled to work for a living,—as nurses, cooks, washerwomen, chambermaids, seamstresses, hucksters, janitresses, and the like. I will say, also, that the condition of this vast host of poor colored people is just as bad as, if not worse than, it was during the days of slavery. Though today we are enjoying nominal freedom, we are literally slaves. And, not to generalize, I will give you a sketch of the work I have to do—and I'm only one of many.

I frequently work from fourteen to sixteen hours a day. I am compelled by my contract, which is oral only, to sleep in the house. I am allowed to go home to my own children, the oldest of whom is a girl of 18 years, only once in two weeks, every other Sunday afternoon—even then I'm not permitted to stay all night. I not only have to nurse a little white child, now eleven months old, but I have to act as playmate or "handy-andy," not say governess, to three other children in the home, the oldest of whom is only nine years of age. I wash and dress the baby two or three times each day; I give it its meals, mainly from a

Source: "More Slavery at the South" by a Negro Nurse, *The Independent* 72 (January 25, 1912), pp. 196–200.

bottle; I have to put it to bed each night; and, in addition, I have to get up and attend to its every call between midnight and morning. If the baby falls to sleep during the day, as it has been trained to do every day about eleven o'clock, I am not permitted to rest. It's "Mammy, do this," or "Mammy, do that," or "Mammy, do the other," from my mistress, all the time. So it is not strange to see "Mammy" watering the lawn in front with the garden hose, sweeping the sidewalk, mopping the porch and halls, dusting around the house, helping the cook, or darning stockings. Not only so, but I have to put the other three children to bed each night as well as the baby, and I have to wash them and dress them each morning. I don't know what it is to go to church; I don't know what it is to go to a lecture or entertainment or anything of the kind; I live a tread-mill life; and I see my own children only when they happen to see me on the streets when I am out with the children, or when my children come to the "yard" to see me, which isn't often, because my white folks don't like to see their servants' children hanging around their premises. You might as well say that I'm on duty all the time—from sunrise to sunrise, every day in the week. I am the slave, body and soul, of this family. And what do I get for this work—this life-time bondage? The pitiful sum of ten dollars a month! And what am I expected to do with these ten dollars? With this money I'm expected to pay my house rent, which is four dollars per month, for a little house of two rooms, just big enough to turn round in; and I'm expected, also to feed and clothe myself and three children. For two years my oldest child, it is true, has helped a little toward our support by taking in a little washing at home. She does the washing and ironing of two white families, with a total of five persons; one of these families pays her $1.00 per week, and the other 75 cents per week, and my daughter has to furnish her own soap and starch and wood. For six months my youngest child, a girl about thirteen years old, has been nursing, and she receives $1.50 per week but has no night work. When I think of the low rate of wages we poor colored people receive, and when I hear so much said about our unreliability, our untrustworthiness, and even our vices, I recall the story of the private soldier in a certain army who, once upon a time, being upbraided by the commanding officer because the heels of his shoes were not polished, is said to have replied: "Captain, do you expect all the virtues for $13 per month?"

Of course, nothing is being done to increase our wages, and the way things are going at present it would seem that nothing could be done to cause an increase in wages. We have no labor unions or organizations of any kind that could demand for us a uniform scale of wages for cooks, washerwomen, nurses, and the like; and, for another thing, if some negroes did here and there refuse to work for seven and eight and ten dollars a month, there would be hundreds of other negroes right on the spot ready to take their places and do the same work, or more, for the low wages that had been refused. So that, the truth is, we have to work for little or nothing or become vagrants! And that, of course, in this State would mean that we would be arrested, tried, and despatched to the "State Farm," where we would surely have to work for nothing or be beaten with many stripes! . . .

Another thing—it's a small indignity, it may be, but an indignity just the same. No white person, not even the little children just learning to talk, no white person at the South ever thinks of addressing any negro man or woman as Mr., or Mrs., or Miss. The women are called, "Cook," or "Nurse," or "Mammy," or "Mary Jane," or "Lou," or "Dilcey," as the case might be, and the men are called "Bob," or "Boy," or "Old Man," or "Uncle Bill," or "Pate." In many cases our white employers refer to us, and in our presence, too, as their "niggers." No matter what they call us—no matter what they teach their children to call us—we must tamely submit, and answer when we are called; we must enter no protest; if we did object, we should be driven out without the least ceremony, and, in applying for work at other places, we should find it very hard to procure another situation. In almost every case, when our intending employers would be looking up our record, the information would be given by telephone or otherwise that we were "impudent," "saucy," "dishonest," and "generally unreliable." In our town we have no such thing as an employment agency or intelligence bureau, and, therefore, when we want work, we have to get out on the street and go from place to place, always with hat in hand, hunting for it. . . .

You hear a good deal nowadays about the "service pan." The "service pan" is the general term applied to "left-over" food, which in many a Southern home is freely placed at the disposal of the cook, or, whether so placed or not, it is usually disposed of by the cook. In my town, I know, and I guess in many other towns also, every night when the cook starts for her home she takes with her a pan or a plate of cold victuals. The same thing is true on Sunday afternoon after dinner—and most cooks have nearly every Sunday afternoon off. Well, I'll be frank with you, if it were not for the service pan, I don't know what the majority of our Southern colored families would do. The service pan is the mainstay in many a home. Good cooks in the South receive on an average $8 per month. Porters, butlers, coachmen, janitors, "office boys" and the like, receive on an average $16 per month. Few and far between are the colored men in the South who receive $1 or more per day. Some mechanics do; as, for example, carpenters, brick masons, wheelwrights, blacksmiths, and the like. The vast majority of negroes in my town are serving in menial capacities in homes, stores and offices. Now taking it for granted, for the sake of illustration, that the husband receives $16 per month and the wife $8. That would be $24 between the two. The chances are that they will have anywhere from five to thirteen children between them. Now, how far will $24 go toward housing and feeding and clothing ten or twelve persons for thirty days? And, I tell you, with all of us poor people the service pan is a great institution; it is a great help to us, as we wag along the weary way of life. And then most of the white folks expect their cooks to avail themselves of these perquisites; they allow it; they expect it. I do not deny that the cooks find opportunity to hide away at times, along with the cold "grub," a little sugar, a little flour, a little meal, or a little piece of soap; but I indignantly deny that we are thieves. We don't steal; we just "take" things—they are a part of the oral contract, expressed or implied. We understand it, and most of the white folks understand it. Others may denounce the service pan, and say that it is used only to support idle negroes, but many a time, when I was a cook, and had the responsibility of rearing my three children upon my lone shoulders, many a time I have had occasion to bless the Lord for the service pan!

Female Perspectives on the Great Migration

With conditions so limited in the South, it is no wonder that many African-Americans were lured by the promise of economic opportunities and greater social freedom in the North. Beginning in the 1910s but greatly hastened by opportunities opened by World War I, more than 500,000 blacks left the South between 1916 and 1919; close to a million more would follow in the 1920s. This exodus is called the "great migration."

Women migrated in fewer numbers than men, and sometimes for different reasons and with different results. While both black men and women sought better economic opportunities, women faced greater economic discrimination and had fewer employment opportunities than men. Many found themselves still doing domestic work once they moved north, although at least for wages significantly higher than before. But economics cannot alone explain the pull of migration. Historians such as Darlene Clark Hine point to a desire for greater personal autonomy and an escape from sexual exploitation, especially at the hands of white Southern employers, as propelling reasons for the move.

More than any other city, Chicago represented the "promised land" for Southern migrants. The terminus of the Illinois Central railroad, which extended deep into the South, it was easily accessible by train. In addition, the *Chicago Defender*, a militantly pro-black newspaper founded in 1905 by Robert Abbott that counted two-thirds of its circulation from outside Chicago, played a key role in conveying information about opportunities to even the remotest corner of the South. The *Defender*'s articles, editorials, and advertisements all presented a picture of Chicago as a city with a vibrant and assertive black community, accompanied by ample opportunities for economic and personal advancement. The *Defender* actively promoted migration, and its pages served as an informal clearinghouse for jobs and other services to help migrants get settled.

Like the demographics of migration in general, fewer women wrote the *Defender* than men, but the letters selected here show some of the characteristics and motivations of women who decided to leave the South. The letters demonstrate the classic "push" and "pull" aspects of migration—the push out of the South because chances for advancement were so limited, and the pull of new opportunities, especially economic. The letters also show the enormous faith that Southern blacks had in the ability of the *Defender* to help them get settled in their new lives, a faith that was often not misplaced.

New Orleans, La., May 7, 1917.

Gentlemen: I read Defender every week and see so much good youre doing for the southern people & would like to know if you do the same for me as I am thinking of coming to Chicago about the first of June. and wants a position. I have very fine references if needed. I am a widow of 28. No children, not a relative living and I can do first class work as house maid and dining room or care for invalid ladies. I am honest and neat and refined with a fairly good education. I would like a position where I could live on places because its very trying for a good girl to be out in a large city by self among strangers is why I would like a good home with good people. Trusting to hear from you.

Jacksonville, Fla., April 28, 1917.

Kind Sir: We have several times read your noted paper and we are delighted with the same because it is a thorough Negro paper. There is a storm of our people toward the North and especially to your city. We have watched your want ad regularly and we are anxious for location with good families (white) where we can be cared for and do domestic work. We want to engage as cook, nurse and maid. We have had some educational advantages, as we have taught in rural schools for few years but our pay so poor we could not continue. We can furnish testimonial of our honesty and integrity and moral standing. Will you please assist us in securing places as we are anxious to come but want jobs before we leave. We want to do any kind of honest labor. Our chance here is so poor.

Mobile, Ala., April 25, 1917.

Sir: I was reading in theat paper about the Colored race and while reading it I seen in it where cars would be here for the 15 of May which is one month from to day. Will you be so kind as to let me know where they are coming to and I will be glad to know because I am a poor woman and have a husband and five children living and three dead one single and two twin girls six months old today and my husband can hardly make bread for them in Mobile. This is my native home but it is not fit to live in just as the Chicago Defender say it says the truth

Source: "Letters of Negro Migrants of 1916–1918," *Journal of Negro History,* Vol. IV, 3 (July 1919) and 4 (October 1919), pp. 317, 318–319, 332, 337–338, 339, 413.

and my husband only get $1.50 a day and pays $7.50 a month for house rent and can hardly feed me and his self and children. I am the mother of 8 children 25 years old and I want to get out of this dog hold because I dont know what I am raising them up for in this place and I want to get to Chicago where I know they will be raised and my husband crazy to get there because he know he can get more to raise his children and will you please let me know where the cars is going to stop to so that he can come where he can take care of me and my children. He get there a while and then he can send for me. I heard they wasnt coming here so I sent to find out and he can go and meet them at the place they are going and go from there to Chicago. No more at present. hoping to hear from you soon from your needed and worried friend.

Atlanta, Ga., April 11, 1917.

Dear Sir: I am a reader of you paper and we are all crazy about it and take it every Saturday and we raise a great howl when we dont get it. Now since I see and feel that you are for the race and are willing to assist any one so I will ask you to please assist me in getting imployment and some place to stop with some good quiet people or with a family that would take some one to live with them. I will do any kind of work. I am a hair dresser but I will do any kind of work I can get to do I am a widow and have one child a little girl 6 years years old I dont know any body there so if you can assist me in any way will be greatly appreciated now this letter is personal please dont print it in your paper. I hope to hear from you soon.

Kissimmee, Fla., May 1, 1917.

Dear Sir: I am a subscriber for the Chicago Defender have read of the good work you are doing in employing help for your large factories and how you are striving to help get the better class of people to the north. I am a teacher and have been teaching five years successful, and as our school here has closed my cousin and I have decided to go north for the summer who is also a teacher of this county. I am writing you to secure for us a position that we could fit and one that would fit us, if there be any that is vacant.

We can furnish you with the best of reference. We would not like to advertise through a paper. Hoping to hear from you at an early date, I am

Alexandria, La., June 6, 1917.

Dear Sirs: I am writeing to you all asking a favor of you all. I am a girl of seventeen. School has just closed I have been going to school for nine months and I now feel like I aught to go to work. And I would like very very well for you all to please forward me to a good job. but there isnt a thing here for me to do, the wages here is from a dollar and a half a week. What could I earn Nothing. I have a mother and father my father do all he can for me but it is so hard. A child with any respect about her self or his self wouldnt like to see there mother and father work so hard and earn nothing I feel it my duty to help. I would like for you all to get me a good job and as I havent any money to come on please send me a pass and I would work and pay every cent of it back and get me a good quite place to stay. My father have been getting the defender for three or four months but for the last two weeks we have failed to get it. I dont know why. I am tired of down hear in this——/ I am afraid to say. Father seem to care and then again dont seem to but Mother and I am tired tired of all of this I wrote to you all because I believe you will help I need your help hopeing to here from you all very soon.

The Story of a Glove Maker

Agnes Nestor

Working in factories was long, tedious work. Working women found that they were at the mercy of foremen, who had the right to hire and fire, speed up or slow down production, and take sexual advantage of working girls who desperately needed to hold on to their jobs. There were other minor, or not so minor, indignities on the job. Workers were often charged fifty cents a week for the power that ran their machines, so-called machine rent. They had to buy their own needles and machine oil. Their working hours were irregular, as was their pay. It was a rare factory that had a union to speak up for the women's demands.

Agnes Nestor's story of a day's work making gloves, written in Chicago around 1898, conveys the texture of working women's lives. Agnes Nestor (1880–1948) came from an Irish Roman Catholic family, never had more than an eighth-grade education, and she spent most of her working life in Chicago. To protest the conditions she describes in this article (especially the issue of machine rent), she impetuously led a walkout of her fellow glove makers. After ten days of picketing, the women won all their demands, including the recognition of a glove makers' union. For the rest of her life, Nestor devoted herself to the International Glove Workers Union, serving in various national capacities. In addition to her union organizing, she was also a successful lobbyist for protective labor legislation, such as the eight-hour day, for women and children in Illinois.

The whistle blows at 7 A.M. but the piece workers have until 7.30 to come in to work. The penalty for coming late (after 7.30 A.M.) is the loss of a half day as the girls cannot then report to work until noon. This rule is enforced to induce the girls to come early but it often works a hardship on them when they are unavoidably delayed on account of the cars, etc. Stormy weather is the only excuse.

Source: Agnes Nestor, "A Day's Work Making Gloves" (1898) in Nestor, *Woman's Labor Leader* (Rockford, Ill.: Bellevue Books Publishing Co., 1954), pp. 37–41.

All the work in the sewing department is piece work so the wages depend upon the speed of the operator. The gloves are made by the dozen and each class of operators has a particular part of them to make. After they are cut they go to the silker, who does the fancy stitching on the backs; then to the closer, who sews in the thumbs and joins the pieces to the palms to form the backs; they then go to several operators each of whom does a small part of the banding; then the gloves come back to the closer to be closed around the fingers. This finishes most of the bandtop gloves but the gauntlets have to go to the binder or hemmer who finishes the tops. Nearly all of the gloves are finished on the wrong side and have to go to another department to be turned and layed off on a heated iron form; this is the finishing process. This is the making of the heavy working and driving gloves.

A few years ago most of the gloves were made throughout by one operator, but by degrees the manufacturers have divided the work into sections until now the closers and girls making the finer driving and fancy gauntlets are the only girls who really have a trade to learn. The other work is very straight and requires more speed than skill.

It is only through our union that we have been able to have the closing work made throughout by the one operator. The employers claim that their object in wanting to have this work done in sections is to make it easier for girls to learn and to make possible a better system in giving out the work. They offered to divide the total price proportionally among the different operators so that there would be no reduction by this arrangement. There was always some reduction in the other sectional work; for instance, a girl received thirty-three cents a dozen for doing all the banding on a certain style of glove. By having this work made in sections and with improved machinery the total price is seventeen cents, necessarily involving a reduction in some sections. We believe we are justified in refusing to have our "closing" work made in sections, if for no other reason than that one part of the "closing" work is very heavy and hard, and when a girl does it all day she is completely tired out, while the putting in thumbs and backing is much lighter and easier work which it is a sort of a rest to do part of the day. So when it is a question of our strength to us and not dollars or cents to the employer, so he claims, then why should we not insist on making our gloves throughout. I am not bringing in the question of breaking up our trade or the monotony and other disagreeable features of section work. One employer even offered us an increased price on the harder part of the work to induce us to accept his system, but even this we refused. You see there is a human as well as a financial question involved in this for us and I think the human is the greater of the two.

It is a curious sight to go through a factory and see in spaces between the windows and on the posts at certain distances apart, eighty-five-cent alarm clocks. The clocks are bought as the result of a collection, which means that each girl puts in five or ten cents.

I have heard and read criticisms of the men who work watching the clock, ready to drop their tools on the minute of quitting time. But the reason our girls buy and watch the clocks is not to see how soon they can quit work, but to see that they do not lose time. It is easy to lose a few minutes and not notice it until the end of the day when we count up our work and pay. Every girl knows just how long it takes her to make any part of the glove. We figure that we can make a pair in a certain number of minutes so we watch the clock to see that we will come out on time with our dozen.

When we begin our day's work we never know what our day's pay will be. We have to figure to make up for time we lose. Although it is not our fault it is at our expense. For instance: a dozen gloves may be cut from very heavy leather and very difficult to sew; or perhaps when we go to the desk for work we may have to stand waiting in line ten to twenty minutes; or the belt of our machine may break and we may have to walk around the factory two or three times before we find the belt boy who, perhaps, is hidden under a table fixing a belt, and then we have to wait our turn; or we go to another desk to get our supplies such as needles, thread, welt, etc. But what we dread most of all is the machine breaking down as we do not know how long it will take to repair it. For this work the machinist takes our name and again we have to wait our turn. The foreman is very willing to allow us to use another machine, but when a girl is accustomed to her own machine it is not an easy matter to sew on any other. For each kind of leather and style of glove we use a different color and number of thread and size of needle; each of these requires a certain tension so that in changing the thread, needles and machine for the various kinds of work again time is taken, our time. Each glove has to be stamped with the girl's number so that a glove can always be traced back to the maker and all "busters" brought to her to repair.

I remember a certain style of glove of which I found I could make a dozen in one hour and a half. There happened to be a large order for this work going through, so that I had a great amount of it. At the end of the day, nine and a half hours, I found that I had only five dozens made. The next day I watched the clock very closely to see where the two hours went the day before. I finished each dozen on "scheduled time" but at the end of this day I found I still had only my five dozens made. I tried this every day for a week, each day trying to work harder, only with the same result and to find myself completely tired out.

A great many employers give as their reason for preferring the piece-work system and establishing it as much as possible, that they are only paying for the work they receive and have more work turned out in a day. This no doubt is true; but it is too often at the expense of the girl. For she pays not only the loss of time but the loss of health too. I am one of the many who are very much against this system for I have seen too many awful results from it. We have a certain amount of strength and energy and if this is to be used up the first few years at the trade what is to become of the workers after that? This system, moreover, encourages a girl to do more than her physical strength will allow her to do continuously. Piece work is worry as well as work.

When I started in the trade and saw the girls working at that dreadful pace every minute, I wondered how they could keep up the speed. But it is not until you become one of them that you can understand. The younger girls are usually very anxious to operate a machine. I remember the first day that I sewed, making the heavy linings. The foreman came to me late in the day and asked how I liked the work. "Oh," I said, "I could never get tired sewing on this machine." But he had seen too many girls "get tired," so he said "Remember those words a few years from now if you stay," and I have.

At half-past nine the whistle blows again and we have five minutes for a light lunch. This time we have to make up so we work until 5:35 P.M. At noon we have only half an hour, which means that the girls have to bring cold lunches. The firm heats a large boiler of water so the girls can make tea or coffee. While half an hour seems a short time for lunch still a great many girls take ten or fifteen minutes of this to trim their gloves or whatever work they can do while the power is shut down. The girls all eat at their places, two or three grouping together. I believe a lunch-room should be provided where we could eat without the sight of gloves and the smell of leather.

There is a big army of foremen, forewomen, and others employed by the various manufacturers just to study and plan how they can save a few cents here and there for the firm. Their methods of saving too often result in a "cut" here and there. As these "cuts" continue to come one after another, the girls must work faster and faster to make up for them, until they have to give up, and then there are other girls ready to take their places in the race. They all have to compete with the "pacemaker." There is only one way of resisting this and that is through the united efforts of the workers in their trade union.

Employers frequently complain about the big expense of "breaking in so much help." If they spent some of this money to make the factory conditions better it would not be necessary to break in so many workers. I believe it would pay them in the end.

One of the valuable features of our trade union is that the workers have an opportunity to meet their employer. It is only by representatives of both employers and employed sitting around the table and talking matters over that they can both recognize and understand each other's rights and interests.

Working Women Write the Jewish Daily Forward

Another window on the struggles of young immigrant working women, this time on New York's Lower East Side, comes from a feature called "A Bintel Brief" in the popular Yiddish-language newspaper, the *Jewish Daily Forward*. Readers shared a variety of trivial, serious, comic, and tragic stories with the editor, who then offered advice or guidance. Especially in the early years after the Bintel Brief column was begun in 1906, many of the stories came from Jewish immigrants who had recently arrived in America and who were seeking help in making the transition from Old World to New. So popular and recognizable did the feature become that it entered the vernacular, with phrases like "It's just like a 'Bintel Brief' story!" often being used in conversations to convey an interesting or poignant story of family life on the Lower East Side.

Unlike the letters to the Chicago *Defender*, which were predominantly from men, women made up a much larger percentage of those who turned to the *Jewish Daily Forward* for help. Although many letter writers focused on family life and relations, working women also used the forum to seek help with job-related problems. The first selection from a 1907 shopgirl raised an issue that was far too familiar to many working women: sexual harassment at work. Speaking up or saying no to a boss's requests for sexual favors could have meant losing your job, and perhaps your family's livelihood, so most women either put up with it or switched jobs to avoid these unwelcome advances.

The second selection from 1914 tells a heart-rending story about the hazards of industrial work. The event she refers to is notorious in history. On March 25, 1911, fire broke out at the Triangle Shirtwaist Factory, located just off Washington Square in lower Manhattan. To keep workers from leaving early, the doors had been kept locked, which prevented quick exit once the fire erupted. About one hundred and fifty workers, mainly young immigrant women, either leapt to their deaths from windows or were burned to death inside. One concrete result of the Triangle Shirtwaist fire was the creation of the New York State Factory Commission in 1912 and the passage of legislation dealing with fire hazards, unsafe working conditions, and wages and hours. This was an important progressive reform but probably little consolation to this survivor, who lost the love of her life in the conflagration and wondered if she had a right to even think about being happy again.

1907

Dear Editor,

I am one of those unfortunate girls thrown by fate into a dark and dismal shop, and I need your counsel.

Along with my parents, sisters and brothers, I came from Russian Poland where I had been well educated. But because of the terrible things going on in

Source: Isaac Metzker, ed., *A Bintel Brief: Sixty Years of Letters from the Lower East Side to the Jewish Daily Forward* (New York: Schocken, 1971), pp. 72–73, 129–131.

Russia we were forced to emigrate to America. I am now seventeen years old, but I look younger and they say I am attractive.

A relative talked us into moving to Vineland, New Jersey, and here in this small town I went to work in a shop. In this shop there is a foreman who is an exploiter, and he sets prices on the work. He figures it out so that the wages are very low, he insults and reviles the workers, he fires them and then takes them back. And worse than all of this, in spite of the fact that he has a wife and several children, he often allows himself to "have fun" with some of the working girls. It was my bad luck to be one of the girls that he tried to make advances to. And woe to any girl who doesn't willingly accept them.

Though my few hard-earned dollars mean a lot to my family of eight souls, I didn't want to accept the foreman's vulgar advances. He started to pick on me, said my work was no good, and when I proved to him he was wrong, he started to shout at me in the vilest language. He insulted me in Yiddish and then in English, so the American workers could understand too. Then, as if the Devil were after me, I ran home.

I am left without a job. Can you imagine my circumstances and that of my parents who depend on my earnings? The girls in the shop were very upset over the foreman's vulgarity but they don't want him to throw them out, so they are afraid to be witnesses against him. What can be done about this? I beg you to answer me.

Respectfully,
A Shopgirl

ANSWER:

Such a scoundrel should be taught a lesson that could be an example to others. The girl is advised to bring out into the open the whole story about the foreman, because there in the small town it shouldn't be difficult to have him thrown out of the shop and for her to get her job back.

1914

Worthy Editor,

I am a girl twenty-two years of age, but I've already undergone a great deal in my life. When I was born I already had no father. He died four months before my birth. And when I was three weeks old my mother died too. Grandmother, my mother's mother, took me in and soon gave me away to a poor tailor's wife to suckle me.

I was brought up by the tailor and his wife, and got so used to them that I called them Mother and Father. When I grew up I learned from the tailor how to do hand sewing and machine sewing too.

When I was sixteen my grandmother died and left me her small dilapidated house. The rabbi of the town sold it for me for three hundred rubles and gave me the money.

In time one of the tailor's apprentices fell in love with me, and I didn't reject his love. He was a fine, honest, quiet young man and a good earner. He had a golden character and we became as one body and soul. When I turned seventeen my bridegroom came to me with a plan, that we should go to America, and I agreed.

It was hard for me to take leave of the tailor's good family, who had kept me as their own child, and oceans of tears were shed when we parted.

When we came to America my bridegroom immediately started to work and he supported me. He was faithful and devoted. I'll give you an example of his loyalty: once, during the summer in the terrible heat, I slept on the roof. But it started to rain in the middle of the night and I was soaked through to the bone. I got very sick and had to be taken to the hospital. I was so sick that the doctor said I could be saved only by a blood transfusion. My bridegroom said immediately that he was ready to give me his blood, and so, thanks to him, I recovered.

In time I went to work at the "famous" Triangle shop. Later my bridegroom also got a job there. Even at work he wanted to be with me. My bridegroom told me then, "We will both work hard for a while and then we'll get married. We will save every cent so we'll be able to set up a home and then you'll be a housewife and never go to work in the shop again."

Thus my good bridegroom mused about the golden future. Then there was that terrible fire that took one hundred and forty-seven young blossoming lives. When the fire broke out, the screaming, the yelling, the panic all bewildered me. I saw the angel of death before me and my voice was choked in my throat. Suddenly someone seized me with extraordinary strength and carried me out of the shop.

When I recovered I heard calming voices and saw my bridegroom near me. I was in the street, rescued, and saw my girl friends jumping out of the windows and falling to the ground. I clung to my bridegroom and rescuer, but he soon tore himself away from me. "I must save other girls," he said, and disappeared. I never saw him alive again. The next day I identified him, in the morgue, by his watch, which had my pictured pasted under the cover. I fainted and they could hardly bring me to.

After that I lay in the hospital for five weeks, and came home shattered. This is the fourth year that I am alone and I still see before me the horrible scenes of the fire. I still see the good face of my dear bridegroom, also the black burned face in the morgue. I am weak and nervous, yet there is now a young man who wants to marry me. But I made a vow that I would never get married. Besides that, I'm afraid that I will never be able to love another man. But this young man doesn't want to leave me, and my friends try to persuade me to marry him and say everything will be all right. I don't believe it, because I think everything can be all right for me only in the grave.

I decided to write to you, because I want to hear your opinion.

Respectfully,
A Faithful Reader

ANSWER:

It is senseless for this girl to sacrifice her life in memory of her faithful bridegroom, since this would not bring him back to life. What the earth covers must be forgotten. She has suffered enough in her life already and is advised to take herself in hand and begin her life anew.

Protective Legislation for Women Workers

Muller v. Oregon

Labor legislation was an important tactic for improving conditions for the nation's workers, but such laws provoked a hostile response from the nation's judicial system. In the 1905 case of *Lochner* v. *New York,* the Supreme Court shot down a New York law limiting the hours that bakers (all men) could work, stating that it was an illegal interference in the right of workers and employers to enter into contracts. But, reformers reasoned, perhaps the courts could be induced to uphold such legislation for women workers because of women's supposed inequality and physical weakness due to maternity. Such reasoning won in the case of *Muller* v. *Oregon* (1908), where the Supreme Court upheld a ten-hour day for women workers in that state.

The brief defending the Oregon law was prepared by Boston lawyer Louis Brandeis and Josephine Goldmark, a researcher for the National Consumers' League (NCL). To preclude a repetition of the *Lochner* decision, the "Brandeis brief" contended that women were distinctive and exceptional. Brandeis and Goldmark filled their brief with sociological data arguing that women were physically weaker than men, that their childbearing and maternal functions warranted protection, and that women were prey to "moral laxity" if overly

Source: *Muller v. Oregon,* 208 U.S. 412, 28 Sup. Ct. 324 (1908). Notes have been omitted.

tired. The Court accepted this reasoning and allowed the law to stand.

This selection from *Muller* v. *Oregon* describes the Oregon law and outlines the judicial history of the case. The reasoning behind the decision is summarized by this statement from the court: "that women's physical structure and the performance of maternal functions place her at a disadvantage in the struggle for subsistence." Historians still debate whether the protection that women gained through such laws outweighed the negative connotations of women as physically weaker than men and set apart as a separate (unequal) class. Legislatures and the courts remained hostile to extending such protection to men, however. In 1917, the Supreme Court upheld an Oregon law that limited hours of labor for male workers, but the decision lacked impact elsewhere. Finally, in 1941, New Deal legislation that set labor standards for both sexes won Supreme Court approval.

Mr. Justice Brewer delivered the opinion of the court:

On February 19, 1903, the legislature of the state of Oregon passed an act (Session Laws 1903, p. 148) the first section of which is in these words:

"Sec. 1. That no female (shall) be employed in any mechanical establishment, or factory, or laundry in this state more than ten hours during any one day. The hours of work may be so arranged as to permit the employment of females at any time so that they shall not work more than ten hours during the twenty-four hours of any one day."

Sec. 3 made a violation of the provisions of the prior sections a misdemeanor subject to a fine of not less than $10 nor more than $25. On September 18, 1905, an information was filed in the circuit court of the state for the county of Multnomah, charging that the defendant "on the 4th day of September, A.D. 1905, in the county of Multnomah and state of Oregon, then and there being the owner of a laundry, known as the Grand Laundry, in the city of Portland, and the employer of females therein, did then and there unlawfully permit and suffer one Joe Haselbock, he, the said Joe Haselbock, then and there being an overseer, superintendent, and agent of said Curt Muller, in the said Grand Laundry, to require a female, to wit, one Mrs. E. Gotcher, to work more than ten hours in said laundry on said 4th day of September, A.D. 1905, contrary to the statutes in such cases made and provided, and against the peace and dignity of the state of Oregon."

A trial resulted in a verdict against the defendant, who was sentenced to pay a fine of $10. The supreme court of the state affirmed the conviction (48 Or. 252, 85 Pac. 855), whereupon the case was brought here on writ of error.

The single question is the constitutionality of the statute under which the defendant was convicted, so far as it affects the work of a female in a laundry. That it does not conflict with any provisions of the state Constitution is settled by the decision of the supreme court of the state. The contentions of the defendant, now plaintiff in error, are thus stated in his brief:

"1. Because the statute attempts to prevent persons sui juris from making their own contracts, and thus violates the provisions of the 14th Amendment, as follows:

    'No state shall make or enforce any law which shall abridge the privileges or immunities of citizens of the United States; nor shall any state deprive any person of life, liberty, or property, without due process of law; nor deny to any person within its jurisdiction the equal protection of the laws.'

"2. Because the statute does not apply equally to all persons similarly situated, and is class legislation.

"3. The statute is not a valid exercise of the police power. The kinds of work prescribed are not unlawful, nor are they declared to be immoral or dangerous to the public health; nor can such a law be sustained on the ground that it is designed to protect women on account of their sex. There is no necessary or reasonable connection between the limitation prescribed by the act and the public health, safety, or welfare."

It is the law of Oregon that women, whether married or single, have equal contractual and personal rights with men. As said by Chief Justice Wolverton, in First Nat. Bank v. Leonard, 36 Or. 390, 396, 59 Pac. 873, 874, after a review of the various statutes of the state upon the subject:

"We may therefore say with perfect confidence that, with these three sections upon the statute book, the wife can deal, not only with her separate property, acquired from whatever source, in the same manner as her husband can with property belonging to him, but that she may make contracts and incur liabilities, and the same may be enforced against her, the same as if she were a *feme sole*. There is now no residuum of civil disability resting upon her which is not recognized as existing against the husband. The current runs steadily and strongly in the direction of the emancipation of the wife, and the policy, as disclosed by all recent legislation upon the subject in this state, is to place her upon the same footing as if she were a *feme sole,* not only with respect to her separate property, but as it affects her right to make binding contracts; and the most natural corollary to the situation is that the remedies for the enforcement of liabilities incurred are made coextensive and coequal with such enlarged conditions."

It thus appears that, putting to one side the elective franchise, in the matter of personal and contractual rights they stand on the same plane as the other sex. Their rights in these respects can no more be infringed than the equal rights of their brothers. We held in Lochner v. New York, 198 U.S. 45, 49 L. Ed. 937, 25 Sup. Ct. Rep. 539, that a law providing that no laborer shall be required or permitted to work in bakeries more than sixty hours in a week or ten hours in a day was not as to men a legitimate exercise of the police power of the state, but an unreasonable, unnecessary, and arbitrary interference with the right and liberty of the individual to contract in relation to his labor, and as such was in conflict with, and void under, the Federal Constitution. That decision is invoked by plaintiff in error as decisive of the question before us. But this assumes that the difference between the sexes does not justify a different rule respecting a restriction of the hours of labor. . . .

That women's physical structure and the performance of maternal functions place her at a disadvantage in the struggle for subsistence is obvious. This is especially true when the burdens of motherhood are upon her. Even when they are not, by abundant testimony of the medical fraternity continuance for a long time on her feet at work, repeating this from day to day, tends to injurious effects upon the body, and, as healthy mothers are essential to vigorous offspring, the physical well-being of woman becomes an object of public interest and care in order to preserve the strength and vigor of the race.

Still again, history discloses the fact that woman has always been dependent upon man. He established his control at the outset by superior physical strength, and this control in various forms, with diminishing intensity, has continued to the present. As minors, though not to the same extent, she has been looked upon in the courts as needing especial care that her rights may be preserved. Education was long denied her, and while now the doors of the schoolroom are opened and her opportunities for acquiring knowledge are great, yet even with that and the consequent increase of capacity for business affairs it is still true that in the struggle for subsistence she is not an equal competitor with her brother. Though limitations upon personal and contractual rights may be removed by legislation, there is that in her disposition and habits of life which will operate against a full assertion of those rights. She will still be where some legislation to protect her seems necessary to secure a real equality of right. Doubtless there are individual exceptions, and there are many respects in which she has an advantage over him; but looking at it from the viewpoint of the effort to maintain an independent position in life, she is not upon an equality. Differentiated by these matters from the other sex, she is properly placed in a class by herself, and legislation designed for her protection may be sustained, even when like legislation is not necessary for men, and could not be sustained. It is impossible to close one's eyes to the fact that she still looks to her brother and depends upon him. Even though all restrictions on political, personal, and contractual rights were taken away, and she stood, so far as statutes are concerned, upon an absolutely equal plane with him, it would still be true that she is so constituted that she will rest upon and look to him for protection; that her physical structure and a proper discharge of her maternal functions—having in view not merely her own health, but the well-being of the race—justify legislation to protect her from the greed as well as the passion of man. The limitations which this statute places upon her contractual powers, upon her right to agree with her employer as to the time she shall labor, are not imposed solely for her benefit, but also largely for the benefit of all. Many words cannot make this plainer. The two sexes differ in structure of body, in the functions to be performed by each, in the amount of physical strength, in the capacity for long continued labor, particularly when done standing, the influence of vigorous health upon the future well-being of the race, the self-reliance which enables one to assert full rights, and in the capacity to maintain the struggle for subsistence. This difference justifies a difference in legislation, and upholds that which is designed to compensate for some of the burdens which rest upon her.

We have not referred in this discussion to the denial of the elective franchise in the state of Oregon, for while that may disclose a lack of political equality in all things with her brother, that is not of itself decisive. The reason runs deeper, and rests in the inherent difference between the two sexes, and in the different functions in life which they perform.

For these reasons, and without questioning in any respect the decision in Lochner v. New York, we are of the opinion that it cannot be adjudged that the act in question is in conflict with the Federal Constitution, so far as it respects the work of a female in a laundry, and the judgment of the Supreme Court of Oregon is affirmed.

FRANCES WILLARD LEARNS TO RIDE A BICYCLE

"As a temperance reformer," Frances Willard wrote, "I always felt a strong attraction toward the bicycle, because it is the vehicle of so much harmless pleasure, and because the skill required in handling it obliges those who mount to keep clear heads and steady hands." But this photograph from the 1890s shows that women who wanted to learn to ride a bicycle had to grapple with the added impediment of cumbersome clothing, such as the heavy, floor-length suit worn by Willard. Even as women were discovering some of the joys of physical exercise, they had to maintain "proper" female attire. (Credit: Courtesy of National Women's Christian Temperance Union)

IN THE COMPANY OF EDUCATED WOMEN

Women college graduates went to great trouble to create rituals and ceremonies to help legitimize their path-breaking decision to pursue higher education. Here graduating seniors in Mount Holyoke's Class of 1902 participate in the annual Ivy exercises. The women's white dresses (which suggest purity, virginity, and traditional womanhood) are kept very visible beneath their academic caps and gowns, which symbolize their new intellectual aspirations. The woman leading on the left is Frances Perkins, who became the first woman to serve in the cabinet when President Franklin D. Roosevelt named her Secretary of Labor in 1933. (Credit: Mount Holyoke College Library/Archives)

EXPANDING HORIZONS OF WOMEN'S WORK

Working in a settlement house was exciting for the young college
graduates who chose to live in poor urban areas and provide services for
the local neighborhood residents. Some settlement houses like Lillian
Wald's Henry Street Settlement in New York served as headquarters for a
corps of visiting nurses and public health workers who reached out to the
poor in their homes. Here a visiting nurse on her rounds (identifiable by
her style of dress and her black medical bag) takes a shortcut between two
tenement buildings. (Credit: Museum of the City of New York)

SERVING WOMEN

Domestic service was still the largest category of paid women's work in the early twentieth century. Matrons had been complaining that "good help was hard to find" throughout the nineteenth century, and the demand for domestic servants often outstripped the supply. Domestic service was so associated with Irish women that the name *Brigit* practically became a generic term for a (usually hapless) Irish immigrant girl. This photograph of a group of household servants is from the early twentieth century. If they were all employed in a single household, it was one of substantial wealth; most households employed only one, perhaps two servants. Their poses do suggest a level of specialization: the woman in the middle is possibly a nursemaid, the cook is front row right, the woman on the upper right seems to be a maid who serves at table, and the woman at the far left with broom and dustbin is probably the scullery maid, the lowest of the jobs on the occupational hierarchy. (Credit: State Historical Society of Wisconsin)

TAKING WORK HOME

This Italian immigrant woman has just picked up a bundle of clothing, which she will probably take home to finish. If she is a married woman with children (it is difficult to tell her age), she will likely have them help with some of the simpler tasks. Notice how dirty the street and sidewalk are. This photograph was taken on New York's Lower East Side in 1910 by Lewis Hine, a pioneer in the field of social documentary photography. The composition is striking, but somewhat misleading. Usually the streets of the Lower East Side were teeming with people and activity. (Credit: George Eastman House, Rochester, #78: 1051: 7)

WOMEN TYPEWRITERS

The typical nineteenth-century office of clerks, stenographers, and accountants was an all-male preserve. But at the end of the century office work became feminized. A large factor was the introduction of the typewriter in the post-Civil War period. Since the typewriter was a new invention, without customary ties to workers of either sex, female typists did not have to overcome the prejudice that they were doing "men's work." These women are taking a Civil Service typing exam in Chicago in 1909 in the hope of finding employment in the expanding government bureaucracy. Winning such a job, with its expectations of neat dress and literacy in English, was a step upward for recent immigrants. (Credit: Chicago Historical Society)

"DO YOU BELIEVE WHAT THEY ARE CHARGING FOR MEAT?!?"

These women on the Lower East Side of New York are discussing the price of meat during one of the protests that periodically rocked immigrant communities in the early twentieth century. The main instigators of such protests were usually married women in their thirties, the time in their life cycle when they would have the maximum number of children at home to clothe and feed. Some reformers tried to suggest that these women learn to substitute other vegetables and cuts of meat for those that had become so expensive, but, especially for Jewish immigrants, certain foods played central roles in religious observances and could not easily be given up. (Credit: Library of Congress)

SUFFRAGISTS TAKE TO THE STREETS

By the 1910s, the woman suffrage movement had mobilized a broad cross section of the American population. In an effort to win new converts to the cause, suffragists adopted the tactic of open-air parades. On the day that Woodrow Wilson arrived in Washington in 1913 for his inauguration, he asked where all the crowds were and was informed that they were watching the suffrage parade. This Philadelphia march, circa 1913, shows the interest of college students and recent graduates in the movement and their willingness to march publicly for the cause, dressed in their caps and gowns. Such parades not only won publicity but bound women together in the camaraderie of collective displays of suffrage spirit. (Credit: Wellesley College Archives)

CHAPTER 4

Feminists, Anarchists, and Other Rebel Girls

During the early twentieth century, radicalism was a flourishing political and intellectual force in American life. Women such as Mother Jones, Emma Goldman, Kate Richards O'Hare, Elizabeth Gurley Flynn, and Margaret Sanger played prominent and visible roles on the Left, especially in such organizations as the Socialist party, which was at the peak of its influence in the early twentieth century. Of its 118,000 members in 1912, between 10 and 15 percent were women. No other political party in United States history has ever been as supportive of women's rights as the Socialist party.

A concrete symbol of the Socialist commitment to women's emancipation was the 1908 formation of the Woman's National Committee, which served as a clearinghouse for women's issues within the party. Despite the prominence of this group, however, Socialist women still experienced problems when they tried to raise women's issues within the context of the class struggle. The usual response was that women's emancipation would occur automatically when class oppression ended, and that attention to women's issues deflected energies away from the more crucial (to male leaders' minds) question of working-class revolution. Socialist men, moreover, often had very traditional ideas about women's place in the home, which belied their public commitments to women's emancipation. Bourgeois women's organizations, on the other hand, were seen as too identified with the class interests of their members' husbands to be dependable allies, despite common ground on such issues as woman suffrage. Socialist women tried to balance feminist and class issues, but could only get so far. The Woman's National Committee was basically defunct by 1913.

While the Socialist party was the focus for much leftist activity in the prewar period, other groups also absorbed radical energies. The Industrial Workers of the World (IWW), established in 1905, represented a new kind of union that sought to organize the working class along Socialist principles. It stressed militant industrial unionism through its chosen weapon of the general strike.

87

One of its most prominent organizers was Elizabeth Gurley Flynn, who had joined the IWW in 1906 at the age of sixteen. A fiery speaker (she was called the "rebel girl" and later used that phrase as the title of her autobiography), Flynn organized workers, led free speech crusades, and participated in the Lawrence and Paterson general strikes.

New York's Greenwich Village was the center for a host of radicals, artists, socialists, writers, and otherwise generally interesting types before World War I. These self-described bohemians experimented with new forms of expression, both sexual (as in free love) and literary (poetry, drama, and the like). Women were at the center of the Greenwich Village scene, in many cases equal partners to the men. One group of women formed a club called Hetero-doxy, which was, in the words of a member, for unorthodox women "who did things, and did them openly." Prominent members included Charlotte Perkins Gilman, journalists Inez Haynes Irwin and Mary Heaton Vorse, and future *Nation* editor Freda Kirchwey. In addition to their general commitment to socialism, these women added feminism to the agenda for the new world that would occur after the hoped-for cultural and political revolution.

Another manifestation of leftist organizing and action was in the fledgling trade union movement. Groups of radical women came together in what historian Meredith Tax has called "the united front of women"—a working coalition of socialists, trade unionists, and feminists who were prominent in such working-class struggles as the Shirtwaist strike in New York in 1909–1910 and the Lawrence textile strike in 1912. The Socialist party played a central role here, but was joined by other organizations such as the Industrial Workers of the World, the Women's Trade Union League, the International Ladies Garment Workers Union, and several bourgeois women's organizations.

This supportive leftist climate, much of it centered in major urban centers with large immigrant populations such as New York, Chicago, and Seattle, allowed for a broad range of individuals to promote their own versions of political and personal liberation. For example, working-class women in New York's Lower East Side neighborhoods organized spontaneous demonstrations to protest the rising cost of living, especially the price of food. Emma Goldman, who saw politics as cooperation with the capitalist state, developed her own strand of revolutionary anarchism in which women's emancipation was a central tenet. Activist Margaret Sanger started out within the Socialist fold, but by 1915 she was working full time on the fledgling birth control movement. Feminist theorist Charlotte Perkins Gilman identified herself as a socialist as she crisscrossed the country lecturing about women's economic independence. What all these intellectuals and activists shared was a hostility to capitalism and a desire to reconstruct industrial, social, and political life along more cooperative lines.

Such activists as Gilman, Sanger, and Goldman were also far to the left of middle-class women's organizations, especially the woman suffrage movement. Groups like the Socialist party and the IWW were more sympathetic to controversial issues relating to women's emancipation and sexuality (such as birth control) than reform movements like suffrage. Some suffragists, in fact, hoped to use the demands of radical women to their advantage. As one suffragist said to Charlotte Perkins Gilman, "What you ask is so much worse than what we ask, that they will grant our demand in order to escape yours."

The working-class activism and intellectual stirrings of the early twentieth century were brought to an abrupt halt by America's entry into World War I. When the Socialist party, the IWW, and other radical groups spoke out against the war, they were victims of a massive denial of civil liberties during wartime. Federal laws banned treasonous materials from the mails and allowed the government to arrest individuals who spoke out against government policies. During the war and the Red scare that immediately followed it, once flourishing groups such as the IWW were decimated through arrests and deportations of leaders and followers. The supportive, questioning climate that had fostered discussions of women's emancipation, birth control, and a general critique of the dominant male power structure abruptly ended. Instead, the period closed with the winning of suffrage, a feminist reform with far less potential to change women's lives.

Housewives Protest High Food Prices

Meredith Tax

The food riots that occurred on New York's Lower East Side in February of 1917 represented one strand of working-class women's activism in early twentieth-century America. Drawing on a tradition of consumer protest (there had been major Kosher meat boycotts in New York City in 1902 and 1912), housewives in this immigrant neighborhood came together in an independent movement to protest an issue that affected them all: the rising price of food, especially onions and potatoes, but soon other vegetables and chicken as well. In less than a month, prices for such commodities had risen between 20 and 30 percent. For working-class housewives, who spent approximately half their budgets on food, such inflation was disastrous. The women decided to act.

The forms of political activism were ones that these predominantly Jewish women felt comfortable with. Their husbands, brothers, and sons might have been more interested in electoral activity or trade union organizing, but the women chose the issue closest to home— food—as a way of challenging the political and economic system. They organized street protests and boycotts of merchants who would not lower their prices; they picketed such merchants and often forcibly prevented customers from entering the shops. They also moved beyond their neighborhoods by holding mass rallies and taking their demands to city hall. For the most part the movement was controlled and maintained by the energies of housewives. The short-term success of the boycott was dramatic: the markets were shut down for two weeks, confirming for many of the participants the efficacy of mobilizing to challenge conditions of their life that they found intolerable.

Historian Meredith Tax offers a fictional description of the 1917 food protests in *Rivington Street* (1982), a novel that conveys the flavor of life on the Lower East Side and the strong roles that working-class immigrant women played in their neighborhoods. The plot centers around the Levy family, especially the lives of the mother Hannah (who figures in this selection as one of the emerging leaders in the food protest) and her oldest daughter Sarah, who becomes a labor organizer during the 1909 Shirtwaist strike.

There was a crash in the street below. Hannah stuck her head out of the window, then, in one fluid motion, stripped off her apron and ran for the door. So did all the other women in the building, clattering down the stairs like bricks falling in their eagerness to reach the street.

A riot had begun outside.

Hannah never found out for sure who pushed over the first cart on Rivington Street that twentieth day of February 1917. Some said it was the anarchist girl, Minnie Fishman, trying to make trouble. Others attributed it to a stranger, a child, an agitator, a gypsy; but all agreed the price of meat was the cause. The peddlers had raised their prices again, and this time people would not stand for it. Food riots had started the day before in Brownsville and Williamsburg, where the police had fought crowds of mothers and children for hours without being able to subdue them. Moreover, Hannah and Yetta Breynes had talked to most of the block about Garfinkle's price-fixing. Word had spread. By the time Hannah got downstairs, all the pushcarts in Rivington Street were toppling and a general free-for-all had broken out, with women pouring into the street from all sides to attack the peddlers with brooms and rolled-up shopping bags.

"What are you telling me, twenty-five cents a pound for chicken!" screamed Yetta Breynes.

"Goniff! Goslin! You've been cheating me for twenty years!"

Soon the onion and potato peddlers, the bread and pickle vendors, were caught up in the melee. Minnie Fishman tied her black shawl to a stick and stood on one of the overturned pushcarts yelling, "Hooray for anarchy, the black flag forever!"

"We should go to the Mayor!" cried Mrs. Ashkenazi from across the street. "We should go down on our hands and knees and beg him to make the prices lower! That's how they do things in America; they go to City Hall!"

Source: Meredith Tax, *Rivington Street* (New York: William Morrow & Co., 1982), pp. 384–387, 390–391. Copyright © 1982 by Meredith Tax. By permission of William Morrow & Co., Inc.

"No, no, we should go to the *Forward*,"[1] cried Yetta Breynes, a loyal reader. "We should ask Ab Cahan what to do."

After an hour of argument and rampaging around, several hundred women surged out of Rivington Street down Essex, to be joined along the way by others as angry and frightened as they until there were at least a thousand of them. Every housewife on the East Side was out in the street that cold Wednesday morning, looking desperately for a way to feed her family. But when they reached the *Forward* building, the women found little help. Ab Cahan advised them not to be violent and offered them the use of the *Forward* hall for a protest meeting that night. Dispirited, they drifted into Rutgers Square, waiting for something to happen.

Minnie Fishman, never one to pass up an opportunity, got up on a park bench. "People, hear my story," she cried. "I was on my way to work this morning when I saw what was going on and how could I resist helping, since I earn only ten dollars a week sewing? My family is starving. My brother is an invalid and can't work. On my ten dollars a week I support him and my mother besides myself. We live in a two-room apartment on Delancey Street. I haven't looked an egg in the face for months. Potatoes are too rich for our blood. We tried to save money by concentrating on cabbage, but so did everybody else, and now even cabbage is twenty cents a pound. How will we live?"

There were cries from the crowd: "Bread! We need bread for our children! What are we going to do?"

"Two things we need: relief and kerosene! The Mayor has to buy food and distribute it for relief! And we have to go after these peddlers and teach them a lesson—not only turn over their carts but pour kerosene on them! That'll show them who they're dealing with!"

"You stop that kind of talk, Minnie Fishman," yelled Mrs. Ashkenazi, getting up on another park bench. "We're Americans. We don't have to listen to your crazy ideas. What we need is a petition; we all sign a paper saying we are starving and send two or three ladies in to give it to the Mayor."

Hannah listened to these suggestions with interest, eager to do anything that would help. Most of the crowd were of a like mind, and without waiting for a consensus to be reached, began to pour out of Rutgers Square down Division Street, toward City Hall.

When they got there, they found the great iron gates barred against them. The Mayor wasn't in, a policeman told them nervously. They should go home. No delegation would be admitted. The women went wild at the sight of those massive, almost European gates. They threw themselves against the bars. They stretched their hands through them imploringly, crying, "Feed our children!" They shook the bars, screaming, "We want food!" in Yiddish. Many had tears streaming down their cheeks. Others held babies or clutched toddlers' hands.

---

[1]The *Forward* was the Socialist party newspaper. See Chapter 3.

Politically inexperienced, not understanding how it was possible to go hungry in the land of plenty, they had assumed the Mayor would help them. They had dreamed he would pass out bread on the spot. They were cruelly disappointed.

"What can we do?" they cried. "Bread! We need bread!"

The policeman told them that if they chose a delegation of five to come back tomorrow, he would make sure they got in to see the Mayor. Bella Ashkenazi was nominated, so was Minnie Fishman; Mrs. Jacob Panken, wife of the well-known socialist lawyer, was added, along with a rabbi's wife, Mrs. Teitlebaum. Then, much to her surprise, Hannah heard her own name being called out. "Mrs. Levy! Hannah Levy!"

"Me?" she said in astonishment.

"Why not?" said Yetta Breynes. "Aren't you Sarah Levy's mother? You should know all about organizing."

A lady Hannah recognized from the market added, "From such a family you must have ideas."

To her own amazement, Hannah heard herself open her mouth and say firmly, "Yes, I do have ideas."

"What are they?" yelled Minnie.

"Well," said Hannah nervously, trying to remember to speak up, "I think we should go around and tell all the ladies not to buy onions or potatoes. Or chicken on *Shabbos*. Today's Wednesday. By *Shabbos* we should have all the streets fixed so nobody buys these things. That will show them what we do when they charge such robbery prices."

"Boycott!" yelled someone. "Nobody buys!" . . .

By Friday, February 23, 1917, there were no onions or potatoes to be seen on the pushcarts of the East Side, and squads of women roamed the street on the watch for chicken. In front of Garfinkle's Kosher Meat, an army of housewives stood guard with picket signs, while Solly Fein and Rosalie howled abuse from the doorway. A sign in the window said, "Roasting fowl, 32¢ lb.," but to no avail: only two women dared cross the picket line to buy their *Shabbos* hens and as they came out of the store, they had their purchases wrested from their hands and ripped to shreds before their eyes.

"What are you going to make for dinner tonight?" asked Yetta Breynes.

"Noodle pudding and vegetable soup," said Hannah.

"With no onions or potatoes."

"I've got beets, celery, carrots, garlic," she sighed. "I might try some of those tomatoes they got in Little Italy."

"You ever taste one?"

"No."

"Juicy," said Yetta. "Very juicy. A little messy but okay for soup."

That Sunday the Levys and the Breyneses joined the rest of the neighborhood in the scheduled march on the Waldorf-Astoria to confront the Governor. Hannah carried a sign reading, "Never Mind Riverside Drive, Give Us Food on the East Side." The crowd of five thousand marchers remained orderly except for one incident when a group of housewives pulled a young man out of his automobile and told him sternly, "You have no right to ride in a car when people are starving." The Governor issued a press statement accusing the food rioters of being unpatriotic antiwar agitators inspired by paid agents of the Kaiser.

On Monday the associated poultry peddlers of the East Side decided to join the boycott. They sent pickets to all the butcher shops that remained open, and to the wholesalers as well. That night a brick crashed through Garfinkle's plate-glass window and someone painted a sign on his wall: "Death to Profiteers."

By the next day, Tuesday, February 27, the price of potatoes and onions had begun to fall. Chicken soon followed. After the boycott had been in effect for a week, potatoes had gone back to six cents a pound, onions to eleven cents, and chicken to nineteen cents. That night Yakhne Breynes caught sight of Tricker Louis Florsheim unobtrusively leaving the building by a side door, carrying a suitcase. She helped him on his way with a shower of well-placed stones.

All through the next week, Hannah Levy and Yetta Breynes kept up an informal guard before the shop. "Garfinkle's the one who started the whole thing," they told shoppers. "He jacked up the meat prices. For him, the boycott is still on." Business picked up in the rest of the street but not at Garfinkle's. Even the credit he offered no longer enticed the housewives of Rivington Street. Three weeks after the meat riot, a sign went up in Garfinkle's still unrepaired store window: "Business Closed For Renovations." A week later, a large horse-drawn van pulled up in front and men began to load furniture into it. Hannah sent Ruby to investigate.

"Moving?" she asked Rosalie Fein.

"You bet," she answered with her nose in the air, "to Central Park West. We're going to open a new butcher shop uptown, where the nice people live."

The sign in the window across the street was replaced by one reading "Store for Rent. Goodwill for Sale. Inquire at AL 2-5900." The store remained empty for some time, however. As Moyshe said, "On Garfinkle's goodwill you could starve to death." But Hannah walked with a new spring in her step. For the first time since 1909, her neighborhood was all hers again.

A Feminist Challenge to the Privatized Home

Charlotte Perkins Gilman

Charlotte Perkins Stetson Gilman (1860–1935) was the leading intellectual of the women's movement in the early twentieth century. Born into the prestigious Beecher family, she struggled through a lonely

childhood and disastrous marriage, which caused a nervous break-
down. Her mental health returned once she separated from her husband (she gave him custody of their young daughter), moved to California, and threw herself into the heady reform climate of the 1890s.
To support herself, she wrote poetry and short stories and lectured ex-
tensively. Her widely read book, *Women and Economics* (1898), argued
for female economic independence, and she developed her iconoclas-
tic views in later books and articles, including fiction. A second marriage in 1900, to her first cousin Houghton Gilman, gave her the personal stability she had been unable to find in her first marriage.

Gilman did not consider herself a feminist, preferring to call herself a sociologist because her vision was not for women alone. In
Gilman's formulation, the interdependence of men and women was
the most important result of human evolution. She was therefore
highly critical of private institutions, such as families and marriage,
that isolated women and prevented their participation in broader social developments. Not only did this stunt women's growth, but it
acted, in her understanding of hereditarian evolution, to retard the development of the human race as a whole.

Women and Economics, from which this selection is drawn, is a mix
of evolution, polemics, common sense, and socialism. It is heavily indebted to Edward Bellamy's utopian novel *Looking Backward* (1889).
Gilman's plans here for collectivist housekeeping show how she
thought a socialist and feminist future might look. Such cooperative
apartment houses would end women's isolation in individual homes,
allow children to interact with others their own age in childcare centers, and make housekeeping and cooking more efficient. Her desire
to assign tasks that best utilized individual talents was in keeping
with her deeply held conviction that all human work was ennobling,
both to society and to the individuals who were performing it. But
notice how she assumes that women will choose occupations "compatible with motherhood." Despite such a lapse into conventional
thinking, Charlotte Perkins Gilman's vision of women and men emancipated from an outmoded private home still makes a compelling contribution to feminist thought.

If there should be built and opened in any of our large cities to-day a com-
modious and well-served apartment house for professional women with families, it would be filled at once. The apartments would be without kitchens; but
there would be a kitchen belonging to the house from which meals could be
served to the families in their rooms or in a common dining-room, as preferred.
It would be a home where the cleaning was done by efficient workers, not hired
separately by the families, but engaged by the manager of the establishment;
and a roof-garden, day nursery, and kindergarten, under well-trained profes-

Source: Charlotte Perkins Stetson (Gilman), *Women and Economics* (Boston: Small, Maynard, and
Company, 1898; reprinted by Harper and Row, New York, 1966), pp. 242–247.

sional nurses and teachers, would insure proper care of the children. The demand for such provision is increasing daily, and must soon be met, not by a boarding-house or a lodging-house, a hotel, a restaurant, or any makeshift patching together of these; but by a permanent provision for the needs of women and children, of family privacy with collective advantage. This must be offered on a business basis to prove a substantial business success; and it will so prove, for it is a growing social need.

There are hundreds of thousands of women in New York City alone who are wage-earners, and who also have families; and the number increases. This is true not only among the poor and unskilled, but more and more among business women, professional women, scientific, artistic, literary women. Our school-teachers, who form a numerous class, are not entirely without relatives. To board does not satisfy the needs of a human soul. These women want homes, but they do not want the clumsy tangle of rudimentary industries that are supposed to accompany the home. The strain under which such women labor is no longer necessary. The privacy of the home could be as well maintained in such a building as described as in any house in a block, any room, flat, or apartment, under present methods. The food would be better, and would cost less; and this would be true of the service and of all common necessities.

In suburban homes this purpose could be accomplished much better by a grouping of adjacent houses, each distinct and having its own yard, but all kitchenless, and connected by covered ways with the eating-house. No detailed prophecy can be made of the precise forms which would ultimately prove most useful and pleasant; but the growing social need is for the specializing of the industries practised in the home and for the proper mechanical provision for them.

The cleaning required in each house would be much reduced by the removal of the two chief elements of household dirt—grease and ashes.

Meals could of course be served in the house as long as desired; but, when people become accustomed to pure, clean homes, where no steaming industry is carried on, they will gradually prefer to go to their food instead of having it brought to them. It is a perfectly natural process, and a healthful one, to go to one's food. And, after all, the changes between living in one room, and so having the cooking most absolutely convenient; going as far as the limits of a large house permit, to one's own dining-room; and going a little further to a dining room not in one's own house, but near by,—these differ but in degree. Families could go to eat together, just as they can go to bathe together or listen to music together; but, if it fell out that different individuals presumed to develope an appetite at different hours, they could meet it without interfering with other people's comfort or sacrificing their own. Any housewife knows the difficulty of always getting a family together at meals. Why try? Then arises sentiment, and asserts that family affection, family unity, the very existence of the family, depend on their being together at meals. A family unity which is only bound together with a table-cloth is of questionable value.

There are several professions involved in our clumsy method of house-keeping. A good cook is not necessarily a good manager, nor a good manager an accurate and thorough cleaner, nor a good cleaner a wise purchaser. Under the free development of these branches a woman could choose her position, train for it, and become a most valuable functionary in her special branch, all the while living in her own home; that is, she would live in it as a man lives in his home, spending certain hours of the day at work and others at home.

This division of the labor of housekeeping would require the service of fewer women for fewer hours a day. Where now twenty women in twenty homes work all the time, and insufficiently accomplish their varied duties, the same work in the hands of specialists could be done in less time by fewer people; and the others would be left free to do other work for which they were better fitted, thus increasing the productive power of the world. Attempts at co-operation so far have endeavored to lessen the existing labors of women without recognizing their need for other occupation, and this is one reason for their repeated failure.

It seems almost unnecessary to suggest that women as economic producers will naturally choose those professions which are compatible with motherhood, and there are many professions much more in harmony with that function than the household service. Motherhood is not a remote contingency, but the common duty and the common glory of womanhood. If women did choose professions unsuitable to maternity, Nature would quietly extinguish them by her unvarying process. Those mothers who persisted in being acrobats, horse-breakers, or sailors before the mast, would probably not produce vigorous and numerous children. If they did, it would simply prove that such work did not hurt them. There is no fear to be wasted on the danger of women's choosing wrong professions, when they are free to choose. Many women would continue to prefer the very kinds of work which they are doing now, in the new and higher methods of execution. Even cleaning, rightly understood and practised, is a useful, and therefore honorable, profession. It has been amusing heretofore to see how this least desirable of labors has been so innocently held to be women's natural duty. It is woman, the dainty, the beautiful, the beloved wife and revered mother, who has by common consent been expected to do the chamber-work and scullery work of the world. All that is basest and foulest she in the last instance must handle and remove. Grease, ashes, dust, foul linen, and sooty ironware,—among these her days must pass. As we socialize our functions, this passes from her hands into those of man. The city's cleaning is his work. And even in our houses the professional cleaner is more and more frequently a man.

The organization of household industries will simplify and centralize its cleaning processes, allowing of many mechanical conveniences and the application of scientific skill and thoroughness. We shall be cleaner than we ever were before. There will be less work to do, and far better means of doing it.

The daily needs of a well-plumbed house could be met easily by each individual in his or her own room or by one who liked to do such work; and the labor less frequently required would be furnished by an expert, who would clean one home after another with the swift skill of training and experience. The home would cease to be to us a workshop or a museum, and would become far more the personal expression of its occupants—the place of peace and rest, of love and privacy—than it can be in its present condition of arrested industrial development. And woman will fill her place in those industries with far better results than are now provided by her ceaseless struggles, her conscientious devotion, her pathetic ignorance and inefficiency.

Wages for Housework

Josephine Conger-Kaneko

Wages for housework have been squarely on the feminist agenda since the 1970s, but that was not the first time the issue had been raised, as this spirited 1913 piece by Socialist writer Josephine Conger-Kaneko demonstrates. It appeared in *Progressive Woman*, the magazine that Conger-Kaneko had founded in 1907 under the original title of *Socialist Woman* with the help of her husband, prominent Japanese socialist Ki-ichi Kaneko. Starting with only twenty-six subscribers, she built circulation to 15,000 at its peak in 1912. Historian Mari Jo Buhle called this magazine and its editor the "single most important source of propaganda and news of the women's sector" for the entire Socialist movement.

Josephine Conger was born in Centralia, Missouri. While attending Ruskin College in Trenton, Missouri, she became an avid convert to socialism. She loved poetry and literature, but she loved journalism more. Building on her experience working for her brother's country newspaper, in 1903 she got a job on the editorial staff of the *Appeal*, the most popular Socialist newspaper in the United States at the time. Her column, which combined inspirational poetry, politics, and a belief in the moral imperative of traditional womanhood, was directed toward women. "A woman can understand anything if presented from a personal standpoint," she once stated.

Josephine Conger-Kaneko was always a strong believer in separate organizations for women within the wider socialist movement. "There is a very great deal that women need to learn about themselves, about their history, and the traditions of their sex," she noted. "These things can best be learned, as a rule, in a separate organization, where the mind can be better centered upon the matter at hand." Her magazine—and her advocacy of women's issues—flourished in the heyday of women's activism from 1908 to 1913 but then fell on hard times when the socialist movement shifted its priorities. *Progressive Woman* ceased publication in 1913.

Does a woman support her husband's employer?

Has anybody ever thought about a woman's part in her husband's contract for his wages?

Has anybody ever thought that when a man gets married he DOESN'T RE-CEIVE A PENNY MORE FOR HIS WORK THAN WHEN HE WAS SIN-GLE, AND THAT THEN HE GOT BARELY ENOUGH TO BOARD AND CLOTHE HIMSELF?

Evidently nobody has thought much about these things. And least of all the woman herself. So, let us see about it.

And you, madam, must see about it with us. It means something to you. It might mean that you are to have a new voile dress next spring, instead of making over that old thing again that you were married in ten years ago.

For that is just what it amounts to—your husband's employer getting the dimes and dollars that should be yours for a new dress and the other things you need so much to lead a normal, happy life.

Here is the situation. Your husband works eight or ten hours a day, and receives a cash return for his work. You work twelve or fifteen hours a day, AND NEVER SEE A CASH RETURN FOR YOUR WORK.

Your husband works to produce saleable goods for the man who employs him. YOU WORK TO KEEP A HOME AND FEED YOUR HUSBAND SO THAT HE CAN KEEP ON WORKING TO PRODUCE SALEABLE GOODS FOR THE MAN WHO EMPLOYS HIM.

Your husband, working for his employer, produces in a year, say $2,500 (the U.S. census statistics say the average worker produces this much in a year) and he gets back in wages $500 (census statistics also say that a man's average wage a year is $500).

Now, YOU make a home for your husband, cook his meals, wash his clothes and mend them; in fact, you keep him in trim and working order so he can produce $2,500 a year for his employer. Your husband gets back from what he makes $500.

WHAT DO YOU GET?

If you hired out to families to do the washing alone, you would get $2 a day and your car fare and lunch. If you went from family to family six days in the week, washing for them, you would get six free lunches and $12.

Working this way, your work is from 8 in the morning till 5 in the afternoon. After you are through with your work you have the evening to yourself, and $2 in your pocket.

Source: Josephine Conger-Kaneko, "Does a Woman Support the Husband's Employer?" *Progressive Woman,* 7.74 (August 1913).

When you work to keep your husband in good order for his employer you don't get through at 5 o'clock, and you don't have your evening for yourself. Nor do you have $2 in your purse at the end of the day.

No. Not exactly.

You work ALL HOURS, at BOARD WAGES. That is, you get a part of the food you cook, and live in the house you keep, and you can have a dress occasionally that you make, FOR WORKING ENDLESS HOURS THAT YOUR HUSBAND MAY BE AN EFFICIENT WORKER FOR HIS EMPLOYER.

And what does your husband's employer get out of it? Taking the U.S. census as a guide, he gets on the average $2,000 out of your husband's work. The employer gets $2,000, your husband gets $500, and YOU GET SOME OF THE FOOD YOU COOK, AND THE RIGHT TO LIVE IN THE HOUSE YOU KEEP.

It is a very nice arrangement—for the employer. Not so very nice for the husband, AND A SLAVE'S LIFE FOR YOU.

But a man needn't get married, some one says. The employer doesn't demand that he be married.

Oh, yes, workingmen have to get married. Not the individual man here and there, perhaps. But the masses of them. That is an undisputable fact, and we would not drag it into this except that some very short-sighted person will raise the question, and thinks he has shattered to star-dust our contention that a woman supports her husband's employer, by saying that A WORKINGMAN NEEDN'T GET MARRIED.

If he DOESN'T MARRY, whose children are going to do the world's work in the future? Not the employer's children. On the contrary, the employer WANTS his employes to marry, and raise up children to work for his heirs when THEY are grown.

So it is an indisputable fact that the workingman must get married. BUT IS IT AN ABSOLUTELY ESSENTIAL FACT THAT THE WOMAN MUST BE THE GOAT AND BEAR THE HARDEST, TOUGHEST, MOST SLAVISH END OF THE DEAL?

THAT IS WHAT SHE IS DOING TODAY!

When a man gets married, does he go to his employer and say: Now, Mr. Employer, I am going to take a partner to help me live as a decent man should live, and so increase my efficiency for my work with you. For her part in our three-cornered deal I think you had better allow me so-and-so.

Does Mr. Young-Man-About-to-Be-Married say that? No, he doesn't. If the boss hears that he is to be married he may unbend his dignity enough to say: "Well, Bill, old man, I hear you are going to hook up with a mighty nice girl. That's right. Every honest fellow should settle down and raise a family." And Bill—well, he just grins. That's all. It's real pathetic, that grin of Bill's. It stands so often for inefficiency. He just don't know what else to do. So when the boss unbends enough to "congratulate" him on the greatest event of his life he grins and feels that a great favor has been bestowed upon him.

But the new little wife! Heaven help her. Bill's grin won't coin into dollars; won't buy new dresses; won't buy baby clothes; won't pay the doctor's bill; won't hire any of the back-breaking work of the house done. The little wife has somehow got to manage to attend to all of these things herself, or go without. And keep Bill going besides, so he can produce saleable goods for the boss.

It's pathetic, but the wives have got to get at the problem themselves. The Bills DON'T KNOW HOW. Their ignorance and stupidity in some things is appalling.

So, next time your husband comes home with $10 in his pocket when he should have $20, ask him where YOUR share is. And don't be put off with the silly answer that you are getting your room and board out of HIS $10 for your share. Tell him you can go out and work by the week and bring home $12, AND YOU WANT TO KNOW WHAT IS GOING TO BE YOUR END OF THE DEAL BETWEEN HIM AND HIS EMPLOYER.

Time was when a man gave his slave men their board and clothes, AND GAVE THE WIVES OF THE SLAVE MEN THEIR BOARD AND CLOTHES ALSO. Today a wage slave gets the equivalent of HIS board and clothes in wages—and the wife of the wage slave gets nothing.

The employer thus gets off a whole lot easier than he did when he owned slaves and was responsible for the physical welfare of the whole family.

THE UNPAID AND GROSSLY EXPLOITED LABOR OF MARRIED WOMEN IN THEIR HOMES MAKES IT POSSIBLE FOR THE EMPLOYER TO PILE-UP IMMENSE PROFITS OUT OF HIS BUSINESS, WHICH, OF COURSE, IS HIGHLY SATISFACTORY TO HIM.

But is it to you, O Woman, who must pay the price?

Margaret Sanger's Epiphany Over Birth Control

Birth control has a long history in America, but the name most closely associated with this cause is that of Margaret Sanger. One of the twentieth century's most influential women, Sanger devoted her career to the promotion and legalization of birth control information.

Margaret Sanger (1879–1966) always had a publicists' flair for drawing lessons from the events of her life. The Sadie Sachs story recounted here proved very effective from the lecture podium, and later in her autobiography. At the time the incident occurred, Sanger was a 29-year-old mother of three children, who was using her training as a public health nurse on New York's Lower East Side. Her specialty was obstetrical cases. Often women would ask her for the "secret" of birth control, and Sanger could only tell them of condoms and withdrawal, both methods which required the cooperation of men and thus were deemed unreliable by her clients. When Sadie Sachs died of the effects of a self-induced abortion, Sanger vowed to devote the rest of her life to making birth control widely available to all classes.

Sanger began her career as a birth control activist in the 1910s while associated with radical groups such as the Wobblies and the Socialist party. She argued that family limitation would improve the lives of working-class people; concerned with increasing women's autonomy, she also wanted to separate intercourse from procreation in order to liberate women's sexuality. Birth control thus met both feminist and revolutionary goals. By 1915, however, Sanger began to concentrate on a strategy of legalization of the distribution of birth control information and devices through doctor-staffed clinics. (Under the Comstock Act of 1873, the dissemination of birth control information was illegal.) In the 1920s and 1930s, she won the right for doctors to dispense such information in clinics, and she successfully challenged federal laws that hindered the practice of birth control. Her organization, the American Birth Control League, became Planned Parenthood in 1942.

Although Margaret Sanger saw birth control as a feminist demand, the legalistic strategy she pursued after 1915 often played down its revolutionary demands for women's autonomy in favor of cooperation with the medical community, a conservative group dominated by men. By making birth control into a medical rather than a feminist issue, Sanger set the stage for the reasoning employed to legalize abortion in the 1973 Supreme Court case of *Roe* v. *Wade*.

During these years in New York trained nurses were in great demand. Few people wanted to enter hospitals; they were afraid they might be "practiced" upon, and consented to go only in desperate emergencies. Sentiment was especially vehement in the matter of having babies. A woman's own bedroom, no matter how inconveniently arranged, was the usual place for her lying-in. I was not sufficiently free from domestic duties to be a general nurse, but I could ordinarily manage obstetrical cases because I was notified far enough ahead to plan my schedule. And after serving my two weeks I could get home again.

Sometimes I was summoned to small apartments occupied by young clerks, insurance salesmen, or lawyers, just starting out, most of them under thirty and whose wives were having their first or second baby. They were always eager to know the best and latest method in infant care and feeding. In particular, Jewish patients, whose lives centered around the family, welcomed advice and followed it implicitly.

But more and more my calls began to come from the Lower East Side, as though I were being magnetically drawn there by some force outside my con-

Source: Margaret Sanger, *An Autobiography* (New York: W. W. Norton, 1938; reprinted by Dover Publications, 1971), pp. 86–92. Reprinted by permission of Michael Sanger.

trol. I hated the wretchedness and hopelessness of the poor, and never experienced that satisfaction in working among them that so many noble women have found. My concern for my patients was now quite different from my earlier hospital attitude. I could see that much was wrong with them which did not appear in the physiological or medical diagnosis. A woman in childbirth was not merely a woman in childbirth. My expanded outlook included a view of her background, her potentialities as a human being, the kind of children she was bearing, and what was going to happen to them.

The wives of small shopkeepers were my most frequent cases, but I had carpenters, truck drivers, dishwashers, and pushcart vendors. I admired intensely the consideration most of these people had for their own. Money to pay doctor and nurse had been carefully saved months in advance—parents-in-law, grandfathers, grandmothers, all contributing.

As soon as the neighbors learned that a nurse was in the building they came in a friendly way to visit, often carrying fruit, jellies, or gefüllter fish made after a cherished recipe. It was infinitely pathetic to me that they, so poor themselves, should bring me food. Later they drifted in again with the excuse of getting the plate, and sat down for a nice talk; there was no hurry. Always back of the little gift was the question, "I am pregnant (or my daughter, or my sister is). Tell me something to keep from having another baby. We cannot afford another yet."

I tried to explain the only two methods I had ever heard of among the middle classes, both of which were invariably brushed aside as unacceptable. They were of no certain avail to the wife because they placed the burden of responsibility solely upon the husband—a burden which he seldom assumed. What she was seeking was self-protection she could herself use, and there was none.

Below this stratum of society was one in truly desperate circumstances. The men were sullen and unskilled, picking up odd jobs now and then, but more often unemployed, lounging in and out of the house at all hours of the day and night. The women seemed to slink on their way to market and were without neighborliness.

These submerged, untouched classes were beyond the scope of organized charity or religion. No labor union, no church, not even the Salvation Army reached them. They were apprehensive of everyone and rejected help of any kind, ordering all intruders to keep out; both birth and death they considered their own business. Social agents, who were just beginning to appear, were profoundly mistrusted because they pried into homes and lives, asking questions about wages, how many were in the family, had any of them ever been in jail. Often two or three had been there or were now under suspicion of prostitution, shoplifting, purse snatching, petty thievery, and, in consequence, passed furtively to the big blue uniforms on the corner.

The utmost depression came over me as I approached this surreptitious region. Below Fourteenth Street I seemed to be breathing a different air, to be in another world and country where the people had habits and customs alien to anything I had ever heard about.

There were then approximately ten thousand apartments in New York into which no sun ray penetrated directly; such windows as they had opened only on a narrow court from which rose fetid odors. It was seldom cleaned, though garbage and refuse often went down into it. All these dwellings were pervaded by the foul breath of poverty, that moldy, indefinable, indescribable smell which cannot be fumigated out, sickening to me but apparently unnoticed by those who lived there. When I set to work with antiseptics, their pungent sting, at least temporarily, obscured the stench.

I remember one confinement case to which I was called by the doctor of an insurance company. I climbed up the five flights and entered the airless rooms, but the baby had come with too great speed. A boy of ten had been the only assistant. Five flights was a long way; he had wrapped the placenta in a piece of newspaper and dropped it out the window into the court.

Many families took in "boarders," as they were termed, whose small contributions paid the rent. These derelicts, wanderers, alternately working and drinking, were crowded in with the children; a single room sometimes held as many as six sleepers. Little girls were accustomed to dressing and undressing in front of the men, and were often violated, occasionally by their own fathers or brothers, before they reached the age of puberty.

Pregnancy was a chronic condition among the women of this class. Suggestions as to what to do for a girl who was "in trouble" or a married woman who was "caught" passed from mouth to mouth—herb teas, turpentine, steaming, rolling downstairs, inserting slippery elm, knitting needles, shoe-hooks. When they had word of a new remedy they hurried to the drugstore, and if the clerk were inclined to be friendly he might say, "Oh, that won't help you, but here's something that may." The younger druggists usually refused to give advice because, if it were to be known, they would come under the law; midwives were even more fearful. The doomed women implored me to reveal the "secret" rich people had, offering to pay me extra to tell them; many really believed I was holding back information for money. They asked everybody and tried anything, but nothing did them any good. On Saturday nights I have seen groups of from fifty to one hundred with their shawls over their heads waiting outside the office of a five-dollar abortionist.

Each time I returned to this district, which was becoming a recurrent nightmare, I used to hear that Mrs. Cohen "had been carried to a hospital, but had never come back," or that Mrs. Kelly "had sent the children to a neighbor and had put her head into the gas oven." Day after day such tales were poured into my ears—a baby born dead, great relief—the death of an older child, sorrow but again relief of a sort—the story told a thousand times of death from abortion and children going into institutions. I shuddered with horror as I listened to the details and studied the reasons back of them—destitution linked with excessive childbearing. The waste of life seemed utterly senseless. One by one worried, sad, pensive, and aging faces marshaled themselves before me in my dreams, sometimes appealingly, sometimes accusingly.

These were not merely "unfortunate conditions among the poor" such as we read about. I knew the women personally. They were living, breathing, human beings, with hopes, fears, and aspirations like my own, yet their weary, misshapen bodies, "always ailing, never failing," were destined to be thrown on the scrap heap before they were thirty-five. I could not escape from the facts of their wretchedness; neither was I able to see any way out. My own cozy and comfortable family existence was becoming a reproach to me.

Then one stifling mid-July day of 1912 I was summoned to a Grand Street tenement. My patient was a small, slight Russian Jewess, about twenty-eight years old, of the special cast of feature to which suffering lends a madonna-like expression. The cramped three-room apartment was in a sorry state of turmoil. Jake Sachs, a truck driver scarcely older than his wife, had come home to find the three children crying and her unconscious from the effects of a self-induced abortion. He had called the nearest doctor, who in turn had sent for me. Jake's earnings were trifling, and most of them had gone to keep the none-too-strong children clean and properly fed. But his wife's ingenuity had helped them to save a little, and this he was glad to spend on a nurse rather than have her go to a hospital.

The doctor and I settled ourselves to the task of fighting the septicemia. Never had I worked so fast, never so concentratedly. The sultry days and nights were melted into a torpid inferno. It did not seem possible there could be such heat, and every bit of food, ice, and drugs had to be carried up three flights of stairs.

Jake was more kind and thoughtful than many of the husbands I had encountered. He loved his children, and had always helped his wife wash and dress them. He had brought water up and carried garbage down before he left in the morning, and did as much as he could for me while he anxiously watched her progress.

After a fortnight Mrs. Sachs' recovery was in sight. Neighbors, ordinarily fatalistic as to the results of abortion, were genuinely pleased that she had survived. She smiled wanly at all who came to see her and thanked them gently, but she could not respond to their hearty congratulations. She appeared to be more despondent and anxious than she should have been, and spent too much time in meditation.

At the end of three weeks, as I was preparing to leave the fragile patient to take up her difficult life once more, she finally voiced her fears, "Another baby will finish me, I suppose?"

"It's too early to talk about that," I temporized.

But when the doctor came to make his last call, I drew him aside. "Mrs. Sachs is terribly worried about having another baby."

"She well may be," replied the doctor, and then he stood before her and said, "Any more such capers, young woman, and there'll be no need to send for me."

"I know, doctor," she replied timidly, "but," and she hesitated as though it took all her courage to say it, "what can I do to prevent it?"

The doctor was a kindly man, and he had worked hard to save her, but such incidents had become so familiar to him that he had long since lost whatever delicacy he might once have had. He laughed good-naturedly. "You want to have your cake and eat it too, do you? Well, it can't be done."

Then picking up his hat and bag to depart he said, "Tell Jake to sleep on the roof."

I glanced quickly at Mrs. Sachs. Even through my sudden tears I could see stamped on her face an expression of absolute despair. We simply looked at each other, saying no word until the door had closed behind the doctor. Then she lifted her thin, blue-veined hands and clasped them beseechingly. "He can't understand. He's only a man. But you do, don't you? Please tell me the secret, and I'll never breathe it to a soul. *Please!"*

What was I to do? I could not speak the conventionally comforting phrases which would be of no comfort. Instead, I made her as physically easy as I could and promised to come back in a few days to talk with her again. A little later, when she slept, I tiptoed away.

Night after night the wistful image of Mrs. Sachs appeared before me. I made all sorts of excuses to myself for not going back. I was busy on other cases; I really did not know what to say to her or how to convince her of my own ignorance; I was helpless to avert such monstrous atrocities. Time rolled by and I did nothing.

The telephone rang one evening three months later, and Jake Sachs' agitated voice begged me to come at once; his wife was sick again and from the same cause. For a wild moment I thought of sending someone else, but actually, of course, I hurried into my uniform, caught up my bag, and started out. All the way I longed for a subway wreck, an explosion, anything to keep me from having to enter that home again. But nothing happened, even to delay me. I turned into the dingy doorway and climbed the familiar stairs once more. The children were there, young little things.

Mrs. Sachs was in a coma and died within ten minutes. I folded her still hands across her breast, remembering how they had pleaded with me, begging so humbly for the knowledge which was her right. I drew a sheet over her pallid face. Jake was sobbing, running his hands through his hair and pulling it out like an insane person. Over and over again he wailed, "My God! My God! My God!"

I left him pacing desperately back and forth, and for hours I myself walked and walked and walked through the hushed streets. When I finally arrived home and let myself quietly in, all the household was sleeping. I looked out my window and down upon the dimly lighted city. Its pains and griefs crowded in upon me, a moving picture rolled before my eyes with photographic clearness: women writhing in travail to bring forth little babies; the babies themselves naked and hungry, wrapped in newspapers to keep them from the cold; six-year-old children with pinched, pale, wrinkled faces, old in concentrated wretchedness, pushed into gray and fetid cellars, crouching on stone floors, their small scrawny hands scuttling through rags, making lamp shades, artificial flowers; white coffins, black coffins, coffins, coffins interminably passing in never-ending succession. The scenes piled one upon another on another. I could bear it no longer.

As I stood there the darkness faded. The sun came up and threw its reflection over the house tops. It was the dawn of a new day in my life also. The doubt and questioning, the experimenting and trying, were now to be put behind me. I knew I could not go back merely to keeping people alive.

I went to bed, knowing that no matter what it might cost, I was finished with palliatives and superficial cures; I was resolved to seek out the root of evil, to do something to change the destiny of mothers whose miseries were vast as the sky.

A Radical View of Women's Emancipation

Emma Goldman

Although Margaret Sanger styled herself as the first advocate of birth control in America, the anarchist and feminist Emma Goldman (1869–1940) had already lectured widely on the subject. Goldman's life was a far cry from Sanger's. Born into a Jewish family in Lithuania, this strong-willed girl emigrated to America in 1885 at the age of sixteen. She found work in New York at the same time she found anarchism and a host of radical causes. She formed a liaison with Alexander Berkman, who spent fourteen years in jail for his part in the attempted assassination of steel magnate Henry Clay Frick in 1892. Meanwhile, Emma Goldman was building a reputation as a revolutionary activist and a feminist committed to free love. (She had a deep capacity for friendships with men and women and had many lovers.) Goldman's speeches, pamphlets, and editorship of the monthly *Mother Earth* (1906–1917) provided forums for her unconventional views.

Emma Goldman defies easy categorization. She was a totally liberated woman long before the word became fashionable; her revolutionary ideology of anarchism made her critical of all institutions. This

Source: Emma Goldman, "The Tragedy of Women's Emancipation," in *Red Emma Speaks: Selected Writings and Speeches by Emma Goldman,* ed. Alix Kates Shulman (New York: Vintage, 1972), pp. 133–142.

selection, "The Tragedy of Women's Emancipation" (1911), criticized the superficial goals of the modern women's movement and provided Goldman's alternative view of women's liberation: "True emancipation begins neither at the polls nor in the courts. It begins in woman's soul."

Goldman's radical activities finally caused her deportation from the United States in 1919. She lived briefly in the Soviet Union, but quickly grew disillusioned with the Soviet experiment. Until her death in 1940, she lived in Europe and Canada, increasingly cut off from her radical roots. Writing her two-volume autobiography, *Living My Life* (1931), recaptured the excitement of those years and brought her un-conventional lifestyle and ideas to new audiences.

I begin with an admission: Regardless of all political and economic theories, treating of the fundamental differences between various groups within the human race, regardless of class and race distinctions, regardless of all artificial boundary lines between woman's rights and man's rights, I hold that there is a point where these differentiations may meet and grow into one perfect whole.

With this I do not mean to propose a peace treaty. The general social antagonism which has taken hold of our entire public life today, brought about through the force of opposing and contradictory interests, will crumble to pieces when the reorganization of our social life, based upon the principles of economic justice, shall have become a reality.

Peace or harmony between the sexes and individuals does not necessarily depend on a superficial equalization of human beings; nor does it call for the elimination of individual traits and peculiarities. The problem that confronts us today, and which the nearest future is to solve, is how to be one's self and yet in oneness with others, to feel deeply with all human beings and still retain one's own characteristic qualities. This seems to me to be the basis upon which the mass and the individual, the true democrat and the true individuality, man and woman, can meet without antagonism and opposition. The motto should not be: Forgive one another; rather, Understand one another. The oft-quoted sentence of Madame de Staël: "To understand everything means to forgive everything," has never particularly appealed to me; it has the odor of the confessional; to forgive one's fellow-being conveys the idea of pharisaical superiority. To understand one's fellow-being suffices. The admission partly represents the fundamental aspect of my views on the emancipation of woman and its effect upon the entire sex.

Emancipation should make it possible for woman to be human in the truest sense. Everything within her that craves assertion and activity should reach its fullest expression; all artificial barriers should be broken, and the road towards greater freedom cleared of every trace of centuries of submission and slavery.

This was the original aim of the movement for woman's emancipation. But the results so far achieved have isolated woman and have robbed her of the fountain springs of that happiness which is so essential to her. Merely external emancipation has made of the modern woman an artificial being, who reminds one of the products of French arboriculture with its arabesque trees and shrubs, pyramids, wheels and wreaths; anything, except the forms which would be reached by the expression of her own inner qualities. Such artificially grown plants of the female sex are to be found in large numbers, especially in the so-called intellectual sphere of our life.

Liberty and equality for woman! What hopes and aspirations these words awakened when they were first uttered by some of the noblest and bravest souls of those days. The sun in all his light and glory was to rise upon a new world; in this world woman was to be free to direct her own destiny—an aim certainly worthy of the great enthusiasm, courage, perseverance, and ceaseless effort of the tremendous host of pioneer men and women, who staked everything against a world of prejudice and ignorance.

My hopes also move towards that goal, but I hold that the emancipation of woman, as interpreted and practically applied today, has failed to reach that great end. Now, woman is confronted with the necessity of emancipating herself from emancipation, if she really desires to be free. This may sound paradoxical, but is, nevertheless, only too true.

What has she achieved through her emancipation? Equal suffrage in a few States. Has that purified our political life, as many well-meaning advocates predicted? Certainly not. Incidentally, it is really time that persons with plain, sound judgment should cease to talk about corruption in politics in a boarding-school tone. Corruption of politics has nothing to do with the morals, or the laxity of morals, of various political personalities. Its cause is altogether a material one. Politics is the reflex of the business and industrial world, the mottos of which are: "To take is more blessed than to give"; "buy cheap and sell dear"; "one soiled hand washes the other." There is no hope even that woman, with her right to vote, will ever purify politics.

Emancipation has brought woman economic equality with man; that is, she can choose her own profession and trade; but as her past and present physical training has not equipped her with the necessary strength to compete with man, she is often compelled to exhaust all her energy, use up her vitality, and strain every nerve in order to reach the market value. Very few ever succeed, for it is a fact that women teachers, doctors, lawyers, architects, and engineers are neither met with the same confidence as their male colleagues, nor receive equal remuneration. And those that do reach that enticing equality generally do so at the expense of their physical and psychical well-being. As to the great mass of working girls and women, how much independence is gained if the narrowness and lack of freedom of the home is exchanged for the narrowness and lack of freedom of the factory, sweat-shop, department store, or office? In addition is the burden which is laid on many women of looking after a "home, sweet home"—cold, dreary, disorderly, uninviting—after a day's hard work. Glorious independence! No wonder that hundreds of girls are so willing to accept the first offer of marriage; sick and tired of their "independence" behind the counter, at the sewing or typewriting machine. They are just as ready to marry as girls of the middle class, who long to throw off the yoke of parental supremacy. A so-called independence which leads only to earning the merest subsistence is not so enticing, not so ideal, that one could expect woman to sacrifice everything for it. Our highly praised independence is, after all, but a slow process of dulling and stifling woman's nature, her love instinct, and her mother instinct.

Nevertheless, the position of the working girl is far more natural and human than that of her seemingly more fortunate sister in the more cultured professional walks of life—teachers, physicians, lawyers, engineers, etc., who have to make a dignified, proper appearance, while the inner life is growing empty and dead.

The narrowness of the existing conception of woman's independence and emancipation; the dread of love for a man who is not her social equal; the fear that love will rob her of her freedom and independence; the horror that love or the joy of motherhood will only hinder her in the full exercise of her profession—all these together make of the emancipated modern woman a compulsory vestal, before whom life, with its great clarifying sorrows and its deep, entrancing joys, rolls on without touching or gripping her soul.

Emancipation, as understood by the majority of its adherents and exponents, is of too narrow a scope to permit the boundless love and ecstasy contained in the deep emotion of the true woman, sweetheart, mother, in freedom.

The tragedy of the self-supporting or economically free woman does not lie in too many; but in too few experiences. True, she surpasses her sister of past generations in knowledge of the world and human nature; it is just because of this that she feels deeply the lack of life's essence, which alone can enrich the human soul, and without which the majority of women have become mere professional automatons. . . .

A rich intellect and a fine soul are usually considered necessary attributes of a deep and beautiful personality. In the case of the modern woman, these attributes serve as a hindrance to the complete assertion of her being. For over a hundred years the old form of marriage, based on the Bible, "Till death doth part," has been denounced as an institution that stands for the sovereignty of the man over the woman, of her complete submission to his whims and commands, and absolute dependence on his name and support. Time and again it has been conclusively proved that the old matrimonial relation restricted woman to the function of man's servant and the bearer of his children. And yet we find many emancipated women who prefer marriage, with all its deficiencies, to the narrowness of an unmarried life; narrow and unendurable because of the chains of moral and social prejudice that cramp and bind her nature.

The explanation of such inconsistency on the part of many advanced women is to be found in the fact that they never truly understood the meaning of emancipation. They thought that all that was needed was independence from external tyrannies; the internal tyrants, far more harmful to life and growth—ethical and social conventions—were left to take care of themselves; and they have taken care of themselves. They seem to get along as beautifully in the heads and hearts of the most active exponents of woman's emancipation, as in the heads and hearts of our grandmothers.

These internal tyrants, whether they be in the form of public opinion or what will mother say, or brother, father, aunt, or relative of any sort; what will Mrs. Grundy, Mr. Comstock, the employer, the Board of Education say? All these busybodies, moral detectives, jailers of the human spirit, what will they say? Until woman has learned to defy them all, to stand firmly on her own ground and to insist upon her own unrestricted freedom, to listen to the voice of her nature, whether it call for life's greatest treasure, love for a man, or her most glorious privilege, the right to give birth to a child, she cannot call herself emancipated. How many emancipated women are brave enough to acknowledge that the voice of love is calling, wildly beating against their breasts, demanding to be heard, to be satisfied. . . .

The greatest shortcoming of the emancipation of the present day lies in its artificial stiffness and its narrow respectabilities, which produce an emptiness in woman's soul that will not let her drink from the fountain of life. I once remarked that there seemed to be a deeper relationship between the old-fashioned mother and hostess, ever on the alert for the happiness of her little ones and the comfort of those she loves, and the truly new woman, than between the latter and her average emancipated sister. The disciples of emancipation pure and simple declared me a heathen, fit only for the stake. Their blind zeal did not let them see that my comparison between the old and the new was merely to prove that a goodly number of our grandmothers had more blood in their veins, far more humor and wit, and certainly a greater amount of naturalness, kindheartedness, and simplicity, than the majority of our emancipated professional women who fill the colleges, halls of learning and various offices. This does not mean a wish to return to the past, nor does it condemn woman to her old sphere, the kitchen and the nursery.

Salvation lies in an energetic march onward towards a brighter and clearer future. We are in need of unhampered growth out of old traditions and habits. The movement for woman's emancipation has so far made but the first step in that direction. It is to be hoped that it will gather strength to make another. The right to vote, or equal civil rights, may be good demands, but true emancipation begins neither at the polls nor in courts. It begins in woman's soul. History tells us that every oppressed class gained true liberation from its masters through its own efforts. It is necessary that woman learn that lesson, that she realizes that her freedom will reach as far as her power to achieve her freedom reaches. It is, therefore, far more important for her to begin with her inner regeneration, to cut loose from the weight of prejudices, traditions, and customs. The demand for equal rights in every vocation of life is just and fair; but, after all, the most vital right is the right to love and be loved. Indeed, if partial emancipation is to become a complete and true emancipation of woman, it will have to do away with the ridiculous notion that to be loved, to be sweetheart and mother, is synonymous with being a slave or subordinate. It will have to do away with the absurd notion of the dualism of the sexes, or that man and woman represent two antagonistic worlds.

Pettiness separates; breadth unites. Let us be broad and big. Let us not overlook vital things because of the bulk of trifles confronting us. A true conception of the relation of the sexes will not admit of conqueror and conquered; it knows of but one great thing: to give of one's self boundlessly, in order to find one's self richer, deeper, better. That alone can fill the emptiness, and transform the tragedy of woman's emancipation into joy, limitless joy.

CHAPTER 5

The Final Push for Suffrage

The woman suffrage movement called on the energies and political skills of three generations of American women. Even as the movement melded into the mainstream of Progressive reform in the early twentieth century, its success was never a foregone conclusion. A combination of factors, including women's patriotic contributions to the home front during World War I, helped to push the Nineteenth Amendment over the top. On election day, 1920, twenty-six million women were eligible to go to the polls as a result.

Dividing the suffrage movement into three distinct periods—1848–1869, 1869–1890, and 1890–1920—helps explain its shifting priorities and tactics over its more than seven decades of existence. The first period, from 1848 to 1869, began at the Seneca Falls convention, the first women's rights convention ever held in the world, where the Declaration of Sentiments included a controversial call for the ballot. Historian Ellen DuBois has pointed out how radical such a demand was in the mid-nineteenth century, because it challenged the separation of the spheres into men's (public) and women's (private). The suffrage plank barely passed the assembled convention.

During the first twenty years of the women's rights movement, it was closely allied with abolitionism and the struggle to end slavery. Disagreements in the immediate post-Civil War period about the priorities of freed blacks versus women's rights led to a severing of this link. With the passage of the Thirteenth, Fourteenth, and Fifteenth Amendments, black people won their freedom and black men won the right to vote. As feminists such as Elizabeth Cady Stanton and Susan B. Anthony pointed out, however, now that the word *male* was in the constitution as a definition of voting rights, it would take another constitutional amendment to enfranchise women.

By 1869, an independent woman suffrage movement had emerged in the United States. The period between 1869 and 1890 was not marked by any great

112

breakthroughs for the cause. Only two states allowed women the vote—the territories of Utah in 1869 and Wyoming in 1870. The suffrage movement on the national level split into two rival wings, mainly over whether to work on a state basis or the federal level. In 1890, the rival wings reunited as the National American Woman Suffrage Association (NAWSA).

By 1890, the suffrage movement was on the threshold of new activism and success. In part, the movement was more palatable because it was less radical. Instead of early demands by feminists such as Stanton for divorce and women's economic emancipation, the movement leaders now stuck very closely to the sole demand of the vote. And increasingly suffragists argued for the vote not as a challenge to conventional notions about women's proper sphere, but as an extension of that sphere. Women cited their domestic orientation as the reason they needed the vote: they could do for the country what they did for their homes and families. Suffragists also played up women's supposed moral superiority. This tactic of accepting conventional views of women and exploiting them was highly successful, especially as the Progressive reform spirit gathered strength.

As late as 1910, the woman suffrage movement had won the vote in only four states, but the tide was turning. New leadership, notably the NAWSA presidency of Carrie Chapman Catt from 1915 to 1920, revitalized the movement with a winning plan. Attention-grabbing tactics, such as suffrage parades and open-air meetings, won publicity. The movement also branched out into immigrant and working-class urban communities to mobilize support. Suffragists effectively pointed out the irony of fighting to make the world safe for democracy in World War I, while the female population remained disfranchised at home. Militant tactics, such as picketing the White House and conducting hunger strikes for the cause, won support.

But probably the main reason women finally won the vote in 1920 was that it was now a far less radical demand than it had been in 1848. Try to imagine how nineteenth century political history would have been revolutionized if women had actually received the vote around the time of the Civil War. Compare that to the small ripple that occurred when women were finally granted the vote in 1920. Women's roles had changed dramatically since the mid-nineteenth century, with women actively participating in work, education, and voluntary organizations outside the home. The meaning of politics had also changed, so that the vote was less a potent symbol of political participation for men by 1920 than it had been at the height of the separate male political culture of the previous century.

Although granting the vote can be seen as a conservative measure that had little impact on women's equality, it is wrong to underestimate what the vote meant to the millions of women who campaigned so hard for its attainment. To the "new women" of the late nineteenth and early twentieth centuries, it was an affront, a slap in the face, that they were not allowed this basic democratic right. Going to the polls would be confirmation of women's new roles as full citizens, the public equals of men. Of course, such sentiments were more likely held by white middle-class women, who shared most of the privileges of their class with men except the vote. But black women and working-class women also campaigned for the vote, seeing it as a tool that could be useful in broader political and economic struggles.

What made the suffrage movement so powerful was that it brought together a diverse range of individuals and organizations in a broad coalition dedicated to a common goal. To attain that goal, women's groups pioneered in innovative political tactics and legislative strategies that showed that women could work together effectively on common causes. While we may look back at the vote and see it as a fairly minor reform, women at the time had a far different perspective.

A Western Suffragist Talks to Her Eastern Sisters

Abigail Scott Duniway

The suffrage movement was comprised of a variety of individuals and organizations—in many ways, that was its greatest strength. One of the most prominent voices in the western states was that of Abigail Scott Duniway (1834–1915). Duniway is another representation of the western pioneering spirit as it applied to women; reflecting her estimation of her place in history, she titled her autobiography *Path Breaking* (1914). Born in Illinois, she made the overland journey to Oregon with her family in 1851 at the age of seventeen. Married soon after, she lived the hard physical life of a young bride (and soon, young mother) on the Oregon frontier. An accident that disabled her husband prodded her to try a variety of jobs to earn money; the most satisfying was the newspaper she ran for sixteen years called the *New Northwest*.

Of the causes which Duniway promoted in her newspaper and her frequent public speaking, none was more prominent than women's rights. Duniway quickly moved into a prominent role in the Oregon suffrage movement, but her outspoken and populist ideas were not always at one with the more conservative leaders of the suffrage movement in the East. This speech, entitled "How to Win the Ballot" and given in 1899 to the National American Woman Suffrage Association national convention in Michigan, was—in Duniway's words—"the shortest way at my command for telling many truths that Eastern readers ought to read." Those "truths" included the reminder that the votes of men were needed to extend the franchise. What really comes through in this speech, however, is the incredible sense of sectional pride linked to the western pioneering spirit.

> Oregon women finally got the vote in 1912, and Abigail Scott Duniway became the state's first registered woman voter.

Coming as I do from the far Pacific, where the sun at night sinks into the sea, to greet a convocation of co-workers from the far Atlantic, where the sun at morn rises out of the sea; and standing here, upon the central swell of the Middle West, where the sun at high noon kisses the heaving bosom of the mighty inland sea that answers back to East and West the echoing song of liberty, I realize the importance of my desire to speak to the entire continent, such tempered words as shall help to further unite our common interests in the great work that convenes us.

The first fact to be considered, when working to win the ballot, is that there is but one way by which we may hope to obtain it, and that is by and through the affirmative votes of men. We may theorize, organize, appeal, argue, coax, cajole and threaten men till doomsday; we may secure their pettings, praises, flattery, and every appearance of acquiescence in our demands; we may believe with all our hearts in the sincerity of their promises to vote as we dictate, but all of this will avail us nothing unless they deposit their affirmative votes in the ballot box.

Every man who stops to argue the case, as an opponent, tells us that he "loves women," and, while wondering much that he should consider such a declaration necessary, I have always admired the loyal spirit that prompts its utterance. But, gentlemen,—and I am proud indeed to see such a fine audience of you here tonight—there is another side to this expression of loyalty. Not only is our movement not instigated in a spirit of warfare between the sexes, but it is engendered, altogether, in the spirit of harmony, and inter-dependence between men and women, such as was the evident design of the great Creator when he placed fathers and mothers, brothers and sisters, in the same home and family. We are glad to be assured that you "love women," but we are doubly glad to be able, on proper occasions, and in every suitable way, to return the compliment. No good Equal Suffragist will any longer permit you to monopolize all the pretty speeches about the other sex. Every good woman in the world likes men a great deal better than she likes women, and there isn't a wise woman in all this goodly land who isn't proud to say so. We like you, gentlemen, and you cannot help it. We couldn't help it if we would; we wouldn't help it if we could. You like us, also, because you cannot help it. God made the sexes to match each other. Show me a woman who doesn't like men, and I will show you a sour-souled, vinegar-visaged specimen of unfortunate femininity, who owes the world an apology for living in it at all; and the very best thing she could do for her country, provided she had a country, would be to steal away and die, in the

Source: Abigail Scott Duniway, *Path Breaking* (Portland, Ore.: James, Kerns, and Abbott, 1914; reprinted in 1971 by Schocken Books, New York), pp. 156–162.

company of the man who doesn't like women. In order to gain the votes of men, so we can win the ballot, we must show them that we are inspired by the same patriotic motives that induce them to prize it. A home without a man in it, is only half a home. A government without women in it is only half a government. Man without a woman is like one-half of a pair of dislocated shears. Woman without man is like the other half of the same disabled implement. Male and female created He them, saith the Higher Law, and to them God gave dominion "over every living thing upon the earth"—except each other. . . .

The fact that men, for the most part, contented themselves in those early days of the Suffrage Movement, with exhibitions of ridicule, I accepted as a good omen. If you wish to convince a man that your opinion is logical and just, you have conquered the outer citadel of his resentment when he throws back his head and opens his mouth to laugh. Show me a solemn-visaged voter, with a face as long as the Pentateuch, and I will show you a man with a soul so little that it would have ample room to dance inside of a hollow mustard seed. Having tickled your opponent with a little nonsense, that at first was necessary to arrest his attention, you must then be careful to hold the ground you have gained. Your next step must be to impress upon all men the fact that we are not intending to interfere, in any way, with their rights; and all we ask is to be allowed to decide, for ourselves, also as to what our rights should be. They will then, very naturally, ask what effect our enfranchisement will have upon their politics. Visions of riotous scenes in political conventions will arise, to fill them with apprehension, as the possibility occurs that women, if enfranchised, will only double the vote and augment the uproar. They will recall partisan banquets, at which men have tarried over cups and pipes until they rolled under the table, or were carried off to bed on shutters. Very naturally, men, everywhere, object to seeing reputable women, and especially their own wives, engaged in such excesses. But our mighty men of the Pacific Northwest are troubled very little by these vagaries. They realize, as they sleep off the results of their latest political banquet, that at every public function in which their wives participate, there is a notable absence of any sort of dissipation. They remember that in former times, before good women had joined them, in the mining camps, mountain towns, and on the bachelor farms, that such scenes as sometimes transpire today, at men's great gatherings, were once so common as to excite little comment. It was the advent of good women in the border territories that changed all this, and eliminated the bad woman from social life, just as the ballot will eventually eliminate the bad woman from political life, where she now reigns supreme among men, having everything her own way. By the very charm of good women's presence they brought these changes about on the Pacific Coast, in social life, till men began to wonder how they had endured the old conditions, before the women joined them. Now, quite naturally, they are learning to apply this rule to politics; and so our men of the Pacific Coast are not alarmed, as many men are in other states, lest women, if allowed to become equal with themselves before the law, will forget their natural duties and natural womanliness. If, however, any man grows timid, and exhibits symptoms of alarm, as they sometimes do (even in Oregon), lest the balloted woman will forsake the kitchen sink, at which she has always been "protected" (without wages), or abandon the cooking stove, the rolling pin, the wash tub and the ironing board, at which she has always been shielded (without salary), we remind him that housekeeping and homemaking are, like everything else, undergoing a complete process of evolution. We show him that there is no more reason why every loaf of bread should be baked in a different kitchen than there is why every bushel of wheat should be ground in a different mill. We show him that the laundry is destined, hereafter, to keep pace with the threshing machine; the creamery with the spinning jenny and power loom; the fruit cannery with the great flour mill; the dish washer with the steam-driven mangle, and the bakery with the ready-made clothing store.

When women have been voters long enough to have acquired recognition of their own equal property rights with men, the servant girl problem will settle itself. When that time comes there will be no more work left to do in the home than the wife and mother can perform with comfort to herself and household; and the servant girls of today will then find systematic employment in the great factories, where food and clothing are manufactured by rule. This evolution has already begun with the woman typewriter. You see her everywhere; pretty, tidy, rosy with a ribbon or flower at her throat, intent upon her work and sure to get her pay. Then can the mother, for the sake of herself, her husband, and children, preserve her health, her beauty, and her mental vigor. Then can she be an adviser in the home, the state, the church, and the school, remaining so to a ripe old age.

But women can never have the opportunity, or the power, to achieve these results, except in isolated cases, till they are voters and lawmakers; and never even then, till they have had time to secure, by legislation, the equal property rights that they have earned with men from the beginning.

Open-Air Meetings: A New Suffrage Tactic

Florence Luscomb

Since the mid-nineteenth century, the suffrage movement had relied on essentially the same tactics: lobbying state and national governments for suffrage bills, organizing women's suffrage organizations on the local, state, and national level, and trying to win publicity for women's cause. But decades of such agitation had seemingly brought the movement no closer to success, so about 1909 suffrage leaders in Massachusetts and other states developed new ways to reach voters and stimulate interest in their cause. Influenced by the tactics of militant British suffragists, Massachusetts women began holding open-air meetings and selling suffrage newspapers on streetcorners like newsboys. Brazenly discarding any lingering notions of protected Victorian womanhood, suffragists took to the streets in what must have been a liberating, if somewhat unsettling, experience.

Florence Luscomb (1887–1985) was one such pioneer. She was already active in the suffrage movement when she graduated from the Massachusetts Institute of Technology with a degree in architecture in 1909. For several years, she combined her architectural career with suffrage work, such as speaking at the open-air meetings described in this speech. In 1917, she took a full-time position as executive secretary of the Boston Equal Suffrage Association for Good Government. For the rest of her life, she was associated with progressive causes.

Such tactics as open-air meetings helped to turn the tide in favor of suffrage. What comes through the strongest in Luscomb's 1909 speech, however, is the sense of camaraderie and shared partnership that characterized the unique political movement that was suffrage.

Right here I want to tell you what outdoor speaking is *not* like. The majority of people who have never been to our open-air meetings have already decided what they are like, down to the minutest detail as to what variety of vegetable is thrown at the speaker. Although every one knows from experience that an American woman can stand in a hall and address American men with dignity and earnestness on her part, and courtesy and interest on theirs, yet, presto, remove the roof and the same woman must become a ranting fanatic, the same men are jeering hooligans. Now I have spoken at more than a score of sky-roofed meetings this summer, to audiences varying from twenty-five to two thousand, at mill gates and at fashionable summer resorts, but have never seen anything which would disgrace an indoor meeting.

The open-air meetings promising so well, they were continued throughout the summer. It was found best to hold two meetings in nearby towns each Saturday; one at four o'clock and the other at seven-thirty. The time and strength required were but little more than one meeting consumed, and far less than would be needed to make two separate trips. Meetings were also held on Wednesday afternoons at various beaches. This being the marketman's day off, the seashore is almost as well attended on that day as on Saturday.

From the success of these meetings around Boston Mrs. Fitzgerald[1] gradually developed the idea of sending out a party which should spend the month of August touring the State and speaking in all the more important towns. The route as laid out went westerly through the Northern towns, swung around and returned through the Southern part of the State, taking in the Marshfield and

Source: Florence Luscomb, unpublished speech, "Our Open-Air Campaign" (1909), in Woman's Rights Collection, Schlesinger Library, Radcliffe College.
[1]Susan Walker Fitzgerald, a Bryn Mawr graduate and the wife of a wealthy Harvard-trained lawyer, was secretary of the Boston Equal Suffrage Association for Good Government (BESAGG).

Barnstable County Fairs. We aspired to go by automobile; we went by trolley. We spoke three times a day, generally in three separate towns, except as an entire day was devoted to such cities as Fall River and New Bedford. The party was made up of four ladies—Mrs. Fitzgerald, commander-in-chief and orator-in-chief, went for the whole month, as did also Miss Edith Haynes, a Boston lawyer. For the first half of the trip Mrs. Dennett (Mary Ware Dennett) and Miss Alfretta McClure accompanied them; and for the last two weeks Miss Katherine Tyng, Radcliffe '00, and I had the pleasure of being the other two members.

The paraphernalia of the trip consisted of one large yellow banner six feet long inscribed in black, "Votes for Women," a jointed flagstaff for the same made to fold in to three pieces, and a heavy, heavy suitcase of literature and buttons. Besides this, each member had her individual suitcase, and there was a bundle of umbrellas.

Picture our party unloading from a street-car in the central square of some little country town. This in itself is a lengthy operation. Then we make for the nearest drug store, deposit all our luggage in one corner, and to compensate for its storage all of us are in duty bound to buy sodas. We have consumed innumerable soft drinks for the sake of the cause, and have become authorities upon the drugstores of Massachusetts. While we drink the drug clerk is cross-examined as to where the best audience can be collected, time of trolleys, hotel for the night, union or non-union, what they manufacture, and a few dozen other similar things. Meanwhile, if the town is large enough for us to require a permit to speak, Mrs. Fitzgerald has interviewed the police. Our leaflets are then unpacked, our flag erected, we borrow a Moxie box from the obliging drug clerk and proceed to the busiest corner of the town square. Our chief mounts the box, the banner over her shoulder, and starts talking to the air, three assorted dogs, six kids, and the two loafers in front of the grocery store just over the way. The rest of us give handbills to all the passersby and to all the nearby stores. Within ten minutes our audience has increased to from twenty-five to five hundred, according to the time and place. We speak in turn for an hour or more, answer questions, sell buttons, and circulate the petition. Then we leave, generally in undignified haste, to catch our car for the next meeting. At New Bedford, all loaded down as we were, we fairly charged for a block down the middle of a street lined on either side by people waiting for their cars.

Such were the afternoon and evening meetings. The noon ones were slightly different in character. These were held at the mill gates in factory towns. If there were several mills in town, or several entrances to the same mill, our party was divided so that sometimes each of the four held an independent meeting. As the workers came out at noon we gave out the bills and announced speaking at half past. They returned early from dinner, and we had a half hour of speaking. These meetings were very interesting. The audience was there ready to be entertained, often sympathetic in advance; and I know some of us enjoyed the experience of being thrown on our own resources, with the entire subject to handle in that short time.

Ordinarily, of course, the arguments were divided up between us to prevent repetition and insure completeness.

During the speaking we circulated the petition as quietly as possible on the outskirts of the crowd. We found it best not to attempt to get many signatures during the speaking as it created too much disturbance. Whenever we had time to stop after the meeting we did canvas the audience pretty thoroughly, but this was not often. For this reason we averaged a smaller percentage of signatures on the trip than at the meetings carried on around Boston, where we were not so hurried.

The trip was by no means all hard work. The first week, while the party was passing through the Berkshires, meetings were far apart, and time for rest and meals scant. Later on, however, in the more thickly settled regions, travelling was not so hard although we never had much time to spare. The motto adopted to describe the trip was, "plain thinking, hard talking, any old kind of living." One other of our collection was, "Gather ye rosebuds while ye may," which being interpreted read, "Sit down every time you get a chance." Nevertheless it was a pleasant trip to travel in the fresh air through pleasant country and picturesque towns.

We were an inexhaustible source of wonder and interest to the small boy. He dogged our footsteps clamouring for literature; he audibly surmised whether we were Salvation Army or Anti-tuberculosis, and the climax of his joy was attained when we allowed him to carry our banner.

Our other constant admirers were the dogs. I feel hardly at home now at a meeting at which there is not at least one dog present, preferably yellow; and when there are a dozen dogs of assorted sizes, colors, and howls, oh, this is bliss! We even reveled in dog-fights; for, as our chief remarked while we were enjoying one such experience, "After all, there is nothing to draw a crowd like a dog-fight." . . .

Was our summer campaign successful? Did it pay? A few figures will answer. We have spoken to 24,900 people, and given literature to thousands of others. The expense of the trolley trip was about one hundred dollars a week, which includes fares and living expenses for four, cost of literature, press notices, and all other incidentals. We held sixty-eight meetings—fifteen of them at factories. Altogether this summer we have held 97 meetings at an average cost of $6.62 a meeting, with an average audience of 257, and have obtained over 2000 signatures to the National Petition. I think you will agree with me that it was a splendid success.

An Anti-Suffrage Monologue

Marie Jenny Howe

Opposition to woman suffrage was diffuse but potent. Liquor interests were afraid women would vote in prohibition, machine politicians feared women voters would turn them out of office, and manufacturers anticipated that newly enfranchised women would force protective legislation and child labor laws which would cut their profits. Conservative religious organizations like the Catholic church were hostile to larger political roles for women. Southerners feared woman suffrage might endanger white supremacy. Perhaps surprisingly, some of the most prominent "antis" were women themselves, who said they did not need or want the vote. The fact that many women, especially middle-class women, were not interested in their own suffrage was one of the most telling weapons that opponents had in their arsenal.

Anti-suffrage sentiment boiled down to the argument that voting, and by extension, exposure to the "muck and mire of politics," violated woman's essential nature, which should be confined to home, maternity, and domesticity. Women's entry into the public sphere, argued a Southern Congressional representative in a 1917 debate, would "disrupt the family, which is the unit of society, and when you disrupt the family, you destroy the home, which is the foundation of the Republic." Opponents of woman suffrage clung defiantly to traditional gender roles, despite the fact that women had already moved far beyond the confines of the home by the early twentieth century. The heat of the debate was in part a reaction to how much had already changed in women's lives.

The suffragists found it fairly easy to punch holes in the often contradictory arguments put forward by the antis, as this satirical *Anti-Suffrage Monologue* by Marie Jenny Howe demonstrates. Howe is especially good at showing the contradictions of anti-suffrage propaganda by arranging her arguments in couplets: "if you don't like one you can take the other." When this pamphlet was published by the National American Woman Suffrage Association in 1913, victory was finally beginning to seem possible.

Please do not think of me as old-fashioned. I pride myself on being a modern up-to-date woman. I believe in all kinds of broad-mindedness, only I do not believe in woman suffrage because to do that would be to deny my sex.

Woman suffrage is the reform against nature. Look at these ladies sitting on the platform. Observe their physical inability, their mental disability, their spiritual instability and general debility! Could they walk up to the ballot box, mark a ballot and drop it in? Obviously not. Let us grant for the sake of argument that they could mark a ballot. But could they drop it in? Ah, no. All nature is against it. The laws of man cry out against it. The voice of God cries out against it—and so do I.

Enfranchisement is what makes man man. Disfranchisement is what makes woman woman. If women were enfranchised every man would be just like every woman and every woman would be just like every man. There would be

Source: Marie Jenny Howe, *An Anti-Suffrage Monologue* (New York: National American Woman Suffrage Association, 1913).

no difference between them. And don't you think this would rob life of just a little of its poetry and romance?

Man must remain man. Woman must remain woman. If man goes over and tries to be like woman, if woman goes over and tries to be like man, it will become so very confusing and so difficult to explain to our children. Let us take a practical example. If a woman puts on a man's coat and trousers, takes a man's cane and hat and cigar and goes out on the street, what will happen to her? She will be arrested and thrown into jail. Then why not stay at home?

I know you begin to see how strongly I *feel* on this subject, but I have some reasons as well. These reasons are based on logic. Of course I am not logical. I am a creature of impulse, instinct and intuition—and I glory in it. But I know that these reasons are based on logic because I have culled them from the men whom it is my privilege to know.

My first argument against suffrage is that the women would not use it if they had it. You couldn't drive them to the polls. My second argument is, if the women were enfranchised they would neglect their home, desert their families and spend all their time at the polls. You may tell me that the polls are only open once a year. But I know women. They are creatures of habit. If you let them go to the polls once a year, they will hang round the polls all the rest of the time.

I have arranged these arguments in couplets. They go together in such a way that if you don't like one you can take the other. This is my second anti-suffrage couplet. If the women were enfranchised they would vote exactly as their husbands do and only double the existing vote. Do you like that argument? If not, take this one. If the women were enfranchised they would vote against their own husbands, thus creating dissension, family quarrels, and divorce.

My third anti-suffrage couplet is—women are angels. Many men call me an angel and I have a strong instinct which tells me it is true; that is why I am an anti, because "I want to be an angel and with the angels stand." And if you don't like that argument take this one. Women are depraved. They would introduce into politics a vicious element which would ruin our national life.

Fourth anti-suffrage couplet: women cannot understand politics. Therefore there would be no use in giving women political power, because they would not know what to do with it. On the other hand, if the women were enfranchised, they would mount rapidly into power, take all the offices from all the men, and soon we would have women governors of all our states and dozens of women acting as President of the United States.

Fifth anti-suffrage couplet: women cannot band together. They are incapable of organization. No two women can even be friends. Women are cats. On the other hand, if women were enfranchised, we would have all the women banded together on one side and all the men banded together on the other side, and there would follow a sex war which might end in bloody revolution.

Just one more of my little couplets: the ballot is greatly over-estimated. It has never done anything for anybody. Lots of men tell me this. And the corresponding argument is—the ballot is what makes man man. It is what gives him all his dignity and all of his superiority to women. Therefore if we allow women to share this privilege, how could a woman look up to her own husband? Why, there would be nothing to look up to.

I have talked to many woman suffragists and I find them very unreasonable. I say to them: "Here I am, convince me." I ask for proof. Then they proceed to tell me of Australia and Colorado and other places where women have passed excellent laws to improve the condition of working women and children. But I say, "What of it?" These are facts. I don't care about facts. I ask for proof.

Then they quote the eight million women of the United States who are now supporting themselves, and the twenty-five thousand married women in the City of New York who are self-supporting. But I say again, what of it? These are statistics. I don't believe in statistics. Facts and statistics are things which no truly womanly woman would ever use.

I wish to prove anti-suffrage in a womanly way—that is, by personal example. This is my method of persuasion. Once I saw a woman driving a horse, and the horse ran away with her. Isn't that just like a woman? Once I read in the newspapers about a woman whose house caught on fire, and she threw the children out of the window and carried the pillows downstairs. Does that show political acumen, or does it not? Besides, look at the hats that women wear! And have you ever known a successful woman governor of a state? Or have you ever known a really truly successful woman president of the United States? Well, if they haven't doesn't that show they couldn't? As for the militant suffragettes, they are all hyenas in petticoats. Now do you want to be a hyena and wear petticoats?

Now, I think I have proved anti-suffrage; and I have done it in a womanly way—that is, without stooping to the use of a single fact or argument or a single statistic.

I am the prophet of a new idea. No one has ever thought of it or heard of it before. I well remember when this great idea first came to me. It waked me in the middle of the night with a shock that gave me a headache. This is it: woman's place is in the home. Is it not beautiful as it is new, new as it is true? Take this idea away with you. You will find it very helpful in your daily lives. You may not grasp it just at first, but you will gradually grow into understanding of it.

I know the suffragists reply that all our activities have been taken out of the home. The baking, the washing, the weaving, the spinning are all long since taken out of the home. But I say, all the more reason that something should stay in the home. Let it be woman. Besides, think of the great modern invention, the telephone. That has been put into the home. Let woman stay at home and answer the telephone.

We antis have so much imagination! Sometimes it seems to us that we can hear the little babies in the slums crying to us. We can see the children in factories and mines reaching out their little hands to us, and the working women in the sweated industries, the underpaid, underfed women, reaching out their arms to us—all, all crying as with one voice, "Save us, save us, from Woman Suffrage." Well may they make this appeal to us, for who knows what woman suffrage might not do for such as these. It might even alter the conditions under which they live.

We antis do not believe that any conditions should be altered. We want everything to remain just as it is. All is for the best. Whatever is, is right. If misery is in the world, God has put it there; let it remain. If this misery presses harder on some women than others, it is because they need discipline. Now, I have always been comfortable and well cared for. But then I never needed discipline. Of course I am only a weak, ignorant woman. But there is one thing I do understand from the ground up, and that is the divine intention toward woman. I *know* that the divine intention toward woman is, let her remain at home.

The great trouble with the suffragists is this; they interfere too much. They are always interfering. Let me take a practical example.

There is the City of New York a Nurses' Settlement, where sixty trained nurses go forth to care for sick babies and give them pure milk. Last summer only two or three babies died in this slum district around the Nurses' Settlement, whereas formerly hundreds of babies have died there every summer. Now what are these women doing? They seek notoriety. They want to be noticed. They are trying to show off. And if sixty women who merely believe in suffrage behave in this way, what may we expect when all women are enfranchised?

What ought these women to do with their lives? Each one ought to be devoting herself to the comfort of some man. You may say, they are not married. But I answer, let them try a little harder and they might find some kind of a man to devote themselves to. What does the Bible say on this subject? It says, "Seek and ye shall find." Besides, when I look around me at the men, I feel that God never meant us women to be too particular.

Let me speak one word to my sister women who are here today. Women, we don't need to vote in order to get our own way. Don't misunderstand me. Of course I want you to get your own way. That's what we're here for. But do it indirectly. If you want a thing, tease. If that doesn't work, nag. If that doesn't do, cry—crying always brings them around. Get what you want. Pound pillows. Make a scene. Make home a hell on earth, but do it in a womanly way. That is so much more dignified and refined than walking up to a ballot box and dropping in a piece of paper. Can't you see that?

Let us consider for a moment the effect of woman's enfranchisement on man. I think some one ought to consider the men. What makes husband faithful and loving? The ballot, and the monopoly of that privilege. If women vote, what will become of men? They will all slink off drunk and disorderly. We antis understand men. If women were enfranchised, men would revert to their natural instincts such as regicide, matricide, patricide and race-suicide. Do you believe in race-suicide or do you not? Then, isn't it our duty to refrain from a thing that would lure men to destruction?

It comes down to this. Some one must wash the dishes. Now, would you expect man, man made in the image of God, to roll up his sleeves and wash the dishes? Why, it would be blasphemy. I know that I am but a rib and so I wash the dishes. Or I hire another rib to do it for me, which amounts to the same thing.

Let us consider the argument from the standpoint of religion. The Bible says, "Let the women keep silent in the churches." Paul says, "Let them keep their hats on for fear of the angels." My minister says, "Wives, obey your husbands." And my husband says that woman suffrage would rob the rose of its fragrance and the peach of its bloom. I think that is so sweet.

Besides did George Washington ever say, "Votes for women?" No. Did the Emperor Kaiser Wilhelm ever say, "Votes for women?" No. Did Elijah, Elisha, Micah, Hezekiah, Obadiah and Jeremiah ever say, "Votes for women?" No. Then that settles it.

I don't want to be misunderstood in my reference to woman's inability to vote. Of course she could get herself to the polls and lift a piece of paper. I don't doubt that. What I refer to is the pressure on the brain, the effect of this mental strain on woman's delicate nervous organization and on her highly wrought sensitive nature. Have you ever pictured to yourself Election Day with women voting? Can you imagine how women, having undergone this terrible ordeal, with their delicate systems all upset, will come out of the voting booths and be led away by policemen, and put into ambulances, while they are fainting and weeping, half laughing, half crying, and having fits upon the public highway? Don't you think that if a woman is going to have a fit, it is far better for her to have it in the privacy of her own home?

And how shall I picture to you the terrors of the day after election? Divorce and death will rage unchecked, crime and contagious disease will stalk unbridled through the land. Oh, friends, on this subject I feel—I feel, so strongly that I can—not think!

A Labor Organizer Speaks Out for Suffrage

Leonora O'Reilly

Although the suffrage movement remained predominantly a middle-class affair, working-class and immigrant women also found a place in its ranks, especially as the movement looked outward for new sources of support in the twentieth century. (Black women, however, were not welcomed in white suffrage organizations and formed their own groups.) This testimony given by labor leader and reformer Leonora O'Reilly before a Joint Senate Committee in April 1912 effectively rebutted the criticisms that women did not want the vote or that the vote was irrelevant to the problems that working women faced in their lives. O'Reilly demolished the argument that women should stay at home by using her own experience to show that many women had no choice but to enter the work force, where they worked under terrible conditions with few weapons to redress their grievances. The vote would be one such weapon.

Leonora O'Reilly (1870–1927) knew what she was talking about. She was born into an Irish family on New York's Lower East Side and had started work not at thirteen, as she says in her testimony, but at eleven. At sixteen, she showed her first interest in the trade union movement by joining the Knights of Labor. It was through organizing a working women's society that she came into contact with middle-class reformers such as Mary Dreier, Margaret Dreier Robins, Lillian Wald, and Grace Dodge. At first she pursued her reform and educational activities while still working in a shirtwaist factory, but Mary Dreier's 1909 gift of a lifetime annuity freed her to devote herself full time to activism on behalf of working women, much of it through the auspices of the Women's Trade Union League. As this testimony hints, Leonora O'Reilly was a charismatic speaker; since she wrote no books and few articles, such documents are all we have to recapture her passionate commitment to labor and women.

Mr. Chairman and gentlemen of the committee: Yes; I have outdone the lady who went to work at 18 by five years. I have been a wage earner since I was a little over 13. I, too, know whereof I speak; that is the reason I do not want to play a bluff game with you any longer. You can not or will not make laws for us; we must make laws for ourselves. We working women need the ballot for self-protection; that is all there is to it. We have got to have it.

We work long, long hours and we do not get half enough to live on. We have got to keep decent, and if we go "the easy way" you men make the laws that will let you go free and send us into the gutter. [Applause.]

We can not believe in man-made laws any longer. We have gone from one assembly to another, from one State senator to another, and we have heard the same old story. You think only of output; there is not a soul among you who cares to save human beings. We have grown rich, as a nation, but we have grown very rotten. As a people—gentlemen, I use the term "rotten" advisedly—for, as far as the working women are concerned, the foundation we are building on is rotten. To purify the life of the Nation we women know we have got to do our part, political as well as industrial duty. Government, as a whole, rests

Source: Statement of Leonora O'Reilly (1912) before Joint Congressional Session of Congress, found in Anne F. Scott and Andrew Scott, *One Half the People* (Philadelphia: J. B. Lippincott, 1975), pp. 126–127.

on industry. You men say to us: "Go back to the home. Your place is in the home," yet as children we must come out of the home at 11, at 13, and at 15 years of age to earn a living; we have got to make good or starve.

"Pay your way" we are taught in school and in church—the greatest thing on earth is to be able to pay your way. Well, if any people on earth pay their way in life we working women do. The return we get is that most of us become physical wrecks along the roadside of life. When you gentlemen hear what it costs a working woman to "pay her way" in life, you sit back in your chairs, say "the story is terrible, but they manage to live somehow." Somehow—that is it, gentlemen. I want to make you realize the *somehow* of life to the hundreds of girls I have seen go down in the struggle. You men do not care. You want this country to get rich, and you do not know the only riches of a nation are its people. [Applause.]

We have gone before legislature after legislature making our pleas for justice. We have seen the game as you play it. What is it? We go there and we are told the same old tommyrot—let men do this for you. I tell you as a bit of business experience if you let anybody do a thing for you they will do you. That is business. [Applause.]

Now, while we have had the colleges opened to women, only one woman in a thousand goes to college, while modern industry claims one woman in every five to-day. It is industrial methods which are teaching the women the facts I am telling you. "Do the other fellow before he gets a chance to do you"— do him so hard that he can not stand up again; that is good business. We know that, and we women are sure that there must be some higher standard for life than business.

We are not getting a square deal; we go before legislature after legislature to tell our story, but they fail to help the women who are being speeded so high in the mills and in factories, from 54 hours to 72 hours in stores in New York, and 92 hours in one week in subcellar laundries. Who cares? Nobody! Nobody does; nobody cares about making laws so long as we get cheap and nasty things in the market. Working women come before you and tell you these things and think you will do something for them. Every man listening is convinced that the girls are telling the truth. It is only when you think of them as your own girls that you have the right to make laws for them. Every man listening wants to do the fair thing, but just as soon as our backs are turned, up comes the representative of the big interest and says, "Lad, you are dead politically if you do what those women ask." They know it is true, and we get nothing, because all the votes are owned.

Every vote you cast is owned, and it is the owned vote which has fought our women. Go before legislatures as you will, the only argument that you can bring in to the man in politics—he is there to go up the ladder, decently if he can, but he will go up anyhow, if he can—the only argument that you can bring to that man is the power of the ballot. When we can say to him, "Man, do this and we will return you so many million votes," he will listen and act.

This is what we want, because it is for the good of the women, because it is for the good of the whole people. It is for that reason that the working woman, facing the hard facts of life and having to fight her way, has come to the conclusion that you men in politics—I am not going to give you any taffy—you men in politics are not leaders, you follow what you think is the next step on the ladder. We want you to understand that the next step in politics, the next step in democracy, is to give to the women of your Nation a ballot. [Applause.]

The working women send me to you with the plain, honest truth; because, working beside you in the same mill or factory, we know you with your evening suit off and your tall hat in the box, or wherever it belongs; you are just a competitor with us there; we tell you the truth there, as I have come to tell you the truth here. Let women have the ballot, in order that you may once more throw the burden which you have carried, or thought you carried, onto them; that is the thing you have done since the beginning of time; when the load was too heavy for you you piled it onto Eve's back. [Applause.] You have got us in a devil of a mess, economic and political. It is so rank it smells to Heaven; but we will come in and help you clean house. We will start all over again, because we belong together shoulder to shoulder. We must get on to a better time. It is only because you will not, in your prejudice and your ignorance, let us into the political field with you that the situation is as bad as it is to-day.

We working women want the ballot, not as a privilege but as a right. You say you have only given the ballot as an expediency; you have never given it as a right; then we demand it as an expediency for the 8,000,000 working women. All other women ought to have it, but we working women must have it. [Applause.]

"Front Door Lobbying" for Suffrage

Maud Wood Park

The women who lobbied for suffrage faced an uphill battle: how as voteless citizens to convince elected representatives to grant them a new right without being able to promise retribution at the polls if their wishes were not taken seriously. Suffragists were determined to serve as a credit to their sex. They quickly earned the nickname of the "front door lobby," which Maud Wood Park remembered as "the half-humorous, half-kindly name given to our Congressional Committee in Washington by one of the press-gallery men there, because, as he explained, we never used backstairs methods."

Maud Wood Park (1871–1955) was the head of the Congressional Committee of the National American Woman Suffrage Association during Carrie Chapman Catt's presidency, and it was under Park's direction that much of the lobbying occurred that led to the final Congressional passage of the Nineteenth Amendment in 1919. These instructions to her fellow lobbyists, and her recollections of the triumphs and setbacks they faced, suggest her skill as an efficient and pragmatic leader. They also show NAWSA's determination to be firm but above all *ladylike*, a sharp contrast to the militants who risked arrest for their public protests and picketing (see next document).

Maud Wood Park spent most of her life working to advance the cause of women in public life. An 1899 graduate of Radcliffe, she was a suffragist even in college and founded the College Equal Suffrage League soon after her graduation. Widowed after a short period of marriage in 1904, she continued an extensive round of suffrage activities in Massachusetts. Carrie Chapman Catt asked her to come to Washington in 1916 for the final stages in the assault on Congress. In 1919, with victory finally in sight, Park became the first president of the newly organized League of Women Voters, where she served until 1924. Her autobiography, appropriately titled *Front Door Lobby*, was published posthumously in 1960.

During January, 1917, our lobby, in addition to members of the Congressional Committee, consisted of twenty-nine women from sixteen different states, who stayed in Washington at their own expense for periods ranging from six days to four weeks. For their use we had our lobby rules drawn up in the following form:

Directions for Lobbyists
I. PREPARATION:
1. Read our records of each member before calling on him. Also read biographical sketch in Congressional Directory. *Records must not be taken from the office.*
2. Provide yourself with small directory. Your own representative is the best source of supply.

II. INTERVIEWING:
1. If the member appears busy ask whether he would prefer to see you at some other time.
2. Be courteous no matter what provocation you may seem to have to be otherwise.
3. If possible learn the secretary's name and have a little talk with him or her. The secretary, if inclined to be interested, should be invited to headquarters.
4. If the member is known to be in favor *show that you realize that fact* and ask him for advice and help with the rest of the delegation. This point is *very important.*

Source: From *Front Door Lobby* by Maud Wood Park, pp. 38–41. Copyright © 1960 by Edna Lamprey Stantial. Reprinted by permission of Beacon Press.

5. Be sure to keep his *party* constantly in mind while talking with him.
6. Be a good listener. Don't interrupt.
7. Try to avoid prolonged or controversial argument. It is likely to confirm men in their own opinion.
8. Do not stay so long that the member has to give the signal for departure.
9. Take every possible means to prevent a member from *committing* himself definitely *against* the Federal Amendment. This is *most important.*
10. Leave the way open for another interview if you have failed to convince him.
11. If the member is inclined to be favorable invite him and his family to headquarters.
12. Remember to hold each interview confidential. Never quote what one member has said to you to another member. It is not safe to talk of your lobby experiences before outsiders or before servants. We can never know by what route our stories may get back to the member and injure our cause with him. We cannot be too cautious in this matter.

III. REPORTS:
1. Do not make notes in offices or halls.
2. Do find opportunity to make notes on one interview before starting another. If necessary, step into the "Ladies" dressing room to do this.
3. Write full report of your interview on the same day giving—
   a. Name and State of member.
   b. Date and hour of interview.
   c. Names of lobbyists and name of person making report.
   d. Member's argument in detail, especially with view to follow-up work.
   e. Any information you may glean about his family or friends that may be useful to the Washington Committee.
   f. Hand-written report to *Miss Bain,* not later than the day following the interview.
   g. Promptness in turning in reports is most important in order that lists and polls may be kept up to date.

When I was sufficiently familiar with the work to have a little sense of humor about it, I condensed those rules into a series of "don'ts":

Don't nag.
Don't boast.
Don't threaten.
Don't lose your temper.
Don't stay too long.
Don't talk about your work where you can be overheard.
Don't give the member interviewed an opportunity to declare himself against the amendment.
Don't do anything to close the door to the next advocate of suffrage.

The last "don't" was the one I dwelt on most in my talks with our workers, partly because it was the most difficult to follow. Knowing that the effect of our work in the case of doubtful members was cumulative, I used to say over and over again, "If we can't do any good, at least we must be sure that we don't do any harm."

Many of our lobby meetings were as entertaining as a good comedy. One of the women had the gift of ironic wit. Another was a capital mimic and gave us side-splitting imitations of some of the men whom she had interviewed. She was wise, too, for she cautioned us never to tell outside that any of our number had ventured to "take off" members of the Congress. I sometimes found it hard to stop my own laughter long enough to give out the next assignments.

Some of the written reports were funny, too. For example, this was turned in by one of our southern lobbyists after she had interviewed a Texas member:

> Polite but positive. Against woman suffrage—any phase of it. Declares that men represent women. When I suggested my being a widow and not having representation, he gallantly offered to represent me. The fact of his living in Texas and my residence being in Kentucky did not dismay him at all, but the proposition was most unsatisfactory to me. Against prohibition and against child labor bill. Has not seen any light at all in progressive legislation.

Another southern interview went into our record in these words:

> Invited us in—polite manner. Believes that woman dwells apart from man— in her nature. "She is different—Nature made it so—all history, science and biology prove it! Look at the barnyard, the 'cockerel' protects the hen, etc. Woman is meant for the home, the hearth and to be sheltered by man." He acknowledged that there were some women outside the home, but men could protect them. The dirty mire of politics for women could not be thought of. He deplored the lack of woman's trust in men, and did not think women wanted to be called "suffragands" (the correlation of the word "brigand"). He is beyond the pale. We parted in a friendly way.

The shortest and most satisfactory report that I remember was of an interview with Hon. Fiorello La Guardia:

He said, "I'm with you; I'm for it, I'm going to vote for it. Now don't bother me," all in one breath.

Suffrage Militant Alice Paul Goes to Jail

The suffrage movement was never monolithic; deep fissures split it over tactics, ideology, race, and even geography, as shown by Abigail Scott Duniway. There was no more emotional or far-reaching split than the one between the National American Woman Suffrage Association and the Congressional Union (CU), a group of militant suffragists led by the charismatic Quaker leader Alice Paul. Several points of conflict emerged: should the suffragists endorse political candidates; should they support a federal amendment, or work for state by state gains; and did dramatic public confrontations, inspired by the example of British militants, help or hinder the suffrage cause?

The Congressional Union was determined to take militant action. In World War I, the CU broke with the more conservative NAWSA and refused to support American entry into the war. More pointedly, militants began picketing the White House protesting President Woodrow Wilson's lack of support for suffrage. Then they began more inflammatory acts, such as burning copies of Wilson's speeches or chaining themselves to the White House fence. Such actions earned them quick arrest for obstructing traffic, and they were sentenced to seven months in jail, an unusually harsh sentence.

Alice Paul (1885–1977) was the leader and inspiration of the jailed suffragists. She and Rose Winslow were the first two suffragists to undertake a hunger strike. Recounting her story in these letters to fellow militant Doris Stevens, Paul conveyed the terrible conditions under which the women suffered and their determination to make themselves into such troublemakers that they would have to be released. Emerging as martyrs, such sacrifices helped push the suffrage amendment to final victory. As Rose Winslow said, "God knows we don't want other women ever to have to do this over again."

Alice Paul masterminded the transfer of energies of the Congressional Union to the postsuffrage National Woman's Party (NWP), of which she was president. The NWP's main goal after 1923 was the passage of an Equal Rights Amendment to the Constitution. Due to her longevity, Alice Paul was an active lobbyist for the ERA when it was rediscovered during the second wave of feminism in the 1960s and 1970s.

It was late afternoon when we arrived at the jail. There we found the suffragists who had preceded us, locked in cells.

The first thing I remember was the distress of the prisoners about the lack of fresh air. Evening was approaching, every window was closed tight. The air in which we would be obliged to sleep was foul. There were about eighty negro and white prisoners crowded together, tier upon tier, frequently two in a cell. I went to a window and tried to open it. Instantly a group of men, prison guards, appeared; picked me up bodily, threw me into a cell and locked the door. Rose Winslow and the others were treated in the same way.

Determined to preserve our health and that of the other prisoners, we began a concerted fight for fresh air. The windows were about twenty feet distant from the cells, and two sets of iron bars intervened between us and the win-

Source: Alice Paul letters quoted in Doris Stevens, *Jailed for Freedom* (New York: Boni and Liveright, 1920; reprinted by Schocken Books, 1976), pp. 215–217, 220–223.

dows, but we instituted an attack upon them as best we could. Our tin drinking cups, the electric light bulbs, every available article of the meagre supply in each cell, including my treasured copy of Browning's poems which I had secretly taken in with me, was thrown through the windows. By this simultaneous attack from every cell, we succeeded in breaking one window before our supply of tiny weapons was exhausted. The fresh October air came in like an exhilarating gale. The broken window remained untouched throughout the entire stay of this group and all later groups of suffragists. Thus was won what the "regulars" in jail called the first breath of air in their time.

The next day we organized ourselves into a little group for the purpose of rebellion. We determined to make it impossible to keep us in jail. We determined, moreover, that as long as we were there we would keep up an unremitting fight for the rights of political prisoners.

One by one little points were conceded to quiet resistance. There was the practice of sweeping the corridors in such a way that the dust filled the cells. The prisoners would be choking to the gasping point, as they sat, helpless, locked in the cells, while a great cloud of dust enveloped them from tiers above and below. As soon as our tin drinking cups, which were sacrificed in our attack upon the windows, were restored to us, we instituted a campaign against the dust. Tin cup after tin cup was filled and its contents thrown out into the corridor from every cell, so that the water began to trickle down from tier to tier. The District Commissioners, the Board of Charities, and other officials were summoned by the prison authorities. Hurried consultations were held. Nameless officials passed by in review and looked upon the dampened floor. Thereafter the corridors were dampened and the sweeping into the cells ceased. And so another reform was won.

There is absolutely no privacy allowed a prisoner in a cell. You are suddenly peered at by curious strangers, who look in at you all hours of the day and night, by officials, by attendants, by interested philanthropic visitors, and by prison reformers, until one's sense of privacy is so outraged that one rises in rebellion. We set out to secure privacy, but we did not succeed, for, to allow privacy in prison, is against all institutional thought and habit. Our only available weapon was our blanket, which was no sooner put in front of our bars than it was forcibly taken down by Warden Zinkhan.

Our meals had consisted of a little almost raw salt pork, some sort of liquid—I am not sure whether it was coffee or soup—bread and occasionally molasses. How we cherished the bread and molasses! We saved it from meal to meal so as to try to distribute the nourishment over a longer period, as almost every one was unable to eat the raw pork. Lucy Branham, who was more valiant than the rest of us, called out from her cell, one day, "Shut your eyes tight, close your mouth over the pork and swallow it without chewing it. Then you can do it." This heroic practice kept Miss Branham in fairly good health, but to the rest it seemed impossible, even with our eyes closed, to crunch our teeth into the raw pork.

However gaily you start out in prison to keep up a rebellious protest, it is nevertheless a terribly difficult thing to do in the face of the constant cold and hunger of undernourishment. Bread and water, and occasional molasses, is not a diet destined to sustain rebellion long. And soon weakness overtook us.

At the end of two weeks of solitary confinement, without any exercise, without going outside of our cells, some of the prisoners were released, having finished their terms, but five of us were left serving seven months' sentences, and two, one month sentences. With our number thus diminished to seven, the authorities felt able to cope with us. The doors were unlocked and we were permitted to take exercise. Rose Winslow fainted as soon as she got into the yard, and was carried back to her cell. I was too weak to move from my bed. Rose and I were taken on stretchers that night to the hospital.

For one brief night we occupied beds in the same ward in the hospital. Here we decided upon the hunger strike, as the ultimate form of protest left us—the strongest weapon left with which to continue within the prison our battle against the Administration. . . .

From the moment we undertook the hunger strike, a policy of unremitting intimidation began. One authority after another, high and low, in and out of prison, came to attempt to force me to break the hunger strike.

"You will be taken to a very unpleasant place if you don't stop this," was a favorite threat of the prison officials, as they would hint vaguely of the psychopathic ward, and St. Elizabeth's, the Government insane asylum. They alternately bullied and hinted. Another threat was "You will be forcibly fed immediately if you don't stop"—this from Dr. Gannon. There was nothing to do in the midst of these continuous threats, with always the "very unpleasant place" hanging over me, and so I lay perfectly silent on my bed.

After about three days of the hunger strike a man entered my room in the hospital and announced himself as Dr. White, the head of St. Elizabeth's. He said that he had been asked by District Commissioner Gardner to make an investigation. I later learned that he was Dr. William A. White, the eminent alienist.

Coming close to my bedside and addressing the attendant, who stood at a few respectful paces from him, Dr. White said: "Does this case talk?"

"Why wouldn't I talk?" I answered quickly.

"Oh, these cases frequently will not talk, you know," he continued in explanation.

"Indeed I'll talk," I said gaily, not having the faintest idea that this was an investigation of my sanity.

"Talking is our business," I continued, "we talk to any one on earth who is willing to listen to our suffrage speeches."

"Please talk," said Dr. White. "Tell me about suffrage; why you have opposed the President; the whole history of your campaign, why you picket, what you hope to accomplish by it. Just talk freely."

I drew myself together, sat upright in bed, propped myself up for a discourse of some length, and began to talk. The stenographer whom Dr. White brought with him took down in shorthand everything that was said.

I may say it was one of the best speeches I ever made. I recited the long history and struggle of the suffrage movement from its early beginning and narrated the political theory of our activities up to the present moment, outlining the status of the suffrage amendment in Congress at that time. In short, I told him everything. He listened attentively, interrupting only occasionally to say, "But, has not President Wilson treated you women very badly?" Whereupon, I, still unaware that I was being examined, launched forth into an explanation of Mr. Wilson's political situation and the difficulties he had confronting him. I continued to explain why we felt our relief lay with him; I cited his extraordinary power, his influence over his party, his undisputed leadership in the country, always painstakingly explaining that we opposed President Wilson merely because he happened to be President, not because he was President Wilson. Again came an interruption from Dr. White, "But isn't President Wilson directly responsible for the abuses and indignities which have been heaped upon you? You are suffering now as a result of his brutality, are you not?" Again I explained that it was impossible for us to know whether President Wilson was personally acquainted in any detail with the facts of our present condition, even though we knew that he had concurred in the early decision to arrest our women.

Presently Dr. White took out a small light and held it up to my eyes. Suddenly it dawned upon me that he was examining me personally; that his interest in the suffrage agitation and the jail conditions did not exist, and that he was merely interested in my reactions to the agitation and to jail. Even then I was reluctant to believe that I was the subject of mental investigation and I continued to talk.

But he continued in what I realized with a sudden shock, was an attempt to discover in me symptoms of the persecution mania. How simple he had apparently thought it would be, to prove that I had an obsession on the subject of President Wilson!

The day following he came again, this time bringing with him the District Commissioner, Mr. Gardner, to whom he asked me to repeat everything that had been said the day before. For the second time we went through the history of the suffrage movement, and again his inquiry suggested his persecution mania clue? [sic] When the narrative touched upon the President and his responsibility for the obstruction of the suffrage amendment, Dr. White would turn to his associate with the remark: "Note the reaction."

Then came another alienist, Dr. Hickling, attached to the psychopathic ward in the District Jail, with more threats and suggestions, if the hunger strike continued. Finally they departed, and I was left to wonder what would happen next. Doubtless my sense of humor helped me, but I confess I was not without fear of this mysterious place which they continued to threaten.

It appeared clear that it was their intention either to discredit me, as the leader of the agitation, by casting doubt upon my sanity, or else to intimidate us into retreating from the hunger strike.

After the examination by alienists, Commissioner Gardner, with whom I had previously discussed our demand for treatment as political prisoners, made another visit. "All these things you say about the prison conditions may be true," said Mr. Gardner, "I am a new Commissioner, and I do not know. You give an account of a very serious situation in the jail. The jail authorities give exactly the opposite. Now I promise you we will start an investigation at once to see who is right, you or they. If it is found you are right, we shall correct the conditions at once. If you will give up the hunger strike, we will start the investigation at once."

"Will you consent to treat the suffragists as political prisoners, in accordance with the demands laid before you?" I replied.

Commissioner Gardner refused, and I told him that the hunger strike would not be abandoned. But they had by no means exhausted every possible facility for breaking down our resistance. I overheard the Commissioner say to Dr. Gannon on leaving, "Go ahead, take her and feed her."

I was thereupon put upon a stretcher and carried into the psychopathic ward.

SUGGESTIONS FOR FURTHER READING

Alpern, Sara. *Freda Kirchwey: A Woman of the Nation.* Cambridge, 1987.

Antler, Joyce. *Lucy Sprague Mitchell: The Making of a Modern Woman.* New Haven, 1987.

Armitage, Susan, and Elizabeth Jameson, eds. *The Women's West.* Norman, Oklahoma, 1987.

Benson, Susan Porter. *Counter Cultures: Saleswomen, Managers, and Customers in American Department Stores, 1890–1940.* Urbana, 1986.

Blair, Karen J. *The Clubwoman as Feminist: True Womanhood Redefined, 1868–1914.* New York, 1980.

Buechler, Steven M. *The Transformation of the Woman Suffrage Movement: The Case of Illinois, 1850–1920.* New Brunswick, 1986.

Buhle, Mari Jo. *Women and American Socialism, 1870–1920.* Urbana, 1981.

Chesler, Ellen. *Woman of Valor: Margaret Sanger and the Birth Control Movement in America.* New York, 1992.

Dudden, Faye. *Serving Women: Household Service in Nineteenth Century America.* Middletown, 1983.

Dye, Nancy Schrom. *As Equals and As Sisters: The Labor Movement and the Women's Trade Union League of New York.* Columbia, Missouri, 1980.

Ewen, Elizabeth. *Immigrant Women in the Land of Dollars: Life and Culture on the Lower East Side, 1890–1925.* New York, 1985.

Faderman, Lillian. *Odd Girls and Twilight Lovers: A History of Lesbian Life in 20th Century America.* New York, 1991.

Fine, Lisa. *The Souls of the Skyscraper: Female Clerical Workers in Chicago, 1880–1930.* Philadelphia, 1990.

Fitzpatrick, Ellen. *Endless Crusade: Women Social Scientists and Progressive Reform.* New York, 1990.

Fowler, Robert Booth. *Carrie Catt: Feminist Politician.* Boston, 1986.

Frankel, Noralee, and Nancy S. Dye, eds. *Gender, Class, Race, and Reform in the Progressive Era.* Lexington, Kentucky, 1992.

Giddings, Paula. *When and Where I Enter: The Impact of Black Women on Race and Sex in America.* New York, 1984.

Glenn, Susan A. *Daughters of the Shtetl: Life and Labor in the Immigrant Generation.* Ithaca, 1990.

Gluck, Sherna B., ed. *From Parlor to Prison: Five American Suffragists Talk About Their Lives.* New York, 1986.

Gordon, Linda. *Woman's Body, Woman's Right: A Social History of Birth Control in America.* New York, 1976.

———, ed. *Women, the State, and Welfare.* Madison, 1990.

Gordon, Lynn D. *Gender and Higher Education in the Progressive Era.* New Haven, 1990.

Greenwald, Maurine Weiner. *Women, War, and Work: The Impact of World War I on Women Workers in the United States.* Westport, 1980.

Higginbotham, Evelyn Brooks. *Righteous Discontent: The Women's Movement in the Black Baptist Church, 1880–1920.* Cambridge, 1993.

Hine, Darlene Clark, ed. *Black Women in America: An Historical Encyclopedia.* New York, 1993.

Horowitz, Helen Lefkowitz. *The Power and Passion of M. Carey Thomas*. New York, 1994.

Jones, Jacqueline. *Labor of Love, Labor of Sorrow: Black Women, Work, and the Family from Slavery to the Present*. New York, 1985.

Kessler-Harris, Alice. *Out to Work: A History of Wage-Earning Women in America*. New York, 1982.

Kroeger, Brooke. *Nellie Bly*. New York, 1994.

Lane, Ann J. *To Herland and Beyond: The Life and Work of Charlotte Perkins Gilman*. New York, 1990.

Lunardini, Christine A. *From Equal Suffrage to Equal Rights: Alice Paul and the National Woman's Party, 1910–1918*. New York, 1986.

Meyerowitz, Joanne. *Women Adrift: Independent Female Wage Earners in Chicago, 1880–1930*. Chicago, 1988.

Morantz-Sanchez, Regina. *Sympathy and Science: Women Physicians in American Medicine*. New York, 1985.

Moynihan, Ruth Barnes. *Rebel for Rights: Abigail Scott Duniway*. New Haven, 1983.

Myres, Sandra L. *Westering Women: The Frontier Experience, 1800–1915*. Albuquerque, 1982.

Orleck, Annelise. *Common Sense and a Little Fire: Women and Working Class Politics in the United States, 1900–1965*. Chapel Hill, 1995.

Palmieri, Patricia Ann. *In Adamless Eve: The Community of Women Faculty at Wellesley*. New Haven, 1995.

Peiss, Kathy. *Cheap Amusements: Working Women and Leisure in Turn-of-the-Century New York*. Philadelphia, 1986.

Perry, Elisabeth. *Belle Moskowitz: Feminine Politics and the Exercise of Power in the Age of Alfred E. Smith*. New York, 1987.

Riley, Glenda. *A Place to Grow: Women in the American West*. Arlington Heights, 1992.

Rosen, Ruth. *The Lost Sisterhood: Prostitution in America, 1900–1918*. Baltimore, 1982.

Rosenberg, Rosalind. *Beyond Separate Spheres: Intellectual Roots of Modern Feminism*. New Haven, 1982.

Scharff, Virginia. *Taking the Wheel: Women and the Coming of the Motor Age*. New York, 1991.

Schwarz, Judith. *The Radical Feminists of Heterodoxy*. Lebanon, 1982.

Scott, Anne F. *Natural Allies: Women's Associations in American History*. Urbana, 1992.

Sicherman, Barbara. *Alice Hamilton: A Life in Letters*. Cambridge, 1984.

Sklar, Kathryn Kish. *Florence Kelley and the Nation's Work: The Rise of Women's Political Culture, 1830–1900*. New Haven, 1995.

Solomon, Barbara Miller. *In the Company of Educated Women: A History of Women and Higher Education in America*. New Haven, 1985.

Tax, Meredith. *The Rising of the Women: Feminist Solidarity and Class Conflict, 1880–1917*. New York, 1980.

Weinberg, Sydney Stahl. *The World of Our Mothers: The Lives of Jewish Immigrant Women*. Chapel Hill, 1988.

Weiner, Lynn Y. *From Working Girl to Working Mother: The Female Labor Force in the United States, 1820–1980*. Chapel Hill, 1985.

Wexler, Alex. *Emma Goldman in America*. Boston, 1984.

Woloch, Nancy. *Women and the American Experience*. New York, 1994.

PART TWO

Individual Choices, Collective Progress

1920–1963

CHAPTER 6

New Dilemmas for Modern Women

"The world broke in two in 1922 or thereabouts," observed writer Willa Cather. In many ways, the period beginning in the 1920s represented a new, more modern orientation to American life. The year 1920 served as a definite watershed for the nation's women, as they gained the vote and embarked on full citizenship and political equality with men. In retrospect, the liberation and freedom women had gained by the 1920s was far from complete; furthermore, important continuities in patterns of women's political participation link the presuffrage and postsuffrage eras. But the 1920s still separate the emerging new woman of the late nineteenth century from her modern equivalent.

The advent of modern times in the United States had as large an impact on the nation's women as its men. By the 1920s, the country had basically completed the process of industrialization and had taken on an increasingly urban orientation. Especially important in distinguishing modern times from earlier nineteenth-century patterns was the dramatic expansion of mass culture, which made it more likely that Americans (at least of the middle class) would share similar experiences throughout the nation. New instruments of mass media, such as radio and the movies, spread the message, as did the expansion of advertising. The automobile epitomized these new values of consumption, economic consolidation, and changing patterns of leisure.

The 1920s is noted for its booming economy, yet this prosperity was unequally distributed: more than 65 percent of households had incomes under $2,000 a year, which severely limited their ability to buy the new automobiles, vacuum cleaners, radios, toasters, and other consumer goods so central to the maintenance of prosperity in the 1920s. Consumer credit (which grew dramatically in the 1920s) could stretch family income only so far. The onset of the Great Depression in 1929 showed the underlying structural weaknesses of the economy.

Women were not only situated within these broader developments—in the words of one historian, "In no other decade of the twentieth century, until the

1970s, have women been so at the center of the major issues." The flapper, whose slim boyish figure and style of dress forms our visual image of women in the decade, served as the symbol of the new values of personal liberation, morality, and consumption. Despite the media's fascination with young women's new lifestyles, the goal for most women continued to be marriage and family life. Most of the advertising in the decade was geared towards accustoming women to that role, as were the movies. The growing acceptance of birth control made it possible for a more companionate ideal to reign in marital relations, and women increasingly turned to experts for help in running their homes or raising their children.

Despite the forces that were liberating women from the home, many cultural messages placed women squarely within the family domain, foreshadowing the "feminine mystique" of postwar America. Married women played vital economic roles as the primary consumers of household goods. Yet these new appliances hardly freed women from domestic toil: often a washing machine or a vacuum cleaner just raised standards of cleanliness, making "more work for mother." Women still spent an average of fifty-one hours a week on household chores, little different from their mothers and grandmothers. And of course, these new appliances were only useful in urban areas where households had electricity. In rural America, few farms were electrified before the 1930s. For families on the fringes of the middle-class ideal promoted in advertising, magazines, and the movies, the modern consumer economy of the 1920s had not yet arrived.

Paid employment occupied a central role in women's lives in the 1920s. The watchwords for many college-educated women were economic independence, but few women found unlimited economic opportunities. Women made up one quarter of the work force, but approximately 86 percent of women worked in only ten occupations, with domestic and personal service leading the list. Women comprised only 3 percent of union members and received between 52 and 55 percent of men's earnings. Women in the professions continued to be concentrated in fields such as nursing, teaching, and social work. Despite the public attention to women's economic liberation that supposedly accompanied the vote, the largest influence on women's employment was the deeply rooted segmentation of the work force.

One trend under way by the 1920s was the increase in married women who worked for pay outside the home. More than any other pattern, this change in women's economic roles shaped the modern era. By 1930, 11 percent of native-born white women, 10.2 percent of foreign-born women, and 37.5 percent of black women who were married were also employed. Professional women may have struggled on an individual basis to balance the demands of career and marriage in order to find personal fulfillment, but most women worked out of necessity. The rising expectations of the new consumer lifestyle propelled some married women into the work force; black women's needs, however, were dictated by economic and family survival.

Equally central to assessing women's experiences in the 1920s is women's continued political activism. The Nineteenth Amendment was treated as a major watershed, the culmination of seven decades of agitation and the beginning of new roles for women in politics and public life. The vote also fostered a false optimism that women were now men's equals as citizens, and by extension, in all other aspects of their lives. But contrary to popular wisdom, the winning of the vote did not cause the disbanding of the women's movement in the 1920s. Some women moved tentatively into the major political parties, but for the most part, women continued to use women's voluntary associations to influence public policy. Without denying the symbolic importance of the vote, historians now emphasize the continuities of women's postsuffrage behavior with the presuffrage patterns. As in the patterns of women's work, it is necessary to look at the long-range trends instead of getting sidetracked by the accomplishments or setbacks of individual decades.

New Voters

Carrie Chapman Catt

Once women won the vote, the organized women's movement stood at a crossroad. When the Nineteenth Amendment removed the goal which had unified a fairly diverse set of organizations and individuals under the suffrage umbrella, women in public life turned their attention to a variety of causes. Many women continued the kind of political mobilization practiced in the nineteenth and early twentieth centuries—that is, working through women's voluntary associations and networks on issue-oriented approaches to politics and social change. Other women branched off in new directions. The most controversial was the National Woman's Party's support for an Equal Rights Amendment, which divided the women's movement after 1923 between those who supported protective labor legislation for women versus feminists who insisted that men and women be treated equally before the law. There was no compromise possible on this issue in the 1920s.

Another challenge posed by the winning of the vote was women's stance towards the political parties. For so long, women had influenced politics from the outside; should they now try to work their way into the inner sanctums of political power in the Democratic and Republican parties? Former suffrage leaders like Carrie Chapman Catt (1859–1947) said yes. In this 1920 address to the newly created League of Women Voters, Catt emphatically argued that women must embrace partisan political activity as part of their new political roles.

Carrie Chapman Catt underestimated the difficulties of integration into the political system. While a few token appointments were made, it was not easy for women to move up the political ladder or exercise power in their own right. By the end of the decade, Emily Newell Blair, named the first woman vice chairman of the Democratic National Committee in 1924, was writing articles with such titles as "Discouraged Feminists in Politics." Catt's call for women to infiltrate the political parties remained an elusive goal in the 1920s and beyond.

Fellow suffragists, we have come to a turn of the road. For about sixty years we have been appealing to political parties to give up the vote, for there was no possible way of ever getting that vote until the political parties were willing that we should have it. I don't think we have ever won the vote in a single state, even by a state referendum, where one or both of the political parties have not tacitly given their consent that it should go through. Certainly ratification would not have been possible without their aid.

Well then, is it our intention to continue on the outside of those political parties where we have been for sixty years and to go on appealing for their favor as we have always been doing? Are we going to petition them as we have always done? Well, if so, what was the use of getting the vote? (Applause.)

It certainly was never any idea of the proposed League of Women Voters that we should remain out of the parties and appeal to them for the things that we wanted to do. The only way to get things in this country is to find them on the inside of the political party. (Applause.) More and more the political parties become the power through which things are accomplished. One cannot get congressional action or legislative action unless the political parties represented there are willing, so powerful are they.

It is not a question of whether they ought to be powerful or ought not to be powerful; they are. It is the trend of the present political development and instead of appealing to them for the things you want, it is better to get on the inside and help yourself to the things you want. (Applause.) . . .

As I read the signs of the present political progress of women within the parties, you are going to have a continuation of the old familiar strife and it is just this: women must persuade men to respect and to have confidence in the capacities of women just as we have been doing for sixty odd years; and on the other hand, they must stimulate other women to forward movement and encourage them to increased self-respect. This is the same old struggle but in a new field. Because women have the vote, it doesn't follow that every man who is an election district ward or a county chairman has suddenly become convinced that women can do things as well as men. Many must be converted to that conclusion and converted by the actual political work of women.

Men will say that it is right for women to vote, but when it comes to administrative work within the party, that is still the exclusive man's business. The mass of women will be hesitant and timid and doubtful of themselves; they

Source: Carrie Chapman Catt, "Political Parties and Women Voters," 1920 address to the League of Women Voters, Carrie Chapman Catt papers, Schlesinger Library, Radcliffe College.

will be content to stand back and not use the power and the brains and the conscience that they have. They will be inclined to think that everything they find ready made in their hands is all right, no matter how wrong it may be. Women must not be content until they are as independent within the party as men are, which isn't saying much. (Laughter and applause.)

That struggle cannot be carried on from the outside. Success can only be found on the inside. For thirty years and a little more, I have worked with you in the first lap of this struggle toward woman's emancipation. I cannot lead or follow in the next lap. I do not wish to advise where I cannot follow. Younger and fresher women must do that work, and because I cannot advise and cannot follow, I only point to the fact that the battle is there, and that I hope you are not going to be such quitters as to stay on the outside and let all the reactionaries have their way on the inside. (Applause.) . . .

You won't be so welcome there, but that is the place to be. (Applause.) And if you stay there long enough and are active enough, you will see something else—the real thing in the center, with the door locked tight, and you will have a hard, long fight before you get behind that door, for there is the engine that moves the wheels of your party machinery. Nevertheless, it will be an interesting and thrilling struggle and well worth while. If you really want women's vote to count, make your way there.

Generational Conflicts

Dorothy Dunbar Bromley

One key to understanding the 1920s is a generational approach. Following the lead of social scientists from the 1920s such as Lorinne Pruette, it is possible to identify at least three generations of women, all of which coexisted (somewhat uneasily, as this selection suggests) in the decade. First, there were the old feminist pioneers, those activists whose lifelong struggle to increase women's options had (at least in the eyes of younger women) deeply embittered them towards men. Then came a middle generation, women in their forties and fifties in the 1920s, who had struggled successfully for woman suffrage and women's professional advancement; while still "woman-identified," they were somewhat less strident in their antagonism towards men.

It was the third generation, the consciously modern women in their twenties and thirties, who captured the public imagination in the decade and have continued to intrigue historians ever since. Journalist Dorothy Dunbar Bromley's 1927 article, "Feminist-New Style," wittily captures the differing perspectives between old and young. Young women wanted little to do with the older generations, whom they characterized as too bitter towards men, lacking style, and generally unsuitable as role models. The new women of the 1920s had different agendas: instead of social reform, they looked to economic independence and professional advancement; instead of bonding with other women, they announced that they much preferred the company of men. Now a life that did not include marriage, children, and a career was seen as incomplete. The key to understanding this new woman (and these are only broad generalizations) is to recognize her highly individualistic approach to both personal and professional life. She would succeed and fail on her own; the women's movement was no longer necessary. Another characteristic of these new-style feminists was the relentlessly white and middle-class character of their self-images and goals; such lifestyles had scant relevance to immigrant, minority, or working-class women. Such personal and professional liberation remained an option only for a privileged elite.

The Queen is dead. Long live the Queen!

Is it not high time that we laid the ghost of the so-called feminist?

"Feminism" has become a term of opprobrium to the modern young woman. For the word suggests either the old school of fighting feminists who wore flat heels and had very little feminine charm, or the current species who antagonize men with their constant clamor about maiden names, equal rights, woman's place in the world, and many another cause . . . *ad infinitum.* Indeed, if a blundering male assumes that a young woman is a feminist simply because she happens to have a job or a profession of her own, she will be highly—and quite justifiably insulted: for the word evokes the antithesis of what she flatters herself to be. Yet she and her kind can hardly be dubbed "old-fashioned" women. What *are* they, then?

The pioneer feminists were hard-hitting individuals, and the modern young woman admires them for their courage—even while she judges them for their zealotry and their inartistic methods. Furthermore, she pays all honor to them, for they fought her battle. But *she* does not want to wear their mantle (indeed, she thinks they should have been buried in it), and she has to smile at those women who wear it to-day—with the battle-cry still on their lips. The worst of the fight is over, yet this second generation of feminists are still throwing hand grenades. They bear a grudge against men, either secretly or openly; they make an issue of little things as well as big; they exploit their sex for the sake of publicity; they rant about equality when they might better prove their ability. Yet it is these women—the ones who do more talking than acting—on whom the average man focuses his microscope when he sits down to dissect the "new woman." For like his less educated brethren, he labors under the delusion that there are only two types of women, the creature of instinct who is content to be a "home-maker" and the "sterile intellectual" who cares solely about "expressing herself"—home and children be damned.

But what of the constantly increasing group of young women in their twenties and thirties who are the truly modern ones, those who admit that a full

Source: Dorothy Bromley, "Feminist-New Style," *Harper's* CLV (October 1927), pp. 552–560. Copyright © 1927 by *Harper's Magazine.* All rights reserved. Reproduced from the October issue by special permission.

life calls for marriage and children as well as a career? These women if they launch upon marriage are keen to make a success of it and an art of child-rearing. But *at the same time* they are moved by an inescapable inner compulsion to be individuals in their own right. And in this era of simplified house-keeping they see their opportunity, for it is obvious that a woman who plans intelligently can salvage some time for her own pursuits. Furthermore, they are convinced that they will be better wives and mothers for the breadth they gain from functioning outside the home. In short, they are highly conscious creatures who feel obliged to plumb their own resources to the very depths, despite the fact that they are under no delusions as to the present inferior status of their sex in most fields of endeavor.

Numbers of these honest, spirited young women have made themselves heard in article and story. But since men must have things pointed out to them in black and white, we beg leave to enunciate the tenets of the modern woman's credo. Let us call her "Feminist—New Style." . . .

In brief, Feminist—New Style reasons that if she is economically independent, and if she has, to boot, a vital interest in some work of her own she will have given as few hostages to Fate as it is humanly possible to give. Love may die, and children may grow up, but one's work goes on forever.

Third Tenet. She will not, however, live for her job alone, for she considers that a woman who talks and thinks only shop has just as narrow a horizon as the housewife who talks and thinks only husband and children—perhaps more so, for the latter may have a deeper understanding of human nature. She will therefore refuse to give up all of her personal interests, year in and year out, for the sake of her work. In this respect she no doubt will fall short of the masculine idea of commercial success, for the simple reason that she has never felt the economic compulsion which drives men on to build up fortunes for the sake of their growing families.

Yet she is not one of the many women who look upon their jobs as tolerable meal-tickets or as interesting pastimes to be dropped whenever they may wish. On the contrary, she takes great pride in becoming a vital factor in whatever enterprise she has chosen, and she therefore expects to work long hours when the occasion demands.

But rather than make the mistake that some women do of domesticating their jobs, *i.e.,* burying all of their affections and interests in them, or the mistake that many men make of milking their youth dry for the sake of building up a fortune to be spent in a fatigued middle-age, she will proceed on the principle that a person of intelligence and energy can attain a fair amount of success—perhaps even a high degree of success—by the very virtue of living a well-balanced life, as well as by working with concentration.

Fourth Tenet. Nor has she become hostile to the other sex in the course of her struggle to orient herself. On the contrary, she frankly likes men and is grateful to more than a few for the encouragement and help they have given her.

In the business and professional worlds, for instance, Feminist—New Style has observed that more and more men are coming to accord women as much responsibility as they show themselves able to carry. She and her generation have never found it necessary to bludgeon their way, and she is inclined to think that certain of the pioneers would have got farther if they had relied on their ability rather than on their militant methods. To tell the truth, she enjoys working with men, more than with women, for their methods are more direct and their view larger, and she finds that she can deal with them on a basis of frank comradeship.

When she meets men socially she is not inclined to air her knowledge and argue about woman's right to a place in the sun. On the contrary, she either talks with a man because he has ideas that interest her or because she finds it amusing to flirt with him—and she will naturally find it doubly amusing if the flirtation involves the swift interplay of wits. She will not waste many engagements on a dull-witted man, although it must be admitted that she finds fewer men with stagnant minds than she does women.

When all is said and done, most of the men of her world are such a decent likable lot that she is hard put to it to understand the sex antagonism which actuates certain "advanced" women who secretly look upon their husbands—and all men—as their natural enemies from whom they must wrest every privilege and advantage possible. Such tactics are a futile waste of energy; now that men have admitted that women can be valuable partners not only in the home, but also in business and civic life, the best thing for women to do is to prove their value.

Fifth Tenet. By the same corollary, Feminist—New Style professes no loyalty to women *en masse,* although she staunchly believes in individual women. Surveying her sex as a whole, she finds their actions petty, their range of interests narrow, their talk trivial and repetitious. As for those who set themselves up as leaders of the sex, they are either strident creatures of so little ability and balance that they have won no chance to "express themselves" (to use their own hackneyed phrase) in a manmade world; or they are brilliant, restless individuals who too often battle for women's rights for the sake of personal glory.

But when a woman in the professions or in public life proves herself really capable, Feminist—New Style will be the first to cheer, and to help her along still farther, by proffering her own support and co-operation. Indeed, she feels that there is to-day a stronger bond among thinking women than ever before. . . .

Seventh Tenet. Empty slogans seem to Feminist—New Style just as bad taste as masculine dress and manners. They serve only to prolong the war between the sexes and to prevent women from learning to think straight. Take these, for instance, "Keep your maiden name." "Come out of the kitchen." "Never darn a sock." After all, what's in a name or in a sock? Madame Curie managed to become one of the world's geniuses even though she suffered the terrible handicap of bearing her husband's name, and it is altogether likely that she darned a sock or two of Monsieur Curie's when there was no servant at hand to do it.

"Keep your maiden name," the slogan which the members of the Lucy Stone League cry from the housetops so lustily, would seem the most inane of all. Will someone kindly tell us why these women don't prove their individuality—and their independence of their husbands—by some sort of real achievement? And would it not be more consistent for them to require that every member not only keep her maiden name but *that she support herself?* . . .

Finally, Feminist—New Style proclaims that men and children shall no longer circumscribe her world, although they may constitute a large part of it. She is intensely self-conscious whereas the feminists were intensely sex-conscious. Aware of possessing a mind, she takes a keen pleasure in using that mind for some definite purpose; and also in learning to think clearly and cogently against a background of historical and scientific knowledge. She aspires to understand the meaning of the twentieth century as she sees it expressed in the skyscrapers, the rapid pace of city life, the expressionistic drama, the abstract conceptions of art, the new music, the Joycian novel. She is acutely conscious that she is being carried along in the current of these sweeping forces, that she and her sex are in the vanguard of change. She knows that it is her American, her twentieth-century birthright to emerge from a creature of instinct into a full-fledged individual who is capable of molding her own life. And in this respect she holds that she is becoming man's equal.

If this be treason, gentlemen, make the most of it.

Creating a Feminist Lifestyle

Crystal Eastman

Feminist Crystal Eastman (1881–1928) bridged the gap between the middle generation of feminists and the young women coming of age in the 1920s. Eastman was a liberated woman from day one. Both her parents were ordained Congregational ministers, and her brother Max became a noted writer and socialist in Greenwich Village in the 1910s and 1920s. Crystal graduated from Vassar in 1903 and worked at a settlement house while getting a law degree from New York University. She was an active opponent of American participation in World War I, and in the 1920s she wrote widely on issues such as international suffragism, peace, and socialism.

What marks Crystal Eastman as a modern woman is her struggle to find expression in her personal life for the feminism and equality that she supported in public. Quipping that feminists were not nuns, she enjoyed men's company, marrying twice. Yet she did not marry until she

Source: Crystal Eastman, "Marriage under Two Roofs," *Cosmopolitan,* December 1923. Quoted in *Crystal Eastman on Women and Revolution,* ed. Blanche Wiesen Cook (New York: Oxford University Press, 1978), pp. 76–83.

was thirty, and this first marriage ended in divorce in 1916. Reflecting her commitment to economic independence, she totally rejected the idea of alimony: "No self-respecting feminist would accept alimony. It would be her own confession that she could not take care of herself." Her second marriage was more compatible and produced two children.

While "Marriage under Two Roofs," a 1923 piece from *Cosmopolitan*, may at first glance seem like a spoof, it is not too different from the lifestyle practiced by Eastman in her second marriage. From 1922 to 1927, she commuted between England, where her husband worked as a journalist, and the United States, where her political and organizational contacts were based. This somewhat unusual arrangement was severed by her husband's sudden death in 1927. Eastman, a self-described workaholic, died the next year of complications from kidney failure at the age of forty-seven.

"You're breaking up our home," my husband said.

"No I'm not. I'm trying to hold it together. You know we've had nothing worthy the name of home for years, and the thing we have is going to pieces so fast that nothing but desperate measures will save it. Try my scheme, then. Only try it, that's all I ask."

We tried it. And it has given us the one serene and happy period of all our married life. We no longer even think of separation, much less talk of it or threaten it. For the first time the fact that we love each other and have two splendid children is making us happy instead of miserable. My husband, who fought the scheme so bitterly, admits this now and often expatiates upon it.

Here is the story as well as I can tell it. To begin with, we had to move. The building in which we had lived for five years was to be torn down. Well, it just seemed to happen without our saying any more about it that we moved into two places instead of one. I took a small flat for myself and the children toward the edge of town where there are playgrounds and green spaces. My husband took a room in a clean rooming house within easy walking distance of his office. The two cost just a bit less than we had had to pay for a place large enough to hold us in reasonable comfort, all together. John's clothes and strictly personal possessions went to the room. Mine and the children's and our furniture, pictures and joint accumulations went to the flat. Technically he lives at one place and I at the other. But of course he keeps a change of clothes and all the essentials for night and morning comfort at my house, as might a favorite and frequent guest.

Every morning, like lovers, we telephone to exchange the day's greetings and make plans for the evening. Two or three times a week we dine together at my house and John stays all night. If we are to dine at a friend's house we usually arrange to meet there and at the end of the evening my husband may come home with me and he may not, according to our mood. If we are going to a theater I meet him in town for dinner, and after the show there are again always two possibilities—going home together like married lovers or parting on the street corner and going off in the night alone to our separate beds. And because neither course is inexorably forced upon us, either one is a bit of a lark. It is wonderful sometimes to be alone in the night and just know that someone loves you. In other moods you must have that lover in your arms. Marriage under two roofs makes room for moods.

Now about the children; for, paradoxical though it may seem, it is having children that complicates marriages so. Many pairs of lovers can have a house in common, a car, a cook, a club and all their Christmas presents; they can eat the same food, see the same plays, go to the same parties, cherish the same friends for years on end and enjoy it. But just introduce one or two children into that home, strong modern personalities, strange ebullient creatures neither his nor hers but mysteriously and indissolubly *theirs*—theirs to love, theirs to teach and train, theirs to be proud of, theirs to be ashamed of—and you have the material for tragedy. Obscure jealousies so often arise, deep resentments may be so long unspoken, rivers of cold misunderstanding may flow forever between the two who were at one before.

Perhaps I exaggerate the difficulty of bringing up children together. If the two parents come from an almost identical background, or if one has had a miserable childhood which he is glad to forget, there may be no difficulty at all. It is when, as in our case, both parents can claim a happy childhood but under totally different auspices, that their joint efforts to raise a family come so often to grief. I think my husband and I have quarreled with more anguish and bitterness over our children than over all other matters put together. But we quarrel no longer. The two-roof plan has made an end of quarreling.

"No wonder!" protests the indignant male. "You've got your way. You have the children, they live with you and you can bring them up as you like. But is that fair?"

Surely, as society is organized today, it is the mother's job to bring up the children. The father's job is to earn the living, and if he belongs as the father in our family does to the intellectual proletariat—people of education with expensive tastes and no capital, who must live by their wits—he will be hard at it for the first fifteen or twenty years of his married life. How can he be more than a "consulting partner" in the twenty-four hour a day job of bringing up children? He can criticize and interfere, or praise and suggest, according to his nature, but he cannot really do the job. Circumstances compel him to leave it to the mother. In big decisions about the children, of course, the father's will counts often more than the mother's, but in the everyday matter of training and association the most he can do is to "use his influence."

And in the usual American middle-class family, when is father's influence most often brought to bear? At breakfast! At breakfast of all times when everyone is already a little on edge from violating his natural instincts—children forced to "hurry up" and "be quiet" and "keep at it" when they long to dawdle and "fool"; mother forced to begin being patient and kind at a time in the day when it is against nature to be patient and kind; father, already heavy with his day's work, forced to spend his last precious half-hour in this crude confusion when his whole being cries out for solitude.

This at least can be said for the two-roof scheme: it automatically relieves father of the family breakfast, and the family breakfast of father! And no hard feelings anywhere. In our family father is now a treat. He might turn up some morning during the week, but if he does it is a surprise and everybody is so good that breakfast is almost a social occasion. Saturday afternoon father usually appears and takes you off for a lark somewhere, and Sunday he is just like a member of the family.

Is there really anything unfair in this arrangement? Are not the father's comments, criticisms and suggestions on the upbringing of his children apt to be better given and better received in the comparative leisure and freedom of Sunday than in the nagging, inescapable contact of a daily breakfast? Must a consulting partner review the raw, unfinished work every day?

At this point, I foresee, the passionate upholder of family life will try to compromise with me. "Why two roofs?" he will argue. "Why not a room for father at the top of the house and his breakfast served there? Is it necessary to drive him right out of the house?"

But I stand my ground. To begin with, for the type of family I am thinking of there seldom is a house. It is a flat, an apartment, a floor or two floors, at most a very small house. If father is lucky enough to have a room of his own it will not be out of hearing. He will always be acutely aware of the children in their noisy process of growing up. And mother will be aware of his presence in the house. The strain will still be there.

Moreover, even though you live in a palace, two rooms will not give you what two roofs will give you. Let us forget breakfast now—imagine it is evening, the long day's work is over, the children are asleep. Speaking from the woman's standpoint, can there be anything more irritating than a husband who shuts himself up in a room and says or intimates, "I want to be alone"? He is there with you in your common home. It is evening. You have been apart all day, and yet he wants to be alone! Outrageous! To sit and read in separate rooms under the same roof! Unnatural! Not to be borne! *Why did he come home if he wanted to be alone?*

Why?

Obviously because he had no home of his own to go to. Now put my scheme into operation. Give him a place of his own, completely outside of your jurisdiction, a place where he keeps his clothes, where he normally sleeps, to which he goes quite simply and naturally whenever he wants to, without explanations and without fear of reproach. At the morning telephone rendezvous you have agreed not to spend the evening together. You may be a little lonely the first few times this happens, but you soon get to like your "vacations" and to plan for them. You may have a friend in for dinner whom your husband takes no pleasure in. You may arrange for some kind of recreation, dancing, music, lecture or what-not for which he has no taste, or you may be tired enough to enjoy a few hours of solitude by your own hearth.

In any case his absence is a refreshment, a chance to be yourself for a while in a rich, free sense which nothing but a separate roof can give you.

Women, more than men, succumb to marriage. They sink so easily into that fatal habit of depending on one person to rescue them from themselves. And this is the death of love.

The two-roof plan encourages a wife to cultivate initiative in rescuing herself, to develop social courage, to look upon her life as an independent adventure and get interested in it. And every Victorian tradition to the contrary, it is thus only that she can retain her charm down the years.

I wish I could set forth as freely and frankly my husband's feeling about this new scheme of life as I can my own. But he is not the sort of man who talks easily about himself. He is what the psychoanalysts call an "introvert." I know from a hundred signs that he likes it, but I can only guess why.

Most women tend to own and manage their husbands too much, and I am not free from that vice. Much of John's depression and irritability which used to be so baffling to me in the old days was due, I am sure, to his having no escape from me, no place where I did not come, no retreat from my influence. Now he has one. Often when we lived under the same roof he must have said to himself, "I love her but I can't stand her. She is too much for me." Now I know he never feels that.

People with very simple natures probably do not suffer from this pressure of one personality on the other in marriage. But for the usual modern type, the complex, sensitive, highly organized city dweller, man or woman, marriage can become such a constant invasion of his very self that it amounts sometimes to torture.

I am the last one to deny that there are successful marriages. I know ideally mated couples who can say to this argument with sincerity:

"But we don't want to get away from each other. We are perfectly happy as we are."

And I can answer only, "Bless you my children; there is nothing in this gospel for you."

Nor is there anything in it for young lovers in the first months of ecstasy and anguish, nor for parents, during the first baby's first year, nor for couples of whom one is a natural door-mat, nor for the excessively domestic man who wants to know the price of everything to a penny, how often the baby falls down and what the cook does on her afternoon off. (Though in this case no doubt the wife needs a retreat.)

No, I am speaking only to those who are discouraged with marriage, who have given it a good trial and found it extremely difficult. But I am sure I shall have a large audience.

Ours is not an extreme case. My husband is a bit temperamental but he has great charm. I am a "strong-minded" woman, perhaps, but not over-strong. We have hosts of friends who find us both good-natured, generous, easy to get along with. We are both of us intelligent. We can both take a joke. And I think we had more genuine love and respect for each other than is common.

Yet marriage was destroying us. We just lived from storm to storm, with tears, an emotional reconciliation and a brief lull of happiness between.

Now that we live under two roofs there are no storms, no quarrels, no tears. Our differences of opinion are not passionate and unbearable. They have an almost rational quality. Criticisms and suggestions are made with the gentleness and reserve that is common between friends. They are received with the open-minded forbearance of one who can be sure of the critic's early departure.

And as for love, we seem to have found it again. The hours we spend together have actually caught back some of the surprising gaiety and warm glow of sweetheart days.

What is the meaning of this all but universal habit of quarreling among the married?

When a friend irritates you or, as we say, gets on your nerves, you do not have to quarrel with her. You know she is going home pretty soon, or you are going home—a natural and inevitable separation will take place.

But with a husband or a wife there is no hope, nothing to look forward to. You cannot good-naturedly walk away, because you have no place to go. *His home*—or her home—*is your home.* This fact increases your irritation five hundredfold, and some outlet must be had.

Stormy quarrels, no matter how tender and intimate the interval between, are wearing to soul and body. But they are not nearly so devastating, I believe, as that much more common type of married quarreling which resolves itself into being a little mean to each other all the time.

Just who is there who does not know at least one couple like that—their conversation with each other made up almost entirely of small slighting remarks, each constantly belittling the achievements and enthusiasms of the other; kindly people in their relations with outsiders but always somewhat bitter and belligerent toward each other? Is anything less enjoyable than visiting in such a home? Is it really good for children to grow up in such an atmosphere?

Perhaps divorce is the only remedy for difficult marriages. But if my theory is correct, if it is the too constant sharing of one home, with no easy and normal method of escape, which primarily makes them difficult, then some loosening of the time-and-space conventions so bound up with marriage is worth trying. Separate beds, separate rooms, have not done much to reconcile people to marriage. Why not take a bold romantic step and try separate roofs?

It will seem to many that in setting forth this new plan for achieving a happy marriage I have avoided the crucial test, that my argument can be challenged at its very heart.

Crudely put, the challenge is: "If my husband sleeps under a separate roof, how do I know that he is always alone?" or again: "If I don't go home every night, how do I know that some other man is not there in my place?" In a literal and exact sense you don't know. That is the answer.

But after all, marriage, like business, is founded on trust.

When a husband goes off to work in the morning, does he *know* that his wife is not going to neglect her children and make love to the plumber? He hopes she isn't, of course, but he cannot be absolutely sure. It would not be practical to ring her up every fifteen minutes to inquire; if he is to get on with his work, he must trust her.

And as for the poor wife, how can she know that her breadwinner is not spending the entire morning kissing the stenographer, unless she squanders what she has saved up for the children's winter coats on a dictograph?

In the most conventional marriage there must be a considerable area of confidence as to the technical faithfulness of the parties. In marriage under two roofs you deliberately extend that area of confidence, that is all.

If one is of a very jealous disposition this may take some courage, but it is courage soon rewarded, for in this matter of marital faithfulness, as all wise women know, increasing the confidence usually lessens the risk. The two-roof scheme demands confidence during those very hours of ease when temptation is greatest; this cannot be denied.

But if it brings happiness where there was misery before, even that risk is well taken, for happiness is the only security.

The New Woman in Fiction

Eudora Ramsey Richardson

Popular culture, especially popular fiction, offers another view of women in the 1920s. In 1923 there were at least 3000 periodicals in the United States with a combined per-issue circulation of more than 128 million; magazines like the *Ladies' Home Journal, Woman's Home Companion,* and *McCall's* had more than a million readers each. A big draw was their fiction. (Since cheap mass paperbacks were not widely available until the very end of the 1930s, most readers turned to magazines for fiction.) Serious authors like Edith Wharton and Willa Cather earned big bucks by serializing their works in popular magazines in the 1920s, and other less well-known authors also found broad audiences in this middlebrow culture.

One genre of popular fiction from the period was the New Woman story. What was different about the New Woman from a Victorian heroine, according to scholar Maureen Honey, was that her desire for self-actualization and meaningful work took precedence over the romance quest. These modern women were not averse to love interests, but they put a higher priority on self-expression and independence. They often fought their battles on their own, rather than working collectively with other women. In Eudora Ramsey Richardson's 1928 story from the *Ladies' Home Journal,* the protagonist Emma Morrison certainly fits that bill. The story's portrayal of the gender-segregated workplace of the 1920s is historically accurate, but if only there were so many happy endings for professionally ambitious women. . . .

Author Eudora Ramsey Richardson held degrees from the University of Richmond and Columbia University and spent most of her life in Virginia. Married and the mother of one daughter, her many interests beyond writing speak to the continuities between women's pre- and post-suffrage activism. She had been a field director of the National American Woman Suffrage Association from 1914 to 1917, was a field representative for the National Federation of Business and Professional Women's Clubs from 1932 to 1935, and was the first president of the Virginia chapter of the American Association of University Women. Her organizational activities and support for feminist causes inform much of her writing, including this story.

Emma Morrison swung herself through the revolving door conscious that the elasticity had gone from her. In the rest room she hung her hat and coat on the usual hook and studied her reflection in the mirror. Yes, she looked her twenty-four years and perhaps one or two more. There were shadows beneath her dark eyes. Listlessly she started toward the rear of the bank.

There he stood—the new trust officer. Emma saw him talking to the president; saw him, and hated his earnest good looks. From the beginning he would be her enemy. She was sick to death of seeing men climb past her. At his new desk across the aisle sat Herbert Harris, yesterday promoted from will soliciting to manager of new business. There was no reason why she should not have been given his former work—anything to take her from the hopeless rut. But no, she was needed in her important service position. Dearly she had paid for having made herself indispensable.

The president smiled and with a stubby forefinger beckoned to Emma. Rotund old gentleman with flabby cheeks and squinting little eyes that looked out from enveloping flesh folds with the obtuse kindliness of a tame elephant, so pleased with the economic scheme! How could he understand unrest of any kind?

"Miss Morrison," the great man patronized, "the new head of the trust department, Mr. Wainwright. You'll find this girl superb, Wainwright. We couldn't do trust business without her."

Emma tried to smile. Thank heaven these men couldn't read the cynical thoughts she had learned so well to suppress, couldn't know that after five years of work praise was not enough.

"I'm afraid I'll have to depend on you at first," John Wainwright replied.

There was nothing surprising in that. Emma was entirely used to being depended upon by officers of the bank.

She murmured something—it couldn't matter what, for no one would be listening—and lifted her great ledger from the drawer.

Source: Eudora Ramsey Richardson, "Men Are Like That," *Ladies' Home Journal* 45, no. 5 (May 1928), reprinted in Maureen Honey, ed., *Breaking the Ties that Bind: Popular Stories of the New Woman, 1915–1930* (Norman: University of Oklahoma Press, 1992), pp. 258–269.

A new trust officer, and Emma Morrison his bookkeeper and untitled assistant—the same old story reënacted! There was no use fighting against the system. Obviously, not having studied law, she could not hope to become trust officer; and there seemed no chance of being transferred to another department in which promotion would be logical . . . .

Emma knew the trust department's entire story. She had kept its books, guarded its records, watched its growth for the five years of its fiduciary existence. It was easy enough to tell it all—to explain the loans and produce the mortgages, the insurance policies. When she had finished, John Wainwright, with elbow on the desk and chin in the palm of his hand, leveled his eyes with hers and was silent for a moment. Then abruptly he rose.

"Thank you," he said. "I'd no idea the work of years could be made clear in an hour."

"Let me know when you're ready to go over the bonds and wills," Emma continued. She tried to speak as impersonally as one might dictate into the gaping mouth of a dictaphone.

"Tomorrow," John Wainwright replied. "I'm due now at the executive meeting."

Emma watched him go. There would be no difference. Like his predecessor, this man would depend on her, and she would remain as stationary as the filing cabinet. The president marched pompously toward the carpeted elegance of the board room. The vice presidents sauntered after with scarcely less grandeur. The cashier followed, and now came the three assistant cashiers. Last of all, like a bantam rooster in the Plymouth Rock's seraglio, strutted Herbert Harris, calling attention to his recent elevation by a throat clearing which seemed to Emma to resemble a faint crow. How utterly absurd ever to have hoped one day to be a part of this procession!

Emma glanced across the elegant tops of many desks behind which revolving chairs evidenced recent desertion. It was the flippancy of others for which she paid. One little stenographer with hair as short as the brains it covered had left her typewriter to talk to the veritable reflection of herself who operated the switchboard. A file clerk coquetted with a youth who kept books. Not a girl was at her place now that the officers' surveillance was lifted. These—these silly children who in their thinking were as far removed from Emma Morrison as the president was from the office boy—helped men to form their estimates of women, chained the ambitious ones to typewriters and adding machines. Emma swallowed hard and returned to her work. . . .

At the door Emma almost ran into the former solicitor of wills who waited watchfully. Though the youth bored her a trifle, she was glad today that he joined her. From fashion plates and the local ad club he had selected all the best selling points with a result 100 per cent American and not unpleasant.

"I feel like celebratin' my new job," he began. "How 'bout dinner downtown and a show?" Emma nodded. It was amazing that this boy liked her— this flapping trousered, pomaded youngster whom she had always helped with whatever inside work his will soliciting involved.

Over dinner Emma inquired politely concerning the new position. "You like the desk with your name on it," she said disconcertingly, "but I'm afraid having to stay in the bank part of the time will bore you terribly."

"You're dead right," the boy replied. "There's a lot about the files I don't understand . . ."

Emma toyed with her salad. The new-business department had been run for a long time in a slipshod fashion. It would be fun to establish a system that would function like the one in the trust department. She would not offer! Long enough she had been cutting the path to success—for others.

Herbert Harris passed his hand across the sleek surface of his head and then fumbled the silver beside his plate. This youth, whose gift for dealing with people of all kinds had won for him his recent promotion, was obviously embarrassed. Emma was sorry for him, foolishly sorry. After all, the boy was a good sort.

"Oh, say, Emma," he began at last, "can't you come over and sort of straighten things out for me? Organize the department? I—I can't get anywhere the way things are."

"You see, Herbert," Emma parried, "I'm very busy just now."

"Yes, I know, but you do your work so easily. Oh, please, Emma!"

"All right. Meet me an hour earlier tomorrow morning."

Several hours later Emma talked things over with her mother. "I'm just discouraged, mother," she choked. "Do you suppose I'll ever accomplish anything?"

"You've done well, honey," Mrs. Morrison consoled. "So young and making a hundred and fifty a month."

"Oh, bother the salary! I want a chance. Ten years from now I'll still be an untitled clerk. Men can see just two types of women—their wives and the stenographers who work just long enough to get some pretty clothes and a husband." At nine o'clock the next morning, however, she was having an excellent time among Herbert's disordered files. John Wainwright had probably been watching her some time when she became aware of his presence just beyond the boundary of the new-business department. There was, of course, no reason for her to be self-conscious, but she was.

"I'm just helping Mr. Harris," she explained evenly, but she patted her hair in that nervous little way she detested. "He claims that getting things systematized isn't his line."

"Decidedly it seems to be yours," John Wainwright added.

"You should have said unfortunately," Emma corrected.

"And why?"

"Because men think what I am doing indispensable but of less importance than the work they like," she replied with a little edge to her voice.

"Their error," was the laconic comment. . . .

The next morning she experienced a mild return of her old cheerfulness. Something would turn up—something must; and in the meantime she was young and healthy and pretty enough and doing work that interested her. Since there was nothing more to explain to John Wainwright, her old routine was undisturbed. Emma was again intent upon doing only that which was expected of her.

The morning held John Wainwright in conference in the outer office. Whenever Emma lifted her eyes, she could see him looking earnestly into the face of the person to whom he talked. His brown hair waved back from a smooth, high forehead; his lean, well-chiseled face was more that of scholar than banker. Impelled by a motive she did not analyze, Emma looked at herself in the mirror of her hand bag. Serious, wide-set eyes, a nose with a bridge too Grecian for the mode American, a chin that balanced the nose, a forehead there was no way to conceal. The lips were not very firm, and they had a provoking way of betraying her by a quiver. But her straight hair was like sun upon ebony.

Then suddenly from the outer office words bored into Emma's consciousness. John Wainwright was considering a request for an increased loan on Alta Vista real estate—a rather remote suburban section which Emma knew to have undergone a reaction following a period of inflated values.

"At the time I requested the loan," a man was arguing, "I needed only about a quarter the house's appraised value. You lend up to fifty per cent, don't you?"

John Wainwright nodded. "In other words, you want us to increase the loan on another first mortgage substituted for the old?"

"Yes," the man replied, "and I'm in need of the money right away."

"Miss Morrison," John Wainwright directed, "will you bring me the data relating to the Craig loan in Alta Vista?"

Emma found the papers, handed them to John Wainwright and returned to her desk. She knew it was all as the man had indicated. The appraisal of the property showed a valuation of $20,000. Only $5000 was lent, but she knew that elsewhere in the files was the record of changed conditions which would certainly make a new appraisal as low as $10,000 and the present loan on the property the maximum the bank was permitted to make.

"Drive out with me and look over the place," Craig urged, and John Wainwright accompanied him immediately.

Emma sat going over the situation in her mind. The trip to Alta Vista would not reveal what she knew to be true—that two proposed factories were ruining the section for residence. John Wainwright had been in the city so short a time that he could not know what Emma had learned through the years. The executive committee of the bank had long ago formed the habit of accepting the recommendation of the trust officer. Wainwright's predecessor had made no mistakes, and only Emma knew of several she had been able to avert. Little good her vigilance had done her. It was absurd to continue—certainly if her opinion were not asked. Let Wainwright take the consequences that would be justly his.

A step in the outer office; voices—Craig's and Wainwright's. Wainwright was agreeing to recommend the loan. An hour of silence on Emma's part, and it would be all over. For once it should be simple to attend to only that which was strictly her business.

In a moment John Wainwright was alone at his desk. Emma could see the scholarly stoop of his shoulders as he bent over the papers before him. His first important step in the bank would be an error. He did not deserve that beginning. Suddenly Emma ceased futile arguing with herself. Automatically she took some papers from the drawer and carried them to the outer office.

"Don't recommend that loan," Emma jerked out the words nervously. "Look at this material and you'll see why."

She handed him all she had gathered together concerning Alta Vista. Five minutes later she heard a long whistle.

"Miss Morrison," John Wainwright said with conviction, "you ought to be trust officer of this bank."

"I haven't an LL.B.," Emma smiled.

Then the smile was lost in the old misgivings. Like all the others, John Wainwright would probably exploit her judgment. There was no use combatting it. Men are like that. And she would go on being exploited. That was her way. Women also are sometimes like that. But Emma was not unhappy. A new exaltation lifted her spirit and sent it soaring.

It was toward noon the next day that John Wainwright sought her for the first time since the epochal interview. Looking up from a monthly statement she was tabulating, Emma saw that he stood by her desk. "The president wants to see you," he said.

John Wainwright's eyes were darker and more deep-set than they had seemed before. His eyebrows came together more closely, and new lines had carved themselves into his face. It was a simple thing he said—"The president wants to see you"—and yet John Wainwright was deeply moved.

Emma left him standing there and crossed to the soft-carpeted sanctum of the bank's chief executive. The portly old gentleman adjusted his pince-nez, consulted his watch, lifted and deposited again the paper weight that lay upon his pile of open letters—all very deliberately—before he asked Emma to be seated.

"To be quite frank," he began at last, "I've had my eyes opened by someone who—er—sees from the perspective of being new to the scene. Never thought of your wanting to be pushed along. Now the boys—you know how they are. If we don't change them once in a while, they leave, but raises generally satisfy the girls. They're all thinking more about getting married than getting famous."

"But some do want to get ahead—want terribly," Emma argued.

The president cleared his throat and continued. "Yesterday Wainwright told the executive committee how you saved him from a bad mistake, mentioned that you straightened things out for the boys whenever they got in tight places, added that you were unhappy about your prospects here."

"He told you that?" Emma gasped, but the president seemed not to hear.

"So I nosed about. Several of the tellers added to the story. The upshot of it is, if you want the chance the men get, it's up to us to give it to you."

"Oh, I do want it!"

"Well, here's the idea. Your genius seems to be for organizing. There're several departments that need going over now. Start in as a kind of efficiency expert, and in a month we'll talk things over. Of course there'll be a bit more salary."

As she passed from the president's office between the pillars that made the aisles of the bank, she saw that doors had been closed to customers and that employees were leaving for luncheon. John Wainwright still sat at his desk while all about him the bank was deserted. He rose to open the little swinging gate, and Emma passed into the enclosure that belonged to the trust department.

"I want to thank you," she said, holding tight to the desk light. "In a few days you have seen what in five years no other man has guessed."

"You should have told them that you were not content to be stranded in the trust department. Men have to be told things like that."

It seemed to Emma that John Wainwright's eyes looked from depths remote yet very near, and she wondered why they filled her with a longing as sharp as pain.

"I did not tell *you,*" she said.

"I knew."

Looking into John Wainwright's eyes, steadily now, Emma understood what his stumbling, inadequate, man-made words could never convey.

"I had known only two types of women till I met you," he continued. "I thought there must be another. One type here—our wives the other—you the third!"

"And I," Emma faltered, "I had only known men without discernment."

For a moment John Wainwright's face was darkly shadowed by the things he could not say. Then a smile broke through, and Emma was at ease again.

"Life is full of little ironies," he said.

"And compensations," Emma added.

"Yes," John Wainwright answered soberly as he went out to meet his wife for luncheon.

Anxious Mothers Write the Children's Bureau

The reality of most women's lives in the 1920s was not shaped by the privilege of creating new feminist lifestyles or winning promotions in the world of business, but by a struggle to fulfill their roles as wives and mothers. This was no easy task. In addition to the problems generated by inadequate income and poverty, women faced very real fears about maternal and infant mortality. Between 1900 and 1930, approximately sixty white women and more than one hundred black women died for every ten thousand live births; infant mortality was also unacceptably high.

After 1912, mothers had a new place to turn: the Children's Bureau of the Department of Labor. Created in response to pressure from settlement leader Lillian Wald and activist Florence Kelley, the Children's Bureau saw saving children as a form of social reform. Its widely read pamphlets, *Infant Care* (1913) and *Prenatal Care* (1914), offered mothers scientific information as well as common sense advice on keeping themselves and their children healthy.

The Children's Bureau took on new responsibilities in the 1920s, when it administered the Sheppard-Towner Maternity and Infancy Protection Act. This pioneering piece of public health legislation supported the distribution of information on nutrition and hygiene, funded conferences, established well-baby clinics, and provided prenatal care for women in rural areas. The Children's Bureau boasted these programs saved sixty thousand children before the program was allowed to lapse by a conservative Congress in 1929.

Individual women were just glad to know that a branch of the government was interested in their concerns and problems. Reflecting the modern tendency to look to experts for advice, women from diverse backgrounds wrote to the Children's Bureau with questions about childcare, birth control (which the staff could not endorse for political reasons), infant hygiene, and other health-related issues. Letters such as the three included here offer a view of daily life in the 1920s, especially women's concerns about their own health and the health of their offspring.

Mrs. M. A., Minnesota
(October 19, 1921)

Dear Miss Lathrop:—

Two or three years ago, I wrote you for some pamphlets on "Care of the Baby" etc. I received them O.K. and found them very useful. But after my last Babe was two years old I gave away one or two of the pamphlets to a relative who has since gone away.

I'm to have another Babe in Jan. and I want very much a pamphlet of some kind containing instructions on the first things to do when the Baby arrives, the tying of naval cord etc. We are 7 1/2 miles from a Dr. and tho that isn't far in summer when cars are running, it's quite a distance in winter, when roads may be bad and one must depend on teams to get the Doctor when needed. I

Source: Raising a Baby the Government Way: Mothers' Letters to the Children's Bureau 1915–1932
by Molly Ladd-Taylor (New Brunswick, N.J.: Rutgers University Press), pp. 55–56, 112–114, 175–179.

want to get some practical directions so that a woman could do all the necessary things if the Dr. was not in time. I thot you would have the latest and best information and would know just what to send me.

My last Baby was born during the War and a flu epidemic, and the two Doctors in our county were both out, miles away when we wanted them. Neither one got back to the office until our Babe was several hours old. I am usually sick just a short time, 3 1/2 hours only with our first boy. The Dr. arrived half an hour too late. The second boy received the Dr.'s attention as there was time, but not the 3rd. Had no Dr. at all, but being a more experienced Mother and having my mother and a neighbor Lady with me, we got along fine. I have 3 boys.

I have been reading quite a bit about the work of the Children's Bureau. Naturally, I am much interested in the things being done for children. I consider them the Nations most important asset, tho I sadly fear that some of our politicians are blind to that fact. In the course of a few years the Babies of today will be directing affairs. How important that they should have some consideration. I wish to say that I appreciate your work very much, tho I am only one of the many common-place "Ma's." I wish you the best of success, and hope that most of us will be able to profit by the needful information obtained thru your office. I'm too far away to "shake hands" so I'll close by signing myself

Sincerely Your Friend.

*   *   *

Mrs. W. M. (February 10, 1925)

Dear Friend:—

I am enclosing a stamp for an answer & am taking the liberty to ask you for advice. You have helped me before & told me I could write & ask your advice anytime.

I am pregnant a little over 6 months. I had a longing for strawberries for breakfast one day; I thought about them before I got up, and while in the bathroom com[b]ing my hair, I wiped out the corners of my eyes with my fingers. I thought, well, it doesn't matter even if I haven't eaten any strawberries yet. I asked a neighbor about it, & she told me I sure must of marked the baby. Is this possible? She told me if you have an appetite for anything & don't eat it, & you put your hand on your face, or scratch your face, that it will mark the baby sure. I'm just worried sick. Its on my mind all the time. I wake up nights & think of things to eat; it seems I just cant get that off my mind & what can you do when you long for watermelon or mush melon, or anything out of season? I cant get these things now. Can that mark or harm the baby in any way? Oh please tell me what to do. All these thoughts about marking the baby when you don't eat what you think of, or long for, just drive me frantic. I think of one thing, & then

I think of something else, but I try to overcome these thoughts, & then I worry every time I wash or put my hand to my face that I'm marking the baby because I couldn't get or didn't eat what I longed for last. Does this come from worry? I never worried about these things the first few mo[n]ths, but her[e] of late I'm just sick from worry. I couldn't tell this to anyone else but you, as I have no mother, & no one else cares. I have kept it to myself, but I just had to go to some one. & I'm sure you will help me. I have your book on "Prenatal Care," but it doesn't say anything about longing for things to eat, so I just had to write and ask your advice. Thanking you very much. Please keep this confidentially. I am.

*   *   *

Mrs. A. E., Minnesota
(August 10, 1932)

Dear Sirs:

About six years ago I made the acquaintance of govt publications Infant Care, Prenatal Care etc. This book Infant Care did me more good than the Dr. I had at the time my baby was born. I did not have a great deal of money and the information in these booklets was [concise] and helpful. I just felt I should write and tell you how grateful I was that one can get even this little bit of free advice from our govt. We should be able to get more medical help and advice from our gov't regarding babies and child raising.

Our Gov't should have a check on doctors. We should be able to write to the Dept. of Labor and get a list of certified doctors who are capable and sincere about handling child birth. I feel that I should write of my experience. In these publications the advice is consult a reputable or family physician. I should like to ask you how one knows who *is* a reputable physician? What check other than public opinion is there on a doctor who is not reputable? Do you realize that doctors are so well organized and the profession has such ethics between themselves that it is almost impossible to check a doctor for malpractice? It requires money and is very hard to prove, so that medical men do about as they please. Is this the way it should be?

I was cared for when my son was born by Dr. B. He is supposed to be a reputable surgeon and qualified for maternity work. I was in the hospital two weeks at the time of his birth. I placed myself under his care about several months before he was born. He never advised a change of diet but I went from 110 lbs to 158 lbs the year he was born. I had a very hard birth, was torn and had three stitches, two surface and one deep tore the floor of the womb. When I left the hospital, Miss L., his head nurse, removed the stitches after they had been in two weeks. Then I went home. Dr. B. did not tell me to come back for further examination later but just let me go. I had milk fever while in the hospital and breast trouble. Then after I got home I was in bed for about two weeks with milk fever. Nothing was done about this.

My baby had colic and green bowels and loose bowels for about a year [and] cried a great deal of the time night and day, necessitating [us] moving because of his crying. The doctor did not advise a change of food for him and I thought often he would die from this. I nursed him until he was thirteen months.

He had scarlet fever when he was eleven months old. It was in the treatment of this that your books on baby care [came] in handy. I followed advice given in Infant Care and he came out of it well and without any complications. He cut all of his teeth by the time he was 13 mon. This Dr. advised me that my baby had heat rash [and] to take off his clothing and make him cooler, over the telephone. I did not follow his advice but became exasperated and called another doctor who pronounced it had scarlet fever.

About two years after my babys birth I did not feel right. I became nervous, the back of my neck and head hurt, and I felt like sitting down all of the time. I went to Dr. B. [and] explained how I felt. He did not give me a thorough examination but quickly pronounced it nervousness and gave me a bromide, which I took for a long time, just covering up my trouble. I broke down completely and went to the hospital again, where no examination was made but a goiter test was given, and I was given iodine all of the time I was there.

Later we moved to St. Paul and a more competent doctor examined me. He said I had not been properly cared for after Child birth and that I was torn. He scraped my womb and took stitches. My health has improved [but] my nervous system is badly shattered. I am sore all through my back and shoulders and the back of my neck. I haven't slept real well for a long time. Now I will never be like I was if I had been properly cared for.

I graduated from a state teachers college and taught successfully four years. I had a very fine record. My son is now healthy and very intelligent, and it is hard for me to bring him up because of this trouble. I would have enjoyed raising him very much if I had stayed well. I came from a family of eight children, was the oldest girl, and helped to raise a family of intelligent brothers and sisters. I worked and saved very hard to get my education. My memory is impaired and my time sense seems to be gone, rendering my accuracy and ability a lot less than it used to be. I am carrying on doing the best that I can.

I want to say again that those government publications were a great consolation and help to me. I have told many about them. When one hasn't much money these things are greatly appreciated.

I have suffered endless torture and unnecessary worry and pain because of this doctors carelessness or ignorance, I don't know which. Life for me will never be as full. I have no come back on him. This same man had a verdict rendered against him on a malpractice case for bone setting some time ago. Now there seems to be nothing but public opinion to combat such practice. This Dr. B. I believe is in the blue book of surgeons.

Doctors all over our land are performing illegal operations too, and there seems to be no way of checking that. All it takes is ready cash for a woman or girl to relieve herself of the responsibility of a baby. This cheapens mother-hood, ruins womanhood and encourages immorality. Operations of all kinds are emphasized because there is money in that, but maternity work is so ne-glected and a great many doctors know so little about baby raising that any old lady who has raised a family can give you better advice.

I have been wanting to put these facts before some body or organization with power and authority for a long time. I feel it my duty. Kindly read this and use your influence to better conditions in this respect. I think a gov't check on hospitals, doctors and operations is coming some day and it will be a good thing. Often times patients are unnecessarily held in hospitals after having op-erations for a longer period than necessary just to run up a bill. Every thing is done so underhanded and secretly among doctors and nurses that it is very hard for a patient to get a square deal.

This comes from the heart and soul of one who has suffered hell on earth because of carelessness and neglect by a doctor in the medical profession. I was an intelligent person seeking all the advice and knowledge I could get about babies and baby raising before my baby came. I was very pleased to get these government publications. I would have come out better, but your publications fail to tell how to detect a reputable physician, and I am marred for life because of this. The Gov't should have a list of qualified tried and true maternity doc-tors that a prospective mother could get by sending for it. This should go along with the publication. Please consider this suggestion.

Sincerely yours.

[P.S.] Kindly advise me what I can do in a case like this if there is no help for me. Please use your influence to prevent further ruination of mothers by such practice.

Female Adolescence

Kate Simon

In the transitional decade of the 1920s, coming of age for young women was full of conflicting messages and values. Movies and advertising trumpeted new styles of consumption and behavior—cigarette smok-ing, makeup, shorter dresses, and rolled down stockings—that seemed shockingly indecent to parents and grandparents. New social mores, like unchaperoned dating and petting, governed relationships be-tween young people. While the new morality had been evolving since the 1890s, it was in the 1920s that young women began to demand a more active role in sexual relationships, including an equal right to ex-perience pleasure. The primary goal for women, however, remained relationships that led to marriage.

The memoirs of travel writer Kate Simon offer a glimpse of adolescence in the late 1920s. In two volumes of autobiography *(Bronx Primitive* and *A Wider World),* Simon reconstructs her childhood in a Jewish immigrant family in the 1920s and early 1930s. Born in 1912, she emigrated with her family from Warsaw to the Bronx before World War I. The main influences on her childhood and adolescence were her family, her immigrant heritage, her schooling, and popular culture, especially the movies. "The brightest, most informative school was the movies," she recalled. "We learned how tennis was played and golf, what a swimming pool was and what to wear if you ever got to drive a car . . . and of course we learned about Love, a very foreign country like maybe China or Connecticut."

Talking big and actually acting that way were two different things. In this excerpt, a fifteen-year-old Kate makes an excursion up to Harlem, where she finds herself in deeper water than she expected. Her return to the Bronx, however, merely precipitates her decision to move out of her family home. This degree of independence (note how her mother tacitly supports the decision by giving her money) was certainly unusual for young women, even if her confused and troubling contacts with sex were not.

A new friend, May, was my number two Carola Polanski (the daughter of our janitors on Lafontaine Avenue and the first and only professional prostitute I've known). May was not as good-looking but a lot smarter, fixing a schedule with a couple of traveling salesmen rather than playing the broader, more hazardous field. Her school attendance was about like mine, full of holes, though she didn't spend her truant time in the library; she curled her hair and polished her nails and slept and shopped. Nor did she shop in Klein's on Union Square as we did, and that rarely. Her clothing looked like the ads of the big stores in the Sunday papers and she had reached the supreme acme of her own place, a one-room kitchenette apartment in Manhattan. Other than a double bed, a small table, and a couple of chairs, it had little furniture and the icebox was almost empty, but this was *living* and I felt honored each time I visited. One Friday evening she asked me if I'd like to go to Harlem; she had a date with some friends there and we'd have a good time. As usual inwardly leaping forward with eager curiosity and at the same time cowering back in fear, I said coolly, "Sure." She, dressed in her low-necked purple satin, squeezed me into a black silk dress with long, tight sleeves. "Black makes you look skinnier and older." After a long subway ride from her place on West Sixteenth Street, we reached Lenox Avenue and made our way among clusters of houses and people I had never known before. They were, for one, several shades of brown, talking, laughing, and dragging at bottles on the stoops of their houses. Their clothing was frilly and brilliant and their children slender sprites who nudged and teased and ran restlessly among them. At one corner, we stopped at a stall lit with kerosene lamps and the shine of fatty meats with a rich hot smell. We had pork sandwiches—particularly delicious because so defiantly nonkosher—and some conversation at the stall and walked on the short distance to the dance hall where May was to meet her friends.

It was a large, low-ceilinged room, dimly lit except where the band sat at one side, under bright lights that glistened on the saxophones and the oiled hair of the drummers. On the opposite side, a series of small lights over the faint gleam of glasses on a bar. (Prohibition concealed the bottles.) On the dimmed dance floor shadowy figures twirled, dipped, kicked, turned, made grotesque shapes as in a dark etching of a witches' sabbath I had seen in an old book. May and I were greeted by a couple of Negro girls. Her chumminess with them, a foreign breed to me, was awesome, as if she had easily floated across a great abyss; my friend May was a citizen of several worlds and I was very proud of her, flattered to be in her company. The girls pointed across the floor and we snaked among the dancing couples until we came to a tall, middle-aged light Negro man walking toward us and, immediately behind him, a younger, darker man. Introductions were made. May began to dance with the younger man and I was taken onto the floor by the older one, a sturdy man with a round, pleasing face. I knew how to dance, somewhat, but usually refused to because I thought I was too fat and felt ugly and was always aware of my feet as Chaplinesque—my father's description. Almost, I could lindy hop, but I had seen it described as "riotous" and as "a flying dance done by couples in which girls are thrown away." I couldn't stand the idea of being thrown, flung like a large, heavy sack, so much manipulated; I resisted, square and stolid. (I often think that fifteen overweight pounds changed the course of my life. For one thing, the sheltering in intellectual pursuits might have come later and less avidly if I could have lindy hopped really sensationally, and I might have known less serious and more playful boys, with whom I might have spent more playful, foolish hours.)

I told the man I didn't know how to dance. With, "I'll teach you, honey," the man put his arm tightly around my waist and I was skimming the floor, turning, bending, swinging, acquiescent to the skillful suggestions of his arms and fingers. He seemed pleased with himself and me and kept me on the floor for another dance and yet another. During the third dance his guiding arm grew tighter, his other arm joined it at my waist, and he began to grind his belly against mine. As I tried to pull away, the arms grew tighter. He smiled down at me. "You're a nice piece. A friend of May's? How come I haven't seen you here before?" Still trying to pull away, as politely as I could, I said that I had never been there before. "Well, I'm glad you finally came. How old are you, honey?" I gave him my stock answer, usually acceptable. "Seventeen." He laughed. "The time of the sweetest, juiciest peaches." Still holding me tight against him, he began to lead me to the edge of the floor, toward a dim area near the bar. He then backed me up against the darkest wall. His hand with the big onyx ring began to rub my breasts while the other arm held me tight to him, his erect penis pounding at my belly. I couldn't run, scream, or try to hit him. Nor did I want to. I had gotten myself into this, maybe actually wanted to, and should have known what to expect. I struggled timidly, but couldn't act offended or angry; it was all my fault. Still clasping, rubbing, pounding, he said huskily, "Let's get out of here. I've got a nice place down the next block and we can come back to dance later." "No, I'm sorry, I have to get home, my father'll kill me if I don't get back soon." "Aw, come on. It's too late to worry about your father." He looked at me, studying my face for a moment or two. "You're scared, aren't you? I'll bet you're a virgin. We'll fix that; no use carrying around a thing you don't need. That cherry's going to be busted one of these days by somebody, why not me?" I didn't know what to say or do, I didn't know how to escape, and if I did were the subway trains running? Where was the station? I was bound in panic, doomed forever, lost to whoredom and disease, as my father had promised. The man, feeling my terror, released me and led me to the bar, where he bought me a bottle of soda which I tried to drink. My strangled throat couldn't swallow it. He stared at me for a long while. "You're no May. You're no seventeen. White girls who come to Harlem come for one thing, black prick—supposed to be bigger than the white thing—to buy or to sell to, and everybody knows it. You're not ready and I hope you'll never be. Come on, let's get your coat now and I'll walk you to the station." As we left the dance hall, he grasped my arm firmly, angrily. "If I ever see you in Harlem again I'll whip the shit out of you, much worse than your father would. I mean it. You know I mean it."

At the station he paid my fare, told me where to change and to stand in the middle of the platform, where I could yell for help to the man in the change booth if anyone bothered me. There was no one else on the platform and no one came except a rat, out of one hole, a nervous shrewd look around, and into another hole. The subways were not then dangerous places, but I was afraid, afraid of the rat, of the station, of the black tunnels on either side of it, of the silence, afraid of my lack of courage, afraid of May's contempt if she would ever bother to see me again. After an endless time, the welcome rumble and the roaring light and I leaped into the nearest door, to sit near a sleeping black woman in a ragged coat held together by safety pins, a shapeless knit hat slipping to her eyes. She roused herself at 149th Street and stumbled out with me, to slant to a bench, asleep as she fell to it. I left her there, bereft of the comfort of her sloping presence, and waited for the East Side train whose slow progress would take me through familiar stations—Freeman Street, Simpson Street, Intervale Avenue—stations that were the addresses of my schoolmates, friendly stations that allayed fear; home, if I would admit it. When I got off at Allerton Avenue, the clock on the candy store window near the station accused me with two-thirty; the street lamp glared balefully. It was an innocent, peaceable neighborhood and there was little reason for fear, but I had acted like a bum, a whore, and I must be assaulted and raped, fulfilling my father's prophecy.

As I ran, my own footsteps were those of a pursuer, someone who would tear me apart.

Relieved by the sound—as soft as I could make it—of the key in our apartment lock and the door shutting behind me, I stood trying to calm my breath in the dark entrance hallway; ebbing panic gave way to resentment over our peculiar sleeping arrangements. The bedroom that might have been mine and my sister's had been given over to my cousin Bessie, for the duration of one of her long separations from her husband; my father's niece of the weak bladder was especially appreciative of the room's proximity to the bathroom. This left a convertible couch in the living room for my younger sister to use, and either my brother or myself with her, depending on who arrived earlier. (Its eccentric machinery suffered when my brother, now a large, well-fleshed adolescent, disturbed its balance as he got in. The couch began to fold slowly of itself, rolling both occupants toward the center and threatening to crush them like insects in a Venus's-flytrap. My resigned sister would wearily call "Sandwich!" and both would pull themselves out to push the sides down again.) The person to arrive home last had to take a cot out of the hall coat closet, extending its folds, dropping its feet quietly to the floor, and reaching high on the closet shelf for blankets and pillows, careful not to pull down a shower of clattering hangers and their coats. I could have pushed my way into my cousin's bed. Unthinkable. With the determination to keep late hours which my brother, a lover of sleep, hadn't yet achieved, I had learned to set up the cot smoothly, without much noise.

It was doubtful that I had awakened them; they must have been awake for some time, to judge from the intensity of the whispering that came from my parents' bedroom, off the hallway. As I lay on the cot, fully dressed, I could hear his voice: "Where does she go? With whom does she run around so late at night? You don't know? Why don't you know? Are you her mother or not? Who but an idiot, a criminal, lets a girl so young run around in the black hours? You're making a prostitute of your own daughter."

"No, I'm not. Maybe you like the idea, you talk about it so much, you've been talking about it since she was ten, even younger. Another father would worry about an accident, maybe, but you always find your way to the same idea—street girl, whore. I know she isn't and won't be and she's a lot older than fifteen. Do you know any other girl who since thirteen has earned her own lunches and carfares and even clothing, a girl who stays on through high school in spite of a father always putting rocks in her way? How long is it that she's taken money from you or me? She's even stopped eating here because you keep talking about how much butter costs and chopped meat, while you feed the fat, ignorant sisters you brought to America. And maybe soon another niece, and who needs her and the expense she'll be. And why is Bessie in the bed that should be your daughter's? She's fighting you and has the right to. She has a right to a father who encourages her, who helps her. Why do strangers, teachers in school, praise her, push her on, while you try to break her legs? She won't let you, she's becoming a *mensch* in spite of you. Leave her alone!"

"Leave her alone? Leave her alone wherever she likes, with whoever she likes? No-goods, street people, dirty people, diseased people, drinkers, maybe gangsters even?"

She broke in on his customary litany of horrors. "Stop it, already. She's foolish, all kids are, but she isn't a fool. Shut up and go to sleep." But he was wound up, driven, and couldn't stop, repeating and repeating, his voice growing louder, his words stronger, more urgent. I could easily picture his distorted face and flailing arms and suddenly imagined that he was about to hit my mother. I jumped off the cot and yelled, "Shut up, you in there. If anybody was going to make me a bum, it would have been your shitty nephew Yankel. Ask him what he tried to do to me. Ask your pal Mr. Silverberg, who took me to the movies to feel me up." I was about to mention Bessie, who had had her kind of fun with me when I was younger, but she was standing at her bedroom door, staring. (And anyhow, my bed experiences with her had been more curious than menacing.) I shouted, "Ask your friend the one-hand-under-the-sheet barber, Tony, who gave us all such cheap haircuts. And it could be that you knew about them all." As I felt again the anguished turns under Tony's pinstriped barber sheet, the twisting under Yankel's thrusting body and onion breath, the imprisonment by Bessie's grabbing thighs, the crawling of Mr. Silverberg's fat spider hands, my fear and shame in Harlem that night, I burst into an explosion of weeping. Sobbing, bellowing, "I always thought you knew it all, and didn't stop them, didn't try to protect me." I pulled my coat on, kicked the cot over, and started out the door. My mother, tight-faced and pale now standing in the hallway, asked where I was going. I didn't know, but I was never coming back. I would let her know when I had a place. She said nothing, she didn't ask me to stay, she didn't cry. When we were out of the apartment, near the stairway, she thrust five dollars into my hand, saying, "Take care of yourself." No embrace, no kiss. We didn't do such things, and in any case I needed to stay untouched, firm, gathered on myself. As I walked down the stairs, Mark opened his door, dressed in his bathrobe. He had of course heard my shouting and weeping, and repeated his offer to find me a room and pay for it; he could be dressed in a moment and we could find a room together. I hated him, too, and his wounded dark-eyed Russian love, another burden to cope with. I told him it was too early in the morning to look, for the time being I would stay with a friend, and dashed down the stairs.

CHAPTER 7

Women Face the Depression

More than any other factor, the Great Depression affected events and lives during the 1930s. Set in motion by the stock market crash in October 1929, the Depression reached its lowest point over the winter of 1932–1933. More than one quarter of the work force was unemployed, and people were literally starving in the nation's cities. Not until the early 1940s did defense mobilization finally pull the economy out of the depression.

The American political system responded to the economic crisis in unprecedented ways. President Herbert Hoover took the first steps to directly involve the federal government in the economy, but he balked at providing federal relief for the unemployed. When Franklin Delano Roosevelt was inaugurated in March of 1933, his New Deal administration accepted federal responsibility for relief, set up public works projects, and regulated the functioning of the stock market and the banks. When the initial measures of the early New Deal failed to end the Depression, Roosevelt embraced more far-reaching reforms, such as the Social Security Act of 1935, which set up old-age pensions, unemployment compensation, and the rudiments of the welfare system that lasted until the 1990s. FDR also put the force of the federal government behind workers' right to join unions by supporting the 1935 Wagner Labor Relations Act. The outpouring of New Deal legislation gave the country a sense of action and won Franklin D. Roosevelt and the Democratic party a landslide victory in 1936. But the New Deal never solved the problem of the Depression.

Oral histories of Americans who lived through the Great Depression often betray what writer Caroline Bird called an *invisible scar.* Even when good times returned during World War II and after, these survivors of the 1930s still feared a return of the economic collapse. Of course, not everyone was devastated by the Depression: middle-class families were more cushioned from the impact, and some wealthy individuals even managed to increase their holdings during the decade. On the other end of the scale, for such groups as blacks and agricultural workers, the hard times of the 1930s were not all that different from normal times. As writer Langston Hughes observed, "The depression brought everybody down a peg or two. And Negroes had but few pegs to fall."

There is also strong evidence that men and women experienced the Depression differently, both in families and on the job. When a man lost his job, he lost his identification as the breadwinner for his family, the male role. But none of the nation's housewives lost their jobs; in fact, their roles in the home took on added significance when husbands were out of work. By substituting their own labor for goods previously purchased, housewives could stretch the family budget over periods of unemployment or cuts in pay. In a study of Muncie, Indiana, sociologists Robert and Helen Lynd saw this phenomenon at work: "The men, cut adrift from their usual routine, lost much of their sense of time and dawdled helplessly and dully about the streets; while in the homes the women's world remained largely intact and the round of cooking, housecleaning, and mending became if anything more absorbing." Yet few wives (or husbands) were comfortable with this affront to traditional gender roles. "We had no choice," one woman remembered. "We just did what had to be done one day at a time." Women's added burdens during the Great Depression solidified their identification with the home and laid the groundwork for the heightened emphasis on domesticity in the postwar period.

Another way that women helped their families in the Depression also challenged traditional gender roles: if husbands were unemployed, married women could take jobs. The number of married women in the paid work force increased fifty percent during the decade.

How could women get jobs in the midst of the Great Depression? The prevailing segmentation of the work force into primarily "men's" and "women's" jobs provided the mechanism. Men were concentrated in heavy industry, manufacturing, coal mining, and construction work—the very sectors that ground to a standstill during the Depression. Women's jobs in clerical work and domestic and personal service were less affected by the downturn; furthermore, since those occupations were typed as women's, unemployed men did not cross over into them. As one commentator observed, "Few of the people who oppose married women's employment seem to realize that a coal miner or steel worker cannot very well fill the jobs of nursemaids, cleaning women, or the factory and clerical jobs now filled by women." Such sex-stereotypes gave women a small measure of protection, but at the unfortunate cost of confirming their concentration in low-paying, low-status jobs. This gender advantage also benefitted white women at the expense of minority women. To make ends meet, white women willingly took jobs usually held by minority women, such as domestic servants. White men also took jobs previously held by minority men.

The politics and government of the New Deal represent a final area where women made a difference in the 1930s. The dramatic expansion of social welfare programs provided jobs and opportunities for women reformers long active in the field. Women played an especially large role in the Works Projects Administration (WPA), the main relief agency, and in the administration of social security, fair labor standards, and welfare. Women also took on larger roles in the revitalized Democratic party.

At the center of many of these developments for women in the New Deal stood First Lady Eleanor Roosevelt. Close by were Secretary of Labor Frances Perkins, the first woman to serve in the cabinet; social reformer-turned-politician Molly Dewson, head of the Women's Division of the Democratic National Committee; and a network of talented women who took on high-level positions throughout the New Deal bureaucracy. But Eleanor Roosevelt was by far the decade's most widely admired woman. Through her newspaper column, her wide-ranging travels, and her advocacy of such disadvantaged groups as blacks, youth, and women, she served as the conscience of the New Deal.

The Despair of Unemployed Women

Meridel LeSueur

In the 1930s, writer Meridel LeSueur chronicled forgotten women, the women who endured the Depression with a very privatized kind of despair. LeSueur's writings, which covered such subjects as strikes, unemployment, and the plight of the farmers, convey the human side of the Great Depression. As one historian observed, "Mass employment is both a statistic and an empty feeling in the stomach. To fully comprehend it, you have to both see the figures and feel the emptiness." Meridel LeSueur helps us to feel the emptiness.

LeSueur, who was born in Iowa in 1900, spent most of her life in the Midwest. Her family's radical roots—in socialism, the Industrial Workers of the World, populism, and farmer-labor organizing—combined with a stubborn frontier spirit to influence her political development, and in the 1920s she joined the Communist party. In the 1930s, Meridel LeSueur was on the staff of the radical magazine *New Masses*, and also wrote for *The Daily Worker, Partisan Review*, and *The Nation*. She was blacklisted during the McCarthy era, only to be rediscovered in the 1960s and 1970s when her writings and speeches found new audiences.

When LeSueur submitted "Women on the Breadlines" to *New Masses* in December 1932, the editors chided her for her "defeatist attitude" and "her nonrevolutionary spirit," but published the piece nonetheless. The scene takes place in 1932, the worst year of the Depression. The situation—the waiting room of a women's employment bureau, populated by a ragged collection of women, young and old, single and married, who desperately need work—defies optimism. When these clients leave the employment agency at the end of the day, still jobless, they will continue their struggle to survive.

The problems of unemployed women (the Women's Bureau estimated their numbers at two million in 1931) were especially acute. The public image of the unemployed worker was a man; women were assumed (incorrectly) to have husbands, brothers, or fathers to take care of them, even though many were heads of households or responsible for dependents. Despite the title of LeSueur's piece, it was rare to see women in line for free food at the soup kitchens. New Deal programs, which did not go into effect until 1933, gave low priority to the needs of single women in cities. Even with LeSueur's haunting piece, these women remained practically invisible.

I am sitting in the city free employment bureau. It's the women's section. We have been sitting here now for four hours. We sit here every day, waiting for a job. There are no jobs. Most of us have had no breakfast. Some have had scant rations for over a year. Hunger makes a human being lapse into a state of lethargy, especially city hunger. Is there any place else in the world where a human being is supposed to go hungry amidst plenty without an outcry, without protest, where only the boldest steal or kill for bread, and the timid crawl the streets, hunger like the beak of a terrible bird at the vitals?

We sit looking at the floor. No one dares think of the coming winter. There are only a few more days of summer. Everyone is anxious to get work to lay up something for that long siege of bitter cold. But there is no work. Sitting in the room we all know it. That is why we don't talk much. We look at the floor dreading to see that knowledge in each other's eyes. There is a kind of humiliation in it. We look away from each other. We look at the floor. It's too terrible to see this animal terror in each other's eyes.

So we sit hour after hour, day after day, waiting for a job to come in. There are many women for a single job. A thin sharp woman sits inside a wire cage looking at a book. For four hours we have watched her looking at that book. She has a hard little eye. In the small bare room there are half a dozen women sitting on the benches waiting. Many come and go. Our faces are all familiar to each other, for we wait here every day.

This is a domestic employment bureau. Most of the women who come here are middle aged, some have families, some have raised their families and are now alone, some have men who are out of work. Hard times and the man leaves to hunt for work. He doesn't find it. He drifts on. The woman probably doesn't hear from him for a long time. She expects it. She isn't surprised. She struggles alone to feed the many mouths. Sometimes she gets help from the charities. If she's clever she can get herself a good living from the charities, if she's

Source: Meridel LeSueur, "Women on the Breadlines," *New Masses,* January 1932.

naturally a lick spittle, naturally a little docile and cunning. If she's proud then she starves silently, leaving her children to find work, coming home after a day's searching to wrestle with her house, her children.

Some such story is written on the faces of all these women. There are young girls too, fresh from the country. Some are made brazen too soon by the city. There is a great exodus of girls from the farms into the city now. Thousands of farms have been vacated completely in Minnesota. The girls are trying to get work. The prettier ones can get jobs in the stores when there are any, or waiting on table, but these jobs are only for the attractive and the adroit. The others, the real peasants, have a more difficult time.

Bernice sits next to me. She is a Polish woman of thirty-five. She has been working in people's kitchens for fifteen years or more. She is large, her great body in mounds, her face brightly scrubbed. She has a peasant mind and finds it hard even yet to understand the maze of the city where trickery is worth more than brawn. Her blue eyes are not clever but slow and trusting. She suffers from loneliness and lack of talk. When you speak to her, her face lifts and brightens as if you had spoken through a great darkness, and she talks magically of little things as if the weather were magic, or tells some crazy tale of her adventures on the city streets, embellishing them in bright colors until they hang heavy and thick like embroidery. She loves the city anyhow. It's exciting to her, like a bazaar. She loves to go shopping and get a bargain, hunting out the places where stale bread and cakes can be had for a few cents. She likes walking the streets looking for men to take her to a picture show. Sometimes she goes to five picture shows in one day, or she sits through one the entire day until she knows all the dialog by heart.

She came to the city a young girl from a Wisconsin farm. The first thing that happened to her, a charlatan dentist took out all her good shining teeth and the fifty dollars she had saved working in a canning factory. After that she met men in the park who told her how to look out for herself, corrupting her peasant mind, teaching her to mistrust everyone. Sometimes now she forgets to mistrust everyone and gets taken in. They taught her to get what she could for nothing, to count her change, to go back if she found herself cheated, to demand her rights.

She lives alone in little rooms. She bought seven dollars' worth of second-hand furniture eight years ago. She rents a room for perhaps three dollars a month in an attic, sometimes in a cold house. Once the house where she stayed was condemned and everyone else moved out and she lived there all winter alone on the top floor. She spent only twenty-five dollars all winter.

She wants to get married but she sees what happens to her married friends, left with children to support, worn out before their time. So she stays single. She is virtuous. She is slightly deaf from hanging out clothes in winter. She had done people's washings and cooking for fifteen years and in that time saved thirty dollars. Now she hasn't worked steady for a year and she has spent the thirty dollars. She had dreamed of having a little house or a houseboat perhaps with a spot of ground for a few chickens. This dream she will never realize.

She has lost all her furniture now along with the dream. A married friend whose husband is gone gives her a bed for which she pays by doing a great deal of work for the woman. She comes here every day now sitting bewildered, her pudgy hands folded in her lap. She is hungry. Her great flesh has begun to hang in folds. She has been living on crackers. Sometimes a box of crackers lasts a week. She has a friend who's a baker and he sometimes steals the stale loaves and brings them to her.

A girl we have seen every day all summer went crazy yesterday at the Y.W. She went into hysterics, stamping her feet and screaming.

She hadn't had work for eight months. "You've got to give me something," she kept saying. The woman in charge flew into a rage that probably came from days and days of suffering on her part, because she is unable to give jobs, having none. She flew into a rage at the girl and there they were facing each other in a rage both helpless, helpless. This woman told me once that she could hardly bear the suffering she saw, hardly hear it, that she couldn't eat sometimes and had nightmares at night.

So they stood there, the two women, in a rage, the girl weeping and the woman shouting at her. In the eight months of unemployment she had gotten ragged, and the woman was shouting that she would not send her out like that. "Why don't you shine your shoes," she kept scolding the girl, and the girl kept sobbing and sobbing because she was starving.

"We can't recommend you like that," the harrassed Y.W.C.A. woman said, knowing she was starving, unable to do anything. And the girls and the women sat docilely, their eyes on the ground, ashamed to look at each other, ashamed of something.

Sitting here waiting for a job, the women have been talking in low voices about the girl Ellen. They talk in low voices with not too much pity for her, unable to see through the mist of their own torment. "What happened to Ellen?" one of them asks. She knows the answer already. We all know it.

A young girl who went around with Ellen tells about seeing her last evening back of a cafe downtown, outside the kitchen door, kicking, showing her legs so that the cook came out and gave her some food and some men gathered in the alley and threw small coin on the ground for a look at her legs. And the girl says enviously that Ellen had a swell breakfast and treated her to one too, that cost two dollars.

A scrub woman whose hips are bent forward from stooping with hands gnarled like watersoaked branches clicks her tongue in disgust. No one saves their money, she says, a little money and these foolish young things buy a hat, a dollar for breakfast, a bright scarf. And they do. If you've ever been without money, or food, something very strange happens when you get a bit of money, a kind of madness. You don't care. You can't remember that you had no money before, that the money will be gone. You can remember nothing but that there is the money for which you have been suffering. Now here it is. A lust takes hold of you. You see food in the windows. In imagination you eat hugely; you taste a thousand meals. You look in windows. Colors are brighter; you buy something to dress up in. An excitement takes hold of you. You know it is suicide but you can't help it. You must have food, dainty, splendid food and a bright hat so once again you feel blithe, rid of that ratty gnawing shame.

"I guess she'll go on the street now," a thin woman says faintly, and no one takes the trouble to comment further. Like every commodity now the body is difficult to sell and the girls say you're lucky if you get fifty cents.

It's very difficult and humiliating to sell one's body.

Perhaps it would make it clear if one were to imagine having to go out on the street to sell, say, one's overcoat. Suppose you have to sell your coat so you can have breakfast and a place to sleep, say, for fifty cents. You decide to sell your only coat. You take it off and put it on your arm. The street, that has before been just a street, now becomes a mart, something entirely different. You must approach someone now and admit you are destitute and are now selling your clothes, your most intimate possessions. Everyone will watch you talking to the stranger showing him your overcoat, what a good coat it is. People will stop and watch curiously. You will be quite naked on the street. It is even harder to try to sell one's self, more humiliating. It is even humiliating to try to sell one's labor. When there is no buyer.

The thin woman opens the wire cage. There's a job for a nursemaid, she says. The old gnarled women, like old horses, know that no one will have them walk the streets with the young so they don't move. Ellen's friend gets up and goes to the window. She is unbelievably jaunty. I know she hasn't had work since last January. But she has a flare of life in her that glows like a tiny red flame and some tenacious thing, perhaps only youth, keeps it burning bright. Her legs are thin but the runs in her old stockings are neatly mended clear down her flat shank. Two bright spots of rouge conceal her pallor. A narrow belt is drawn tightly around her thin waist, her long shoulders stoop and the blades show. She runs wild as a colt hunting pleasure, hunting sustenance.

It's one of the great mysteries of the city where women go when they are out of work and hungry. There are not many women in the bread line. There are no flop houses for women as there are for men, where a bed can be had for a quarter or less. You don't see women lying on the floor at the mission in the free flops. They obviously don't sleep in the jungle or under newspapers in the park. There is no law I suppose against their being in these places but the fact is they rarely are.

Yet there must be as many women out of jobs in cities and suffering extreme poverty as there are men. What happens to them? Where do they go? Try to get into the Y.W. without any money or looking down at heel. Charities take care of very few and only those that are called "deserving." The lone girl is under suspicion by the virgin women who dispense charity.

I've lived in cities for many months broke, without help, too timid to get in bread lines. I've known many women to live like this until they simply faint on the street from privations, without saying a word to anyone. A woman will shut herself up in a room until it is taken away from her, and eat a cracker a day and be as quiet as a mouse so there are no social statistics concerning her.

I don't know why it is, but a woman will do this unless she has dependents, will go for weeks verging on starvation, crawling in some hole, going through the streets ashamed, sitting in libraries, parks, going for days without speaking to a living soul like some exiled beast, keeping the runs mended in her stockings, shut up in terror in her own misery, until she becomes too super-sensitive and timid to even ask for a job.

Bernice says even strange men she has met in the park have sometimes, that is in better days, given her a loan to pay her room rent. She has always paid them back.

In the afternoon the young girls, to forget the hunger and the deathly torture and fear of being jobless, try to pick up a man to take them to a ten-cent show. They never go to more expensive ones, but they can always find a man willing to spend a dime to have the company of a girl for the afternoon.

Sometimes a girl facing the night without shelter will approach a man for lodging. A woman always asks a man for help. Rarely another woman. I have known girls to sleep in men's rooms for the night on a pallet without molestation and be given breakfast in the morning.

It's no wonder these young girls refuse to marry, refuse to rear children. They are like certain savage tribes, who, when they have been conquered, refuse to breed.

Not one of them but looks forward to starvation for the coming winter. We are in a jungle and know it. We are beaten, entrapped. There is no way out. Even if there were a job, even if that thin acrid woman came and gave everyone in the room a job for a few days, a few hours, at thirty cents an hour, this would all be repeated tomorrow, the next day and the next.

Not one of these women but knows that despite years of labor there is only starvation, humiliation in front of them.

Mrs. Grey, sitting across from me, is a living spokesman for the futility of labor. She is a warning. Her hands are scarred with labor. Her body is a great puckered scar. She has given birth to six children, buried three, supported them all alive and dead, bearing them, burying them, feeding them. Bred in hunger they have been spare, susceptible to disease. For seven years she tried to save her boy's arm from amputation, diseased from tuberculosis of the bone. It is almost too suffocating to think of that long close horror of years of child-bearing, child-feeding, rearing, with the bare suffering of providing a meal and shelter.

Now she is fifty. Her children, economically insecure, are drifters. She never hears of them. She doesn't know if they are alive. She doesn't know if she is alive. Such subtleties of suffering are not for her. For her the brutality of hunger and cold. Not until these are done away with can those subtle feelings that make a human being be indulged.

She is lucky to have five dollars ahead of her. That is her security. She has a tumor that she will die of. She is thin as a worn dime with her tumor sticking out of her side. She is brittle and bitter. Her face is not the face of a human being. She has borne more than it is possible for a human being to bear. She is reduced to the least possible denominator of human feelings.

It is terrible to see her little bloodshot eyes like a beaten hound's, fearful in terror.

We cannot meet her eyes. When she looks at any of us we look away. She is like a woman drowning and we turn away. We must ignore those eyes that are surely the eyes of a person drowning, doomed. She doesn't cry out. She goes down decently. And we all look away.

The young ones know though. I don't want to marry. I don't want any children. So they all say. No children. No marriage. They arm themselves alone, keep up alone. The man is helpless now. He cannot provide. If he propagates he cannot take care of his young. The means are not in his hands. So they live alone. Get what fun they can. The life risk is too horrible now. Defeat is too clearly written on it.

So we sit in this room like cattle, waiting for a nonexistent job, willing to work to the farthest atom of energy, unable to work, unable to get food and lodging, unable to bear children—here we must sit in this shame looking at the floor, worse than beasts at a slaughter.

It is appalling to think that these women sitting so listless in the room may work as hard as it is possible for a human being to work, may labor night and day, like Mrs. Gray wash streetcars from midnight to dawn and offices in the early evening, scrub for fourteen and fifteen hours a day, sleep only five hours or so, do this their whole lives, and never earn one day of security, having always before them the pit of the future. The endless labor, the bending back, the water-soaked hands, earning never more than a week's wages, never having in their hands more life than that.

It's not the suffering of birth, death, love that the young reject, but the suffering of endless labor without dream, eating the spare bread in bitterness, being a slave without the security of a slave.

American Women Ask Eleanor Roosevelt for Help

Many Americans have always been poor, and for them the Great Depression of the 1930s meant hard times as usual. But there were quite a few Americans who had been getting by all right until 1929, and then, through no fault of their own, found themselves down and out. These "newly poor" were in many ways the most damaged by the depression experience.

Many Americans asked for help directly from the White House. Both Franklin and Eleanor Roosevelt encouraged ordinary citizens to write to them with their observations and troubles. People responded in unprecedented numbers; letters poured into the White House at a rate of five to eight thousand a day throughout the New Deal, all of which were answered or passed on to the appropriate government agency for action. People really felt that the Roosevelts cared about their problems and would try to correct injustices once they knew about them.

It was in that spirit that these women wrote to Eleanor Roosevelt with their problems. A California woman told a story of downward social mobility, an upstate New York woman asked for a layette of baby clothes, a black Mississippian requested a loan, a Pennsylvania woman asked for the First Lady's cast-off clothes, and a twelve-year-old girl asked for roller skates because "my friends at school have skates and laugh because I don't have some." Although Eleanor Roosevelt's exact responses to these pleas are not known, she probably forwarded these requests to the appropriate relief authorities or local charities. When such requests came accompanied by a cover letter from the White House, they often got results.

Eureka, Calif.
June 14, 1934

Mrs. F. D. Roosevelt
Washington, D.C.

Dear Mrs. Roosevelt:

I know you are overburdened with requests for help and if my plea cannot be recognized, I'll understand it is because you have so many others, all of them worthy.

But I am not asking for myself alone. It is as a potential mother and as one woman to another.

My husband and I are a young couple of very simple, almost poor families. We married eight years ago on the proverbial shoe-string but with a wealth of love. We both wanted more than anything else to establish a home and maintain that home in a charming, quiet manner. I had a job in the County Court House before I married and my husband was, and is, a surveyor. I kept my job as it seemed the best and only way for us to pay for a home as quickly as we could. His work was not always permanent, as surveyors jobs seldom are, but we managed to build our home and furnish it comfortably. Perhaps we were

Source: Robert S. McElvaine, ed., *Down & Out in the Great Depression: Letters from the Forgotten Man* (Chapel Hill: University of North Carolina Press, 1983), pp. 54–55, 62–63, 86–87, 164, 116.

foolish to put all our money into it but we felt it was not only a pleasure but a saving for the future.

Then came the depression. My work has continued and my salary alone has just been sufficient to make our monthly payments on the house and keep our bills paid. But with the exception of two and one-half months work with the U.S. Coast and Geodetic Survey under the C.W.A., my husband has not had work since August, 1932.

My salary could continue to keep us going, but—I am to have a baby. We wanted one before but felt we should have more assurance for the future before we deliberately took such a responsibility. But now that it has happened, I won't give it up! I'm willing to undergo any hardship for myself and I can get a leave of absence from my job for a year. But can't you, won't you do something so my husband can have a job, at least during that year? I realize there is going to be a lot of expense and we have absolutely nothing but our home which still carries a mortgage of $2000. We can't lose that because our baby will need it. And I can't wait until the depression is over to have a baby. I will be 31 in October and I'll soon be too old.

We had such high hopes in the early spring that the Coast and Geodetic work would continue. Tommy, my husband, had a good position there, and we were so happy. We thought surely our dreams of a family could come true. Then the work ended and like "The best laid plans of mice and men" our hopes were crushed again. But now Fate has taken it into her own hands and left us to work it out somehow. I'm happy, of course, but Tommy is nearly out of his head. He has tried every conceivable prospect but you must know how even pick and shovel jobs do not exist.

If the Coast and Geodetic work could continue or if he could get a job with the Bureau of Public Roads,—anything in the surveying line. A year is all I ask and after that I can go back to work and we can work out our own salvation. But to have this baby come to a home full of worry and despair, with no money for things it needs, is not fair. It needs and deserves a happy start in life.

As I said before, if it were only ourselves, or if there were something we could do about it, we would never ask for help. We have always stood on our own feet and been proud and happy. But you are a mother and you'll understand this crisis.

Tommy is competent and dependable. He has a surveyor's license and was level man for the U.S. Coast and Geodetic work in this (Humboldt) county. He will go away from home for work, if necessary, but, dear Mrs. Roosevelt, will you see if you can arrange for a job for him? It sounds impossible, I know, but I am at a point where I *ask* the impossible. I have to be selfish now.

I shall hope and pray for a reply and tell myself that you are the busiest woman in America, if I don't receive it. I am going to continue to work as long as I can and then—an interval of waiting. God grant it will be serene and untroubled for my baby's sake.

> *Very sincerely yours,*
> *Mrs. M. H. A.*
> *Eureka,*
> *Humboldt County,*
> *California*

                                    *   *   *

> Troy, N.Y.
> Jan. 2, 1935.

Dear Mrs. Roosevelt,

About a month ago I wrote you asking if you would buy some baby clothes for me with the understanding that I was to repay you as soon as my husband got enough work. Several weeks later I received a reply to apply to a Welfare Association so I might receive the aid I needed. Do you remember?

Please Mrs. Roosevelt, I do not want charity, only a chance from someone who will trust me until we can get enough money to repay the amount spent for the things I need. As a proof that I really am sincere, I am sending you two of my dearest possessions to keep as security, a ring my husband gave me before we were married, and a ring my mother used to wear. Perhaps the actual value of them is not high, but they are worth a lot to me. If you will consider buying the baby clothes, please keep them (rings) until I send you the money you spent. It is very hard to face bearing a baby we cannot afford to have, and the fact that it is due to arrive soon, and still there is no money for the hospital or clothing, does not make it any easier. I Have decided to stay home, keeping my 7 year old daughter from school to help with the smaller children when my husband has work. The oldest little girl is sick now, and has never been strong, so I would not depend on her. The 7 year old one is a good willing little worker and somehow we must manage—but without charity.

If you still feel you cannot trust me, it is allright and I can only say I donot blame you, but if you decide my word is worth anything with so small a security, here is a list of what I will need-but I will need it very soon.

2 shirts, silk and wool. size 2

3 pr. stockings, silk and wool, 4 1/2 or 4

3 straight flannel bands

2 slips—outing flannel

2 muslim dresses

1 sweater

1 wool bonnet

2 pr. wool booties

2 doz. diapers 30 × 30—or 27 × 27

1 large blanket (baby) about 45" or 50"

3 outing flannel nightgaowns

If you will get these for me I would rather no one knew about it. I promise to repay the cost of the layette as soon as possible. We will all be very grateful to you, and I will be more than happy.

Sincerely yours,
Mrs. H. E. C.

* * *

Tupelo. Miss
Feb. 4th 1935

Mr President and Wife

Im about to ask you A Question that I hate to trouble you with. but Ive tried hard to get by With out any assistance but Ive Nearly got to road end, I Just Cant make my way as I will explain. Now Mr President I owe Several different people that are compeling me to pay them They are Sending Squires an colectors To me every Week I hate not to pay them but I Just can not Ive a Job. but owing from 8 to 12 different ones It make it difficult To pay be Sides the fuel food House rent That has to be paid each week an fuel each Time it is ordered then Mr president the food is a Necessity We have to have that to keep going on our Jobs. every thing is very high in Tupelo but Im thankful To have a Job. Making Something but not nearly enough To pay those Bills I owe. Im not Writing Just because I can write for I have tried to borrow from the white people here and they say they have not got any money So I cannot get help from them as I used to. Now I am asking you please to help Me. Ive a little child 4 years a mother 62 years an She has ben Sick for 15 or 18 years Ive got along all right till the middle of last year up till now. It has been hard for 7 or 8 month doctor Bills Groceries coal Bill I do not ask for Money for foolish thing an I do not ask you to give it to me. I am only asking a loan an I will pay you as you desire Me to by the week or by the month only as you say. but please mr president keep This confidential as I would loose my Job. you See Mr President I can pay one person easier Than a lots of people. These Bill has got a head of me when I didnt have any work as they are demanding their pay please if It will not Trouble you to much help me I will appreciste it More than Any Thing. My bill Totals $150.00 that is for The Thing That I have Necessaraly needed not one bit of foolishness for I Tries to put every cent to good use please

help me in the Name of the lord an I will pay you back. I have not got any thing
for Security but my honor if you will Trust me Thank you

A Colored Friend down in Tupelo Miss
G. T. [female]
General delivery

P.S. please answer direct to me

*   *   *

Philadelphia Pa.
Feb'y 19, 1935.

Dear Mrs. Roosevelt:

After Seeing So many of your pictures in the Magazines and papers, and
seeing that you always look so well dressed, a thought came to me. that you
may have a few old discarded dresses among the ones that you have tired of
that you would like to get rid of, and do some one good at the same time. I have
waited and waited for work until every thing I had is about finished. I can sew
and would only be too glad to take two old things and put them to gether and
make a new one. I don't care what it is, any thing from an old bunch of stockings to an old Sport Suit or an old afternoon dress, in fact. Any-thing a lady 40
years of age can wear. I will await an early reply.
     Thanking you in advance.

Mrs. E. T.
Phila. Pa.

*   *   *

Blacksburg S.C.
January 19. [1934]

Dear Mrs. Roosevelt,

Mrs. Roosevelt will you send me and my sister, Ruth, a pair of ball bearing roller skates? Our friends have skates and we are not able to buy them. We
sure will thank you if you will.

yours trully,
L. L. [female]

P.S. I am twelve years old and in the sixth grade at Blacksburg Grammar school. My friends at school have skates and laugh because I dont have some.

your's trully
L.

The Dust Bowl

Ann Marie Low

In addition to the ravages of the Great Depression, during the 1930s residents of the Great Plains endured the worst drought recorded in the climatological history of the United States. The "dirty thirties" saw crops wither and livestock die when the rains failed to material-ize. Then the loosened soil was swirled into huge dust storms that de-scended on towns like tornadoes, turning day into night and en-veloping residents in clouds of dirt, soot, and dust. Only in 1941 did the drought end, simultaneously with war mobilization, breaking the grip of the Depression.

Although the states of Oklahoma, Texas, and Arkansas were the hardest hit by the drought, the northern plains did not escape its im-pact. This memoir by Ann Marie Low, *Dust Bowl Diary*, describes her family's experience in the Badlands of southeastern North Dakota. Born in 1912, Ann Marie kept diaries from 1927 to 1937 that record both a young woman's coming of age and the devastation wrecked by drought and depression on American agriculture.

The story that Ann Marie Low recorded in her diary reflected the frustrations of farm life for an ambitious young woman who nonethe-less was devoted to her family and their commitment to keeping their farm going. The diary describes the daily struggle with the dust storms that invaded North Dakota, and it conveys the hard work (usually without benefit of electricity) that was the lot of women on the farm. One of three children, Ann Marie took teaching jobs to help out with family finances, especially to help pay for her siblings' educations. Al-though she acknowledges several marriage proposals, she saw mat-rimony as a threat to women's independence. The last entry in her diary, dated June 4, 1937, when she was twenty-five years old, records her frustration at her lost youth and the bleak prospects for the future: "This is a round that will go on forever. At least it will go on until my youth is gone. *Somehow, I've got to get out!!*"

Source: Reprinted from *Dust Bowl Diary*, by Ann Marie Low, pp. 95–98, by permission of the Uni-versity of Nebraska Press. Copyright 1984 by the University of Nebraska Press.

April 25, 1934, Wednesday

Last weekend was the worst dust storm we ever had. We've been having quite a bit of blowing dirt every year since the drouth started, not only here, but all over the Great Plains. Many days this spring the air is just full of dirt coming, literally, for hundreds of miles. It sifts into everything. After we wash the dishes and put them away, so much dust sifts into the cupboards we must wash them again before the next meal. Clothes in the closets are covered with dust.

Last weekend no one was taking an automobile out for fear of ruining the motor. I rode Roany to Frank's place to return a gear. To find my way I had to ride right beside the fence, scarcely able to see from one fence post to the next.

Newspapers say the deaths of many babies and old people are attributed to breathing in so much dirt.

May 7, 1934, Monday

The dirt is still blowing. Last weekend Bud [her brother] and I helped with the cattle and had fun gathering weeds. Weeds give us greens for salad long before anything in the garden is ready. We use dandelions, lamb's quarter, and sheep sorrel. I like sheep sorrel best. Also, the leaves of sheep sorrel, pounded and boiled down to a paste, make a good salve.

Still no job. I'm trying to persuade Dad I should apply for rural school #3 out here where we went to school. I don't see a chance of getting a job in a high school when so many experienced teachers are out of work.

He argues that the pay is only $60.00 a month out here, while even in a grade school in town I might get $75.00. Extra expenses in town would probably eat up that extra $15.00. Miss Eston, the practice teaching supervisor, told me her salary has been cut to $75.00 after all the years she has been teaching in Jamestown. She wants to get married. School boards will not hire married women teachers in these hard times because they have husbands to support them. Her fiancé is the sole support of his widowed mother and can't support a wife, too. So she is just stuck in her job, hoping she won't get another salary cut because she can scarcely live on what she makes and dress the way she is expected to.

Dad argues the patrons always stir up so much trouble for a teacher at #3 some teachers have quit in mid-term. The teacher is also the janitor, so the hours are long.

I figure I can handle the work, kids, and patrons. My argument is that by teaching here I can work for my room and board at home, would not need new clothes, and so could send most of my pay to Ethel [her sister] and Bud.

In April, Ethel had quit college, saying she did not feel well.

May 21, 1934, Monday

Ethel has been having stomach trouble. Dad has been taking her to doctors though suspecting her trouble is the fact that she often goes on a diet that may affect her health. The local doctor said he thought it might be chronic appendicitis, so Mama took Ethel by train to Valley City last week to have a surgeon there remove her appendix.

Saturday Dad, Bud, and I planted an acre of potatoes. There was so much dirt in the air I couldn't see Bud only a few feet in front of me. Even the air in the house was just a haze. In the evening the wind died down, and Cap came to take me to the movie. We joked about how hard it is to get cleaned up enough to go anywhere.

The newspapers report that on May 10 there was such a strong wind the experts in Chicago estimated 12,000,000 tons of Plains soil was dumped on that city. By the next day the sun was obscured in Washington, D.C., and ships 300 miles out at sea reported dust settling on their decks.

Sunday the dust wasn't so bad. Dad and I drove cattle to the Big Pasture. Then I churned butter and baked a ham, bread, and cookies for the men, as no telling when Mama will be back.

May 30, 1934, Wednesday

Ethel got along fine, so Mama left her at the hospital and came to Jamestown by train Friday. Dad took us both home.

The mess was incredible! Dirt had blown into the house all week and lay inches deep on everything. Every towel and curtain was just black. There wasn't a clean dish or cooking utensil. There was no food. Oh, there were eggs and milk and one loaf left of the bread I baked the weekend before. I looked in the cooler box down the well (our refrigerator) and found a little ham and butter. It was late, so Mama and I cooked some ham and eggs for the men's supper because that was all we could fix in a hurry. It turned out they had been living on ham and eggs for two days.

Mama was very tired. After she had fixed starter for bread, I insisted she go to bed and I'd do all the dishes.

It took until 10 o'clock to wash all the dirty dishes. That's not wiping them—just washing them. The cupboards had to be washed out to have a clean place to put them.

Saturday was a busy day. Before starting breakfast I had to sweep and wash all the dirt off the kitchen and dining room floors, wash the stove, pancake griddle, and dining room table and chairs. There was cooking, baking, and churning to be done for those hungry men. Dad is 6 feet 4 inches tall, with a big frame. Bud is 6 feet 3 inches and almost as big-boned as Dad. We say feeding them is like filling a silo.

Mama couldn't make bread until I carried water to wash the bread mixer. I couldn't churn until the churn was washed and scalded. We just couldn't do anything until something was washed first. Every room had to have dirt almost shoveled out of it before we could wash floors and furniture.

We had no time to wash clothes, but it was necessary. I had to wash out the boiler, wash tubs, and the washing machine before we could use them. Then every towel, curtain, piece of bedding, and garment had to be taken outdoors to have as much dust as possible shaken out before washing. The cistern is dry, so I had to carry all the water we needed from the well.

That evening Cap came to take me to the movie, as usual. Ixnay. I'm sorry I snapped at Cap. It isn't his fault, or anyone's fault, but I was tired and cross. Life in what the newspapers call "the Dust Bowl" is becoming a gritty nightmare.

The Life Cycle of a White Southern Farm Woman

Margaret Jarman Hagood

The lives of white tenant farm women in the South shared certain similarities with the lives of rural women everywhere: harsh conditions, isolation, and unpredictable cash flow depending on the harvest. The agricultural system in the South was dominated by an overdependence on cash crops such as cotton or tobacco and by a sharecropping system where black and white farm families often worked land owned by white landowners. Gender roles were clearly defined. Women had full responsibility for running the household, while men oversaw farm duties. Wives also did field work during certain seasons, although husbands rarely (if ever) reciprocated by helping out with household chores. In addition, southern white women had a fertility rate (6.4 live births per married woman, excluding stillbirths and abortions), which was almost three times the national average.

Sociologist Margaret Jarman Hagood (1907–1963) first uncovered this high fertility rate while researching her doctoral dissertation in statistics at the University of North Carolina. Curious about the social and economic context, she embarked on sixteen months of interviews with 254 white southern women. Since she herself was from Georgia, married and the mother of a child, she found that women felt comfortable discussing intimate details (such as contraception and childbirth) with her. The results of her study were published in 1939 as *Mothers of the South*.

Hagood's chapter, "Of the Tenant Child as Mother to the Woman," utilizes the concept of *life cycle* to trace the experiences of

Mollie Goodwin as she matures and marries. The life cycle approach captures the development of this individual over time and suggests how her life story interacts with broader themes such as farm tenancy, adolescence and education, work roles, marriage patterns, and fertility.

The story of the tenant child begins more than a quarter of a century ago. On Monday ten-year-old Mollie woke up when her mother lifted the stove lid and began making the fire. She slipped from underneath the cover easily, so as not to disturb her little brother, and took down her last year's red dress, which had been fleecy and warm, but now was slick and thin. . . .

Mollie's plump arms stretched tight the seams of her outgrown dress, and as she leaned over to pick up fresh wood for the fire, she felt her dress split at the shoulder. She wondered what she would do the washing in if she couldn't get into the old dress next Monday or the one after that. Her father's rule was that her two new dresses of the same cotton fleece lined material, one red and one blue, must never be worn except for school or Sunday School. She had no sisters to hand down clothes to her, for the other four children were boys. Some girls she knew wore overalls for working, but her father would not allow that either. A wicked thought came to her mind—maybe if she had nothing to wear to wash in next Monday, she wouldn't have to wash and instead could go to school with her brothers. She could iron on Tuesday inside the house in her underwear—then a vision of her mother bending over the wash tubs, moaning with the pain in her back, made her put aside the daydream of a washless Monday.

After breakfast Mollie's older brother cut wood and started a fire under the wash pot while she and the brother next younger drew and carried water from the well. Then the boys left for the mile walk to the one-teacher school and Mollie started back for the house to get up the clothes. She lingered on the way, debating whether her father's overalls, stiff with a week's accumulation of winter mud and stable stains, were harder to wash than the baby's soiled diapers. They *were* harder, but the odor from the diapers made you feel you couldn't go on. It was a sensory symbol of babies, of her sick mother, of crying, little brothers, and now was vaguely mixed with her distaste for what two girl friends had told her at recess last week about how babies come. Mollie tried not to think about this and hoped she never had any babies.

The school bell's ringing interrupted her musing and reminded Mollie of how much she wanted to be there. Her dress was as new as any in school and its color still bright. The teacher had smiled approvingly at Mollie last week when the visiting preacher pinched her dimpled cheek and said, "Miss Grace, you have a fine looking bunch of little girls." Mollie thought now of having, when she was grown, a dress like Miss Grace's Sunday one. The bell stopped ringing and Mollie resolved to stop thinking and to work very hard and fast. Once before she had finished all the washing in time to go back with the boys after dinner. And so she scrubbed with all her force against the washboard and paid no attention to the pain from her knuckles scraped raw.

By dinner time all the clothes were on the line and the first ones out already frozen stiff. Mollie, numbed by cold and fatigue, ate peas, fat pork, and cornbread without joining in the family talk. When she got up from the table, her back ached—she wondered how many years of washing it would take to make it as bent over as her mother's. She changed to her new dress in time to set off for the afternoon session of school. She pulled herself together to respond to the teacher's beaming look of approval for having come to school that afternoon, and then relaxed into a lethargy from weariness and missed words she knew in the Third Reader and was spelled down quickly. . . .

One stormy winter night three months before Mollie was twelve, she was put to bed early. Her father moved the trundle bed from the main room and all the children went to sleep in the kitchen—all but Mollie. She had a terrible feeling of impending disaster to her mother and herself. When she had asked her mother about babies not long before, her mother had told her she was going to have another and that something would happen to Mollie soon, too. From the front room Mollie heard groans and knew her mother was suffering. Her own body began to ache. Her mother's sounds grew louder and each time an anguished scream reached Mollie's ears, a shooting pain went through her. Hardly daring, Mollie reached down under the cover and felt that her legs were wet. All the boys were asleep and so she drew back the cover and in the moonlight saw black stains which had come from her body. Suddenly she thought she was having a baby. She tried to scream like her mother, but the terror of the realization paralyzed her. Fright overwhelmed her until she was no longer conscious of pain. She remained motionless for a long time, knowing and feeling nothing but a horrible fear of disgrace and dread. Then she became aware that the moaning in the next room had stopped and that someone had unlatched the kitchen door. Trembling, she eased out of bed and crept into her mother's room. There was a new baby lying on one side, but she slipped into the other side of the bed and nestled against her mother. The relaxing warmth and comfort of another's body released the inner tensions and Mollie melted into tears and weak, low sobs. Her mother stroked her but said nothing. She lay there for some minutes until the Negro "granny" said she must leave her mother and led her back to bed. Early in the morning she hid the soiled bedclothes in a corner until she could wash them secretly in the creek and found some cloths in her mother's drawer which she asked for without giving any reason. Not for two years, when a girl friend told her, did she have any instruction about how to fix and wear sanitary pads.

*   *   *   *   *

The summer Mollie was fourteen her mother persuaded Ben to buy her a silk dress. Mollie had worked so well that year that her father, in an appreciative mood, took her to town and let her select the material, which was a glamorous, changeable, rose and green taffeta. Mrs. Bynum helped her make it, and when her father consented to take the whole family to a Fourth of July celebration ten miles away, Mollie's cup overflowed with joy. She rolled up her hair in rags the night before. She helped bathe and dress the younger children two hours before leaving time so that she might extract the full delight from dressing leisurely in her new clothes for the first time. By eight o'clock in the morning, the family, now nine, piled into the wagon and set off. To keep from going through the county seat, they cut through a shorter, back road, which was rocky and went over steep hills. The boys got out and pushed on the worst places, but Mollie sat on the bench with her mother and father—accorded special privileges because of her new dress. The jolting and hot sun bearing down were unnoticed for the joy anticipated in being the most beautifully dressed girl at the celebration. Mollie was scarcely aware of her family in the wagon as she rode along with her head in the clouds.

They reached the tabernacle, where there were to be political speeches interspersed with hymn singing contests between churches. Mollie hopped down lightly and was about to run over to join a group of girls she knew when her mother, climbing over the edge of the wagon more slowly, called her back and took her a few steps away from the wagon.

"Your dress is ruined behind," she whispered to Mollie, "you'll have to set still over here by this tree all day." Excitement and the jolting had brought on her menstrual period early and the realization of this brought about a flush of hot shame which obliterated the festive scene of picnic tables and merry people. Mollie's heart seemed to close up and with it her capacity to perceive or respond. Passively she allowed herself to be led to a sheltered spot under an oak with protruding roots which afforded a seat. The loss of her life's triumph and the indescribable embarrassment kept her from comprehending meanings. She felt that she was dead and after awhile she leaned against the tree and slept. No one approached, for there seemed to be a tacit understanding of her plight. Late in the afternoon she rode home without speaking to her family. The next day she and her mother were unable to remove the stain from her dress and the beautiful taffeta was never worn. Her father never bought her another silk dress.

*   *   *   *   *

Two years later, Mollie finished the seventh grade at sixteen. . . . That summer one of Mrs. Bynum's many nieces went to a town in another county to work in a tobacco factory and her sister reveled in telling Mollie about the money she made and spent. They planned what sort of things Mollie could buy if she were to go to work in town. After weeks of whispered plans, the sister in town arranged for Mollie to have a job weighing and wrapping cigarettes. Without telling even her mother, Mollie bundled up her clothes and left early one morning, just as the cotton picking season was beginning. A neighbor boy drove her to town and she went to a relative of Ben's to board.

For four months Mollie worked in the tobacco factory and exulted in making $20 a week. This was during the post-war boom period and labor was scarce. As fast as the money came in, she spent $15 for a coat, $11 for hightop shoes, $8 for a hat, and smaller amounts for slippers, dresses, beads, and brooches. There were five other women boarding in the same house and Mollie's greatest delight was in the just-before-bedtime lunches they shared. Each one chipped in a nickel every night for cheese, crackers, and fancy canned things. Mollie had never before eaten "store bought" food and had never had even one cent to spend on self-indulgence. After she had bought an entire outfit of new clothes, she went to a county fair with the women. A boy who worked in the cigarette factory asked her to go with him, but she thought she would have a better time with the other women. This boy always hung around Mollie in the factory and said things she thought were fresh, but the landlady wouldn't allow her to go out with him. Once in December he asked Mollie to marry him but she laughed and said, "Why should I marry and keep house and have babies when I've got such a good job and can buy myself such fine clothes?" . . .

The following summer Mollie's mother gave birth to her ninth child. It was in the daytime and the baby came in a hurry. No one was in the house except Mollie and the sick brother in the back room. Ben had gone for a doctor but not soon enough and the doctor did not get there in time. The suffering woman begged for help but Mollie did not know what to do. She even pled with Mollie to kill her and put an end to her tortures. Finally the baby was born, but with the covers pulled up so that Mollie could not see. The mother wrapped the baby up and let it lie there until the doctor came and cut the cord.

*   *   *   *   *

With a sick brother, a sickly mother, and a new baby in the house, Mollie had a busy summer. About the only times she had off from household duties were when she spent the night with her cousins or with Mrs. Bynum's nieces. On one such night the young people all went to watch a Negro revival meeting. While they were standing on the outside listening to the shouting through the windows, a man who knew some of the boys came up and joined them. His name was Jim and he was ten years older than Mollie, but he "took a shine" to her from their first meeting. For the rest of the summer he rode his mule for nine miles to come to see her whenever she could spend a night away from home, as Ben was still adamant about no sports coming to his house.

In the fall the brother was better and the original plan for Mollie to go to school in town was feasible. Because Ben had no buggy of his own, and because he wished so much to have his favorite daughter at home on week-ends, he finally consented for Jim to drive her out on Fridays and back to town on Sundays. His mule was the fastest one for miles around, but walked very slowly when Jim was taking Mollie home. This was when they did their courting, for Jim was never permitted to linger after delivering Mollie to her parents. He pressed his suit with urgency, for he was nearly thirty and felt it was time for him to be getting married. Mollie wasn't enjoying going back to school after being out for a year, since she was older than the town girls in her grade and felt awkward with them. She liked Jim although she never felt gay or excited with him the way she did with younger boys. She still did not want to think of marrying and settling down to repeat her mother's life—ruining her health and looks with overwork and child-bearing. She made one last appeal to her father to let her go back to work in the cigarette factory, for her one-time job has remained to this day a symbol of money for clothes and luxuries. Ben would not consent, however; he said that factories were no place for his womenfolks and that she could never go back. And so Mollie gave Jim a lukewarm "yes" and they planned to marry on Christmas Day. . . .

Five years later Mollie was pregnant for the third time. She felt very hopeful because this was "the kickingest baby you ever felt." Her first child had been a girl, but a terrible disappointment to Mollie in looks. At four she was big, cumbersome, awkward, and slow moving, resembling her two-hundred-pound father so much that he was frequently told, "You couldn't deny that child if you wanted to!" The second baby was a boy, weakly and always crying just like the little brother Mollie used to sleep with and take care of. The alertness of the child she was now carrying promised better success.

Mollie showed more interest in everything that spring and summer. Jim's family had left them to go live and work in a cotton mill town and for the first time they were "tending" a farm and living in a house alone. Their family of four was the smallest she had ever cooked, cleaned, and washed for, and their tobacco crop looked good in July. She was glad Jim was raising tobacco instead of cotton because it meant more money in the fall. He was still kind about buying her one Sunday dress every year with the first tobacco money he got. Mollie was still pretty at twenty-three and during her nine months of pregnancy she often daydreamed of the child, who was to be a pert, attractive daughter whom she could dress daintily.

In midsummer when her time was nearing, the baby suddenly stopped moving one night, "right short like." Mollie knew that minute the baby was dead and alarmed she woke up Jim and told him about it. He reassured her, but on her insistence the next morning went to town and told the doctor about it. The doctor said there was nothing to do but wait, although it was eleven days before labor set in. The delivery was difficult for the dead fetus had begun disintegrating. The body was too much in pieces to be dressed for burial but they showed Mollie the face of her little girl and she thought it was the prettiest she had ever seen. Blood poison, complications, and a long illness afterwards made Mollie temporarily infertile and she had no more children for ten years.

* * * * *

At thirty-seven Mollie is again pregnant. She is not bitter about it, although she wishes doctors would tell you what to do when they say, "Now you shouldn't have any more children." . . .

Mollie doesn't worry too much about the child yet to be born. She is sorry about the trouble it will be, but she accepts the "Lord's will" here as she does when they have a bad crop year. She no longer expects to realize the goals of life herself, but has transferred her efforts to achieving them for her daughter. Last year she even chose to forego the Sunday dress in order to buy a fur-trimmed coat for her baby. And yet Mollie is cheerful, except when impatient with her two older children, and works routinely at her farm and housework without complaint.

A Mexican-American Childhood during the Depression

Carlotta Silvas Martin

The border is an apt metaphor for Mexican-American life, capturing the fluidity of crossing back and forth between two countries and two cultures. Carlotta Silvas Martin was born in 1917 in Superior, Arizona, a rural mining town. Her father, Miguel López Silvas, had been born in Mexico but often picked up work across the border. He met his future wife, Elena Amanda Romero, who was of Mexican heritage but had been born in Arizona, at the boardinghouse run by her mother for miners working at the Magma Copper Company in Superior. Many Mexican-American women, like immigrant women in Eastern cities, found that taking in boarders could add important cash to the family income. Even when men were employed, life was always hard in these mining towns.

Things got even worse during the Great Depression of the 1930s, as Carlotta Silvas Martin remembered. She was living with her grandmother, which was not unusual among Mexican-American families, when hard times struck. Her oral history documents how the community worked together to get by; note that her grandmother for a time had a relief job with the WPA, the main New Deal relief agency. But the depression was not on everybody's mind twenty-four hours a day. Life continued as usual for the teenaged Carlotta Silvas, a life shaped by religion, tradition, and community, plus new elements like popular culture and movies.

After graduating from Superior High School, Carlotta Silvas attended Arizona State University and then returned to Superior, where she wrote a popular column called "Aqui y Alla" (Here and There) for the local newspaper. In 1955 she married Walter Martin, a mining engineer, and had two children. The family's decision to move to Mesa so their children could attend school was typical of the migration *el rancho al barrio* (from ranch, or rural area, to city) of many Mexican-Americans of her generation. But in a further migration, Carlotta Silvas Martin returned to Superior in the 1980s. The town had changed dramatically since the mine shut down in 1984. "It was a thriving town," she remembered, "and now it is barren, like a desert." The memories of women of her generation are increasingly our only windows on a world almost lost.

My mother had two small babies on her hands. When I became sickly, Grandmother Josefa took me home with her, and I never returned to my parents. From the time I can remember I was raised by my "Nani." In those years it was very common for grandmas to raise kids.

My grandmother worked very hard; I grew up during the Depression. My kids asked me why I can't ride a bike and I'd say, "That's the last thing I would ask for!" During the Depression my grandmother would give Armida, my Uncle Ernesto's wife, a dollar a day. With that she'd buy potatoes, lard, and beans. They had thirteen children, and she'd feed us all. That was the menu— *papas fritas, frijoles,* and *tortillas.* Aunt Armida made big piles of hot tortillas and we sat on those long benches and she gave them to us as she made them. Every once in a blue moon she bought a quarter's worth of hamburger and fried it with potatoes. That was a real treat!

During the Depression my grandmother sewed piecework for the WPA. I'd go by the building on my way to and from school and see her sitting at the sewing machine. My dad helped when he could, but the miners only made four dollars a day. Uncle Ernesto worked also. He used to dig graves.

My mother was very kind; she was known for her charity. She gave people food during the Depression. My dad used to buy one-hundred-pound sacks of sugar, flour, and potatoes, and my mother would portion it in little bags and give them to the people who were in need.

When my mother's father died, Doña Isabel, who never went out anywhere because she was partially paralyzed, went to my grandfather's wake. Mother asked her, "Ay, why are you coming out in this cold and windy weather?" "Because, Elena," she answered, "I owe you favors. If I owed you money, I would pay you, but I can only repay the kind favors that you have done for me by accompanying you in your grief." Many of the people in our little mining town were very ethical and high-class people in their own way.

Another young man was telling me the other day: "Carlotta, I never liked Superior because I suffered so much hunger there, but your parents were always very kind to us." "Yes," I told him. "They were kind to everybody."

The Depression years were very, very, hard. I remember seeing the people passing on the way to California from Oklahoma, Arkansas, and Missouri.

Source: Patricia Preciado Martin, ed., *Songs My Mother Sang to Me: An Oral History of Mexican-American Women,* pp. 202–204, 206, 210–212, 215–216. Published by The University of Arizona Press, copyright © 1992. Reprinted by permission of the publisher.

At that time we lived on Queen Creek, and everyone went by there. It hurt me to see the people in their rickety old cars, their clothes in tatters, escaping from the drought and the dust bowls. . . .

My early childhood years were spent playing in Queen Creek near my grandmother's home. It was so pretty—a green oasis shaded by huge cottonwood trees that made my playground a cool haven. Clean, clear water ran in the creek all the time. Sometimes, after a heavy rainstorm, the creek would flood as high as the bridge and then miraculously turn into a trickle the very next day. But now it's dirty, and there are no trees. My grandmother's house was located on the "American" side of town, but there was nothing they could do about it because she was there before anybody else and had staked her claim. Later on she sold the lot for five hundred dollars and moved the lumber and built another house on a lot she had on Heiner Street. I grew up playing with Anglo children and speaking English. Most of my friends were the Mahoneys, a big Irish family from Utah.

When it was time for me to go to school I was assigned to Harding School, which was the school for the non-English-speaking children on the Mexican side of town. We were segregated; there was a place called McKelveyville by Harding School, and those Anglo children were sent to Roosevelt School and the Mexican children who lived closer to Roosevelt had to go down to Harding. I'll admit, there was a lot of discrimination in those years. An ice plant located just below the present Hing's Market on Main Street seemed to be the unofficial boundary between the "American" side (we were all Americans!) and the "Mexican" side.

Superior's Mexican side of town could have been considered a barrio, but to me it was a lovely environment. The people were very united; they intermingled a lot. There was never a need to lock doors. I don't ever recall my seeing a key to any of the doors in either my parents' or grandmother's homes. . . .

There was a strong feeling of community among the Mexican people of Superior. The fraternal organizations had socials and picnics as well as dances. When someone died, they all turned out in their uniforms and banners—all very formal.

We also celebrated Las Fiestas Patrias—el 16 de septiembre, el 5 de mayo, and also July 4. Some men in town knew a great deal about Mexican history and politics, and they were very involved in these celebrations. We'd have patriotic speeches, a queen and princesses, a parade with floats, a dance, and a picnic with races and pie contests. On September 16 they'd blow up some dynamite, and the blast would represent "El Grito de Dolores," which was the cry for independence from Spain by Miguel Hidalgo.

We had a theater at one time in Mexican town. It had a very nice stage and seated about three hundred people. It burned down and was never rebuilt. Touring stock companies came from Los Angeles and presented beautiful plays in Spanish—comedies, dramas, and musical reviews. You know who used to come here—Rita Hayworth! Her name was Rita Cansino then. She toured with her father. They sang together and she danced. That was in the early thirties.

I belonged to a women's group called "Las Mexicanitas." We did a lot of community service. We raised money for scholarships; we donated the altar and railing when they built the new St. Francis Church and raised money for the St. Mary's Community Center. We put on plays and skits and variety shows. One year I wrote a play in Spanish and English called "The Apparition of Our Lady of Guadalupe." Martin Fierro, the high school Spanish teacher, did the men's voices, and I did the women's voices. My husband, Walter, and I went up to the flats and collected manzanita bushes. Walter put them on stands, and we decorated them with paper roses. Then we blacked out the stage lights, and when the lights were turned on the Virgen de Guadalupe was standing there. Everyone said, "Ahhhhhhh." It was so beautiful. It was such a big success we had to put it on twice.

The first movie theater was in American town. Later we also had a movie house in Mexican town that had movies in Spanish. That's about the only time my mother would go out. How she enjoyed those movies!

My father was a very honorable man; his word was his bond. He was a very hard worker and was respected. Some of the men didn't like to work with him because he was such a perfectionist at his job. At one time he was a contract miner and worked in a very lucrative spot. He was a good provider. But then, that's not all there is to life. He was in charge of the money, but my mother had to save for any of the extras. Sometimes he would just blow it away. When he retired in 1950 he had worked for the mining company forty-three years and had never been laid off. If he went out and drank, which he did do, he'd go to work the next day. People would tell time by him. He had a lunch pail with a canvas strip that he swung on his back. By six o'clock every morning, he was going up the hill on Pinal. People would say, "Ay, ya son las seis. Allí va el Mique Silvas." (Oh, it's six o'clock; there goes Mikey Silvas.). . . .

I married my husband, Walter Martin, in 1955. He is an Alaskan native and a mining engineer. We have two children, a son, Jonathan, and a daughter, Elena. I moved to Mesa for sixteen years so my children could attend school there. Our daughter is a music teacher at Lehi Elementary School in Mesa, and our son is a surveyor for Magma Copper Company.

I moved back to Superior three years ago, but so much has changed since the mine closed down in 1984. John Mitchell's was a beautiful department store with quality merchandise. There were appliance stores, two drugstores, and some nice restaurants. The Magma Hotel was a very nice place; the theater was going full blast. Every two weeks when the miners got paid, there was money flowing all over the place. It was a thriving town, and now it is barren, like the desert. Even the Kress' Dime Store has closed, and that was the meeting place for people.

I used to go and visit people that I have known since I was a little girl, but now so many of the people have gone away or died. I hardly go out anymore.

To me that's one of life's sadnesses—to lose the people you've known all your life.

A lot of the children of the Mexican families from Superior have done very, very well. A lot of professional people have come out of our little mining community—doctors, lawyers, educators, and political leaders. A professor at ASU told me that young people from the mining towns always did well because they had support of their parents.

My sister's son, Aaron Kizer, is an attorney. I remember once when Aaron was a little boy he was singing "Anything you can do, I can do better." When my dad heard him singing that song, he asked me, "¿Que está cantando el muchacho?" I explained it to him. He got such a big kick out of that. He'd be so thrilled today if he knew how well our children have done.

Women and Labor Militancy

Genora Johnson Dollinger

The 1930s are rightly remembered as the decade when the labor movement became an institutionalized part of American life. This breakthrough occurred because of labor militancy engendered by the harsh conditions of the Depression as well as New Deal legislation such as the 1935 Labor Relations Act, which put the force of the federal government behind labor's right to organize. Women participated in this upsurge in labor organization, increasing their numbers in unions from barely 250,000 in 1929 to more than 800,000 just ten years later.

The success of the Congress of Industrial Organizations (CIO) was a major factor in the growth of the labor movement in the 1930s. One of the earliest targets was the auto industry in Michigan. A successful 44-day sit-down strike against General Motors (where workers occupied the plants, but refused to work) led to recognition for the fledgling United Auto Workers union. Although women were only a fraction of auto workers, they played a major role in the Flint sit-down strikes that led to the victory.

Genora Johnson Dollinger, a twenty-three-year-old wife of a GM striker and mother of two small children, mobilized five hundred women during the strike, mainly the wives, sisters, and girlfriends of the male strikers. These women called themselves the Women's Emergency Brigade and wore distinctive red berets and armbands. Their activities included responsibility for picket lines, staffing soup kitchens and first aid stations, and occasionally taking more militant action, such as breaking windows to protect strikers from tear gas. The women played a special role in deflecting the potential for violence and bloodshed, all in the name of protecting their men. As journalist Mary Heaton Vorse observed, "They were fearless and seemingly tireless. One and all were normal, sensible women who were doing this because they had come to the natural conclusion that it must be done if they and their children were to have a decent life."

The pride that these women felt in their contributions comes through in Genora Johnson Dollinger's story. So too does the hostility of the male union leaders, who quickly consigned the women back to the home once the emergency had passed.

I was raised in the city of Flint, Michigan. There are roads and streets in that city named for my family because they were among the early settlers there.

Actually, this was an advantage when the strike came. I could not successfully be labeled an outside union agitator brought in to cause trouble. My father was well-known and well-to-do—a portrait photographer who invested in real estate.

I was twenty-three years old on December 30, 1936, when the strike started. It lasted forty-four days, a very dramatic forty-four days, until February 11, 1937.

It was New Year's Eve when I realized women had to organize and join in the fight. I was on the picket lines when the men's wives came down. They didn't know why their husbands were sitting inside the plant. Living in a company town, you see, they got only company propaganda through the press and radio. So when they came down on New Year's Eve, many were threatening to divorce their striking husbands if they didn't quit and get back to work to bring home a paycheck.

I knew then that union women must organize on their own in order to talk with these wives.

At that time, I was a housewife myself with two sons, aged six and two. I had been exposed to socialist doctrine when I was very young . . . sixteen or seventeen, when I met my husband Kermit's father. He'd come from South Dakota bringing certain socialist ideas. So Carl Johnson, the father, and Kermit and I formed a socialist party branch in Flint. I knew what was going on within the AFL craft unions because our socialist party headquarters was in the Labor Temple where all their activities took place. Everybody knew me down there, and I had some pretty firm ideas about the responsibilities of industry to the factory worker.

So when the strike began, I already had many friends among the auto workers; and I was fairly well known by others in town, including the local newspaper, because of my father's position. . . .

When the strike started, my mother—without my father's knowledge—agreed to take care of my two little boys, and other friends helped, as well. I was then relatively free, and immediately went to Roy Reuther and Robert

Travis—those were the UAW organizers—and I volunteered to help. I was told to go to the kitchen and peel potatoes, but I said there were plenty of others who could do that, including some of the men. So they gave me a job setting up a press clipping bureau. I kept busy for a couple of days until I found out there was a person going over all the work I'd done. I decided anyone sitting with a pair of shears could handle that job, so I organized a sign painting department. We made signs and set up a children's picket line—and that's what the history books show. I remember one sign, my own little snow-suited two-year-old holding it high: "My daddy strikes for us little tykes." That picture went from one end of the nation to the other. Anyway, a professional sign painter friend of mine took that over, and that's when I got busy organizing the women.

Now remember, Chevrolet, A/C Sparkplug, and Buick were working—Fisher plants 1 and 2 were struck. On December 30, the police attempted to break the strike at Fisher 2. You see, the men were sitting-in on the second floor, and food was brought up to them by ladder—'cause the plant police had control of the bottom floor. On that night, the police decided to cut off the food, and the next thing we knew they started throwing tear gas at the plant to get the men out. That fight became famous as the Battle of Bull's Run and it went on into the long night. The street was barricaded on both sides by union men. The local GM-controlled radio was broadcasting that a riot—some people thought a revolution—had broken out in the city. People came to watch the police shooting us with rifle bullets, buckshot, and tear gas. We had nothing but rocks and car door hinges, but we picked up the tear gas bombs and heaved them back at the police before they exploded. Men were going down, and fourteen people were shot that night, one seriously. I saw blood flowing.

But before this happened union men had herded all the women to safety—all except me. I said, "I've got just as strong weapons as you've got. You've got no guns, neither have I. I can fight as well as you." I was the only woman too stubborn to leave, so I stayed down there. We were putting cold water on our faces in order to brave the sea of tear gas. Victor Reuther was in charge of the sound truck that night and the batteries were running down. They couldn't last but a few more minutes. Remember, the public had no other access to union information, so the sound car was a very valuable weapon for us. In this way we broadcast our message to the 3,000 people on both sides of the barricades, telling them why we were striking, the profit General Motors was making, and the unbearable conditions the men were working under. . . .

At this point Victor privately told some of us, "We may have lost this battle, but we're not losing the war." He seemed to be preparing us for defeat on this night. It was then I asked him: "Victor, can I speak to them?" And he replied, "We've got nothing to lose." He was a fine person, but still I could feel that he didn't think a woman could do much in this situation.

I got up on the sound car—I know it was an electrifying thing . . . a woman's voice calling to the people of Flint after so many hours of fighting . . . and I said,

"I'm talking especially to you women out there. You didn't know that mothers"—I meant myself—"are being fired on by the police. The police are cowards enough to fire into the bellies of unarmed men. Aren't they also cowards to fire at mothers of little children? I'm asking you women out there behind the barricades to break through those police lines. Come down here and stand with your brothers, your sons, your sweethearts, your husbands and help us win this fight."

And so help me, I could hardly believe it—one woman started walking toward us. The police grabbed at her and she walked right out of her coat. She marched down, other women following her—the police didn't dare shoot all those women in the back. Then the union men broke through. The battle was over and the union had won.

The women had saved the day. It was then that I realized how much power women had, and I proceeded to organize the Women's Emergency Brigade.

This was an independent move. It was not under the direction of the union or its administrators—I just talked it over with a few women—the active ones—and told them this is what we had to do.

Women might, after all, be called upon to give their lives. That was exactly the appeal I made while we were forming the brigade—I told the women, "Don't sign up for this unless you are prepared. If you are prone to hysteria or anything like that you'd only be in our way." I told them they'd be linking arms and withstanding the onslaughts of the police and if one of our sisters went down shot in cold blood there'd be no time for hysteria.

Around 500 women answered that call. We bought red berets and made arm bands with the white letters "EB" for Emergency Brigade. It was a kind of military uniform, yes, but it was mainly identification. We wore them all the time so we'd know who to call on to give help in an emergency. I had five lieutenants—three were factory women. I chose them because they could be called out of bed at any hour, if necessary, or sleep on a cot at the union hall. Mothers with children couldn't answer calls like that—although they did sign up for the brigade. Even a few grandmothers became brigadiers and, I remember, one young girl only sixteen.

We had no communication system to speak of. Very few people had telephones so we had to call one woman who was responsible for getting the messages through to many others.

We organized a first aid station and child care center—the women who had small children to tend and couldn't join the EB took care of these jobs.

Listen, I met some of the finest women I have ever come across in my life. When the occasion demands it of a woman and once she understands that she's standing in defense of her family—well, God, *don't fool around with that woman then.*

The brigade developed in such a short period of time. Some of them we soon sent to Lansing, Pontiac, and other outlying automobile factory towns where the police were beating the heads of men attempting to organize a union. We went in carloads to give them courage. Women played important roles. . . .

I saw women stand up under circumstances where big men ran around the corner and hid under a car. I have seen them rise up when I would not have believed they could.

I'd get up in the men's meetings and say, "Bring your wives down here." I'd tell them, "Your wives should come out and join us so they will understand what their husbands are fighting for." I explained it would make for closer companionship within the family.

Finally, you know, everything just came to a head. With so many workers' homes without sufficient food and heat in the freezing January temperatures, and powerful General Motors benefiting from the unequal contest . . . well, it came time for a major decision. Plant 4, the largest plant in the Chevrolet division of ten plants, produced all the motors for Chevrolet throughout the country. That plant became our target. We knew if we could close it down, profits would be cut and that would bring General Motors to the bargaining table. We also knew that 4 was the plant they guarded the most vigilantly—so what historians have called the finest labor strategy of the twentieth century was devised.

We pretended to strike one of the other Chevrolet plants, Plant 9, which was far removed on the other side of the whole complex and had that action drawing all the company police, city police, and Pinkerton agents . . . a diversionary tactic, you see. The Women's Emergency Brigade was there and they broke the windows to allow air to get in to the tear-gassed union men. Women just played a fantastic role over there at Plant 9.

Now, my husband Kermit's assignment was to shut down Plant 4, the target plant. But I dared not let the brigade know about it because it had to be such a tight secret. The whole union movement had been infiltrated with company spies. After the Plant 9 action, I sent the brigade back to headquarters and with my five lieutenants, walked around the city streets that paralleled the big Chevrolet compound—very leisurely, very casually—so that no one would notice us too much. The rest of the brigade marched back to the headquarters so our absence wasn't noticed.

We strolled over to Plant 4 which the union men were attempting to shut down. I was very nervous because I knew it was a life and death matter for my husband and the other men inside. By the time we got over there there was a great deal of confusion. It was a huge place—imagine a plant with 8,000 workers. They had to seal doors that were as big as the sides of houses—gondolas of steel parts had to be brought up in order to barricade some doors, while others were welded shut. They were having a helluva time.

The plant foreman and his hired agents were giving them trouble. There were fist fights breaking out all over the place. The men yelled to us, "My God, we're having an awful time. Don't let anybody come in through the front gate on Chevrolet Avenue." Naturally, that was a big order, so I sent one of my lieutenants to call headquarters. "Tell the brigade to come at once," I told her. And the five of us left strung ourselves across the front gate.

When the city police got word what was happening they came, seventy-five of them, and found us women on the gate. We defied them . . . told them they would have to go in over our dead bodies.

And we used psychology on them. Eighty percent had relatives working under those horrible conditions in the plants. "Look," I said, "if you worked in this plant, and you were being driven crazy, and your health was broken down, wouldn't you expect your wife to come down here to see what she could do?"

It threw them off their guard and they began answering my arguments, just long enough. By the time they got provoked and said, "Well, we've got a job to do," and started pushing us, at that point the brigade came down Chevrolet Avenue. There came hundreds of those red berets bobbing up and down with the American flag at their head, singing "Solidarity Forever." The sound of it, from all those voices, just flooded the whole area.

They quickly set up an oval picket line in front of the main gate. This meant the police would have to club and shoot these women, and they had no stomach for that. Then the truck arrived filled with union men, and God, it dawned on me, *we'd saved the gate.*

The union had closed the huge and valuable Plant 4 with another sit-down strike. Soon after, Governor Frank Murphy declared martial law and ordered negotiations started. On February 11th, an agreement was reached recognizing unions in GM plants across the nation. That was a much greater victory than our small, inexperienced union ever expected to win.

After the settlement, I was sent on a public speaking tour of the major unions on the Eastern coast for at least a month, and when I returned to Flint, I collapsed completely and I had to go into a sanatorium. Did I mention that I had TB during this time?

The union raised money to send me to a sanatorium in the Adirondacks. But when I came back, I found erosion had taken place. The brigade had been disbanded with the victory. Maybe it's a good thing I wasn't around during this period because the husbands began saying, "Well, you women did a wonderful job, but now your duty is back there getting those kids in school, getting the wash done, and regular meals again. . . ."

Oh, the union had tremendous respect for us, but after the strike was over they said in effect, "Thank you, ladies, so much." And at the top level of the International Union they turned the women's group into a mockery that I couldn't even be a part of. They had courses in styling clothes, coiffure, and makeup—things which, of course, some women had an interest in—but that wasn't our whole interest nor did it represent our real concerns.

A few of the women tried to hang on, and they were meeting in homes and that sort of thing. But it was a phantom thing, and I decided I didn't want to carry on that way.

It's a measure of the strength of those women of the Red Berets that they could perform so courageously in an atmosphere that was often hostile to them. We organized on our own without the benefit of professional leadership, and yet, we played a role, second to none, in the birth of a union and in changing working families' lives forever.

EQUAL TIME FOR CHIVALRY

The independent woman of the 1920s felt herself to be man's equal, so why shouldn't she doff her hat to him as she passed him on the street? After all, men had been greeting women in that way for centuries. But notice that the hats being doffed in this photograph are decidedly stylish—in the cloche style—and that the women's hair underneath them is clearly bobbed because their necks are visible. This summer scene (the women's dresses, if not terribly stylish, are lightweight and comfortable) suggests the trappings of independence that women adopted in the decade. (Credit: UPI)

THE AVIATOR AS FEMINIST HEROINE

For many Americans, Amelia Earhart (1897–1937) symbolized women's emancipation and modern roles. A former settlement house volunteer as well as a pioneer in the field of aviation, Earhart, in 1932, became the first woman to fly across the Atlantic alone. Her short, bobbed hair and appearance of easy self-assurance, plus a strong physical resemblance to aviator Charles Lindbergh, earned her the nickname *Lady Lindy*. She was presumed lost at sea somewhere in the Pacific in 1937 while attempting a round-the-world flight, although her plane was never recovered. (Credit: UPI)

WOMEN IN A SOUP LINE

Although it was rare to see women on a bread line in the Great Depression, these Mexican-American women have gone around the back of a private agency called the International Institute in San Antonio, Texas, to receive a handout of free soup. The year is 1937, and the Depression still grips the nation. Although the federal government offered some assistance to San Antonians through the Works Progress Administration (WPA), it was never enough to assist all those who qualified, and many families were forced to rely on private agencies. The smiles on the faces of these women show their gratitude for this help, probably the difference between feeding their families and going to bed hungry that night. (Credit: *San Antonio Light* Collection, University of Texas Institute of Texas Cultures, San Antonio)

STRIKING SOLIDARITY

Women from the United Auto Workers' Women's Auxiliary demonstrate their solidarity with their sisters from Flint during the sit-down strikes of 1937. If this picture had been in color, it would have shown the bright green caps of the Detroit women, which contrasted with the red berets worn by the Flint auxiliary. The nightsticks that the women carry suggest their vaguely paramilitary role, although one of their placards reminds the citizens of Flint "We Are against Violence." Another banner takes a stand for equal pay for equal work. (Credit: Wayne State University Archives)

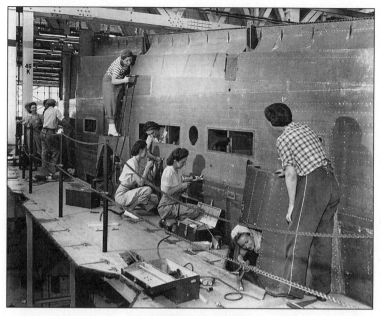

WARTIME WORKERS

When men went off to war, women moved into the jobs left behind in the defense industries. These women work in an aviation plant owned by Douglas Aircraft in Chicago in 1943. Note that most of the women are young, and all are white; black workers (if employed at all) would have been likely sent to other, less desirable jobs in the plant. Notice also that all the women are dressed in pants. And there is not a man in sight! (Credit: UPI)

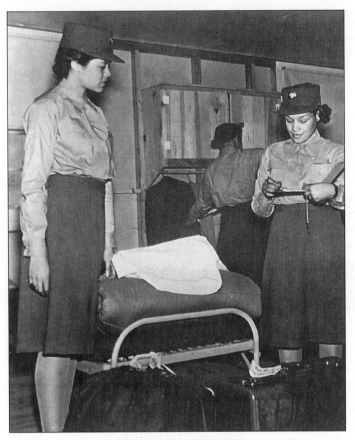

THE JIM CROW ARMY

These women are members of the 33rd Post Headquarters Company of the Women's Army Auxiliary Corps (WAACs), stationed at Fort Huachuca, Arizona, during World War II. Black women made up approximately 10 percent of the WAACs, although they were rigidly assigned (as were black men in the armed forces) to separate units. This barracks, into which the new recruit is settling, would have been segregated, and she would have eaten in an all-black mess hall and exercised at black-only recreational facilities. Also, it would have been highly unlikely that her unit would have seen duty overseas. (Credit: Schomburg Center for Research in Black Culture, New York Public Library)

Women Want Homes Like This!

A FRIENDLY doorway that always says "Welcome!"... a lovely door-garden where sunshine and flowers suggest the happiness and contentment inside ... not just a house, but a *home* where you have time to relax and enjoy life.

These are things we all want.

And in these days of tired bodies and troubled minds it's good for one to think about them now and then—about the new

kind of a home you will have after victory. Cooking, dishwashing, laundry and housecleaning will still go on, of course, but they will be done the easy, efficient, electrical way without drudgery ... there'll be time to fuss with flowers.

But just now new home things must wait—there's a war to win first. So put your money in war bonds—buy another and another and another. Each extra dollar does an extra bit

to speed victory. And each dollar you spend *after* victory will help provide jobs for the soldiers returning to peace-time industry.

Until the war is won General Electric will continue making only "tools of victory." But when that job is finished we will go back with added enthusiasm to the job we like best—making better electrical equipment for your home that will bring you better living at less cost.

GENERAL ELECTRIC

DELAYED DREAMS

Since so few consumer goods were manufactured during the war mobilization, industry leaders used advertisements to ask customers to delay their dreams until after the war was won. "Everything Electric for After-Victory Homes" proclaims this General Electric ad from *Life* magazine, February 7, 1944. While the text is filled with statements linking wartime sacrifices with the promised affluence of a postwar world, the image presented (happy baby, cheerful [white] mother, lushly landscaped garden, large house, even the picket fence) was a reality for only a minority of American families at war's end. (Credit: By permission of General Electric Company)

CIVIL RIGHTS ACTIVISM IN AN ERA OF CONFORMITY

Rosa Parks represents the large role that black women played in the Civil Rights revolution that rocked American society in the 1950s and beyond. Here she is fingerprinted at the Montgomery, Alabama, police station in 1955 after being arrested for failing to give up her seat on a city bus to a white person. "I felt it was just something I had to do," Parks said simply. Black activist Eldridge Cleaver captured the broader significance of her personal stand: "Somewhere in the universe a gear in the machinery shifted." (Credit: Wide World Photos, Inc.)

CHAPTER 8

Rosie the Riveter and Other Wartime Women

World War II had an unmistakable impact on American society. The task of fighting and winning a global war greatly accelerated the growth of the federal bureaucracy that had begun during the New Deal; federal budgets and functions never returned to their prewar levels. Nor did the United States return to its prewar stance of isolation from international relations. The war also encouraged dramatic social changes on the home front, especially an increase in mobility as people flocked to war jobs or entered the armed services. African Americans were able to lay the groundwork for the postwar civil rights revolution by equating segregation with Nazi white supremacist ideology. Most importantly, defense mobilization brought a return to prosperity after a decade of depression.

The specific impact of the wartime experience on the nation's women is less clear-cut. Some historians have argued that the war represented a major turning point for women because of their dramatic roles in the war effort, especially in defense plants. Others have focused on the persistence of sexism and discrimination against women on the job, in families, and in society as a whole. The weight of the evidence in this historical debate tilts towards analyzing women's wartime experiences in light of long-term trends of employment, demographics, and family roles, rather than seeing the war as a dramatic period of social change.

One of the difficulties of coming to an assessment of the impact of World War II on women is that the impact varies depending on which women are examined. Despite all the media attention to the "Rosie the Riveters" who took on defense jobs, the majority of American women were homemakers during the war. The war permeated every aspect of their daily life. Popular culture and advertising were saturated with patriotic war themes, especially the movies. Household management was challenging during wartime, notably coping with the high inflation rate and the shortages and rationing of most durable consumer

213

goods, food, and gasoline. Women also performed volunteer services for their communities.

Many women were more directly involved in the war effort. For example, 350,000 women joined the armed services, supplying approximately 2 percent of the total fighting forces. Equally dramatic were changes for the nation's female workers. The female work force grew by 50 percent between 1940 and 1945. These war workers were drawn both from the ranks of women already working (they used the opportunity to leave such traditional female jobs as domestic and personal service for higher-paying industrial work) and new workers, including recent students and former full-time homemakers who joined the war effort for reasons both of patriotism and economics. The wartime economic and social climate was especially liberating for single women, who experienced increasing autonomy and independence in the conduct of their personal lives. Such opportunities were also an important breakthrough for black workers of both sexes, who until the war-induced labor shortage had been barred from most manufacturing and industrial jobs.

These women workers were welcomed into the work force, a stark contrast to the public disapproval that greeted women during the Depression. But much of the public support derived from the conviction that these women workers were only temporary, that they would happily trade their overalls and welding tools for aprons when the men came home from war. Women workers had other ideas. When surveyed, the vast majority wanted to keep their new jobs. In the reconversion process, women did in fact lose many of the gains made during wartime, but they did not return to the home—they just went back to the traditional kinds of female jobs they had always held. After a slight dip after the war, the percentage of women who worked began a steady climb upwards. By 1950, 28.6 percent of adult women were working (down from the wartime peak of 37 percent), comprising 30 percent of the work force. In the postwar period, women showed an increasing propensity to combine marriage and work, a trend first noticed during the Depression but vastly accelerated during wartime.

World War II left other legacies for the nation's women. Because women's work was seen as temporary, there was no underlying shift in public attitudes about women's traditional responsibilities for home and family. In fact, "the unshaken claim of family" was probably intensified by the war: after the years of home front dislocation, returning soldiers and their spouses welcomed a return to normalcy. The marriage and birth rates, which had been artificially suppressed during the Depression, had already begun to rise during the war and would shoot up soon afterwards. So did the divorce rate.

Concentrating on women's displacement from industrial jobs and the continuity of traditional attitudes about women's place leads to fairly negative assessments about the impact of the war on women's lives. Such a view, however, is too shortsighted, for it misses what the wartime experience meant to individual women. Historian Sherna Gluck, who collected oral histories from female war workers in California, found this common thread to many women's recollections: "I never realized what I could do." Gluck posits that this increase in self-esteem and belief in women's own capabilities spilled over into more egalitarian family and marital relations in the postwar years, but was not translated into a direct challenge of the status quo in the public realm: "Changes in consciousness are not *necessarily* or *immediately* reflected in dramatic alterations in the public world. They may be very quietly played out in the private world of women, yet expressed in a fashion that can both affect future generations and eventually be expressed more openly when the social climate is right." Taking this perspective on the impact of the war on individual women's lives, World War II may turn out to have been more of a watershed for women than historians have realized.

Rosie the Riveter

Fanny Christina Hill

No image captured the popular view of women's contributions to the war effort better than Norman Rockwell's *Saturday Evening Post* cover of "Rosie the Riveter": a patriotic housewife who dons overalls and goes to work in a defense plant "for the duration." Yet, there was no one Rosie the Riveter: she was a recent high school graduate taking her first job or a mother with a son in the service; she had been working before the war or was taking her first full-time job after years of homemaking; she was single or married, white or black or Latina, middle- or working-class. What unified the experiences of these women was that they proved to themselves (and the country) that they could do a "man's job," and could do it well.

The experiences of black women in the defense industry are especially instructive. World War II's labor shortage opened up skilled work in industry, providing better working conditions and dramatic increases in pay over black women's previous concentration in domestic service or farm labor. The jobs opened to blacks, however, were always less desirable than those available to whites. But the process of whites working alongside blacks (and, to a lesser degree, Latinas) encouraged a breaking down of social barriers and a healthy recognition of diversity.

The oral history of Fanny Christina (Tina) Hill illuminates these broader trends. A black woman who was born in Texas but migrated to California, she had been trapped in domestic service until at age 24 she got a job at North American Aircraft. Her memoir balances excitement at the opportunity with an awareness of the discrimination blacks faced on the job. Her story also confirms the need to look be-

yond just the war years to understand the life cycles of the Rosie the
Riveters. After quitting work near war's end to have a child, she returned to North American Aircraft in 1946 (one of the minority of
wartime women who got their jobs back), remaining there until her
retirement in 1980. As her final comment underscores, Tina Hill realizes that World War II had a positive impact on her life.

I don't remember what day of the week it was, but I guess I must have started
out pretty early that morning. When I went there, the man didn't hire me. They
had a school down here on Figueroa and he told me to go to the school. I went
down and it was almost four o'clock and they told me they'd hire me. You had
to fill out a form. They didn't bother too much about your experience because
they knew you didn't have any experience in aircraft. Then they give you
some kind of little test where you put the pegs in the right hole.

There were other people in there, kinda mixed. I assume it was more
women than men. Most of the men was gone, and they weren't hiring too many
men unless they had a good excuse. Most of the women was in my bracket,
five or six years younger or older. I was twenty-four. There was a black girl
that hired in with me. I went to work the next day, sixty cents an hour.

I think I stayed at the school for about four weeks. They only taught you
shooting and bucking rivets and how to drill the holes and to file. You had to
use a hammer for certain things. After a couple of whiles, you worked on the
real thing. But you were supervised so you didn't make a mess.

When we went into the plant, it wasn't too much different than down at
the school. It was the same amount of noise; it was the same routine. One difference was there was just so many more people, and when you went in the
door you had a badge to show and they looked at your lunch. I had gotten accustomed to a lot of people and I knew if it was a lot of people, it always meant
something was going on. I got carried away: "As long as there's a lot of people here, I'll be making money." That was all I could ever see.

I was a good student, if I do say so myself. But I have found out through
life, sometimes even if you're good, you just don't get the breaks if the color's
not right. I could see where they made a difference in placing you in certain
jobs. They had fifteen or twenty departments, but all the Negroes went to Department 17 because there was nothing but shooting and bucking rivets. You
stood on one side of the panel and your partner stood on this side, and he would
shoot the rivets with a gun and you'd buck them with the bar. That was about
the size of it. I just didn't like it. I didn't think I could stay there with all this
shooting and a'bucking and a'jumping and a'bumping. I stayed in it about two
or three weeks and then I just decided I did *not* like that. I went and told my
foreman and he didn't do anything about it, so I decided I'd leave.

Source: Reprinted with permission of Twayne Publishers, an imprint of Simon & Schuster Macmillan, from *Rosie the Riveter Revisited,* by Sherna Berger Gluck, pp. 37–42. Copyright © 1987 by
Sherna Berger Gluck.

While I was standing out on the railroad track, I ran into somebody else out there fussing also. I went over to the union and they told me what to do. I went back inside and they sent me to another department where you did bench work and I liked that much better. You had a little small jig that you would work on and you just drilled out holes. Sometimes you would rout them or you would scribe them and then you'd cut them with a cutters.

I must have stayed there nearly a year, and then they put me over in another department, "Plastics." It was the tail section of the B-Bomber, the Billy Mitchell Bomber. I put a little part in the gun sight. You had a little ratchet set and you would screw it in there. Then I cleaned the top of the glass off and put a piece of paper over it to seal it off to go to the next section. I worked over there until the end of the war. Well, not quite the end, because I got pregnant, and while I was off having the baby the war was over. . . .

Negroes rented rooms quite a bit. It was a wonderful thing, 'cause it made it possible for you to come and stay without a problem. My sister and I was rooming with this lady and we was paying six dollars a week, which was good money, because she was renting the house for only twenty-six dollars a month. She had another girl living on the back porch and she was charging her three dollars. So you get the idea.

We were accustomed to shacking up with each other. We had to live like that because that was the only way to survive. Negroes, as a rule, are accustomed to a lot of people around. They have lived like that from slavery time on. We figured out how to get along with each other.

In the kitchen everybody had a little place where he kept his food. You had a spot in the icebox; one shelf was yours. You bought one type of milk and the other ones bought another type of milk, so it didn't get tangled up. But you didn't buy too much to have on hand. You didn't overstock like I do today. Of course, we had rationing, but that didn't bother me. It just taught me a few things that I still do today. It taught me there's a lot of things you can get along without. I liked cornbread a lot—and we had to use Cream of Wheat, grits, to make cornbread. I found out I liked that just as well. So, strange as it may seem, I didn't suffer from the war thing.

I started working in April and before Thanksgiving, my sister and I decided we'd buy a house instead of renting this room. The people was getting a little hanky-panky with you; they was going up on the rent. So she bought the house in her name and I loaned her some money. The house only cost four thousand dollars with four hundred dollars down. It was two houses on the lot, and we stayed in the little small one-bedroom house in the back. I stayed in the living room part before my husband came home and she stayed in the bedroom. I bought the furniture to go in the house, which was the stove and refrigerator, and we had our old bedroom sets shipped from Texas. I worked the day shift and my sister worked the night shift. I worked ten hours a day for five days a week. Or did I work on a Saturday? I don't remember, but I know it was ten hours a day. I'd get up in the morning, take a bath, come to the kitchen, fix my lunch—I always liked a fresh fixed lunch—get my breakfast, and then stand outside for the ride to come by. I always managed to get someone that liked to go to work slightly early. I carried my crocheting and knitting with me.

You had a spot where you always stayed around, close to where you worked, because when the whistle blew, you wanted to be ready to get up and go to where you worked. The leadman always come by and give you a job to do or you already had one that was a hangover from the day before. So you had a general idea what you was going to do each day.

Then we'd work and come home. I was married when I started working in the war plant, so I wasn't looking for a boyfriend and that made me come home in the evening. Sometimes you'd stop on the way home and shop for groceries. Then you'd come home and clean house and get ready for bed so you can go back the next morning. Write letters or what have you. I really wasn't physically tired.

Recreation was Saturday and Sunday. But my sister worked the swing shift and that made her get up late on Saturday morning, so we didn't do nothing but piddle around the house. We'd work in the garden, and we'd just go for little rides on the streetcar. We'd go to the parks, and then we'd go to the picture show downtown and look at the newsreel: "Where it happens, you see it happen." We enjoyed going to do that on a Sunday, since we was both off together.

We had our little cliques going; our little parties. Before they decided to break into the white nightclubs, we had our own out here on Central Avenue. There were a ton of good little nightclubs that kept you entertained fairly well. I don't know when these things began to turn, because I remember when I first came to Los Angeles, we used to go down to a theater called the Orpheum and that's where all the Negro entertainers as well as whites went. We had those clip joints over on the east side. And the funniest thing about it, it would always be in our nightclubs that a white woman would come in with a Negro man, eventually. The white man would very seldom come out in the open with a black woman. Even today. But the white woman has always come out in the open, even though I'm sure she gets tromped on and told about it. . . .

Some weeks I brought home twenty-six dollars, some weeks sixteen dollars. Then it gradually went up to thirty dollars, then it went up a little bit more and a little bit more. And I learned somewhere along the line that in order to make a good move you gotta make some money. You don't make the same amount everyday. You have some days good, sometimes bad. Whatever you make you're supposed to save some. I was also getting that fifty dollars a month from my husband and that was just saved right away. I was planning on buying a home and a car. And I was going to go back to school. My husband came back, but I never was laid off, so I just never found it necessary to look for another job or to go to school for another job.

I was still living over on Compton Avenue with my sister in this small little back house when my husband got home. Then, when Beverly was born, my sister moved in the front house and we stayed in the back house. When he came back, he looked for a job in the cleaning and pressing place, which was just plentiful. All the people had left these cleaning and pressing jobs and every other job; they was going to the defense plant to work because they was paying good. But in the meantime he was getting the same thing the people out there was getting, $1.25 an hour. That's why he didn't bother to go out to North American. But what we both weren't thinking about was that they did have better benefits because they did have an insurance plan and a union to back you up. Later he did come to work there, in 1951 or 1952.

I worked up until the end of March and then I took off. Beverly was born the twenty-first of June. I'd planned to come back somewhere in the last of August. I went to verify the fact that I did come back, so that did go on my record that I didn't just quit. But they laid off a lot of people, most of them, because the war was over.

It didn't bother me much—not thinking about it jobwise. I was just glad that the war was over. I didn't feel bad because my husband had a job and he also was eligible to go to school with his GI bill. So I really didn't have too many plans—which I wish I had had. I would have tore out page one and fixed it differently; put my version of page one in there.

I went and got me a job doing day work. That means you go to a person's house and clean up for one day out of the week and then you go to the next one and clean up. I did that a couple of times and I discovered I didn't like that so hot. Then I got me a job downtown working in a little factory where you do weaving—burned clothes and stuff like that. I learned to do that real good. It didn't pay too much but it paid enough to get me going, seventy-five cents or about like that.

When North American called me back, was I a happy soul! I dropped that job and went back. That was a dollar an hour. So, from sixty cents an hour, when I first hired in there, up to one dollar. That wasn't traveling fast, but it was better than anything else because you had hours to work by and you had benefits and you come home at night with your family. So it was a good deal.

It made me live better. I really did. We always say that Lincoln took the bale off of the Negroes. I think there is a statue up there in Washington, D.C., where he's lifting something off the Negro. Well, my sister always said—that's why you can't interview her because she's so radical—"Hitler was the one that got us out of the white folks' kitchen."

Women in the Armed Forces

Marion Stegeman

Of the more than fifteen million Americans who entered the armed services during World War II, approximately 350,000 were women. Like the Rosie the Riveters, women who joined the armed forces experienced new challenges, greater geographical mobility, and increased responsibility. The largest number served in the Women's Army Corps (WACS)—140,000—followed by 100,000 volunteers for the WAVES (Women Appointed for Volunteer Emergency Service) in the Navy. There were women's branches of the Marines and Coast Guard, and one thousand WASPs (Women's Airforce Service Pilots) did stateside and noncombat air duty.

Avenger Field in Sweetwater, Texas, was the place to be if you were a woman and a pilot in World War II. The letters that Marion Stegeman wrote home convey the excitement of being a WASP, a thrill that was part patriotism but mainly the sheer joy of flying. They also convey the disappointments, like a friend "washing out" (being asked to leave) or, worse, the death of classmates in training exercises. In all, thirty-eight WASPs lost their lives during the war.

Marion Stegeman had learned to fly in a Civilian Pilot Training Program while a student at the University of Georgia, from which she graduated with a degree in journalism and art in 1941. She became a WASP because she "wanted to be part of the action." After her training at Sweetwater, she was stationed at Love Field in Dallas. But, as her last letter shows, she realized that there was no future for women as pilots in the armed services and in 1944 she resigned to marry her boyfriend Ned Hodgson, a Marine stationed in Texas. After the war, they settled in Fort Worth to raise a family, both their lives dramatically and irrevocably affected by their service during World War II.

Sweetwater, Texas
April 24, 1943

Dearest Mother,

The gods must envy me! This is just too, *too* to be true. (By now you realize I had a good day as regards flying. Nothing is such a gauge to the spirits as how well or how poorly one has flown.) Where was I? Oh, yes, I'm far too happy. The law of compensation must be waiting to catch up with me somewhere. Oh, God, how I love it! Honestly, Mother, you haven't *lived* until you get way *up* there—all alone—just you and that big, beautiful plane humming under your control. I just sit there and sing at the top of my lungs while I'm climbing up to 4,000 feet—or however high I want to go. Of course, I'm too busy to sing while in the middle of aerobatics—but you ought to hear me let loose when I'm "clearing my area" between maneuvers. (We always clear the area first to make sure there are no planes underneath or close by—safety foist!)

The only thing that I know that's going to happen that I won't like is that they are changing my instructors some day soon. Mine is going on to the B.T.'s (Basic trainers—one step ahead of primary trainers) but maybe I'll get him again when I get to the B.T.'s. Hope so! I have no idea who my new instructor will be—I hope I'll like him as much as I do this one. He'll have to be pretty good and mighty nice though, to beat Mr. Wade's time. . . .

Smackers and much love to John, Janet, Joanna and you—M.

* * *

Sweetwater, Texas
[May 31, 1943]

Mother, Darling—

Get set! Prepare yourself! Because here comes another one of those slap-happy, nonsensical (??) ecstatic letters! OOOOOOO, Mom. I'm so happy I could die.

By now you know I've either (1) had a good day at flying or (2) passed a check ride. It just so happens that both are correct!

Honestly, mater, I was so scared when I climbed into that cockpit to take my first civilian check ride on the B.T. that I thought I'd vomit all over the controls. I had been running to the johnny for a nervous B.M. every ten minutes. One girl, seeing me dash in to the john for the fourth or fifth time (prior to my check ride) said to me, "You either are about to have a check ride or you're going on a cross country. Which is it?" It seems that it affects us gals the same way!

Anyway, I gave the check pilot a good ride and he told my instructor he might have an H.P. (hot pilot) on his hands. But since the only H.P's are dead pilots—proved by experience, he got his terminology mixed, but anyway, he meant it as a compliment. Happy day!

Then I went up for a ride with my instructor, and he told me to climb in the *back* seat which meant I was to do instrument (under the hood) flying—which is a very great compliment, since you aren't supposed to get instrument instruction until you are either qualified to solo or have already soloed! So he must think I'm ready to handle it alone as soon as I have the required eight hours, which makes me veddy, veddy happy indeed! I can hardly wait. He told me he thought I had the feel of the airplane now, and that I was cooking on the front burner! Also, he let me do a few slow rolls in the *B.T.* from the *back seat*—and he said they were *perfect.* Of course I came out from under the hood to do the slow rolls. . . .

While I was still under the hood, later, he said, "O.K. I'll take it, then you come out from under the hood when I tell you to." So he messed around awhile, then said, "All right, Come out!" So I came out from under the hood and *I was still under the hood!* He had flown right into the middle of a huge white cloud. More fun! So he flew the instruments until we were out of the cloud and could see again. . . .

So you see, your baby chile is enjoying life to the fullest. I have *everything* I want: my family loves me (and I'm sorta fond of it); I've got wonderful roommates—real *friends;* I'm doing what I love better than anything in the world; I'm so healthy and feel so good that it's revolting; and the men love me and I love the men! EEEEEEEEE, law! What a life! . . .

I love you all—M.

*   *   *

Sweetwater, Texas
[June 10, 1943]

Mother, Dear,

. . . I went on my fourth solo cross-country ("X-C") yesterday and at last something happened to break the monotony. Each trip is around 400 miles and takes about three hours, and they really get boring. But yesterday a strong wind blew me off course and made me temporarily uncertain. I decided to head out for home anyway, but things started looking *wrong,* and the check points didn't jibe with the map. I buzzed a couple of towns but couldn't find the names of them anywhere, so I turned around and went back to a town I had just passed over that had an airport. I knew it was either Ballinger or another town north of Ballinger, both of which had army airports. The roads leading out of each town made a similar pattern and the fields were located in the same place in relation to the towns. So I entered the traffic pattern with a bunch of P.T's and landed. I could've tried to get on home, but I didn't have a heck of a lot of gas and I was bored with it all anyway, and didn't want to waste time. The Army cadets and instructors nearly fell out of their planes when they saw a *girl* taxiing by in a *B.T.!* I beamed at them all and got out at a hangar where I telephoned our squadron commander, after I had found it was Ballinger, after all.

While I was waiting for the call to go through, some Lt. came up and said, "You're from Sweetwater?" I said, yace, and he went on: "Have you seen Major McConnell?" I said, "No, he's not at Sweetwater any more." (He was our commanding officer before being transferred.) The Lieutenant grinned and said, "I know. He's the C.O. here, and I bet you knew it all along." His last remark was untrue, though I *had* heard that he was at Ballinger, but had forgotten it. He's a young, attractive bachelor, so I don't blame the Lt. for thinking I had stopped over on purpose for a visit with the Major. (It turned out one girl had preceded me there by about a half hour, having secretly planned deliberately to stop over and see him. Sh-H-H! No one knows.) Anyway, I nearly fainted from the news and trucked on over to see the Commanding Officer.

Meanwhile I had gotten Avenger Field on the phone. I forgot to tell you: when I taxied up and brought the plane to a stop, I dropped my map on the bottom of the cockpit, and I thought: Ah! I'll just pretend this happened while I was in the air, and then I will have had a good excuse to land. (They tell us always to put the airplane down if we lose our air map.) So that was my story after I realized that Ballinger was almost directly on course and if I didn't have some alibi they'd never believe I didn't have an ulterior motive in landing. So everyone but my roommates think I lost my map in the bottom of the plane and landed to retrieve it.

The Sqn. Cmdr. here (when I got him on the phone) told me I had done the right thing and to come on home if I could get clearance to take off from Ballinger. So I sacheted over to Major McConnell's office and got the most cordial greeting, I've ever had. He said, "Sure I'll clear you, but I refuse to do it for a couple of hours." So he took me to the PX for cokes and cigarettes and showed me around the post. He devoted his entire time to me, and then—and then!—flew formation home with me! I had a wonderful time and the girls were really impressed and refuse to believe it wasn't all planned. The major's parting words, before he took off for Ballinger after delivering me here safely, were: "Next time make it late in the afternoon!" . . .

Darling, I do miss you so! Please don't worry about me when you miss me, though, because, honestly, I'm so happy and having so much fun it's worth any chance in the world I could take. And, actually, I'm not doing anything dangerous at all. I fly well-kept-up planes in a country where no one will shoot me down, so I'm not really brave at all, though you may keep on thinking so if you like!

LOVE YA, M.

*   *   *

Sweetwater, Texas
[Summer 1943]

Mother dear,

. . . Mother, the most heart-breaking thing has happened. Jane . . . the older roommate—washed out yesterday. The check pilots said the B.T. was just too much for her to handle, that it was no reflection on her flying. . . . Some people just aren't capable of handling the faster, heavier ships and still they make good pilots on lighter planes. Poor Jane, though! Next to Shirley and Sandy she was my favorite, and I'll sure miss her and her inimitable sense of humor. She was loads of fun and it just about broke my heart to watch what she was going through while waiting for what she knew was to be her last ride. Of course, this doesn't hit her as hard as it would someone like the other roommates because Jane has a husband and daughter—but, as she put it, that didn't keep her "from being heartsick." Poor gal cried for two days, and I cried right with her most of the time. . . .

Love you *deely.* M.

*   *   *

[Sweetwater, Texas
Late summer, 1943]

Dear Mom,

. . . Mother, this was to be a short letter, but now something has happened that I must tell you about.

You may just as well get used to hearing about these things, Mom, because so long as I'm in the flying racket they are bound to happen. Two of my classmates and their instructor were killed yesterday afternoon near Big Spring. . . .

This is no doubt another of those undetermined causes that brings about crashes, and no one will ever know what it was. Maybe it was one of those rare structural failure cases—no one knows. It seems likely, since the instructor was in the plane—Or it could have been that the girls were changing seats in mid air and one of them could've grabbed the wheel for support, thus stalling the plane. There are endless possibilities—Most of them things that *could* have been avoided, as most crashes seem to be. . . .

Don't worry about it, though, Mom, because it's very unusual for anything so mysterious to happen (especially *here*) and they're inspecting all the airplanes before we go up in them again.

As I've told you before, we *do* take chances, but they are small compared to those that thousands take every day all over the world. And we could fall down in our bathtubs at home and be killed, or get in a car and meet death. It's just not up to us to say where or when. You believe that, don't you? We'll talk about it more when I get home. . . .

I love you, Marion

*   *   *

Tallahassee, Florida
March 30, 1944

Mother, dear:

(1) General Arnold [Henry H. "Hap" Arnold, Chief of the Army Air Forces] says openly that the Army Air Forces has more than enough pilots.

(2) There are experienced instructors now being forced into the foot army—and others out of jobs.

(3) If I go into the Army, they could chain me to a typewriter for the duration plus six months, in spite of anything they might promise.

(4) I can't see myself running around saluting and kow-towing and obeying orders from [those who] . . . will really dish out the works to those of us who have been in only a year and will be mere Second Lieutenants. I can do what I'm told gracefully now only because—underneath it all—I know I don't *have* to.

Summary: All this adds up to a great deal of rationalization that has been taking place since I last saw my love. I want to marry him—now! Of course, though, I'd stay on the job indefinitely as a civilian, because I owe so much, but since the Army is forcing me to become a puppet or resign, I'm tempted to go my own way,—mine and Ned's.

I don't think the airplane will replace the man, do you?

It may be days, weeks, or months before it is necessary for me to decide. How's about a long letter of advice from you—and also please ask Aunt Helvig and Grannie what they think.

I love you, M.

Wartime Migration

Harriette Arnow

One of the most far-reaching changes on the homefront during World War II was the dramatic increase in migration. Just the sheer fact of mobilizing 15 million men and women for military service encouraged a huge amount of internal migration, as people left their homes (often for the first time) to report to service camps and training centers. In addition, the Census Bureau estimated that another 15.3 million Americans moved during wartime, with more than half of those crossing state lines. The largest single influx was westward to the state of California, the site of much of the new defense mobilization and hence jobs. During the war alone, California gained 1.4 million newcomers.

Harriette Arnow's novel, *The Dollmaker* (1954), conveys the dislocation and confusion that often accompanied such wartime uprootings. Set in the closing years of World War II (although the war is barely mentioned), the book traces the story of the Nevels family as they leave rural Kentucky for war-induced industrial opportunities in Detroit. Clovis, the husband, excited about the prospects for higher wages and a better life in a big city, initiates the move, even though

Source: Reprinted with the permission of Simon & Schuster from *The Dollmaker* by Harriette Simpson Arnow, pp. 171–73, 181, 186–90. Copyright © 1954 by Harriette Simpson Arnow, Renewed 1982 by Harriette Simpson Arnow.

his wife Gertie's dream is to own a farm of her own. In this excerpt, Gertie and her children have just arrived in Detroit at the home Clovis has rented for them. We see Detroit, and by extension, modern urban industrial life, through the eyes of a rural migrant. We follow her fumbling attempts to acquaint herself with such unfamiliar consumer items as gas stoves, bottled milk, and city water. We also see the poverty and barrenness of the urban landscape: no yard, railroad near by, tiny house with flimsy walls and little furniture, never enough money, even with everything bought on credit.

This novel does not offer a happy ending. One of Gertie's children runs away back to Kentucky, and another is killed by a train. The family sinks deeper in debt, as Clovis finds himself working only sporadically while expenses rise due to wartime inflation. The novel ends with Gertie Nevels, a skilled woodcarver, turning a large Christ figure she has been creating into cheap trinkets and wooden dolls that she can sell to make ends meet, thus supplying the ironic title of *The Dollmaker*.

Gertie stood, her outspread hands pressed against the door, closed behind her. She realized she stood in the kitchen of her new home, but it seemed more like a large closet with rows of uncurtained shelves above a sink, and smotheringly crowded with curious contrivances. A few feet in front of her was a doorless doorway into a small hall-like living room. In this room, no more than a dozen feet past the doorway, was another outside door, exactly opposite and exactly like the one behind her. The place seemed all halls and walls and doors and windows.

"It's so little, Mom. We cain't never cook an eat an—" Clytie's voice wavered, then died as she stared at a large black heating stove in a corner by the doorway.

Gertie continued to stand a moment longer, staring, choking, swallowing hard to prove to herself that she was not choking. "I figger," she said in a moment, "that it's about twenty-five feet frum inside to outside. If it jist wasn't broke up so, but we can—" Clytie, she realized, had disappeared like the rest of the children. She heard their cries and comments of exploration behind the kitchen walls. She drew a deep breath, then took the few steps to the other outside door. She opened the inner door, and scraped a hole in the dirt and frost on the outer door. She saw across a narrow strip of soot-blackened snow another building exactly like her own, telephone wires and poles, smoke, steel-mill light, and steam. She suddenly bent close to the glass, smiling. Quickly, she scraped the hole larger, then looked again; dim it had been through the steam and the smoke, and far away on the other side of the railroad fence, but it was a hill. She turned away; when seen more clearly the hill had become a great pile of coal.

She struck her shin bone against a chair as she closed the door. She bent to rub the pain, sharp in her half numb leg, and in bending her hips struck a corner of the low head of a cot-like bed. There was between the door and wall room for the head of the narrow bed, and on the other side of the door almost room for a chair. Touching the chair was a sofa, holding three cushions of some slippery, rubbery material. The wood of the sofa, like that of the chair, was a pale but shiny oak.

She stood a moment, her hands clenched by her sides, then carefully walked through the narrow space between bed and sofa. Two halls, scarce wider than her shoulders, led to the bathroom and the three bedrooms. Two of these were big enough for a double bed and four chairs each. The other was smaller still, but into it two single beds were jammed so close together there was no room to walk between them.

Clytie bumped her as she turned away. "Mom, they ain't no dressers, an no looken glass, but I bet they's twenty chairs, all alike. An jist one table fer all our cooken an eaten."

Clytie's voice had grown closer and closer to sobs, and Gertie patted her shoulder. "I recken th gover'ment thinks people won't be a doen much in their houses but setten an sleepen. An anyhow it won't be fer long an—" she was comforting when Enoch's laughter and Amos's frightened scream came from the other side of the kitchen. She bumped into the stove as she whirled toward the sound. Amos, water dripping from his hair, came running, with Enoch behind him, explaining between giggles, "He clumb into a little box uv a thing, Mom, an turned a round thing an water squirted all over."

Cassie trailed behind them, whimpering, "Th water stinks, Mom."

"It's city water, silly," Clytie explained. "It's purified like in th health books, and that thing in th bathroom, it's a shower, like in th catalogue."

Gertie tried a glass of water, but after one taste emptied it into the sink with a suspicious frown. "They's somethen in it besides water. It's worse'n that on th train."

Enoch was holding a match he had found above the kitchen sink and begging: "Light th gas, Mom. It'll warm up Amos, an we're all freezen."

Gertie turned to consider the little cooking stove in a corner of the kitchen. The top was hardly a fourth as big as that of her range cookstove back home, and no warming oven at all. Enoch, climbed on the edge of the sink to watch, pointed out the knobs she must turn, while Clytie warned, "Watch out, Mom. Vadie Tucker—recollect she'd been in Cincinnati—said a body had to be mighty careful a gas."

Gertie struck a match, and held it waveringly, looking first at the row of small black handles, then at the blank wall behind. "It ain't got no pipe. Mebbe it ain't ready to light."

"I'll bet gas stoves don't need pipes. Go on, turn one," Enoch urged.

"I don't know which is which," Gertie said in a whimpering voice, new to her.

Enoch turned a knob just as her match went out. She reached for another, while Enoch cried: "Hurry up, Mom. I'm turnen em all on."

She struck the match and held it toward the burners, all hissing now. Flame leaped at her; the corner of the kitchen seemed a wall of flame. She, like the children, jumped away, but her head struck a corner of the row of open shelves across from the stove. She saw stars and whirling lights, smelled smoke, and heard the screams of the children. Then Reuben was slapping her forehead. Clytie was throwing a glass of water on her, and Enoch was laughing. "Mom, you look so funny. Your hair's all swinged." . . .

The fire was singing soon, not loud, as the wind in the telephone wires, but with a good hearty crinking of iron and hissing of flame; and Gertie began the job of feeding the children out of the curious packages Clovis had left on the kitchen table. Tin cans she had seen, but never milk in a bottle. The children, warmed now, and all, even Reuben, happier after the coming of Maggie, crowded round her, hungry for bread and milk. Clytie got glasses, and the three quarts of milk and two loaves of bread were gone in an instant. Only Cassie wrinkled her nose, and declared the milk tasted funny. "It's pasteurized, silly," Clytie said, "like in th health books at school."

"An it's made in a factory," Enoch said.

"But they's a cow somewhere's behind it," Clytie said. . . .

The dusk had deepened until the flickering steel-mill lights made a bloody brightness on the windows, when there came another banging on the door. Clovis. He looked peaked, she thought, but hardly had a chance to look at him before the children came swarming over him, so crowding the tiny kitchen that she backed against the icebox, watching. Clytie was almost crying, and even Amos, little as he was, remembered his daddy as if he'd never been away.

She felt a sharp thrust of guilt. It was in truth like her mother said: the children had a right to live with their father. Seemed like sometimes they loved him better than her, especially Enoch and Clytie. But then she'd always been the one to give them the work and the scoldings. Clovis had brought the fun— trips in the coal truck, the river in summer, grape hunting in the fall. She'd never had the time.

In a moment he looked across their heads and smiled. "Supper ready, Gert? I'm starved fer some a yer good cooken. I ain't had a bite a fried meat, seems like, since I got up here."

"I ain't got no fried meat," she said, "but I've got supper."

"I'm figgeren on some good eaten. You ought tu have a heap a ration points. You never used none at home."

They pulled the table out from the wall, and there was room for Clovis and the older children to squeeze into their chairs, with space enough left at the corners for Amos and Cassie to stand. Gertie never sat down, but, as she had often done at home, stood between table and stove waiting on them all. Clovis, she saw, was displeased with the food. He looked resigned and disgusted as he had used to be when she left eggs out of the cornbread in order to have a few more to sell. Some of Sophronie's beans were left, and they were good, better than her own scrambled eggs and cornbread. The eggs had stuck for lack of grease and the bread, badly baked to begin with, was dry and hard and lifeless, as the meal that had gone into it.

He chirked up when Clytie praised the new dishes, and Enoch started carrying on about the wonders of the radio, and Cassie admired his new work clothing. Gertie, sorry that after he had bought so many things for them she didn't have a better kind of supper, said, trying hard to act pleased, "You've done good, real good, Clovis, to buy so much stuff, an send us th truck money besides."

He looked at her with a great showing of surprise. "Law, woman, you shorely don't think I've paid fer all this. Up here everybody buys everything on time."

She had fixed herself a plate of cornbread and beans, set it on the rim of the sink, and started to eat, standing up. But now she turned away from the food, asking, "How much we owe, Clovis?"

"Gert, don't start a worryen. Jist git it into yer head that I'm a maken big money. I ain't no sweeper maken th lowest. I done what I aimed to do, got on as a machine repair man. An it shore took some tall talken, an a heap a white lies. But it was worth it. I git in a heap a overtime, too. Do you know what my pay check-ull be this week?" he went on, laying down his knife and fork and twisting about in his chair to look at her, "Why, better'n a hundred dollars."

She heard the admiring gasp of Reuben, hurt and sullen as he still was from his attempts to borrow kindling. Big as he was, he'd worked many a day for seventy-five cents. Clytie, her voice all jerky with surprise and delight, was exclaiming, "Oh, Pop—why we're rich. That's way more'n a schoolteacher makes back home in a month."

"I don't make it ever week," Clovis explained, "an recollect that's afore hospitalization, an union dues, an OAB, an taxes. An right now, with everything tu buy, it ain't no fortune. It took saven to git a down payment on all this an on a car, too."

Gertie backed against the sink, heard her plate of beans and cornbread flop off the rim into the dishwasher, but did not look around. "But Clovis," she began haltingly, not wanting to darken the family joy, "if'n you've already run intu debt 'fore me an th youngens comes, why how can you manage with us? An we cain't, jist cain't keep on a liven in this little hole. Cain't you git along without a car?"

He pushed his plate away. "Gert, we ain't hardly seen each other 'fore you start a quarrelen about money an th place I got fer ye. What was you expecten—a castle in Grosse Pointe where them rich dagoes lives? I was lucky, mighty lucky, tu git this. They ain't hardly standen room in Detroit—I'd meant tu surprise th youngens with a ride when the weather was fitten." He held out his cup for more coffee. "But I've already got me a car. It's in th parken place now. A body cain't git along in this town thout a car."

The delighted squeals of the children, all save Reuben, only subsided under his animated discussion of the car, especially the sweetness of the motor's running, now that he had worked on it. Gertie had heard little past the words "got me a car." She turned and looked down at the gray dishwater. If just for one minute she could walk outside, go to the barn, the spring, somewhere— walk, see her father, get away from the gas smell, the water smell, the steamy heat; the hard white light beating into her eyeballs. She turned toward the outside door. A corner of the pulled out table barred her way. She looked toward the passway. Clovis's chair was there. Her empty hands found the dishrag. Somehow she washed the dishes. Hemmed in, shut down, by all this—and debts.

The evening in the hot, overcrowded, noise-laden place seemed endless. She answered questions about back home, learned that Sophronie's man, Whit Meanwell, worked in the same Flint plant as Clovis, though on a different job and shift. She wanted to ask Clovis questions: how much did they owe, how much was the interest on the debts for the car and the house plunder, where was the school, and how far away? But the radio was on, and she talked but little.

As soon as the children were asleep, Clovis had no thought for answering questions. Amos had been put to bed on the cot in the middle room, so that Gertie and Clovis were alone in the room beside the kitchen. Still, she was conscious of the restless sleep of the children on the other side of the thin walls. They were all so close together it didn't seem decent. The whole place wasn't as big as either of the two main rooms at the Tipton Place.

She shut her eyes and tried to think that she was there when Clovis fell quickly into a deep, satisfied sleep. She drowsed and dreamed of pines talking. The talking rose, became the roar of a fast through train, its screeching whistle rising above the roar as it neared the through street. This was followed at once by the tumultuous sound of its passing, so close it seemed in the very house. Amos and Cassie screamed out in fright, then as the sounds subsided they sank gradually into a whimpering half-sleep. There remained only the quiverings—the windows, the steel springs of the bed, the dishes, a chair touching the wall.

There came at last a silence so complete she could hear the ticking of the clock under the bed, and the snoring of Sophronie's children behind the wall of the girls' bedroom. The feeling that had followed her at times since she had got on the train came back in the silence—she had forgotten something, something very important. But what? She was sorting out the things she'd left behind when she found herself lifted on one elbow, listening.

Someone was moving about on the other side of the wall. She heard running water, the soft thud of a pot going over the gas flame, the creak and slam of an icebox door—breakfast getting sounds. Soon she heard the opening and closing of the outside door, and whoever it was did not come back. He had not taken time to eat his breakfast. He was most likely the husband of that

Sophronie in the sleazy nightgown. She was too lazy to get up and cook break-fast.

She drowsed, but sleep enough never came to drown the strangeness of the bed or the closeness of the air. It seemed only a little while before she found herself listening again. A singing it was in the alley now. Tipsy he was, and a tenor, "They'll be pie in a sky—" A woman's voice cut him off, something like the girl Maggie's, but near crying, "Please, Joseph, please. Du neigh-bors—"

"Quitcha tucken," the man said, and a door on the other side of the alley slammed.

"Tucken." What was "tucken," she wondered. Then the door next her own was opened quietly, but slammed shut so loudly that Clovis turned in his sleep. She heard the opening of the oven door, the little whoosh of the lighting gas, then the opening and closing of the icebox door. A chair was pulled out fol-lowed by the hissing sound of the cap jerked off a bottle of something fizzy like pop. She heard a chair tip back against the wall, so close through the thin-ness seemed like she could feel it. She could see the man's chair leaning against the wall, his cold feet warming in the oven, as he drank from the bottle. She heard the soft clink of glass on steel as he put it down. But where had he been and why, at this time of night? She sat straight up in bed with wonder and sur-prise when the voice came, low, more like a sigh than a voice, "Oh, Lord, that moven line," for the voice was a woman's voice, Sophronie's.

The sounds of the other side of the wall or her own abrupt movement awak-ened Clovis enough that he mumbled sleepily: "Don't be afeared, Gert. Th doors locks good."

"Oh, I ain't afeared," she whispered. "It's that Sophronie. Why, she's jist got in home."

He clamped one ear against the pillow, put an arm over the other. "When else would a woman on th three-tu-twelve shift git home?"

Japanese Relocation

Monica Sone

The internment of 110,000 Japanese-Americans from 1942 to 1945 rep-resented the largest denial of civil liberties during the war. After the Japanese attack on Pearl Harbor in December 1941, the federal gov-ernment ordered all Japanese-Americans relocated from the West Coast war zone to internment camps in the interior. The Japanese community did not strenuously contest this policy, fearing further reprisals and charges of treason or spying; public opinion, federal of-ficials, and (in 1944) the Supreme Court all upheld the detention as a necessary military decision during wartime. Only after the war, and among later generations, did the shame of this episode sink in.

Monica (Itoi) Sone's autobiography, *Nisei Daughter* (1953), tells the story of Japanese relocation from the perspective of a young woman in Seattle, Washington. (The Japanese character *sei* means generation; by adding a number as a prefix, such as *Issei, Nisei, Sansei,* and most recently, *Yonsei,* it enumerates the successive generations.) The Issei generation, Monica's parents, were permanently barred from citizenship by the 1924 law which cut off immigration from Japan (and China) completely. But their American-born children, the Nisei, were citizens, and much more part of American culture than their parents. This autobiography, like many stories of immigrant children and their parents, concerns the struggle to balance the dual heritages. As the war hysteria mounts, Monica can only describe herself as "a despised, pathetic two-headed freak," but at story's end she feels that her Japanese and American parts have now melded into one.

This section describes the Itoi family's forced evacuation to a temporary encampment called Camp Harmony; later they will be moved to a settlement in Idaho. They are now Family #10710, trying to make the best of a terrible situation. Monica Sone's memoir suggests the generational conflicts between elders and their children, and it conveys the strain that the prison-like barrack conditions imposed on family life and parental authority. It also displays the physical and mental resourcefulness necessary to survive this enforced internment. Although her parents spent the entire war in the camp, Monica Sone was allowed to leave in 1943 to attend college in Indiana.

When our bus turned a corner and we no longer had to smile and wave, we settled back gravely in our seats. Everyone was quiet except for a chattering group of university students who soon started singing college songs. A few people turned and glared at them, which only served to increase the volume of their singing. Then suddenly a baby's sharp cry rose indignantly above the hubbub. The singing stopped immediately, followed by a guilty silence. Three seats behind us, a young mother held a wailing red-faced infant in her arms, bouncing it up and down. Its angry little face emerged from multiple layers of kimonos, sweaters and blankets, and it, too, wore the white pasteboard tag pinned to its blanket. A young man stammered out an apology as the mother gave him a wrathful look. She hunted frantically for a bottle of milk in a shopping bag, and we all relaxed when she had found it.

We sped out of the city southward along beautiful stretches of farmland, with dark, newly turned soil. In the beginning we devoured every bit of scenery which flashed past our window and admired the massive-muscled work horses plodding along the edge of the highway, the rich burnished copper color of a browsing herd of cattle, the vivid spring green of the pastures, but eventually the sameness of the country landscape palled on us. We tried to sleep to escape from the restless anxiety which kept bobbing up to the surface of our minds. I awoke with a start when the bus filled with excited buzzing. A small group of straw-hatted Japanese farmers stood by the highway, waving at us. I felt a sudden warmth toward them, then a twinge of pity. They would be joining us soon.

About noon we crept into a small town. Someone said, "Looks like Puyallup, all right." Parents of small children babbled excitedly, "Stand up quickly and look over there. See all the chick-chicks and fat little piggies?" One little city boy stared hard at the hogs and said tersely, "They're *bachi*—dirty!"

Our bus idled a moment at the traffic signal and we noticed at the left of us an entire block filled with neat rows of low shacks, resembling chicken houses. Someone commented on it with awe, "Just look at those chicken houses. They sure go in for poultry in a big way here." Slowly the bus made a left turn, drove through a wire-fenced gate, and to our dismay, we were inside the oversized chicken farm. The bus driver opened the door, the guard stepped out and stationed himself at the door again. Jim, the young man who had shepherded us into the busses, popped his head inside and sang out, "Okay, folks, all off at Yokohama, Puyallup."

We stumbled out, stunned, dragging our bundles after us. It must have rained hard the night before in Puyallup, for we sank ankle deep into gray, gluttinous mud. The receptionist, a white man, instructed us courteously, "Now, folks, please stay together as family units and line up. You'll be assigned your apartment."

We were standing in Area A, the mammoth parking lot of the state fairgrounds. There were three other separate areas, B, C and D, all built on the fair grounds proper, near the baseball field and the race tracks. This camp of army barracks was hopefully called Camp Harmony.

We were assigned to apartment 2-I-A, right across from the bachelor quarters. The apartments resembled elongated, low stables about two blocks long. Our home was one room, about 18 by 20 feet, the size of a living room. There was one small window in the wall opposite the one door. It was bare except for a small, tinny wood-burning stove crouching in the center. The flooring consisted of two by fours laid directly on the earth, and dandelions were already pushing their way up through the cracks. Mother was delighted when she saw their shaggy yellow heads. "Don't anyone pick them. I'm going to cultivate them."

Father snorted, "Cultivate them! If we don't watch out, those things will be growing out of our hair."

Just then Henry stomped inside, bringing the rest of our baggage. "What's all the excitement about?"

Sumi replied laconically, "Dandelions."

Henry tore off a fistful. Mother scolded, *"Arra! Arra!* Stop that. They're the only beautiful things around here. We could have a garden right in here."

"Are you joking, Mama?"

I chided Henry, "Of course, she's not. After all, she has to have some inspiration to write poems, you know, with all the *'nali keli's.'* I can think of a poem myself right now:

> Oh, Dandelion, Dandelion,
> Despised and uprooted by all,
> Dance and bob your golden heads
> For you've finally found your home
> With your yellow fellows, *nali keli,* amen!"

Henry said, thrusting the dandelions in Mother's black hair, "I think you can do ten times better than that, Mama."

Sumi reclined on her seabag and fretted, "Where do we sleep? Not on the floor, I hope."

"Stop worrying," Henry replied disgustedly.

Mother and Father wandered out to see what the other folks were doing and they found people wandering in the mud, wondering what other folks were doing. Mother returned shortly, her face lit up in an ecstatic smile, "We're in luck. The latrine is right nearby. We won't have to walk blocks."

We laughed, marveling at Mother who could be so poetic and yet so practical. Father came back, bent double like a woodcutter in a fairy tale, with stacks of scrap lumber over his shoulder. His coat and trouser pockets bulged with nails. Father dumped his loot in a corner and explained, "There was a pile of wood left by the carpenters and hundreds of nails scattered loose. Everybody was picking them up, and I hustled right in with them. Now maybe we can live in style with tables and chairs."

The block leader knocked at our door and announced lunchtime. He instructed us to take our meal at the nearest mess hall. As I untied my seabag to get out my pie plate, tin cup, spoon and fork, I realized I was hungry. At the mess hall we found a long line of people. Children darted in and out of the line, skiing in the slithery mud. The young stood impatiently on one foot, then the other, and scowled, "The food had better be good after all this wait." But the Issei stood quietly, arms folded, saying very little. A light drizzle began to fall, coating bare black heads with tiny sparkling raindrops. The chow line inched forward.

Lunch consisted of two canned sausages, one lob of boiled potato, and a slab of bread. Our family had to split up, for the hall was too crowded for us to sit together. I wandered up and down the aisles, back and forth along the crowded tables and benches, looking for a few inches to squeeze into. A small Issei woman finished her meal, stood up and hoisted her legs modestly over the bench, leaving a space for one. Even as I thrust myself into the breach, the space had shrunk to two inches, but I worked myself into it. My dinner companion, hooked just inside my right elbow, was a bald headed, gruff-looking Issei man who seemed to resent nestling at mealtime. Under my left elbow was a tiny, mud-spattered girl. With busy runny nose, she was belaboring her sausages, tearing them into shreds and mixing them into the potato gruel which she had made with water. I choked my food down.

We cheered loudly when trucks rolled by, distributing canvas army cots for the young and hardy, and steel cots for the older folks. Henry directed the arrangement of the cots. Father and Mother were to occupy the corner nearest the wood stove. In the other corner, Henry arranged two cots in L shape and announced that this was the combination living room-bedroom area, to be occupied by Sumi and myself. He fixed a male den for himself in the corner nearest the door. If I had had my way, I would have arranged everyone's cots in one neat row as in Father's hotel dormitory.

We felt fortunate to be assigned to a room at the end of the barracks because we had just one neighbor to worry about. The partition wall separating the rooms was only seven feet high with an opening of four feet at the top, so at night, Mrs. Funai next door could tell when Sumi was still sitting up in bed in the dark, putting her hair up. *Mah, Sumi-chan,* Mrs. Funai would say through the plank wall, "are you curling your hair tonight again? Do you put it up every night?" Sumi would put her hands on her hips and glare defiantly at the wall.

The block monitor, an impressive Nisei who looked like a star tackle with his crouching walk, came around the first night to tell us that we must all be inside our room by nine o'clock every night. At ten o'clock, he rapped at the door again, yelling, "Lights out!" and Mother rushed to turn the light off not a second later.

Throughout the barracks, there were a medley of creaking cots, whimpering infants and explosive night coughs. Our attention was riveted on the intense little wood stove which glowed so violently I feared it would melt right down to the floor. We soon learned that this condition lasted for only a short time, after which it suddenly turned into a deep freeze. Henry and Father took turns at the stove to produce the harrowing blast which all but singed our army blankets, but did not penetrate through them. As it grew quieter in the barracks, I could hear the light patter of rain. Soon I felt the "splat! splat!" of raindrops digging holes into my face. The dampness on my pillow spread like a mortal bleeding, and I finally had to get out and haul my cot toward the center of the room. In a short while Henry was up. "I've got multiple leaks, too. Have to complain to the landlord first thing in the morning."

All through the night I heard people getting up, dragging cots around. I stared at our little window, unable to sleep. I was glad Mother had put up a makeshift curtain on the window for I noticed a powerful beam of light sweeping across it every few seconds. The lights came from high towers placed around the camp where guards with Tommy guns kept a twenty-four hour vigil. I remembered the wire fence encircling us, and a knot of anger tightened in my breast. What was I doing behind a fence like a criminal? If there were accusations to be made, why hadn't I been given a fair trial? Maybe I wasn't considered an American anymore. My citizenship wasn't real, after all. Then what was I? I was certainly not a citizen of Japan as my parents were. On second thought, even Father and Mother were more alien residents of the United States than Japanese nationals for they had little tie with their mother country. In their twenty-five years in America, they had worked and paid their taxes to their adopted government as any other citizen.

Of one thing I was sure. The wire fence was real. I no longer had the right to walk out of it. It was because I had Japanese ancestors. It was also because some people had little faith in the ideas and ideals of democracy. They said that after all these were but words and could not possibly insure loyalty. New laws and camps were surer devices. I finally buried my face in my pillow to wipe out burning thoughts and snatch what sleep I could.

Women of Wartime Los Alamos

Ruth Marshak

Among American women affected by wartime dislocations, one of the most unusual situations concerned the Manhattan Project, the secret government project that designed, assembled, and tested the first atomic weapons. In 1943 many of the country's top physicists and scientists were sent to a remote area called Los Alamos thirty-five miles west of Santa Fe, New Mexico. This being the 1940s, all of these scientists were men, but the U.S. Army (which ran the project) allowed them to bring their families. As this selection from Ruth Marshak opens, she and her husband (who was Deputy Head of a theoretical physics group) had been sworn to secrecy about where they were going, and they had no idea what would await them when they arrived.

The men were quickly absorbed into their research, leaving the women to cope with problems of housekeeping and childcare in this remote and somewhat primitive location. In many ways it was like living in a company town. Many of the women's memories concern such mundane details as how big their house (or more accurately, trailer or hut) was, the difficulty of doing laundry, and problems with their domestic workers, local Pueblo Indian women hired for $1.50 a half-day. But complaints were balanced by the beautiful scenery and recreational opportunities, and Saturday evenings of square dancing and camaraderie with other Los Alamos residents thrown together in this unusual wartime situation.

The Manhattan Project grew rapidly, its population swelled by new recruits and by the burgeoning baby boom caused by the fertile young scientific couples, who arrived with young children or quickly had more on the way. The first baby was born in August, 1943, and eighty more arrived the next year. Babies kept coming at the rate of about 10 a month, keeping the staff pediatrician quite busy and allowing project residents to joke about "rural free delivery." Many of the women were recruited to staff the childcare center or teach in the school. Ruth Marshak, for example, taught third grade and also worked in the Housing Office. Her recollections, originally written in 1946, are typical of the mix of the travails of daily life and wartime patriotism of the women and men who were part of the Manhattan Project.

A physicist's wife in peacetime and a physicist's wife in wartime are, I have discovered, two very different things. In the years before our country was at war, this wife's interests were identical with those of any other academic lady. She went to faculty teas, fretted over her budget, and schemed for her husband's advancement. Although a physicist was inclined to work rather longer hours than his colleagues in other departments of the university, his wife's life was no different from that of the wife of a history professor. It was a good life, too.

Even before the Pearl Harbor attack, however, the physicist's routine had changed. Defense projects were started in college laboratories; armed guards began to pace the thresholds of physics buildings. One's husband grew more secretive about his work, and one knew that his job must be important, for he was immune from the draft. The physicist's wife realized that her husband, in wartime, was more than just a college professor—his was a key profession in the defense of his country.

Some physicists remained at home to teach the few students who were left in the universities. Others worked on subcontracts for the Army or the Navy in their own laboratories. But many were forced to leave home in order to do their part in developing and perfecting the weapons of war. They went to a giant installation at the Massachusetts Institute of Technology to work on radar. They went to Washington as Naval Ordnance men. They went to the Aberdeen Proving Grounds. Then, sometimes, the wives who accompanied them found that they were moving to a destination without a name.

I was one of the women thus bound for an unknown and secret place. "I can tell you nothing about it," my husband said. "We're going away, that's all." This made me feel a little like the heroine of a melodrama. It is never easy to say goodbye to beloved and familiar patterns of living. It is particularly difficult when you do not know what substitute for them will be offered you. Where was I going and why was I going there? I plied my husband with questions which he steadfastly refused to answer.

"Be very careful what you say," he warned me over and over again. As if I, confused and distraught, knew anything which might be of aid and comfort to the enemy! German agents could probably tell me a thing or two, I reflected bitterly. I went about my packing in a daze. Many questions quivered on my

Source: Ruth Marshak, "Secret City," in Jane S. Wilson and Charlotte Serber, eds., *Standing By and Making Do: Women of Wartime Los Alamos* (Los Alamos: Los Alamos Historical Society, 1988), pp. 1–2, 3–5, 8–9, 10–11, 19. Reprinted by permission of the publisher.

lips, but I would have to wait two years to find out most of their answers. "What's it all about?" I cried to my husband. "At least tell me why we are going away?"—That was in 1943, and only when an atomic bomb ripped Hiroshima in the fall of 1945 did I really understand.

When I left home, I had never even heard the name, "Los Alamos." I gradually became aware, however, that we were going to the Southwest. My husband had received a letter of instructions which said, in part, "Go to 109 East Palace Street, Santa Fe, New Mexico. There you will find out how to complete your trip." What should I expect? Rattlesnakes? Outdoor privies? My concern as a housewife over the mechanics of living seemed rather petty in the face of the secrecy surrounding our destination. I felt akin to the pioneer women accompanying their husbands across the uncharted plains westward, alert to danger, resigned to the fact that they journeyed, for weal or for woe, into the Unknown. The analogy is incomplete, for I rode, not in a covered wagon, but in a red coupe, comfortably, over silver highways. The hazards of the road were not Indians but the broken glass that menaced our thin, irreplaceable tires.

Just before reaching New Mexico, we stopped at a gasoline station in Colorado. The attendant looked over the loaded car, examined our license plates, and asked us where we were heading. We replied that we were bound for New Mexico. The man studied my husband and said, "Oh, you folks must be going to that secret project!" He needed no encouragement to launch into a detailed and accurate description of our new home. Thus for my husband's caution! We proceeded on our way, feeling considerably less important. . . .

The day after we arrived in Santa Fe, we went to 109 East Palace for our passes. We received our instructions from Mrs. McKibbin, who was in charge of the office. I learned nothing new, really. I had already realized that when my husband joined the Manhattan Project it would be as if we shut a great door behind us. The world I had known of friends and family would no longer be real to me. Why, my parents were not even allowed to come to Santa Fe on a pleasure trip! The only bridge between us would be the shadowy one of censored letters. By a rapid transmutation, my husband and I had become different people. He could not even admit that he was a physicist; his profession was "engineer." Now we were part of the top secret of the war, that great secret which lay behind our innocent rural address: P.O. Box 1663, Santa Fe, New Mexico.

P.O. Box 1663 went by many names. Those who lived there were inclined to call it Los Alamos or the mesa. People in Santa Fe referred to it as the Hill. In Manhattan District jargon it was known as Site Y, and although another designation, Zia Project, never really caught on, everyone said, familiarly, "Here on *the* Project." A mournful GI once wailed, "Lost—almost," and the populace laughed, but few called it that. People coming to the Project often spoke of it as Shangri-La.

The first thing I learned about my new home was that it was not, as I had supposed, in the desert, but rather was on the top of a mesa thirty-five miles from Santa Fe. The most direct road to it was a treacherous washboard running through the Indian pueblo of San Ildefonso, over the muddy Rio Grande, and then up a series of narrow switchbacks. As we neared the top of the mesa, the view was breathtaking. Behind us lay the Sangre de Cristo Mountains, at sunset bathed in changing waves of color—scarlets and lavenders. Below was the desert with its flatness broken by majestic palisades that seemed like the ruined cathedrals and palaces of some old, great, vanished race. Ahead was Los Alamos, and beyond the flat plateau on which it sat was its backdrop, the Jemez Mountain Range. Whenever things went wrong at Los Alamos, and there was never a day when they didn't, we had this one consolation—we had a view.

A mile or two before reaching the settlement itself, we had to show our temporary passes to the MP on duty. He jotted our pass and car license numbers on the record for the day. Passes were to be a solemn business in our lives. A lost pass meant hours of delay in the guard's hutment, an elemental little structure, its stark walls decorated with starkly naked pinup girls. The expiration date of a pass was apt to creep up, finding one unaware on just the day one had planned an outing. Many a tearful woman or belligerent gent found themselves stopped at the guardhouse, while the rest of the party sailed gaily by. The fence penning Los Alamos was erected and guarded to keep out the treasonable, the malicious, and the curious. This fence had a real effect on the psychology of the people behind it. It was a tangible barrier, a symbol of our isolated lives. Within it lay the most secret part of the atomic bomb project. Los Alamos was a world unto itself, an island in the sky.

So we arrived at the place we would call home. My first impression was discouraging. The rickety houses looked like the tenements of a metropolitan slum area; washing hung everywhere, and the garbage cans were overflowing. Dust rose in great clouds around our car. Later, we learned that the homes were not as hideous as they had seemed at first. Often, they had large yards and attractive interiors. Always, the mountains were behind them, and there was no time of year when the mountains were not beautiful. . . .

Los Alamos is about 7200 feet above sea level. Many people found the altitude a bit uncomfortable at first. Typical manifestations were a shortness of breath and insomnia. I happened to feel fine, but the altitude affected my cooking and baking. It took much longer for water to boil, so my first few meals were on the tardy side. Cakes rose beautifully in the oven, but fell magically the moment they were removed. I'd never enjoyed baking anyhow, so I now had an excuse not to bake at all. There were, however, no commercial bakeries on the Hill.

After one grew acclimated to the altitude, one began really to enjoy the Los Alamos climate. Los Alamos was a secret place, and the job of its large Security Division was to avoid publicity, not to court it. Had it had a Chamber of Commerce or a bigger booster club, however, wonderful advertisements might have been written about its weather. The sun shone almost every day. Although summer days might be warm, they were never unendurable, for the air was dry. Winters were without penetrating cold. The citizens of our community seemed to draw vigor from the air. They not only worked inhuman hours to perfect the bomb; they also had energy to dissipate on skiing and horseback riding, mountain climbing and folk dancing, and gay parties which lasted until dawn.

The social life of the Hill was surely one of its redeeming features. I found much friendliness and informality, but I discovered also that Los Alamos was not a casteless society. Lines were drawn principally, not on wealth, family, or even age, but on the position one's husband held in the Laboratory. . . .

The Tech Area was a great pit which swallowed our scientist husbands out of sight, almost out of our lives. The men were drawn to their work not only by curiosity and zeal, but also by an inspiring patriotism. They worked as they had never worked before. They worked at night and often came home at three or four in the morning. Sometimes, they set up Army cots in the laboratories and did not come home at all. Other times, they did not sleep at all. Few women understood what the men were seeking there or comprehended the magnitude of the search. The loneliness and heartache of some scientists' wives during the years before the atomic bomb was born were very real. . . .

In a broader sense, for most of us elders, the Los Alamos experience was one of the most educational of our lives. Sequestered, regimented, we had to make the most of the little we had. Perhaps it was a good thing, three years ago when I left home and started westward, that I knew so little of what awaited me. There was much amiss in the ugly town where the bomb was born. Yet I have only to think of the neighborliness and warmth and esprit de corps of Los Alamos to be heartily glad for the chance that took me there. Nor is it surprising that most people enjoyed their years on the mesa. Los Alamos was our town, our own creation. To no other community will we ever give so much of ourselves.

CHAPTER 9

The Fifties: The Way We Were?

On the surface, the 1950s is full of seeming contradictions for American women. For example, a heightened emphasis on domesticity, which Betty Friedan tagged *the feminine mystique,* coexisted alongside a steady, indeed dramatic increase in the number of married women working outside the home. Another contradiction is the stark contrast between women's supposed political apathy and nonparticipation in the 1950s and the explosion of social turmoil in the 1960s and 1970s, especially the revival of feminism. Historians are still trying to unravel the mysteries of the decade (which in terms of women's history more accurately refers to the period between 1946 and 1963, a generational cohort). Tentative findings suggest a far more complex picture than our nostalgic views of "Father Knows Best," hula hoops, and '57 Chevies provide.

After two decades of dislocation from depression and war, traditional family values looked fairly appealing to the younger generation coming of age in the 1940s. The average age of marriage for women dropped to twenty, and a third of all women in 1951 were married by nineteen. The birth rate, after steadily declining since 1800, and falling below the replacement level briefly during the Depression, suddenly shot up and stayed high well into the early 1960s. (Demographers call this phenomenon the *baby boom.*) American women on average were now having close to four children. The baby boom was accompanied by the growth of suburbia, one of the most far-reaching trends of postwar America; by 1960, more people lived in suburbs than cities. And the baby boom took place in a period of general affluence—Americans experienced a 25 percent rise in real income between 1946 and 1959. This affluence in turn heightened the cultural emphasis on consumption, which characterized postwar society. The way that such factors reinforced the identification of women with the home was well captured by Betty Friedan in her bestselling *The Feminine Mystique* (1963), which more than any other source has shaped our views of women's lives in the 1950s.

One key to unraveling the experiences of women in the 1950s is to remember that the prescriptive literature that Betty Friedan drew on to write *The Feminine Mystique* does not necessarily reflect the reality of women's lives. For one thing, many families could not afford to live the child-centered suburban lifestyle glorified in the pages of *Good Housekeeping* or *McCall's*. What relevance did it have to black or Latina women trapped in urban ghettoes, farm women still living in rural areas, or even working-class families, where such a lifestyle would have represented an almost unattainable standard of upward mobility? Looking at it another way, perhaps the popular culture so relentlessly and shrilly pushed this domestic ideal precisely because so many women were no longer willing or able to accept its basic tenet that women belonged at home. Nowhere is this more suggestive than in explaining the continuing increase in women who worked outside the home.

Women continued to enter the work force throughout the postwar period, especially married women who should have been the prime candidates for the "togetherness" glorified by the feminine mystique. Some women worked for personal reasons (they needed the stimulation of interaction on the job), but most women worked for economic ones: supporting the consumer lifestyle of postwar America often required two incomes, even in a time of rising affluence. And women worked for structural reasons related to the maturation of the American economy: the economy needed clerical and service workers, precisely the occupations women have traditionally filled. So despite the prescriptive ideology telling women to stay home, many women found sufficient reasons to make different choices. When the life choices of these women are included in the history of the decade, the experiences of women in the 1950s look far more diverse and heterogeneous than one would ever expect from only reading the popular literature.

Another area where we need to modify our simplistic views of the 1950s is as a period of political apathy. To be sure, there were few large scale protest movements in this time of complacency and satisfaction with the rewards of the American way of life. But that does not mean that the decade was devoid of political action. The most obvious example is the developing civil rights movement, which gained strength throughout the 1950s. Women, both black and white, played important roles in the early stages of this struggle. Also important were the efforts of the peace movement against nuclear testing and in favor of disarmament. Such activism makes the contrast between the apathetic 1950s and the turbulent 1960s harder to sustain.

The root problem, it seems, to our interpretation of women in the decade is that we see the 1950s only in terms of one group of women: young mothers with small children. If historians looked at that age cohort in any decade, they would not likely see much activity beyond the home, because those are the years when women's child-rearing responsibilities are most extensive. But the 1950s were not just populated by young mothers in their twenties; a generational approach reminds us that there were older women whose life patterns were set in the 1920s, 1930s, and 1940s for whom the feminine mystique is hardly the most relevant analytical tool.

It is also important to let the archetypical women of the fifties grow up and get on with their lives rather than being forever frozen in time. Because of their young age at marriage, these postwar wives and mothers finished their intensive child-rearing responsibilities (even if they have four children) by their late thirties. Given the demographic aging of the population, that left women approximately thirty-five years of their lives when domestic responsibilities would be less central. Many full-time suburban housewives of the 1950s later entered the work force, joining the significant minority who had already done so by the 1950s. When we take this broader view of women's lives in the postwar period, the picture does not look as vapid and devoid of progress. Once again, small, incremental change has the power to shape the lives of women in twentieth-century America.

The Feminine Mystique, from the Woman Who Coined the Phrase

Betty Friedan

Betty Friedan first confronted "the problem that has no name" in 1956–57 when she compiled and analyzed questionnaires for her fifteenth reunion at Smith College. Six years later, she expanded on the themes she had seen in her classmates' lives in her witty and polemical expose, *The Feminine Mystique*. "As she made the beds, shopped for groceries, matched slipcover material, ate peanut butter sandwiches with her children, chauffeured Cub Scouts and Brownies, lay beside her husband at night—she was afraid to ask even of herself the silent question—'Is this all?' " The root of the dissatisfaction, Friedan argued, lay in the postwar allegiance to the ideal of the feminine mystique: the ideology that "the highest value and only commitment for women is the fulfillment of their own femininity."

Friedan's portrait drew a responsive chord among the millions of Americans who read her book, but historians approach Friedan's view of the 1950s with some caution. Her portrait is drawn impressionistically from the lives of a very small elite of highly educated, white, middle-class suburban homemakers. Even among that group, there were many women who did not feel neurotic and harried the way Friedan's subjects did—many members of the League of Women Voters in the 1950s, for example, combined community work with suburban family life quite successfully. Friedan's portrait has little relevance to the lives of working-class women and absolutely nothing to say about blacks and Latinas.

What no one disputes, including Betty Friedan herself, is that her book was drawn very closely from her own experiences. A graduate of Smith College in 1943, she gave up a psychology fellowship in order to marry. She worked as a journalist in the early years of her marriage, but was fired from that position when she became pregnant. This piece, which was written in 1974, describes Friedan's own memories of being a suburban housewife.

In 1949 I was concentrating on breast-feeding and wheeling Danny, my first baby, to the park, and reading Dr. Spock. I was beginning to wonder if I really wanted to go back to work, after all, when my maternity leave was up. I bought a pressure cooker and *The Joy of Cooking* and a book by George Nelson about *The Modern House*. One Saturday, though we had no money, we went out to Rockland County and looked at old barns that my husband might be able to convert into a house. And I wrote my mother that I wanted the sterling silver—which she had offered us as a wedding present and I had scorned as too bourgeois—after all.

That was the year it really hit, the feminine mystique, though at the time we didn't know what it was. It was just that our lives seemed to have shifted in dimension, in perspective. The last of our group, which had come to New York after Smith and Vassar and shared an apartment in the Village, was getting married. During the war, we'd had jobs like "researcher" or "editorial assistant," and met GIs at the Newspaper Guild Canteen, and written V-mail letters to lonesome boys we'd known at home, and had affairs with married men—hiding our diaphragms under the girdles in the dresser. And we had considered ourself part of the vanguard of the working-class revolution, going to Marxist discussion groups and rallies at Madison Square Garden and feeling only contempt for dreary bourgeois capitalists like our fathers—though we still read *Vogue* under the hair dryer, and spent all our salaries on clothes at Bergdorf's and Bendel's, replacing our college Braemar sweaters with black cashmere and Gucci gloves, on sale.

And then the boys our age had come back from the war. I was bumped from my job on a small labor news service by a returning veteran, and it wasn't so easy to find another job I really liked. I filled out the applications for Time-Life researcher, which I'd always scorned before. All the girls I knew had jobs like that, but it was official policy that no matter how good, researchers, who were women, could never become writers or editors. They could write the whole article, but the men they were working with would always get the by-line as writer. I was certainly not a feminist then—none of us were a bit interested in women's rights. But I could never bring myself to take that kind of job. And what else was there? The wartime government agencies where some of us had worked were being dissolved. The group on Waverly Place was break-

Source: Betty Friedan, "The Way We Were—1949," *New York Magazine* (1974), in Friedan, *It Changed My Life* (New York: Dell, 1976), pp. 26–37. © 1974 by Betty Friedan. Reprinted by permission of Curtis Brown Ltd.

ing up—Maggie, Harriet, Madelon, everyone was getting married (and Abe Rosenthal was waiting greedily to move into that apartment so that *he* could get married).

It was very hard to find an apartment right after the war. I had left the group and found a funny apartment in the basement of a townhouse on West 86th. You had to go through the furnace room to get to it, there were pipes on the ceiling, and the cold water didn't work in the bathroom so you had to run the hot an hour ahead to take a bath. It didn't even have a kitchen, but since I had no interest in cooking, I didn't mind. It had a brick wall and lots of shelves, and a terrace door, and when Carl Friedan came back from running the Soldier Show Company in Europe to start a summer theater in New Jersey, his best friend, whom I worked with, said he knew a nice girl with an apartment. He brought me an apple and told me jokes which made me laugh, and he moved in. We got married in City Hall, but went through it again with a rabbi in Boston for his mother's sake. And while I was in the hospital having Danny, he painted the pipes on the ceiling and made a kitchen out of the closet and moved our bed into the living room so Danny could have a nursery.

After the war, I had been very political, very involved, consciously radical. Not about women, for heaven's sake! If you were a radical in 1949, you were concerned about the Negroes, and the working class, and World War III, and the Un-American Activities Committee and McCarthy and loyalty oaths, and Communist splits and schisms, Russia, China and the UN, but you certainly didn't think about being a woman, politically. It was only recently that we had begun to think of ourselves as women at all. But that wasn't political—it was the opposite of politics. Eight months pregnant, I climbed up on a ladder on a street corner to give a speech for Henry Wallace. But in 1949 I was suddenly not that interested in political meetings.

Some of us had begun to go to Freudian analysts. Like the lady editor in Moss Hart's *Lady in the Dark,* we were supposedly discovering that what we really wanted was a man. Whatever the biological, psychosexual reality, a woman was hardly in a mood to argue with that message if (a) she was lonesome and tired of living alone, or (b) she was about to lose her job or (c) had become disillusioned with it. In 1949, nobody really had to tell a woman that she wanted a man, but the message certainly began bombarding us from all sides: domestic bliss had suddenly become chic, sophisticated, and whatever made you want to be a lady editor, police reporter, or political activist, could prevent or destroy that bliss—bourgeois security, no longer despised.

The magazines were full of articles like: "What's Wrong with American Women?"; "Let's Stop Blaming Mom"; "Shortage of Men?"; "Isn't a Woman's Place in the Home?"; "Women Aren't Men"; "What Women Can Learn from Mother Eve"; "Really a Man's World, Politics"; and "Nearly Half the Women in *Who's Who* are Single."

The short stories in those women's magazines we still read under the hair dryer were all about miserable girls with supposedly glamorous jobs in New

York who suddenly saw the light and went home to marry Henry. In "Honey, Don't You Cry" (*McCall's,* January 1949), the heroine is reading a letter from her mother: "You should come home, daughter. You can't be happy living alone like that." In "The Applause of Thousands" (*Ladies' Home Journal,* March 1949), the young woman *pities* her poor mother who dreamed of being an actress; she is going to get married before she can even be tempted by such dreams.

I remember in particular the searing effect on me, who once intended to be a psychologist, of a story in *McCall's* in December 1949, called "A Weekend with Daddy." A little girl who lives a lonely life with her mother, divorced, an intellectual know-it-all psychologist, goes to the country to spend a weekend with her father and his new wife, who is wholesome, happy, a good cook and gardener. And there is love and laughter and growing flowers and hot clams and a gourmet cheese omelet and square dancing, and she doesn't want to go home. But, pitying her poor mother typing away all by herself in the lonesome apartment, she keeps her guilty secret that from now on she will be living for the moments when she can escape to that dream house in the country where they know "what life is all about."

I remember about that time running into a real psychologist, a woman slightly older than I was whom I had known in graduate school. She had been brilliant and ambitious. Unlike me, she had taken the fellowships and gotten her Ph.D. What was she doing now? "I am married," she said with great self-satisfaction, "and I am pregnant." When I asked, she said that she had picked her husband up on the subway. And I understood, because in 1949 I was also becoming infected by the mystique, that it almost didn't matter who the man was who became the instrument of your feminine fulfillment. I was awed by the strength and sincerity of her new psychological awareness, that she would even find him on the subway.

That year saw the last of the spirited, brave, adventurous heroines who had filled the magazines and movies in the thirties and forties—the Claudette Colbert, Myrna Loy, Bette Davis, Rosalind Russell, and Katharine Hepburn types. These heroines, in the end, got their man, but they were usually working toward some goal or vision of their own, independent and determined and passionately involved with the world. They were less aggressive in pursuit of a man, less kittenish than the Doris Day little housewife that followed, and the men were drawn to them as much by their spirit as by their looks. "Career woman" in the fifties became a pejorative, denoting a ball-busting man-eating harpy, a miserable neurotic witch from whom man and child should flee for very life.

In March 1949, the *Ladies' Home Journal* printed the prototype of the innumerable paeans to "Occupation: Housewife" that were to flood the women's magazines into the sixties. It began with a woman complaining that when she has to write "housewife" on the census blank, she gets an inferiority complex. ("When I write it I realize that here I am, a middle-aged woman, with a university education, and I've never made anything out of my life. I'm just a housewife.") Then the author of the reply, who somehow never is a housewife (in this case Dorothy Thompson, newspaperwoman, foreign correspondent, famous columnist), roars with laughter. The trouble with you, she scolds, is that you don't realize that you are expert in a dozen careers, simultaneously. "You might write: business manager, cook, nurse, chauffeur, dressmaker, interior decorator, accountant, caterer, teacher, private secretary—or just put down philanthropist. . . . All your life you have been giving away your energies, your skills, your talents, your services, for love." But still, the housewife complains, I'm nearly fifty and I've never done what I hoped to do in my youth—music. I've wasted my college education.

Ho-ho, laughs Miss Thompson, aren't your children musical because of you, and all those struggling years while your husband was finishing his great work, didn't you keep a charming house on $3,000 a year and paper the living room yourself, and watch the market like a hawk for bargains? And in time off, didn't you type and proofread your husband's manuscripts, play piano duets with the children to make practicing more fun, read their books in high school to follow their study? "But all this vicarious living—through others," the housewife sighs. "As vicarious as Napoleon Bonaparte," Miss Thompson scoffs, "or a queen. I simply refuse to share your self-pity. You are one of the most successful women I know."

That year the *Ladies' Home Journal* serialized Margaret Mead's *Male and Female,* with its deceptively tempting version of a South Sea world where a women succeeds and is envied by men, just by "being" a woman.

> In Bali, little girls between two and three walk much of the time with purposely thrust-out little bellies, and the older women tap them playfully as they pass. "Pregnant!" they tease. So the little girl learns that . . . some day she will have a baby, and having a baby is, on the whole, one of the most exciting and conspicuous achievements that can be presented to the eyes of small children in these simple worlds, in some of which the largest buildings are only fifteen feet tall. . . . Furthermore, the little girl learns that she will have a baby not because she is strong or energetic or initiating, not because she works and struggles and tries, and in the end succeeds, but simply because she is a girl and not a boy, and girls turn into women, and in the end—if they protect their femininity—have babies. . . . In our Occidental view of life, women, fashioned from man's rib, can at the most strive unsuccessfully to imitate man's superior powers and higher vocations.

That it was slightly schizophrenic to try to live through your pregnant belly, as it were, in an increasingly complex world where the largest buildings were a lot taller than fifteen feet—well, we only woke up to that later. In 1949 we were suckers for that apple—we could cop out from the competition, the dull, hard work of "man's higher vocations," by simply "playing our role as women." No more need to rock the boat, risk failure or resentment from men.

That year, the *Ladies' Home Journal* also serialized *Cheaper by the Dozen,* the story of the lady engineer who applied her scientific know-how to raising that newly fashionable large family. Very good reporters were given the assignment of documenting in minute detail every detail of the daily life of the newly glamorous American housewife—cooking in her own kitchen, with all her new appliances. It was also reported in the fall of 1949 that "something new in birth rates has occurred in the U.S. Between 1940 and 1947, the reproductive rate of women college graduates increased 81%, compared with an increase of only 29% among women who had completed only grade school."

It certainly did not occur to any of us then, even the most radical, that companies which made a big profit selling us all those washing machines, dryers, freezers and second cars, were overselling us on the bliss of domesticity in order to sell us more things. Even the most radical of us, in our innocence, wanted those pressure cookers.

We were even more innocent in our sophistication as women. Though I was virtually a virgin myself when I came to New York after college, it was my lot to arrange abortions for our entire Smith group. Why me? Because I was the radical, also a psychologist and unshockable (I knew all the Freudian words). More practically, as a newspaperwoman, I was supposed to know my way around. The men I worked with during the war, necessarily over draft age, were *Front Page* types who taught me to write a jazzy lead after three martinis at lunch. They were avuncular to my innocence, with occasional lecherous lapses. The first time I said, "Trav, you have to help me. A friend of mine is pregnant," the whole office sprang into action. I was told, in serious, sinister secrecy, where to take my "friend." It also cost $1,000 and they were concerned where my "friend" would get the money. Six months later, I had to come to them again. This time, the reaction was not so warm. It was years before I realized that they had assumed each "friend" needing an abortion was *me*.

I myself never had an abortion, though I personally accompanied several of these friends to scary, butchery back rooms, and shared their fear and distrust of the shifty, oily, illegal operators, and sat outside the room and heard the screams and wondered what I'd do if they died, and got them into taxis afterward. Dear Virginias who read this now—when our efforts have gotten you legal abortion in New York, and an historic Supreme Court decision affirming your right to control your own body, and sexual privacy, and birth control and abortion—you can't imagine how humiliating, traumatic, horrible it was, to need an abortion in 1949. Nor can you whose parents buy you the pill understand the awkward indignity of getting a diaphragm in New York, in 1949, if you weren't married—and sometimes even if you were.

My last task, as the group broke up, was to find an Episcopal priest to marry Maggie and Roger in a fancy church acceptable to her mother. But in 1949 not even a young pacifist minister would perform the ceremony for a man who had been divorced. It was harder to find such a minister than an abortionist. Divorce was unthinkable, in our very buying of the feminine mystique. In fact, no woman I knew personally had been through divorce herself in 1949, and that was still true fifteen years later when the first threat of its personal possibility paralyzed me with terror in the security of my own suburban dream house.

"Security" was a big part of what began to happen in 1949. "Security," as in "risks," was in the headlines, as in atomic secrets, Communist espionage, the House Un-American Activities Committee, loyalty oaths, and the beginning of blacklists for writers. Was it unconscious political retreat that so many who had talked so bravely, and marched, suddenly detoured to the security of the private four walls of that house in suburbia—everything that was "bourgeois." Suddenly we stopped using the word "bourgeois." We were like our parents, it seemed. Suddenly we were very interested in houses and *things:* chairs, tables, silverware. We went to the Museum of Modern Art to study furniture and displays of modern architecture, and bought our first possessions— Eames chairs, a blond free-form sculptured Noguchi dining table, and a Herman Miller couch-day bed with a plain tweed-covered mattress and bolsters, so modern, so different from the overstuffed, tufted davenport at home (whose comfort I have now gone back to).

Toward the end of the year I read a story in the *Times* about a new garden apartment community in Queens called Parkway Village, built for the UN with some vacancies for ex-GIs. It was almost like having your own home: the apartments had French doors opening on to a common lawn where the children could go out and play by themselves, instead of having to be taken to the park. And there was a cooperative nursery school. During my lunch hour I took the subway to the wilds of Queens, and so began the fifteen-year trek of my own particular nuclear family away from the city, to that garden apartment in Queens, to a rented barn in Sneden's Landing, to our own eleven-room Charles Addams Victorian house in Rockland County, where my children (increased to three) grew up, and I chauffeured, and did the P.T.A. and buffet dinners, and hid, like secret drinking in the morning, the book I was writing when my suburban neighbors came for coffee, *The Feminine Mystique.*

I felt that I would never again, ever, be so happy as I was living in Queens. The floors were parquet, and the ceilings were molded white plaster, no pipes, and the plumbing worked. The rent was $118.50 a month, for four and one-half rooms, and we thought that was enormous. And now our friends were the other couples like us, with kids at the nursery school who squealed at each other from the baskets of the grocery carts we wheeled at the supermarket. It was fun at first, shopping in those new supermarkets. And we bought barbecue grills, and made dips out of sour cream and dried onion soup to serve with potato chips, while our husbands made the martinis as dry as in the city and cooked hamburgers on the charcoal, and we sat in canvas chairs on our terrace and thought how beautiful our children looked, playing in the twilight, and how lucky we all were, and that it would last forever.

There were six families in our group, and if your child smashed his finger in the manhole cover and you weren't home, one of the others would take him to the doctor. We had Thanksgiving and Christmas and Passover Seders as a joint family, and in the summer rented houses together, on Lake George and Fire Island, that we couldn't afford separately. And the support we gave each

other hid the cracks in our marriages—or maybe kept them from getting serious. As it is, of the six families, three couples are now divorced, one broken
by suicide.

Having babies, the Care and Feeding of Children according to Doctor
Spock, began to structure our lives. It took the place of politics. But the mystique was something else—that college graduates should make a *Career* of
motherhood, not just one or two babies, but four, five, six. Why even go to college?

I remember the zeal with which we took the classes at the Maternity Center. Our husbands were envious, but then with natural childbirth the husbands
could take the classes too, and breathe along, and show off at dinner parties,
doing the exercises on the floor. And then there was the moral, political seriousness of our breast-feeding. In the summer of '49, I was frowned on for
breast-feeding in public, on the front steps of my husband's summer theater.
It wasn't fashionable then. But it's so *natural,* we gloried, feeling only scorn
for our superficial selfish sisters who thought breast-feeding was animal and
would spoil their figures. (Actually, I did not breast-feed in public—I'd retire
to the back row of the darkened theater where they were rehearsing. But I did
sit out on the front steps afterwards, burping him in the sun.) And how proud
I was, continuing the breast-feeding nearly all that year, even after the milk
began to give out and I had to sterilize bottles anyway. And how furious I was,
when they called from the office and insisted that I come back to work, one
month before the year's maternity leave was over, because it was messing up
vacation schedules.

So twenty-five years later when that grown-up boy is having trouble with
his girl, and—knowing Freudian words himself, if not yet Dr. Spock—says his
insecurity in love is all my fault, I still feel the pains of the guilt caused by leaving my first baby with a nurse when I went back to work. Would all that guilt
have been necessary if Dr. Spock hadn't said, in the section on "Should Mother
Work?": "In most cases, the mother is the best one to give him this feeling of
'belonging,' safety and security. . . . If a mother realizes clearly how vital this
kind of care is to a small child, it may make it easier for her to decide that the
extra money she might earn, or the satisfaction she might receive from an outside job, is not so important after all."

To be honest, those years were not all products of the "mystique." I still
remember the marvelous dark night in the spring of 1949 when we were wheeling Danny home in the baby carriage. I looked down as we passed under a
streetlight, and he was smiling at me, and there was recognition in his eyes. A
person was there, and he knew me.

Besides, the reality of the babies, the bottles, the cooking, the diapering,
the burping, the carriage-wheeling, the pressure cooker, the barbecue, the playground, and doing-it-yourself was more comfortable, more safe, secure, and
satisfying—that year and for a lot of years thereafter—than that supposedly
glamorous "career" where you somehow didn't feel wanted, and where no mat-

ter what you did you knew you weren't going to get anywhere. There was a guilty feeling, too: it was somehow your fault, *pushy* of you, to want that good assignment for yourself, want the credit, the by-line, if the idea, even the writing, had been yours. *Pushy,* too, if you felt rejected when the men went out to lunch and talked shop in one of those bars where women were not allowed— even if one of those same men asked you out to lunch, alone, in the other kind of restaurant, and held your hand, or knee, under the tablecloth. It was uncomfortable, unreal in a way, working in that kind of office with "career" still driving you, but having no words to deal with, even *recognize,* that barrier that you could never somehow break through, that made you invisible as a person, that made them not take you seriously, that made you feel so basically unimportant, almost unnecessary, and—buried very deep—so angry.

At home, you *were* necessary, you were important, you were the boss, in fact—the mother—and the new mystique gave it the rationale of career.

The concrete, palpable actuality of the carpentry and cooking you could do yourself, and the surprising effectiveness of the changes you could make happen in school boards and zoning and community politics, were somehow more real and secure than the schizophrenic and even dangerous politics of the world revolution whose vanguard we used to fancy ourselves. The revolution was obviously not going to *happen* that way in America by 1949: the working class wanted those pressure cookers, too. It was disillusioning, to say the least, to see what was happening in the trade unions, and in Czechoslovakia and the Soviet Union, even if the myth of the Communist menace was mostly an excuse for red-baiting. In 1949, McCarthyism, the danger of war against Russia and of fascism in America, and the reality of U.S. imperial, corporate wealth and power all made men and women who used to have large visions of making the whole world over uncomfortable with the Old Left rhetoric of revolution.

Suburbia, exurbia, with the children as an excuse—there was a comfortable small world you could really do something about, politically: the children's homework, even the new math, compared to the atomic bomb.

The feminine mystique made it easier for a woman to retreat smugly, without the pangs of conscience and self-contempt a man might feel while using all his wits to sell cigarettes that would cause cancer, or deodorants. We could be virtuous and pure of compromise, and even feel a smug contempt for the poor man who could not so easily escape the ulcerous necessity of really conforming and competing. For a long while, it looked as if women had gotten the better of that bargain. It was only later that some of us discovered that maybe we had walked as willing victims into a comfortable concentration camp.

Shortly after 1949, I was fired from my job because I was pregnant again. They weren't about to put up with the inconvenience of another year's maternity leave, even though I was *entitled* to it under my union contract. It was unfair, *wrong* somehow to fire me just because I was pregnant, and to hire a man instead. I even tried calling a meeting of the people in the union where I worked. It was the first personal stirring of my own feminism, I guess. But the other women were just embarrassed, and the men uncomprehending. It was my own fault, getting pregnant again, a *personal* matter, not something you should take to the union. There was no word in 1949 for "sex discrimination."

Besides, it was almost a relief: I had begun to feel so guilty working, and I really wasn't getting anywhere in that job. I was more than ready to embrace the feminine mystique. I took a cooking course and started studying the suburban real-estate ads. And the next time the census taker came around, I was living in that old Charles Addams house we were fixing up, on the Hudson River in Rockland County. And the children numbered three. When the census taker asked my occupation, I said self-consciously, virtuously, with only the faintest stirrings of protest from that part of me I'd turned my back on— "housewife."

Balancing Work and Family

Betty Jeanne Boggs

Besides the heightened media emphasis on domesticity, the other major trend of the 1950s was the growing number of women who were working outside the home. Women made up 29 percent of the work force in 1950 and 35 percent in 1965; whereas one fifth of wives worked in 1950, the figure approached one third by 1960. Women's work was not necessarily a challenge to the values of home and family, however, since many women justified taking jobs in order to improve their family lifestyle. But it did point to the emerging centrality of paid work to women's lives, especially for married women whose children were in school.

Betty Jeanne Boggs is one of the women who alternated work with home responsibilities in the 1950s. Born in 1926, she had been a Rosie the Riveter in the aircraft industry in California during World War II. When the war ended, she returned to her native Seattle to resume her education, marry, and raise a family. She had always had nontraditional aspirations (she wanted to be a test pilot and major in aeronautical engineering) and began a career as a lab technician. But after her second child was born, she left the work force completely, although not without a great deal of ambivalence, as this selection shows. After her children were older, she went back to school to earn her masters in fine arts; as a sculptor, she works with heavy metals in ways that hark back to her experiences in World War II.

Betty Boggs's story once again reminds us of the importance of looking at women's life cycles. If we looked only at the 1950s, we might say, she dropped out to raise a family and thus conformed to the roles expected. But she did not stay a homemaker forever, nor did many of the women who were the young suburban housewives of the

1950s. Either by choice or necessity, many of their lives took different turns in the 1960s, 1970s, and beyond.

I worked in a war plant and it was one of the things you did when your country was at war, and it had been an enjoyable experience. Even today, I'm very proud of that job. I can always say "Hey, I was a riveter during World War II!". . . .

The job I got after that, I was working in downtown Portland, like a file clerk. Office work—you had to dress up, you had to behave yourself in a certain way, and it just didn't seem to be as productive. I liked working with my hands, and I didn't mind dressing in pants and blouse or shirts or overalls or jumpsuits. But that office, oh, a total bore!

I would much rather have worked in a factory. There was a shipyard, I remember, and some small companies, but I wasn't given the chance to think about it. My mother made me quit that job. She was trying to have me where she could watch me. See, when I was working down at that office, I would meet a lot of "boots" who were getting ready to get on the ship that was being launched there at the shipyard. They would be in town for maybe two or three months. I didn't see any sense in rebelling. So we went across the river to Vancouver Barracks, which was an army post, and I went to work as a dental assistant.

When I went to work there, I went from sailors over to meeting soldiers. Gee, there was no lack of knowing men, for goodness sakes. I was right at the source of supply—and whoopie! You'd wade in barefoot and have a great time! It was always movies and there was a roller-skating rink in Portland. If you didn't like roller skating, okay, then there was ice skating and there was hockey we could go to. We'd go sight-seeing a little bit and we could go on picnics. There was a lot of recreation.

We left the Portland area because she thought I was dating too many servicemen. But what I could never figure out, what was her reasoning in having me work there at Vancouver Barracks if she didn't want me to date servicemen? That put me right in the lap of the whole works.

I started to major in math, and you know how people'll ask, "Well, what are you going to do with it? Are you going to teach?" "Oh, is that all you can do, is teach?" "Well, there's not much else you can do with it because you're a woman." Always this—"because you're a woman." So I thought, "Teach? I can't imagine me being up in front of a class trying to teach kids." Still there was this shyness. So I think I finished calculus and also got through physics.

I was working part time at a scientific supply house. They brought in an auditor and his desk was next to mine. Naturally, you get to talking. He told me that at Stanford University they had a test which you could write for. You answer all these questions: "What are you best suited for?" So I wrote for the

Source: Reprinted with permission of Twayne Publishers, an imprint of Simon & Schuster Macmillan, from *Rosie the Riveter Revisited* by Sherna Berger Gluck, pp. 113–120. Copyright © 1987 by Sherna Berger Gluck.

test. When the results came back, the two top things—it was equal—was either an artist or a laboratory technician. I had never given either one of them any thought. In fact, a laboratory technician—I'd never even heard of it. Then it went down to a dentist, a librarian. Oh, I think even an engineer was kind of high. Anyway, it introduced new ideas.

So I thought, okay, look into a laboratory technician. That's when I changed my major from math into biological science. That made a big difference because before, in math, I just couldn't figure out—what am I going to do with it? Also my social life sort of got in the way. I knew a fellow at that time, and he kept telling me he couldn't figure out why I was taking calculus. He was in one of my calculus classes and his presence bothered me. I just didn't quite get a hold of the idea of calculus as well as if I'd been in there by myself. In the engineering classes, I may have been the only girl but I wasn't going on dates with them, and I seemed to get those subjects a lot better. Anyway, in chemistry I felt, "This is my place." It has that nice feeling to it. . . .

My girlfriend, Shirley, was in a couple of my classes and we would do things together. Pretty soon she started talking about this character she met in one of her classes, and his name was Josh. Being a lab technician, there was a club that you joined, and she and I would go to these meetings. Josh was there because he was going to be premed. He would take us both home from these meetings, and I gradually got acquainted with him. There was nothing going on at first, except that he had such a terrific sense of humor that I just really was quite fascinated by him.

I didn't go out with him until February. It was one of these dances where the girls ask the boys. He will deny it to this day—I'm glad he's not here because he can't argue with me—but I stopped to talk to him in the hall and he said something about going to that dance, and I said, "Well, I just hadn't thought of who I'm going to take." And he said something like "I think it would be nice if you took me." So that was the first date with him, and from then on there wasn't anybody else. We got married September the first, and so here we are a hundred years later. . . .

Josh said, "I want you to finish school, and then I'll go back and won't have to work because you'll work full time. We can live better off of your salary than we can this other way and I can get through faster."

California, having different rules and regulations as far as lab technicians go—you had to graduate and then you intern and then you take the state test. There was just a lot of other classes I had to take. It was almost like starting school all over again, because it was more bacteriology and more chemistry, parasitology and embryology. Finally I graduated from San Jose State in 1953.

I was going to intern at the County Hospital in San Jose. I just about had that lined up when one of my friends in class says, "Betty, I got a job through the Sylvania Electronics Company and it's right near where you live. I'm going to get married and I'm not going to take the job. Why don't you go over and talk to them? That way I don't have to face them and tell them that I'm getting married and leaving them in the lurch."

So they hired me. It was only like two and a half miles from my house, and it was working in a chemistry and plating lab instead of a medical lab, which appealed to me even more. I would test the plating tanks and make sure that all the chemicals were made up. If we had to have a new tank or if one had to be emptied and cleaned out, I would make that up. As far as the plating, I would do a lot of experimenting. We were doing little, oh, klystron tubes and traveling wave tubes. It was a hush-hush thing. They had a jet that we were working on and a lot of test equipment for it. The engineers would bring in something: "I need just a little tiny gold plating on this little mark right here." We had two or three different types of plating: the copper, nickel, cadmium, silver, and gold. I took care of all of that.

I started out at two hundred dollars and something. I remember I got a raise to three hundred dollars, and there was some other engineer that was provoked because he didn't get as big a raise as I did. About a year after that, they transferred my boss to another part of that lab. I was then supervisor. Because I had a degree and was a white-collar worker and working out in the plant, they gave me the title of engineer. There was a couple of girls under me, maybe one or two. The most I had reporting to me at one time were ten girls. They had lead-girls, but as far as being a supervisor, I think I was the only woman. From what I've been told, I was supposed to be the first woman engineer, which naturally was very thrilling to me.

When they talk about women's lib, boy, oh boy, this is where the whole darn thing came in. If I'd known then, I really would have told the son of a gun off and I really would have run him right into the president's office. He was the production manager, and I think he was one of these people that came out of the plant back in West Virginia. He didn't have a college education but was one that came up through the ranks. Not that there's anything wrong with it, but when it affects the male ego, then there's a lot wrong with it. He could not stand to think that there was a woman white-collar worker, and he didn't like it one bit. He thought that I should be at home, and he hassled me every way he possibly could. He hassled me right up until practically the day I quit.

When we married, Josh's health wasn't that great and we got a sperm count. He was just so sterile at that time, we just sort of figured, okay, kids are for everybody else. We didn't do anything for or against. I don't think we even gave it any thought like "Well, are we going to adopt later on?" It was like "Oh, I guess kids are for everybody else, and maybe one of these days we'll sit down and think about it seriously."

Then when I did get pregnant: "Wow, I'm pregnant!" It was bewildering, in a way. Like "Oh, for heaven sakes!" So I will jokingly say to this day, "Well, shrugging the shoulders did it."

Then I was really torn up. For one thing, I wanted to stay home with the baby; two, I wanted to help Josh get through; three, I really enjoyed that job. I just didn't know what to do about it, because I enjoyed working and yet I thought I should really be home with that baby. My mind was sort of made up for me because Josh kept saying, "I've got to get through school. It's better that you work. I can spend all my time studying and get through engineering. When I get through, then we'll take it from there."

We kept trying to find baby-sitters and I think I went through five of them. That was a chore because you just didn't want any old body. At that time there weren't any of those places where they have preschool—which would really have worked out nice. So I'd find somebody that could take him for a while. I was paying ten dollars a week at that time for child care. Then the last one, oh gad, she was taking care of some other little baby about the same age as my son. She caused more trouble than any of the others put together: "Don't do this, don't do that. No, no, no."

When I stayed home with Tad when he was a little over two years old, his attitude was rather antagonistic. I'd go to be affectionate with him and he'd just kind of close up. I thought, "Okay, doggone child, you're going to love me and you're going to be affectionate. I'm just going to keep working away at you."

Josh had a good relationship built up, because he'd have Tad to himself. Sometimes he'd be home earlier and then he would pick up Tad, or he'd have a day off and he'd keep Tad with him, or if he was out working in the yard, he'd have Tad with him. And he took care of him. He never once hesitated to change diapers or to feed the baby. Absolutely no holding back as far as caring for him. The only thing I think that held him back was if he had a lot of homework.

I felt terrible—terrible, because I really enjoyed my job; good, because I could be at home. It was really a mixed emotion. You wanted to be in two places at one time and how can you resolve that? So in one way it was resolved for me, because then I didn't go back to work. I was at home with the kids all the time.

We took them everywhere. We never went on a trip that we left them at home. We didn't do any camping at that time, but we'd go to parks, we'd take them to the city—San Francisco—we'd picnic. Of course, Josh and I always did a lot together right from the time we got married. In fact, people are going to think I'm archaic when I mention this, but I would never go anywhere unless he could go. We always had the philosophy, "Well, why should I go enjoy myself when you're not here to enjoy it with me?" I think we've carried that out even today.

I gave it some thought that someday I would go back to work, but I didn't really think about it too much, 'cause my time was taken up pretty much by the kids. I don't regret one moment of ever staying home with them, because to me, it's very important that I was there. I think it has paid off. My daughter has told me, she's glad I didn't work. I think it's important for a woman to do something, 'cause I think she's got a brain, the same as a man. But I can't quite come to grips with women working full time and having children. It's either one way or the other, 'cause I feel that there's a lot of problems nowadays that are caused by women working and you've got everybody else raising your kids.

I think a mother should be there the first couple of years of a child's life, and like high school, I definitely think that she should be there. I know they're old enough to take care of themselves, but it seems to make a difference. You just sense it: a parent cares, they're there.

Female Entrepreneurship in the 1950s

Helen Stone Hovey

Another way to complicate the picture of the 1950s is to realize that even women who stayed at home were not necessarily totally domestic. Magazine articles, books, newspaper columns, and government publications gave women practical advice on how to make money out of their homes, and more than a million women took the challenge. One of the biggest success stories was Lillian Vernon Katz, who in 1951 while pregnant with her first child used $2000 of wedding gifts to open the mail order catalogue business that still bears her name today. In general, however, female entrepreneurs operated on a smaller scale. Some of the most popular ventures included food, beauty products and services, gifts and fashion, and services like babysitting or real estate.

The 1953 book by Helen Stone Hovey, *Making Money in Your Kitchen: Over 1600 Products that Women Can Make,* is typical of the books geared toward women in the decade. Its tone is upbeat and almost inspirational, combining recipes and tips with case histories of women who turned their special domestic skills into profitable businesses. "The American way of life proves the possibilities of individual ability," says Hovey. As she says, all this can be had for an initial investment of only $1.00. Who could beat that?

Often women's income-producing efforts are dismissed as "pin-money," just adding a bit of extra money to enhance a family's standard of living. But while some women in the 1950s might have couched their business undertakings in domestic tones or downplayed them as just a hobby, for many others these economic opportunities represented a vital contribution to family income. And whether you were Lillian Vernon or just a local caterer selling your favorite apple pie, it is not hard to imagine that many women found this work satisfying as well as profitable. Once again, the home and domesticity look a lot less claustrophobic than Betty Friedan implied.

This book is for the stay-at-home women who wish to earn extra money. Women *can* make money by selling *good* homemade food if their cooking skills are superior.

Source: Helen Stone Hovey, *Making Money in Your Kitchen: Over 1600 Products that Women Can Make* (New York: Wilfred Funk, 1953), pp. 1–3, 11–12, 13.

This book is filled with practical and helpful answers to such basic questions as what to make and how to market a product after it is made.

Also, this book will describe a wide variety of small products that have been launched at home. These products were launched at home with a minimum amount of money but full measures of patience, effort, and willingness to accept small financial return. It is these that are the substitute for a large amount of capital.

Since World War II, the number of working women has increased to about 22 million. Some women are working to support themselves and their families, others are working to help with the medical bills, to buy a home, or to educate their children. They may add a little to the savings account and make possible some of the little luxuries such as music lessons for Susy, a new carpet, and a well-earned family vacation. About 1 1/2 million women are profitably self-employed at home. Remaining at home has many advantages such as eliminating the cost of working clothes, transportation, meals out, and the confusion of frantic housekeeping activities after working hours. Yes, a few extra dollars can make a lot of difference in the life of the average homemaker.

"Women have everything it takes to succeed in small, independent enterprises—imagination, courage, and a capacity for hard work," said a wise person. Every homemaker has a kitchen and some good ideas, but those women who have had the will power and courage to put ideas into practice and to realize profits from them are the ones who have earned the extra money—even become the "heroines" of success stories.

An analysis of hundreds of women who have been successful in small but profitable home-kitchen businesses shows certain very definite things. For example, it is not a matter of age since all ages succeed. It is not a matter of nationality or race since all groups are represented. It is not a matter of location since all states have city and country representation. It is not a matter of occupational training or special aptitudes beyond pride in a product and average skills. With a profitable hobby in foods you cannot help but be successful IF you inform yourself about opportunities in your community needs and make the contacts which will benefit you.

The profitable kitchen career refers to the small business which may be operated by the average woman in her home. It can easily average $50 a month, more or less, depending upon the time and effort devoted to it and the skill in handling foods. Incidentally, skills may be developed with interest and consistent effort. The profit does not only refer to the cash-in-hand, which is both desirable and necessary for many. It also refers to self-satisfaction, prestige, and recognition in the community for creditably serving a need as well as commendation from both family and friends.

Success in a Kitchen Career

What do you prepare especially well? What do your family and friends never fail to compliment? Many surveys show that the real money-makers are the foods that definitely save a busy woman's time and energy such as an Italian meat sauce, homemade bread, and foods that she cannot easily prepare or may lack a special knack for preparing such as checkerboard party sandwiches or mayonnaise. The selection of the right product may easily make the difference between success and failure.

1. Capital. Perhaps the very best feature of a home-kitchen venture is the very small amount of capital needed. For example, the cost of ingredients for a cake to be used for tasting samples, for a few jars of marmalade, for a batch of creamy fudge, or for a luscious blueberry pie can easily be under a dollar. It doesn't take much of an adventurous spirit or a gambling instinct to risk less than $1.00 for tasting samples, does it?

After the original less-than-$1.00 investment for tasting samples you will need little more for your next step. It may be the price of a small advertisement in the local paper or it could be even less—a few dozen postal cards to friends and acquaintances or a few brief telephone calls announcing your venture. If you have prepared food for church bazaars, community suppers, parent-teacher groups, or if you have established yourself as a hostess, it is even more simple to start a home business. The oft-quoted Chinese proverb seems to fit here: "The journey of a thousand miles is begun by taking the first step." You will be pleased to see how many friends and acquaintances will wish you well and help you with that first step and the others that follow.

2. Contacts. Throughout this book and especially in the later chapters you find listed numerous food products that are suitable for sale. You will find many examples of women who have pioneered and blazed trails for you to follow. Sometimes an outstanding food editor, such as Clementine Paddleford of the *New York Herald Tribune,* will give publicity to a product if it shows unusual merit, and many women have had the fortunate experience of either that sponsorship or other similar excellent ones. If they have found a chance to earn money in their kitchens, it is unquestionable that you can do likewise and, at the same time, have great pleasure as well as extra dollars for your efforts.

3. Ideas by the Dozen. Sometimes the homemaker contemplating a business venture will feel inadequate because she thinks she may be unable to furnish new ideas for all occasions. However, it is certain that a listing of holidays and special-occasion days should convince the doubting ones that ideas for food services and food products are numberless. Suggestions can be used for catering for parties with both suitable foods and decorations. An advertisement in the newspaper suggesting holiday foods has brought orders in almost every instance.

Each season of the year suggests special food activities. When the peak for fruits and vegetables comes we think of canning and freezing. The fall suggests preparation of relishes and pickles. The summer suggests picnic boxes, frozen desserts, and food for showers and weddings. The fall also suggests many school activities, the preparation of fruitcakes, box suppers, and other foods for community activities. All year there are scores of birthdays, club parties, weddings, christenings, reunions, sport events, and other reasons for celebrations. All are more fun if the food is especially good.

Working with food is a satisfying, interesting, and challenging experience. To be able to prepare excellent food means that you have skillful and competent hands, good judgment, an appreciation of art principles, the thoroughness of a chemist, and some special blessing from above. Also, in every community, with the ability to prepare and serve food attractively comes a certain prestige.

Women Strike for Peace

Ethel Barol Taylor

Although the 1950s are often labeled a period of apathy and conservatism, the decade was hardly the political wasteland usually portrayed. Ethel Barol Taylor's lifelong activism began in reaction to the dropping of the atomic bombs on Hiroshima and Nagasaki in 1945, the very bombs that the husbands of the women at Los Alamos had worked so hard to produce. As a mother, Taylor was profoundly concerned about the effect of atomic weapons on the human race, especially the harmful effects of fallout released into the atmosphere. Soon she found other women who shared her concerns.

In 1961 more than 50,000 women came together in a nationwide Women's Strike for Peace (WSP) to build support for a treaty to ban nuclear testing. Like Ethel Barol Taylor, who quickly found her home in this movement, participants were mainly white, middle-class, college-educated women from left to liberal political backgrounds; most were married with small children. Their appeal was unabashedly maternalist; that is, they used their status as wives and mothers, especially their concern for children, as the reason why they should have a political say about such vital issues as peace and nuclear testing. As Taylor attests, they dressed the part, always going to sit-ins and protests in hats and white gloves, symbols of middle-class ladies. This was a very effective appeal, and WSP's mobilization was a major factor in the passage of the 1963 treaty banning nuclear testing.

But along the way, Women's Strike for Peace drew the attention of the House Un-American Activities Committee (HUAC), the major congressional body charged with investigating concerns about internal communist subversion. Historians refer to the domestic witch-hunting of the postwar period as McCarthyism for one of the most vocal anti-communists, Senator Joseph McCarthy of Wisconsin, but the phenomenon was broader than one man. In the Cold War climate, any peace activism was seen as suspicious and potentially helpful to the Soviet Union.

Here Ethel Barol Taylor retells the story of what happened when HUAC subpoenaed fourteen WSP women to quiz them on the supposedly communist leanings of their organization. HUAC was no match for the women, as newspaper headlines like "It's Ladies Day at

Capitol" and "Peace Gals Make Red Hunters Look Silly" affirmed. The full caption of the Herblock cartoon mentioned in the text says it even better: "I came in late, which was it that was un-American—women or peace?"

I was catapulted into the peace movement with the dropping of the bomb on Hiroshima. I was pretty apolitical up to that point. I used to get up in the morning and start polishing the furniture until I was polishing the polish. I thought, "There must be more to life than this."

I had a daughter, who was a small child at the time of the bombing of Hiroshima. When I read that the blast was so hot that in some circumstances it incinerated people and left just a shadow against a stone wall, creating instant fossils, I was numbed. I realized there were wars and there were wars, but this kind of war must never happen again.

There were others who felt as I did, and a few of us got together and talked. We formed a little group of women to study issues. I think even then, even though I was not political, I had this feeling that because women are not in positions of power and they have no role in policy-making, that maybe what we had to do was to make policy outside of government and demand of government that it listen to us.

A columnist once wrote a piece about me, and she called it "Rebel in White Gloves" because in the early days of Women Strike for Peace, women in the demonstrations, who were generally middle-class women, wore white gloves and hats. We used to do things like sit down and not move in the middle of the street, or whatever, but we would have our hats and white gloves on. I always thought that was a real protection until once we had an action, and hundreds of people went to Washington as a symbolic takeover of Congress. We walked and we came to a narrow street. The police said, "Cross this street and you get arrested." Well, I realized then that, what could they do? They're not going to electrocute me. They're not going to shoot me. It was much easier to cross that street than not to cross that street, so I crossed that street. Then we sat on the ground and waited to be arrested. We sat down, but we decided we weren't going to be yanked by our armpits, we were going to walk like ladies to the police van. We did. We got to the jail, and they opened the back door of the van. I looked out, and there was a five-foot drop to the ground. I waited for the policeman to help me down. The policeman came around and said, "Jump, sister." So I jumped into an entirely new world.

I didn't realize when I first got involved, when our government dropped the bomb on Hiroshima and Nagasaki, that this was going to be a lifetime commitment. I think if I had realized it I might have thought twice, because it's a terrible business to be in.

Source: Reprinted with permission of Twayne Publishers, an imprint of Simon & Schuster Macmillan, from *Peacework: Oral Histories of Women Peace Activists* by Judith Porter Adams, pp. 12–14, 17, 18. Copyright © 1991 by G.K. Hall & Co.

I think most of the pressures were because of the issues, not just because I was a woman—although there were those pressures too. You can really go nuts working for something and never have a success, never see enough change. Camus said, and I'm paraphrasing, that just because a thing is hopeless doesn't mean you don't get involved. That sounds gloomy. We have had some successes, but when I first got in, there were two bombs and they were both ours. Now there are 50,000 in the world. Someone once said, "Ethel, that's going to look lousy on your resumé." I think I developed an early anger that leaders had such contempt for the people they were supposed to be leading. That anger really has sustained me.

My anger is directed towards leaders who threaten the lives of children now and those yet unborn with their inhumane policy of nuclear weapons. We started because of children, because the scientists and doctors said that the strontium 90 and iodine 131 from the atomic tests would poison our children's milk and cause cancer. When we first organized we sent out a call throughout the streets with leaflets saying, "Take your children off milk." We sent our children's baby teeth to a lab in St. Louis to determine if strontium 90 was present. We were concerned about an epidemic, like polio before vaccines, except that polio is viral and these were man-made epidemics. Those who were then children now have children themselves.

My work in Women Strike for Peace sustains me. Outside of my family and my friends, WSP to me is the most important entity. It started out as a one-day action. We would meet every week around my dining room table to plan our "strike." There was a sugar bowl in the middle of the table for contributions toward the action. Some women stopped going to the hairdresser and did their own hair and put the money in the bowl. Some put birthday checks in. In one remarkable case, a woman who had very little money would occasionally give blood to the Red Cross and put the five dollars in the bowl. There was a wonderful outpouring of feeling and sisterhood. We were the harbingers of the women's movement—our weekly round table discussions were certainly consciousness raising. It was really an amazing experience. We never pledged solidarity, but we really were solid.

It was like an electric current running through the country with these women who decided that this couldn't just be a one-day action; it would have to go on. That has been our strength and weakness, to try to make a permanent organization out of a one-day action. WSP is more than an organization; it's a state of mind. I've never been part of a group—and I've been in a lot of them— where there was such a feeling of sisterhood. That is not to say that we don't sometimes get furious at each other.

In 1962 some WSP members were brought before the House Un-American Activities Committee [HUAC]. In order to show solidarity, many of us wrote to the chair of the committee asking for an opportunity to testify. The hearing was in 1962. It was pure theater. There is a wonderful cartoon about the HUAC hearings and WSP. There are these two guys sitting up at the HUAC table, and one of them says, "What are we against, women or peace?" They were against both. When some of us walked in, the guards were standing out in the hall outside the hearing room minding baby carriages and babies. We all carried red roses, and each time a woman would step down from testifying, we would present her with a bouquet, and we would applaud. The committee kept threatening to clear the room. They were in real trouble! They couldn't get out of the sessions, and they became more and more permissive because we were all so good-natured. The committee was just ridiculed away. It was a tremendous victory against the hearings.

When Dagmar Wilson was asked if there were Communists in WSP, she responded very pleasantly by saying something like, "We welcome everyone as long as they are for disarmament." That was quite a statement to make. I can't really speak for the women who faced the committee, and what the effect was on their lives, but it wasn't like the early McCarthy days, when people informed on others because they feared for their jobs—or the brave ones who refused to buckle under were ruined professionally. Then there was the real unadulterated fear and panic, because once you were blacklisted, that was it. But these were middle-class women whose jobs did not depend on whether or not they were cleared by this committee. I'm sure the HUAC experience for the women questioned was pretty scary, but the great difference was the tremendous, enthusiastic support they received publicly. We had a clipping service of all of the newspapers that covered the hearings. It was all "hats off to the ladies," as I remember. . . .

I think one of the amazing things about my own personal life is that on the day of that first protest, where we were challenged to cross the street, it was easier to do it than not to do it. The next time it was a natural thing to do. So many women in the movement did things that they never thought would be possible to do because of the deep feelings they had against war. . . .

I've survived by maintaining a sense of humor. It's better to laugh than to cry. I always got a tremendous amount of satisfaction and strength from the women with whom I worked. We can't always see immediate results from our work, but we have had an effect; we women have been dedicated and have made these issues ones that the government has to reckon with.

Civil Rights Activists

Rosa Parks and Virginia Foster Durr

Civil rights was the major social movement to rock the complacency of the 1950s. Although seeds of change for black Americans had been planted during World War II, it was the 1954 Supreme Court decision on school desegregation in *Brown* v. *Board of Education of Topeka* that marked the beginning of civil rights as a national issue.

On December 1, 1955, Montgomery, Alabama, seamstress Rosa Parks was arrested on a city bus for failing to give up her seat to a white person. The local National Association for the Advancement of Colored People (NAACP), headed by E. D. Nixon and to which Parks belonged, decided to challenge the constitutionality of the segregation ordinance. To further build support in the black community, Nixon and others called for a one-day boycott of the buses on December 5th, the day of Parks's trial. More than 90 percent of Montgomery's black community stayed off the buses that day, and for the following 381 days, in a show of solidarity. A new leader emerged in the process: the twenty-six-year-old Rev. Martin Luther King, Jr., who had recently become pastor of Montgomery's Dexter Avenue Baptist Church. The Supreme Court eventually ruled that Alabama laws requiring segregation on buses were unconstitutional, and on December 21, 1956, the city of Montgomery begrudgingly complied.

The quiet determination of Rosa Parks not to give up her seat comes through in her description here of the events that fateful day. The story is then picked up by Virginia Foster Durr, a liberal white Alabaman and early crusader against the poll tax, who with her lawyer husband Clifford Durr was deeply committed to the cause of civil rights. Durr's story (she was personally acquainted with Parks through the NAACP) shows the roles that whites played in the developing civil rights movement, as well as demonstrating how the bus boycott affected the relations between white women and their black servants.

I had left my work at the men's alteration shop, a tailor shop in the Montgomery Fair department store, and as I left work, I crossed the street to a drugstore to pick up a few items instead of trying to go directly to the bus stop. And when I had finished this, I came across the street and looked for a Cleveland Avenue bus that apparently had some seats on it. At that time it was a little hard to get a seat on the bus. But when I did get to the entrance to the bus, I got in line with a number of other people who were getting on the same bus.

As I got up on the bus and walked to the seat I saw there was only one vacancy that was just back of where it was considered the white section. So this was the seat that I took, next to the aisle, and a man was sitting next to me. Across the aisle there were two women, and there were a few seats at this point in the very front of the bus that was called the white section. I went on to one stop and I didn't particularly notice who was getting on the bus, didn't particularly notice the other people getting on. And on the third stop there were some people getting on, and at this point all of the front seats were taken. Now in the beginning, at the very first stop I had got on the bus, the back of the bus was filled up with people standing in the aisle and I don't know why this one va-

Sources: The interview with Rosa Parks is reprinted by permission of The Putnam Publishing Group from *My Soul is Rested* by Howell Raines. Copyright © 1977 by Howell Raines; *Outside the Magic Circle: The Autobiography of Virginia Foster Durr,* edited by Hollinger F. Barnard, pp. 279–283. Copyright © 1985 The University of Alabama Press. Reprinted by permission of the publisher.

cancy that I took was left, because there were quite a few people already standing toward the back of the bus. The third stop is when all the front seats were taken, and this one man was standing and when the driver looked around and saw he was standing, he asked the four of us, the man in the seat with me and the two women across the aisle, to let him have those front seats.

At his first request, didn't any of us move. Then he spoke again and said, "You'd better make it light on yourselves and let me have those seats." At this point, of course, the passenger who would have taken the seat hadn't said anything. In fact, he never did speak to my knowledge. When the three people, the man who was in the seat with me and the two women, stood up and moved into the aisle, I remained where I was. When the driver saw that I was still sitting there, he asked if I was going to stand up. I told him, no, I wasn't. He said, "Well, if you don't stand up, I'm going to have you arrested." I told him to go on and have me arrested.

He got off the bus and came back shortly. A few minutes later, two policemen got on the bus, and they approached me and asked if the driver had asked me to stand up, and I said yes, and they wanted to know why I didn't. I told them I didn't think I should have to stand up. After I had paid my fare and occupied a seat, I didn't think I should have to give it up. They placed me under arrest then and had me get in the police car, and I was taken to jail and booked on suspicion, I believe. The questions were asked, the usual questions they ask a prisoner or somebody that's under arrest. They had to determine whether or not the driver wanted to press charges or swear out a warrant, which he did. Then they took me to jail and I was placed in a cell. In a little while I was taken from the cell, and my picture was made and fingerprints taken. I went back to the cell then, and a few minutes later I was called back again, and when this happened I found out that Mr. E. D. Nixon and Attorney and Mrs. Clifford Durr had come to make bond for me.

*   *   *   *   *

This particular afternoon, Mrs. Parks later told me, she was exhausted. The bus she took went out to the housing project and was full of blacks, but some white men got on. The bus driver turned around and said, the way they always said, "Niggers, move back." And she just sat. The driver stopped the bus and came up to her. He said, "Did you hear me say to move back?" She said yes. He said, "Are you going to move back?" She said no. He called the police, and they came and arrested her and took her to jail. She was booked and put behind bars.

We got home about five o'clock from the office. Only Lulah was at home then, and she always had coffee ready for us. Lucy had graduated from high school and had gone to college, and we had sent Tilla north to school. Lulah was pretty lonesome because she didn't have any friends in the neighborhood, so we always tried to get home on time. We had just walked in and poured some coffee when the telephone rang. It was Mr. Nixon. He said, "Mr. Durr, will you call the jail and see why Mrs. Parks has been arrested?" The police recognized his voice as being that of a black man, and they wouldn't tell him anything. They treated him with the utmost disdain. Cliff called the jail and said he was Clifford J. Durr and he was a lawyer. They knew who he was, I think. He asked why Mrs. Parks was in jail. They told him she'd been booked on the city segregation ordinance. So Cliff called Mr. Nixon back. Mr. Nixon asked if Cliff would go down with him to make bail. Cliff said, "Mr. Nixon, I don't have anything to make bail with." We didn't own any property at that time, and we only had three or four hundred dollars a month to live on. Mr. Nixon said, "That's all right. I can make bail, if you'll just go with me." He was afraid they wouldn't let him make bail. I was determined to go, too, so I put on my coat and came running out.

I waited for them while they made bail. Everything went very smoothly. They brought Mrs. Parks out from behind the bars. That was a terrible sight to me to see this gentle, lovely, sweet woman, whom I knew and was so fond of, being brought down by a matron. She wasn't in handcuffs, but they had to unlock two or three doors that grated loudly. She was very calm. I asked her how they had treated her and she said, "Very nicely." Just at that moment her husband arrived. He was very excited and upset. She went home with him in the car that some friend had brought. We told her we would follow her home in Mr. Nixon's car and would discuss the case in her apartment.

We all went to her apartment, and after she had freshened up and had a little supper, Cliff and Mr. Nixon and Mrs. Parks and her husband and her mother and I discussed the case. Of course, Mr. Nixon wanted her to make a test case of it. Mr. Nixon remembers her as being extremely reluctant to do so, but I remember that it was her husband who was so reluctant. He kept saying over and over again, "Rosa, the white folks will kill you. Rosa, the white folks will kill you." It was like a background chorus, to hear the poor man, who was as white as he could be himself, for a black man, saying, "Rosa, the white folks will kill you." I don't remember her being reluctant.

Part of the city bus ordinance said that the white people got on in the front and sat from the front back; the black people got on in the back and sat from the back toward the front. No signs were posted and the center was always a no-man's land. When more whites got on, the bus driver would make the blacks get up and go stand up in the back. But the city ordinance included a phrase that said the bus driver couldn't order a black to give up a seat unless there was another seat available farther back in the black section. In other words, he couldn't just say, "Nigger, get back." Cliff asked Mrs. Parks if she wanted to test the constitutionality of the law itself or if she wanted him to try to get her off on the fact that the bus driver hadn't been following the law. She said she wanted to test the constitutionality of the law.

Cliff told Mrs. Parks he thought he could get the charges dropped, if that's what she wanted, to prevent her going through a long court session. Cliff told her, "Now if you're going to fight this on a constitutional basis, you will have to get the NAACP to finance it because it's going to cost you a fortune. It'll have to go all the way up to the Supreme Court of the United States and it's going to cost a lot of money. You don't have it and of course we don't have it." Certainly the Montgomery NAACP or even the Alabama NAACP didn't have it, but Fred Gray, a lawyer for the NAACP in Montgomery, had connections with the NAACP Legal Defense Fund in New York. So that night it was decided that Mrs. Parks would challenge the bus ordinance on constitutional grounds, and Fred Gray would represent her. It would be an NAACP case and Cliff would do all he could to help Fred, but Cliff would not be the lawyer of record.

Mrs. Parks was brought up to trial on the Monday after her arrest. In the meantime, Mr. Nixon had organized a boycott of the buses on the day of her trial. It was supposed to be just a one-day boycott. I can very well remember going to a meeting Mr. Nixon had that Sunday afternoon at a black church. It was an NAACP meeting and Mr. Nixon asked me to come. I remember that he was very emotional. He said to the people, "I'm a Pullman porter and every time I go on my job, I put on an apron or a jacket." He said, "You know, we've been wearing aprons for three hundred years. It's time we took off our aprons." I always thought that was a vivid phrase. He asked them not to get on the bus the next day. He had spread the word to all the preachers and they all told their congregations to stay off the buses on that Monday, the day of Mrs. Parks's trial. They announced they would have a meeting at the Holt Street Baptist Church on Monday night.

Fred Gray represented Mrs. Parks in the courtroom. She was found guilty and fined. Then he announced they were going to appeal the case.

That night I left the house to go to the mass meeting. Mr. Nixon had had to go off on his run as a Pullman car porter, and Martin Luther King was selected to be the speaker. There must have been ten or fifteen thousand black people crowding in and around that church. At that time I felt on very friendly terms with all the black community. I hadn't the slightest feeling of fear being the only white person, but I couldn't get into the church because of the crowd. King made a magnificent speech that electrified the black people. He became their undoubted leader that night.

The Parks case went on and on, and so did the boycott. The black people formed car pools, and the city tried cracking down on them by arresting the drivers for going two miles an hour over the speed limit. The police were harassing them. So Cliff got in touch with Fred Gray, and they decided to transfer the case to federal court. It came before a three-judge panel: Judge Rives and Judge Johnson declared the ordinance unconstitutional; Judge Lynne dissented, saying the panel shouldn't declare the ordinance unconstitutional until a higher court had ruled in that area of the law. Then the case went to the Fifth Circuit Court of Appeals and then to the Supreme Court. Finally the Supreme Court declared the ordinance unconstitutional, and the Negroes began to ride the buses again.

The boycott lasted the entire year, December 1955 until December 1956. I would see the black women walking to work every morning and walking back at night. It was like the black tides would come up out of the black section of town and go to work and then sweep back again. We would offer the women rides when we saw them walking, particularly out in the country club area where the distances were rather great. I would say to a complete stranger, "Would you like a ride?" They'd say, "Yes, thank you very much." They'd get in the car, and I'd ask them where they lived. They always lived on the west part of town. I'd say, "I'm glad to see that you're supporting the boycott." "No, ma'am. I hadn't nothing to do with that boycott. The lady I work for, she wasn't feelin' so good this afternoon, so that's why I was walkin' home." "No, ma'am, I don't have nothin' to do with that boycott. It's just that her little girl's sick." One reason after another, but they wouldn't admit they were supporting the boycott.

Then the policemen began giving tickets to the white women who were taking black women home. I had a washwoman who came once a week, an older lady who belonged to the Church of Christ. She admired Dr. King greatly. She said she had seen the angels come down and stand on his shoulders every Monday night. In everything he said he was speaking with the voice of God. Now, everything she did was also dictated by the voice of God. She got so she talked to God so much that she didn't do much ironing. She was really a sweet old lady, but she was a religious fanatic. I was taking her home one afternoon and we were stopped. I knew positively I had stopped at the stop sign, but a policeman came roaring up to me. He said that I had stopped too late. I'd gone two or three feet over the line. I knew there was no use in arguing, so I told him I was sorry and got my ticket and took this old lady home. I had to pay five dollars. This incident was typical of what happened over and over again all over town.

The mayor of the city, Tacky Gayle, issued a plea for the white women of Montgomery to stop taking their black maids home. He said they could break the boycott if the white women would stop taking their black maids home, or even stop hiring them. Well, you have never heard a roar of indignation in your life as came from the white women of Montgomery. They were just furious at Tacky Gayle. They said, okay, if Tacky Gayle wants to come out here and do my washing and ironing and cleaning and cooking and look after my children, he can do it, but unless he does, I'm going to get Mary or Sally or Suzy. And they said, "Sally has never had a thing to do with that boycott in the first place. She told me she only stays off the buses because she's scared of those hoodlums that might hurt her."

A vast deceit went on. Everybody knew everybody else was lying, but to save face, they had to lie. The black women had to say they weren't taking any part in the boycott. The white women had to say that their maids didn't take any part in the boycott. We had a good example of that in Mary, Mrs. Durr's old cook who came from Hardaway, in Macon County. She'd been with the

Durrs for years and now was Mrs. Durr's nurse. Mrs. Durr by that time was quite old and feeble and had to stay in bed, but a lot of people would drop by in the afternoons. Mary would sit in the room.

Mrs. Durr was a beautiful old woman, all propped up in bed, with a pink bed jacket and a pink ribbon in her hair and looking so pretty. Her mind was failing her, but she was still able to carry on a conversation. One afternoon when I was in the room somebody said to Mary, "Mary, I hope you don't have anything to do with that boycott." Mary said, "No, ma'am, I hadn't had nothing to do with that boycott. There's my sister Olla. She don't live very far from her job so she just walks to work. And my brother, he's got a job at the cotton mill and he just goes to work with some other men who are driving a car. And my other sister she just walks to work cause it's so close. No, ma'am, none of us has a thing to do with that boycott. We just stays off the buses." The white people really believed that. They didn't see through it at all.

In truth, Mary was a passionate advocate of the boycott. She'd meet us as we came in the driveway to ask how the bus boycott was getting on, how Dr. King was. She couldn't read and write, but she listened to the radio. That afternoon after the guests had left and Mary was fixing supper, Cliff and I said to her, "Mary, you are the biggest storyteller in the world. You know very well you're supporting the boycott and all of your family are. Why in the world did you make up that tale about how none of you were, and you were all walking just because you wanted to?" She laughed and she said, "Well, I tell you, Mr. Cliff, I tell you, I learned one thing in my life and that is, when your hand's in the lion's mouth, it's just better to pat it on the head." That expressed the feeling in the black community. The black women needed those jobs. They weren't paid very much, but that's all the income many of them had. They couldn't afford to say, "I'm supporting the boycott." So the white women lied and the black women lied. And the maids kept coming and the white women kept driving them back and forth to work.

Desegregating the University of Georgia, 1961

Charlayne Hunter-Gault

Civil rights activists faced some of their toughest challenges in desegregating the Southern educational system, despite the 1954 Supreme Court decision that ended the separate-but-equal doctrine. In January, 1961, Charlayne Hunter and Hamilton Holmes became the first two black students to enroll at the University of Georgia in Athens. It had taken two years of legal battles by the NAACP's Legal Defense and Educational Fund lawyers Constance Baker Motley and Vernon Jordan to get to that point. Even when the students won the legal right to register for classes, they faced a hostile reaction on campus that threatened to erupt in violence.

This selection by Charlayne Hunter, published in a black magazine called *The Urbanite*, describes the riot that occurred on her second night in the women's dorm. The violence led to her being suspended, supposedly for her own safety, and hustled out of the Athens campus and back to Atlanta in the dead of night. Her piece, written soon after the event, captures the undercurrent of fear surrounding her arrival on campus, but also her determination not to cave in to the pressure. It also balances the bigotry of her classmates with the bravery of a few students and faculty who tried to make her feel welcome. After this incident, she was reinstated by the courts almost immediately and finished the semester under somewhat more settled, but still far from friendly, circumstances.

As a child, Charlayne Hunter decided she wanted to be a journalist, a goal that she was able to fulfill after college. She is now best known as Charlayne Hunter-Gault, the widely respected national correspondent for PBS's MacNeil/Lehrer News Hour and the author of *In My Place*, the 1992 memoir of her childhood and her role in the struggle to desegregate the University of Georgia campus. In 1988, twenty-five years after her graduation, she became the first black to deliver the commencement address in the school's two-hundred year history.

The lobby of the dormitory was almost empty, but after I had gone to my room many of the girls came down as they had the day before—to welcome, observe, inspect. Mrs. Porter, the housemother, came down and told the girls not to stay too long because I was tired. She had advised me earlier that it would be best to have my dinner in my room that night. This, again, seemed only a normal precaution, considering the circumstances.

It began getting dark around six o'clock. After the last of the girls had gone, everything became amazingly quiet inside the dorm. I picked up a book and tried to study, but then firecrackers began popping outside, as they had the night before. I decided there was nothing to do but go to bed, despite the racket outside. Mrs. Porter came in again to see if I had eaten and to ask how I was feeling. She suggested that I keep the blinds closed and stay away from the windows. "We expect some trouble," she said.

Later, as I went into the hall for a drink of water, I caught a glimpse of the faculty members the students had nicknamed "The Baby-Sitting Crew," because they had volunteered to patrol the building. It seemed to me the group was larger than it had been the night before. I returned to my room. After a while, the noise outside gradually grew larger and uglier. Though I did not know it at the time, a hotly disputed last-minute defeat of the basketball team at the hands of Georgia Tech had helped create anything but a mood of sweet rea-

Source: Charlayne Hunter-Gault, *In My Place* (New York: Farrar, Straus, Giroux, 1992; Vintage paperback edition, 1993), pp. 181–185. Reprinted by permission of Sterling Lord Literistic, Inc.

sonableness in the crowd that had marched from the gym to the dormitory. Reading or sleeping was out of the question. I was in the first room of the duplex apartment. Suddenly there was a loud crash in the bedroom. Not stopping to think, I rushed in, only to be stopped in my tracks by another crash, as a Coca-Cola bottle followed the brick that had ripped through the window a moment before. Jagged splinters of window glass and fragments of the bottle had spattered across my dress, slippers, and the skirts and blouses that I had not yet had time to unpack.

Strangely, I was not at all afraid at this moment. Instead, I found myself thinking, as I stood there in the midst of the wreckage, So this is how it is.

At this time, I did not know that all the students had been told by the riot planners to turn off the lights in their rooms when it got dark. With the rest of the building in darkness, the three brightly lit windows of my apartment must have made an inviting target for the mob out on the lawn.

I heard the dean's voice in the hall and called out to him, but he didn't hear me. I met a campus patrolman in the hall and told him what had happened. As he went into my room to investigate, I continued down the hall to a counselor's office a couple of doors away. There in the darkness I went to the window and looked out. All I could see was a moving mass—not a face that could be recognized as belonging to a separate person. Even the voices seemed to run together in one confusion of shouts and jeers.

Turning from the window, I saw that the partition between the counselor's office and the lobby was open. The crashing of the glass and the screams of one girl on the floor above, who had been struck by a brick as she looked out her window, had brought most of the girls into the lobby. Some of them passed back and forth, looking to see how I had reacted to all of this.

I realized that it was nearing time for the eleven o'clock news and that my mother in Atlanta would be waiting up for it. I called her and told her that I was all right. Though I knew she could hear the noise in the background, she seemed relatively calm. But I could not get her to promise that she would go to bed at once, without waiting to look at the television news program.

After I hung up, [Paula Leiter], one of the most genuine persons it has been my good luck to meet came down and began talking to me. Though it was clear that she herself was nervous, she did all she could under the circumstances to take my mind off what was going on. This was anything but easy, since by now the hostility from outside was being echoed by some of the girls inside the dorm. Perhaps it was partially out of hysteria, or partially because the girl upstairs had been hurt. At any rate, a group of girls began tramping in a continuous circle, yelling insults first at me and then at the schoolmate who had come in to befriend me.

It was hard to sit there and listen to some of the things that were said about me without being able to answer. I was told I was about to become "a Black martyr, getting fifty dollars a day for this from the NAACP"—a piece of news that would have considerably surprised my family.

The city police outside, after having waited in vain for the state patrol, finally resorted to tear gas. The gas fumes began seeping into the dorm, and the girls were told to change the linen on their beds. This prompted deliberately loud offers of a dime or a quarter to Charlayne for changing the sheets of these same residents who professed to believe that I was already being paid at a rate of over six dollars an hour, if figured on the basis of an eight-hour day.

My new friend was beginning to get drowsy, though she tried not to show it, and I suggested that she go to bed, assuring her that I would be all right. After she had left, I wondered how many people, myself included, would have had the courage to do what she had done.

Mrs. Porter came in, looking worn-out from the ordeal of trying to console over 150 overwrought girls. She gave me an orange. "It's a sweet orange," she said. "You might enjoy it."

Mrs. Porter left as I began peeling the orange. Before I had finished, she was back again. This time, she was serious and unsmiling. Slowly and sympathetically, she told me that the dean had said I would have to leave. I was to be taken to Atlanta, so that I would be safe. I don't think I heard the rest of what she said. I suddenly felt totally sick and miserable. All I could think was: I've failed, I've failed. I began to cry and, hard as I tried, I couldn't stop. Mrs. Porter patted me on the arm and told me not to cry and not to worry. "Everything will be all right," she said. Needless to say, I could not really believe this.

I packed quickly, not even bothering to remove the pieces of glass from my suitcase. Dean Williams came to my room and repeated what Mrs. Porter had said. Feeling empty inside, I followed him out of the room, stopping only to pick up my Madonna from the table beside the bed. Afterward, it bothered me to think that people looking at the newspaper pictures would mistakenly think I was crying because of fear, but at that moment I was too sick to care.

The girls were all quiet now. They were huddled together in the lobby as I went by. A few of them started to hiss, but they were immediately shushed into silence by the others. The state troopers had finally arrived. (It was after midnight.) As we came out into the chilly night air, I saw the gray patrol cars parked at the curb. The husky, red-faced troopers in their gray uniforms and broad-rimmed hats were impassive and coolly official in speech and manner. We stopped to pick up the Dean of Women at her residence. I remember saying something about being sorry to inconvenience her at that hour, to which she answered that she couldn't sleep from worrying about what was going on. When we arrived at the house at which Hamp was living, he was on the phone talking to Attorney Hollowell in Atlanta. (Until the call from Hollowell came, he had been asleep, unaware of what was happening a mile away.)

Hamp wanted to drive his car home. I tried at first to reason with him, telling him I thought it was dangerous; that he could be more easily isolated, even if there were patrolmen in front of and behind him; we didn't know how much we could trust them. "They could just pick you off," I said. But Hamp loved that car, which his grandfather had given him when he got into Georgia, and he was not about to leave it. I knew that Hamp didn't like scenes, but I was desperate. So somewhere between reality and drama, I found a zone of hysteria that was persuasive. I had my hands on his shoulders and was shaking him frantically and screaming, "You've got to go in the car with me . . . You can't drive . . . You've got to come with me!" Finally, somewhat embarrassed by this performance, which he couldn't quite decipher, he gave in.

As we sped along the often bumpy highway toward home, Hamp and I had little to say. Neither of us could get used to the idea that we had been "suspended." Yet what could we say or do about it? I remember almost nothing of the trip itself. Before I knew it, we were in Atlanta, turning into my block and pulling up in front of the porch where a local Black man had stood so many months ago telling me that I should give up the idea of trying to go to the University of Georgia. The news of our coming home had preceded us, and a few close friends had gathered at the house. Most reassuring of all, my mother, her hair all done up in braids, came out with open arms to welcome both Hamp and me and to take some of the sting out of our forced homecoming.

SUGGESTIONS FOR FURTHER READING

Anderson, Karen. *Wartime Women: Sex Roles, Family Relations, and the Status of Women During World War II.* Westport, 1981.

Bailey, Beth. *From Front Porch to Back Seat: Courtship in 20th Century America.* Baltimore, 1988.

Blackwelder, Julia Kirk. *Women of the Depression: Caste and Culture in San Antonio, 1929–1939.* College Station, Texas, 1984.

Blee, Kathleen. *Women of the Klan: Racism and Gender in the 1920s.* Berkeley, 1991.

Breines, Wini. *Young, White, and Miserable: Growing Up Female in the Fifties.* Boston, 1992.

Brown, Dorothy M. *Setting a Course: American Women in the 1920s.* Boston, 1987.

Cook, Blanche Wiesen. *Eleanor Roosevelt: Volume I, 1884–1933.* New York, 1992.

Cott, Nancy F. *The Grounding of Modern Feminism.* New Haven, 1987.

Crawford, Vicki, Jacqueline Ann Rouse, and Barbara Woods, eds. *Women in the Civil Rights Movement: Trailblazers and Torchbearers, 1941–1965.* New York, 1990.

D'Emilio, John, and Estelle Freedman. *Intimate Matters: A History of Sexuality in America.* New York, 1988.

Ehrenreich, Barbara. *The Hearts of Men: American Dreams and the Flight from Commitment.* New York, 1983.

Fass, Paula. *The Damned and the Beautiful: American Youth in the 1920s.* New York, 1977.

Faue, Elizabeth. *Community of Suffering and Struggle: Women, Men, and the Labor Movement in Minneapolis, 1915–1945.* Chapel Hill, 1991.

Gluck, Sherna B. *Rosie the Riveter Revisited: Women, the War, and Social Change.* Boston, 1987.

Gordon, Felice D. *After Winning: The Legacy of the New Jersey Suffragists, 1920–1947.* New Brunswick, 1986.

Hall, Jacqueline Dowd. *Revolt against Chivalry: Jessie Daniel Ames and the Women's Campaign against Lynching.* New York, 1979.

Hartmann, Susan M. *The Home Front and Beyond: American Women in the 1940s.* Boston, 1982.

Hoff-Wilson, Joan, and Marjorie Lightman. *Without Precedent: The Life and Career of Eleanor Roosevelt.* Bloomington, 1984.

Honey, Maureen, ed. *Breaking the Ties That Bind: Popular Stories of the New Woman, 1915–1930.* Norman, OK, 1992.

———. *Creating Rosie the Riveter: Class, Gender, and Propaganda during World War II.* Amherst, 1984.

Janiewski, Dolores E. *Sisterhood Denied: Race, Gender, and Class in a New South Community.* Philadelphia, 1985.

Jones, Jacqueline. *Labor of Love, Labor of Sorrow: Black Women, Work, and the Family from Slavery to the Present.* New York, 1985.

Kaledin, Eugenia. *Mothers and More: American Women in the 1950s.* Boston, 1984.

Kessler-Harris, Alice. *Out to Work: A History of Wage-Earning Women in America.* New York, 1982.

Litoff, Judy Barrett, and David C. Smith. *We're in This War, Too: World War II Letters from Women in Uniform.* New York, 1994.

Lynd, Helen Merrill, and Robert S. Lynd. *Middletown: A Study in Contemporary American Culture.* New York, 1929.

Martin, Patricia Preciado, ed. *Songs My Mother Sang to Me: An Oral History of Mexican-American Women.* Tucson, 1992.

May, Elaine Tyler. *Homeward Bound: American Families in the Cold War Era.* New York, 1988.

Meyerowitz, Joanne, ed. *Not June Cleaver: Women and Gender in Postwar America, 1945–1960.* Philadelphia, 1994.

Milkman, Ruth. *Gender at Work: The Dynamics of Job Segregation by Sex during World War II.* Urbana, 1987.

Modell, John L. *Into One's Own: From Youth to Adulthood in the United States, 1920–1975.* Berkeley, 1989.

Muncy, Robyn. *Creating a Female Dominion in American Reform, 1890–1930.* New York, 1991.

Neff, Mary. *Preserving the Family Farm: Women, Community, and the Foundations of Agribusiness in the Midwest, 1900–1940.* Baltimore, 1995.

Palmer, Phyllis. *Domesticity and Dirt: Housewives and Domestic Servants in the United States, 1920–1945.* Philadelphia, 1989.

Rossiter, Margaret. *Women Scientists in America: Struggles and Strategies to 1940.* Baltimore, 1982.

Ruiz, Vicki L. *Cannery Women, Cannery Lives: Mexican Women, Unionization, and the California Food Processing Industry, 1930–1950.* Albuquerque, 1987.

Rupp, Leila J., and Verta Taylor. *Survival in the Doldrums: The American Women's Rights Movement, 1945 to the 1960s.* New York, 1987.

Scharf, Lois. *To Work and To Wed: Female Employment, Feminism, and the Great Depression.* Westport, 1980.

———. *Eleanor Roosevelt: First Lady of American Liberalism.* Boston, 1987.

Showalter, Elaine, ed. *These Modern Women: Autobiographical Essays from the 1920s.* Old Westbury, NY, 1978.

Swerdlow, Amy. *Women Strike for Peace: Traditional Motherhood and Radical Politics in the 1960s.* Chicago, 1993.

Todd, Ellen Wiley. *The "New Woman" Revised: Painting and Gender Politics on Fourteenth Street.* Berkeley, 1993.

Wandersee, Winifred. *Women's Work and Family Values, 1920–1940.* Cambridge, 1981.

Ware, Susan. *Beyond Suffrage: Women in the New Deal.* Cambridge, 1981.

———. *Holding Their Own: American Women in the 1930s.* Boston, 1982.

———. *Still Missing: Amelia Earhart and the Search for Modern Feminism.* New York, 1993.

Westin, Jeane. *Making Do: How Women Survived the 30s.* Chicago, 1976.

PART THREE

The Personal Becomes Political

1963 to the Present

CHAPTER 10

The Revival of Feminism

The *sixties,* as the term is commonly used to describe a period of political up-heaval and dissent, did not really start in 1960 nor did it end in 1970. The women's movement helps to correct this chronology. Just as the civil rights movement pushes the period of activism back to its beginnings in the 1950s, so does the women's movement extend the activism well past the end of the decade.

In 1960, feminism was a topic of interest only to a small minority of American women. Over the next fifteen years feminism became a major item on the national agenda. The revival of feminism initially followed two different paths—through "women's rights" and "women's liberation." By the 1970s, however, those distinctions had blurred and supporters began to talk about "the women's movement" or "feminism" without dividing it into two branches. The widening public discussion of women's issues continues today, although the terms of the debate have changed over the intervening decades.

Several events set the stage for the revival of feminism as a national issue in the early 1960s. The establishment of the Presidential Commission on the Status of Women by President John F. Kennedy in 1961 brought together women and men concerned about women's issues; although its final recommendations were rather limited, just the fact of its existence raised expectations that women's issues were going to be addressed. The publication of Betty Friedan's *The Feminine Mystique* in 1963 suggested a groundswell of popular dissatisfaction with women's lives that could be tapped for an emerging political movement.

An especially important event was the passage of the 1964 Civil Rights Act, which had as great an impact on women as it did on blacks. The key provision was Title VII, which in its original formulation outlawed discrimination in public accommodations or employment on the basis of race, color, religion, or national origin. At the last moment, *sex* was added as a category, mainly as a delaying tactic by a southern congressman who hoped to kill the entire bill. But the amendment passed (women's activists had already been planning to introduce a similar standard), and women had an important legal tool to challenge discrimination on the job.

The Civil Rights Act set up the Equal Employment Opportunity Commission to deal with complaints, but dissatisfaction with how the EEOC was implementing its mandate against sex discrimination led to the founding of the National Organization for Women in 1966. NOW best represents the women's rights branch of feminism. Composed mainly of professional women who had long been active in politics and public life, its members considered themselves a civil rights organization for women. Their main goal was, in the words of their statement of purpose, "to take action to bring women into full participation in the mainstream of American society now, exercising all the privileges and responsibilities thereof in truly equal partnership with men." By the 1970s, NOW had grown to the largest feminist organization in the country, a position it still holds today.

Women's liberationists came to feminism by a different path. Radical women, who tended to be much younger than the politicos of NOW, had been active in the civil rights movement in the early 1960s. Their experiences on the front line of voter registration drives and protest marches increased their self-confidence, but also fed their frustration about the way that women were treated within the movement. For example, women were automatically expected to take notes at meetings, make coffee, do all the housework, and often be available as sexual partners for male co-workers. But women found it difficult in the mid-1960s to pinpoint their generalized dissatisfactions, because they lacked the ideological context of feminism to frame the questions. Civil rights activists began tentatively by comparing women's position to that of blacks, but when they tried to raise such issues with their male colleagues, both black and white, they were rebuffed.

By the mid-1960s, whites had been kicked out of the civil rights movement, which was entering its black power phase. Radical women did not find the male-dominated New Left much more congenial. As the men debated ending the war in Vietnam and taking over the universities, women continued to be expected to make coffee and take notes. By 1967 and 1968, groups of radical women in several cities across the country had begun to come together to share common concerns. At first, none of them thought they were founding a separate women's movement, but when the New Left refused to include a commitment to fighting sexism as part of its agenda, the women walked out.

Around 1969 and 1970, the media discovered feminism. With wide coverage of such events as the August 26, 1970, marches and demonstrations to honor the fiftieth anniversary of the suffrage amendment, the media brought the stimulating ideas of feminism to a far wider audience than had been reached by the members of NOW or the small constituencies of the New Left. Women started to join the movement or call themselves feminists who had not been part of either women's rights or women's liberation, and the distinctions between the two branches began to blur.

There was also a certain breaking down of barriers because each side was learning from the other. Radical women, who had devoted much of their energy to critiquing patriarchal institutions such as marriage and the family, saw the relevance of such legislative changes as increased child care services or protection of battered women. The women of NOW, on the other hand, while still wedded to working within the system, began to embrace a broader critique of women's place in American society than could be cured simply by legal reform. By 1970, feminism was on the way to becoming a mass movement.

The symbol of the new women's movement was the Equal Rights Amendment. No longer a divisive issue between feminists as it had been in the 1920s, the ERA seemed a perfect vehicle for mobilizing the nation around a commitment to equality and a strong tool to correct the legal disabilities under which women still labored. (The text of the amendment reads, "Equality of rights under the law shall not be abridged on account of sex.") In large part in response to the new political muscle of organized feminism, the ERA passed the Congress in 1972 and was sent to the states for what was predicted as a speedy ratification. At that point, the women's movement was at high tide, taking as its mindset the title of Robin Morgan's bestselling 1970 book, *Sisterhood Is Powerful.*

Founding the National Organization for Women, 1966

At a 1966 convention in Washington, D.C. of state commissions mandated in the aftermath of the Presidential Commission on the Status of Women, Betty Friedan, lawyer Pauli Murray, ERA supporter Marguerite Rawalt, Women's Bureau staffer Catherine East, Wisconsin activist Kay Clarenbach, and others met in Friedan's hotel room to draw up plans for what they saw as a civil rights organization for women. The immediate backdrop was frustration over the failure of the Equal Employment Opportunity Commission (EEOC) to take action against sex discrimination as required under Title VII. More generally, these women had become increasingly aware of the discrimination that women faced in American life and they wanted to organize a pressure group to seek change. As Friedan later put it dramatically, "The absolute necessity for a civil rights movement for women had reached such a point of subterranean explosive urgency by 1966, that it only took a few of us to get together to ignite the spark—and it spread like a nuclear chain-reaction."

The National Organization for Women was officially launched in October 1966, with Betty Friedan as its first president; it counted three hundred charter members, of whom perhaps one quarter were men.

NOW's statement of purpose reprinted here is a classic document of liberal feminism: rather than challenging the system, it asks for women's full inclusion into the mainstream of American society; rather than being antagonistic to men, it strives towards a "truly equal partnership." But its recommendations are more wide ranging than the Presidential Commission's just three years before, and its tone conveys an urgency about action now.

It is interesting to note what issues are not mentioned in the NOW document, notably the Equal Rights Amendment and support for reproductive rights. By its second national convention in November of 1967, NOW had added those demands to its "Bill of Rights for Women," but only after heated debate. Showing the ability of the women's movement to mobilize a constituency, NOW grew from one thousand members in 1967 to over forty thousand just seven years later.

We, men and women who hereby constitute ourselves as the National Organization for Women, believe that the time has come for a new movement toward true equality for all women in America, and toward a fully equal partnership of the sexes, as part of the world-wide revolution of human rights now taking place within and beyond our national borders.

The purpose of NOW is to take action to bring women into full participation in the mainstream of American society now, exercising all the privileges and responsibilities thereof in truly equal partnership with men.

We believe the time has come to move beyond the abstract argument, discussion and symposia over the status and special nature of women which has raged in America in recent years; the time has come to confront, with concrete action, the conditions that now prevent women from enjoying the equality of opportunity and freedom of choice which is their right as individual Americans, and as human beings.

NOW is dedicated to the proposition that women first and foremost are human beings, who, like all other people in our society, must have the chance to develop their fullest human potential. We believe that women can achieve such equality only by accepting to the full the challenges and responsibilities they share with all other people in our society, as part of the decision-making mainstream of American political, economic and social life.

We organize to initiate or support action, nationally or in any part of this nation, by individuals or organizations, to break through the silken curtain of prejudice and discrimination against women in government, industry, the professions, the churches, the political parties, the judiciary, the labor unions, in education, science, medicine, law, religion and every other field of importance in American society.

Source: Statement of Purpose, National Organization for Women (1966), quoted in Betty Friedan, *It Changed My Life* (New York: Dell, 1976), pp. 124–130. Reprinted by permission of the National Organization for Women. This is a historical document (1966) and does not reflect the current language or priorities of the organization.

Enormous changes taking place in our society make it both possible and urgently necessary to advance the unfinished revolution of women toward true equality, now. With a life span lengthened to nearly seventy-five years, it is no longer either necessary or possible for women to devote the greater part of their lives to child rearing; yet childbearing and rearing—which continues to be a most important part of most women's lives—is still used to justify barring women from equal professional and economic participation and advance.

Today's technology has reduced most of the productive chores which women once performed in the home and in mass production industries based upon routine unskilled labor. This same technology has virtually eliminated the quality of muscular strength as a criterion for filling most jobs, while intensifying American industry's need for creative intelligence. In view of this new industrial revolution created by automation in the mid-twentieth century, women can and must participate in old and new fields of society in full equality—or become permanent outsiders.

Despite all the talk about the status of American women in recent years, the actual position of women in the United States has declined, and is declining, to an alarming degree throughout the 1950's and 1960's. Although 46.4 percent of all American women between the ages of eighteen and sixty-five now work outside the home, the overwhelming majority—75 percent—are in routine clerical, sales, or factory jobs, or they are household workers, cleaning women, hospital attendants. About two-thirds of Negro women workers are in the lowest paid service occupations. Working women are becoming increasingly—not less—concentrated on the bottom of the job ladder. As a consequence, full-time women workers today earn on the average only 60 percent of what men earn, and that wage gap has been increasing over the past twenty-five years in every major industry group. In 1964, of all women with a yearly income, 89 percent earned under $5,000 a year; half of all full-time year-round women workers earned less than $3,690; only 1.4 percent of full-time year-round women workers had an annual income of $10,000 or more.

Further, with higher education increasingly essential in today's society, too few women are entering and finishing college or going on to graduate or professional school. Today women earn only one in three of the B.A.'s and M.A.'s granted, and one in ten of the Ph.D.'s.

In all the professions considered of importance to society, and in the executive ranks of industry and government, women are losing ground. Where they are present it is only a token handful. Women comprise less than 1 percent of federal judges; less than 4 percent of all lawyers; 7 percent of doctors. Yet women represent 53 percent of the U.S. population. And increasingly men are replacing women in the top positions in secondary and elementary schools, in social work, and in libraries—once thought to be women's fields.

Official pronouncements of the advance in the status of women hide not only the reality of this dangerous decline, but the fact that nothing is being done to stop it. The excellent reports of the President's Commission on the Status of Women and of the state commissions have not been fully implemented. Such commissions have power only to advise. They have no power to enforce their recommendations, nor have they the freedom to organize American women and men to press for action on them. The reports of these commissions have, however, created a basis upon which it is now possible to build.

Discrimination in employment on the basis of sex is now prohibited by federal law, in Title VII of the Civil Rights Act of 1964. But although nearly one-third of the cases brought before the Equal Employment Opportunity Commission during the first year dealt with sex discrimination and the proportion is increasing dramatically, the commission has not made clear its intention to enforce the law with the same seriousness on behalf of women as of other victims of discrimination. Many of these cases were Negro women, who are the victims of the double discrimination of race and sex. Until now, too few women's organizations and official spokesmen have been willing to speak out against these dangers facing women. Too many women have been restrained by the fear of being called "feminist."

There is no civil rights movement to speak for women, as there has been for Negroes and other victims of discrimination. The National Organization for Women must therefore begin to speak.

WE BELIEVE that the power of American law, and the protection guaranteed by the U.S. Constitution to the civil rights of all individuals, must be effectively applied and enforced to isolate and remove patterns of sex discrimination, to ensure equality of opportunity in employment and education, and equality of civil and political rights and responsibilities on behalf of women, as well as for Negroes and other deprived groups.

We realize that women's problems are linked to many broader questions of social justice; their solution will require concerted action by many groups. Therefore, convinced that human rights for all are indivisible, we expect to give active support to the common cause of equal rights for all those who suffer discrimination and deprivation, and we call upon other organizations committed to such goals to support our efforts toward equality for women.

WE DO NOT ACCEPT the token appointment of a few women to high-level positions in government and industry as a substitute for a serious continuing effort to recruit and advance women according to their individual abilities. To this end, we urge American government and industry to mobilize the same resources of ingenuity and command with which they have solved problems of far greater difficulty than those now impeding the progress of women.

WE BELIEVE that this nation has a capacity at least as great as other nations, to innovate new social institutions which will enable women to enjoy true equality of opportunity and responsibility in society, without conflict with their responsibilities as mothers and homemakers. In such innovations, America does not lead the Western world, but lags by decades behind many European countries. We do not accept the traditional assumption that a woman has to choose between marriage and motherhood, on the one hand, and serious participation in industry or the professions on the other. We question the present expectation that all normal women will retire from job or profession for ten or fifteen years, to devote their full time to raising children, only to reenter the job market at a relatively minor level. This in itself is a deterrent to the aspirations of women, to their acceptance into management or professional training courses, and to the very possibility of equality of opportunity or real choice, for all but a few women. Above all, we reject the assumption that these problems are the unique responsibility of each individual woman, rather than a basic social dilemma which society must solve. True equality of opportunity and freedom of choice for women requires such practical and possible innovations as a nationwide network of child-care centers, which will make it unnecessary for women to retire completely from society until their children are grown, and national programs to provide retraining for women who have chosen to care for their own children full time.

WE BELIEVE that it is as essential for every girl to be educated to her full potential of human ability as it is for every boy—with the knowledge that such education is the key to effective participation in today's economy and that, for a girl as for a boy, education can only be serious where there is expectation that it will be used in society. We believe that American educators are capable of devising means of imparting such expectations to girl students. Moreover, we consider the decline in the proportion of women receiving higher and professional education to be evidence of discrimination. This discrimination may take the form of quotas against the admission of women to colleges and professional schools; lack of encouragement by parents, counselors and educators; denial of loans or fellowships; or the traditional or arbitrary procedures in graduate and professional training geared in terms of men, which inadvertently discriminate against women. We believe that the same serious attention must be given to high school dropouts who are girls as to boys.

WE REJECT the current assumptions that a man must carry the sole burden of supporting himself, his wife, and family, and that a woman is automatically entitled to life-long support by a man upon her marriage, or that marriage, home and family are primarily woman's world and responsibility—hers, to dominate, his to support. We believe that a true partnership between the sexes demands a different concept of marriage, an equitable sharing of the responsibilities of home and children and of the economic burdens of their support. We believe that proper recognition should be given to the economic and social value of homemaking and child care. To these ends, we will seek to open a reexamination of laws and mores governing marriage and divorce, for we believe that the current state of "half-equality" between the sexes discriminates against both men and women, and is the cause of much unnecessary hostility between the sexes.

WE BELIEVE that women must now exercise their political rights and responsibilities as American citizens. They must refuse to be segregated on the basis of sex into separate-and-not-equal ladies' auxiliaries in the political parties, and they must demand representation according to their numbers in the

regularly constituted party committees—at local, state, and national levels—
and in the informal power structure, participating fully in the selection of candidates and political decision-making, and running for office themselves.

IN THE INTERESTS OF THE HUMAN DIGNITY OF WOMEN, we will
protest and endeavor to change the false image of women now prevalent in the
mass media, and in the texts, ceremonies, laws, and practices of our major social institutions. Such images perpetuate contempt for women by society and
by women for themselves. We are similarly opposed to all policies and practices—in church, state, college, factory, or office—which, in the guise of pro-
tectiveness, not only deny opportunities but also foster in women self-
denigration, dependence, and evasion of responsibility, undermine their
confidence in their own abilities and foster contempt for women.

NOW WILL HOLD ITSELF INDEPENDENT OF ANY POLITICAL
PARTY in order to mobilize the political power of all women and men intent
on our goals. We will strive to ensure that no party, candidate, President, senator, governor, congressman, or any public official who betrays or ignores the
principle of full equality between the sexes is elected or appointed to office. If
it is necessary to mobilize the votes of men and women who believe in our
cause, in order to win for women the final right to be fully free and equal human
beings, we so commit ourselves.

WE BELIEVE THAT women will do most to create a new image of
women by *acting* now, and by speaking out in behalf of their own equality,
freedom, and human dignity—not in pleas for special privilege, nor in enmity
toward men, who are also victims of the current half-equality between the
sexes—but in an active, self-respecting partnership with men. By so doing,
women will develop confidence in their own ability to determine actively, in
partnership with men, the conditions of their life, their choices, their future and
their society.

Feminist Guerilla Theater, 1968

Robin Morgan

Radical women presented a stark contrast to the National Organization for Women, the difference between dresses, makeup, and stockings versus jeans, T-shirts, and long hair. Women's liberation was all
mass and no organization; groups formed and disbanded spontaneously, often not knowing of each other's existence; there were no
leaders. Members tended to be young women in their twenties (only
later did the women's movement reach the college campuses) who
were far more hostile to men than the women's rights branch of the
movement. They believed in revolution, not reform, of the dominant
system.

Women's liberation first gained media attention with this protest
organized by the Radical Women of New York at the Miss America

Pageant in September 1968. In the spirit of counterculture street theater (such as had occurred at that summer's Democratic convention in Chicago, but without the violence), the protesters planned such antics as crowning a live sheep as Miss America and throwing items of women's oppression into a freedom trash can. The language in the following reprint of the broadside the feminists distributed is characteristic of the 1960s, with such words as *groovy, busted, dig that,* and *male chauvinism.* Its reasoning also closely links beauty pageants to other key issues of the 1960s, such as racism, a critique of affluence, and the war in Vietnam.

The protest was staged as a media event. When organizers announced they would speak only to women reporters, who were greatly underrepresented in journalism at the time, the demand helped to raise media interest in the event, and it became front page news. Such media coverage had a twofold effect. It spread the notion that women's liberation was growing (although *movement* is too strong a word for the loose structures of 1968), which in turn brought more women into the cause. At the same time, the media portrayed the protestors in fairly negative terms, such as coining the term *bra-burners* to denote all radical feminists, even though no bras were burned. Media coverage was thus a double-edged sword.

On September 7th in Atlantic City, the Annual Miss America Pageant will again crown "your ideal." But this year, reality will liberate the contest auction-block in the guise of "genyooine" de-plasticized, breathing women. Women's Liberation Groups, black women, high-school and college women, women's peace groups, women's welfare and social-work groups, women's job-equality groups, pro-birth control and pro-abortion groups—women of every political persuasion—all are invited to join us in a day-long boardwalk-theater event, starting at 1:00 P.M. on the Boardwalk in front of Atlantic City's Convention Hall. We will protest the image of Miss America, an image that oppresses women in every area in which it purports to represent us. There will be: Picket Lines; Guerrilla Theater; Leafleting; Lobbying Visits to the contestants urging our sisters to reject the Pageant Farce and join us; a huge Freedom Trash Can (into which we will throw bras,* girdles, curlers, false eyelashes, wigs, and representative issues of *Cosmopolitan, Ladies' Home Journal, Family Circle,* etc.—bring any such woman-garbage you have around the house); we will also announce a Boycott of all those commercial products related to the Pageant, and the day will end with a Women's Liberation rally at midnight when Miss America is crowned on live television. Lots of other surprises are being planned (come and add your own!) but we do not plan heavy disruptive tactics and so do not expect a bad police scene. It should be a groovy day on the Boardwalk in the sun with our sisters. In case of arrests, however, we plan

*Bras were never burned. Bra-burning was a whole-cloth invention of the media.—Ed. [Morgan]

to reject all male authority and demand to be busted by policewomen only. (In Atlantic City, women cops are not permitted to make arrests—dig that!)

Male chauvinist-reactionaries on this issue had best stay away, nor are male liberals welcome in the demonstrations. But sympathetic men can donate money as well as cars and drivers.

Male reporters will be refused interviews. We reject patronizing reportage. *Only newswomen will be recognized.*

The Ten Points

We Protest:

1. *The Degrading Mindless-Boob-Girlie Symbol.* The Pageant contestants epitomize the roles we are all forced to play as women. The parade down the runway blares the metaphor of the 4-H Club county fair, where the nervous animals are judged for teeth, fleece, etc., and where the best "specimen" gets the blue ribbon. So are women in our society forced daily to compete for male approval, enslaved by ludicrous "beauty" standards we ourselves are conditioned to take seriously.

2. *Racism with Roses.* Since its inception in 1921, the Pageant has not had one Black finalist, and this has not been for a lack of test-case contestants. There has never been a Puerto Rican, Alaskan, Hawaiian, or Mexican-American winner. Nor has there ever been a *true* Miss America—an American Indian.

3. *Miss America as Military Death Mascot.* The highlight of her reign each year is a cheerleader-tour of American troops abroad—last year she went to Vietnam to pep-talk our husbands, fathers, sons and boyfriends into dying and killing with a better spirit. She personifies the "unstained patriotic American womanhood our boys are fighting for." The Living Bra and the Dead Soldier. We refuse to be used as Mascots for Murder.

4. *The Consumer Con-Game.* Miss America is a walking commercial for the Pageant's sponsors. Wind her up and she plugs your product on promotion tours and TV—all in an "honest, objective" endorsement. What a shill.

5. *Competition Rigged and Unrigged.* We deplore the encouragement of an American myth that oppresses men as well as women: the win-or-you're worthless competitive disease. The "beauty contest" creates only one winner to be "used" and forty-nine losers who are "useless."

6. *The Woman as Pop Culture Obsolescent Theme.* Spindle, mutilate, and then discard tomorrow. What is so ignored as last year's Miss America? This only reflects the gospel of our society, according to Saint Male: women must be young, juicy, malleable—hence age discrimination and the cult of youth. And we women are brainwashed into believing this ourselves!

7. *The Unbeatable Madonna-Whore Combination.* Miss America and Playboy's centerfold are sisters over the skin. To win approval, we must be both

sexy and wholesome, delicate but able to cope, demure yet titillatingly bitchy. Deviation of any sort brings, we are told, disaster: "You won't get a man!!"

8. *The Irrelevant Crown on the Throne of Mediocrity.* Miss America represents what women are supposed to be: unoffensive, bland, apolitical. If you are tall, short, over or under what weight The Man prescribes you should be, forget it. Personality, articulateness, intelligence, commitment—unwise. Conformity is the key to the crown—and, by extension, to success in our society.

9. *Miss America as Dream Equivalent To—?* In this reputedly democratic society, where every little boy supposedly can grow up to be President, what can every little girl hope to grow to be? Miss America. That's where it's at. Real power to control our own lives is restricted to men, while women get patronizing pseudo-power, an ermine cloak and a bunch of flowers; men are judged by their actions, women by their appearance.

10. *Miss America as Big Sister Watching You.* The Pageant exercises Thought Control, attempts to sear the Image onto our minds, to further make women oppressed and men oppressors; to enslave us all the more in high-heeled, low-status roles; to inculcate false values in young girls; to use women as beasts of buying; to seduce us to prostitute ourselves before our own oppression.

NO MORE MISS AMERICA

The Politics of Housework

Pat Mainardi

One of the major contributions of the women's liberation movement was the idea of consciousness-raising, that is, using group discussions of women's personal experiences to understand how sexism (a word just coming into use in 1968) shaped their lives. Credit for the consciousness-raising tactic belongs to a group of radical women in New York who called themselves the Redstockings. In their 1969 Manifesto, they asserted: "We regard our personal experience, and our feelings about that experience, as the basis for an analysis of our common situation. . . . Consciousness-raising is not 'therapy,' which implies the existence of individual solutions and falsely assumes that the male-female relationship is purely personal, but the only method by which we can ensure that our program for liberation is based on the concrete realities of our lives."

Painter Pat Mainardi was a member of Redstockings, and this piece on "The Politics of Housework" grew out of her experience. One of the slogans of the women's movement was that "the personal is political," and nowhere was that more clear than in who did the housework. In such sessions, many women who considered themselves liberated realized that the men with whom they were sharing their lives, as husbands or lovers, were often resistant to changing old patterns if they (the men) had something to lose. Her humorous, yet pointed, recounting of such dialogues in her own household shows the uneasiness and tension that could occur when women took the revolution home.

Dismissed by men as a trivial issue, housework in fact goes to the heart of a patriarchal family structure that deposits all responsibility for household management and child care on women. Furthermore, the discussion pinpoints the parallels between housework and women's work in general: its low status, its repetitiveness, its dull and boring nature. Women's liberation argued that not just women should change, but men must as well. And the change should occur not just in the public realm of law and politics, but in the private realm of family life and sexuality.

Liberated women—very different from women's liberation! The first signals all kinds of goodies, to warm the hearts (not to mention other parts) of the most radical men. The other signals—*housework.* The first brings sex without marriage, sex before marriage, cozy housekeeping arrangements ("You see, I'm living with this chick") and the self-content of knowing that you're not the kind of man who wants a doormat instead of a woman. That will come later. After all, who wants that old commodity anymore, the Standard American Housewife, all husband, home and kids. The New Commodity, the Liberated Woman, has sex a lot and has a Career, preferably something that can be fitted in with the household chores—like dancing, pottery, or painting.

On the other hand is women's liberation—and housework. What? You say this is all trivial? Wonderful! That's what I thought. It seemed perfectly reasonable. We both had careers, both had to work a couple of days a week to earn enough to live on, so why shouldn't we share the housework? So I suggested it to my mate and he agreed—most men are too hip to turn you down flat. "You're right," he said, "It's only fair."

Then an interesting thing happened. I can only explain it by stating that we women have been brainwashed more than even we can imagine. Probably too many years of seeing television women in ecstasy over their shiny waxed floors or breaking down over their dirty shirt collars. Men have no such conditioning. They recognize the essential fact of housework right from the very beginning. Which is that it stinks. Here's my list of dirty chores: buying groceries, carting them home and putting them away; cooking meals and washing dishes and pots; doing the laundry, digging out the place when things get out of control; washing floors. The list could go on but the sheer necessities are

Source: Pat Mainardi, "The Politics of Housework." From *Sisterhood Is Powerful: An Anthology of Writings from the Women's Liberation Movement,* edited by Robin Morgan, pp. 502–506. Copyright © 1970 by Robin Morgan. By permission of Edite Kroll Literary Agency.

bad enough. All of us have to do these things, or get some one else to do them for us. The longer my husband contemplated these chores the more repulsed he became, and so proceeded the change from the normally sweet considerate Dr. Jekyll into the crafty Mr. Hyde who would stop at nothing to avoid the horrors of—*housework.* As he felt himself backed into a corner laden with dirty dishes, brooms, mops, and reeking garbage, his front teeth grew longer and pointier, his fingernails haggled and his eyes grew wild. Housework trivial? Not on your life! Just try to share the burden.

So ensued a dialogue that's been going on for several years. Here are some of the high points:

"I don't mind sharing the housework, but I don't do it very well. We should each do the things we're best at."

Meaning: Unfortunately I'm no good at things like washing dishes or cooking. What I do best is a little light carpentry, changing light bulbs, moving furniture *(how often do you move furniture?).*

Also Meaning: Historically the lower classes (black men and us) have had hundreds of years experience doing menial jobs. It would be a waste of manpower to train someone else to do them now.

Also Meaning: I don't like the dull stupid boring jobs, so you should do them.

"I don't mind sharing the work, but you'll have to show me how to do it."

Meaning: I ask a lot of questions and you'll have to show me everything everytime I do it because I don't remember so good. Also don't try to sit down and read while I'm doing my jobs because I'm going to annoy hell out of you until it's easier to do them yourself.

"We used to be so happy!" (Said whenever it was his turn to do something.)

Meaning: I used to be so happy.

Meaning: Life without housework is bliss. *(No quarrel here. Perfect agreement.)*

"We have different standards, and why should I have to work to your standards. That's unfair."

Meaning: If I begin to get bugged by the dirt and crap I will say "This place sure is a sty" or "How can anyone live like this?" and wait for your reaction. I know that all women have a sore called "Guilt over a messy house" or "Household work is ultimately my responsibility." I know that men have caused that sore—if anyone visits and the place *is* a sty, they're not going to leave and say, "He sure is a lousy housekeeper." You'll take the rap in any case. I can outwait you.

Also Meaning: I can provoke innumerable scenes over the housework issue. Eventually doing all the housework yourself will be less painful to you than trying to get me to do half. Or I'll suggest we get a maid. She will do my share of the work. You will do yours. It's women's work.

"I've got nothing against sharing the housework, but you can't make me do it on your schedule."

Meaning: Passive resistance. I'll do it when I damned well please, if at all. If my job is doing dishes, it's easier to do them once a week. If taking out laundry, once a month. If washing the floors, once a year. If you don't like it, do it yourself oftener, and then I won't do it at all.

"I *hate* it more than you. You don't mind it so much."

Meaning: Housework is garbage work. It's the worst crap I've ever done. It's degrading and humiliating for someone of *my* intelligence to do it. But for someone of *your* intelligence . . .

"Housework is too trivial to even talk about."

Meaning: It's even more trivial to do. Housework is beneath my status. My purpose in life is to deal with matters of significance. Yours is to deal with matters of insignificance. You should do the housework.

"This problem of housework is not a man-woman problem! In any relationship between two people one is going to have a stronger personality and dominate."

Meaning: That stronger personality had better be *me.*

"In animal societies, wolves, for example, the top animal is usually a male even where he is not chosen for brute strength but on the basis of cunning and intelligence. Isn't that interesting?"

Meaning: I have historical, psychological, anthropological, and biological justification for keeping you down. How can you ask the top wolf to be equal?

"Women's liberation isn't really a political movement."

Meaning: The Revolution is coming too close to home.

Also Meaning: I am only interested in how *I* am oppressed, not how I oppress others. Therefore the war, the draft, and the university are political. Women's liberation is not.

"Man's accomplishments have always depended on getting help from other people, mostly women. What great man would have accomplished what he did if he had to do his own housework?"

Meaning: Oppression is built into the System and I, as the white American male receive the benefits of this System. I don't want to give them up.

Postscript

Participatory democracy begins at home.

Thoughts on Indian Feminism

Kate Shanley

As a result of the consciousness raising from the civil rights and feminist movements, nonwhite women in the United States (who make up approximately 20 percent of the population) have had greater reasons to reach out to each other as women. Within each minority group, women have faced the simultaneous oppressions of race and gender (and since many minority women are also poor, of class) and consistently refused to rank one oppression above another. And yet when it has come to making links with the predominantly white feminist movement, suspicion and misunderstanding have reigned.

Kate Shanley's piece, "Thoughts on Indian Feminism," suggests reasons why such alliances have often been fraught with problems at the same time it argues that such coalitions are beneficial, indeed necessary, for feminism. Native-American women fear being made into tokens or mascots for a white woman's movement, and all too often have had the experience of seeing their concerns marginalized or ignored by white feminists. Shanley points to the different agenda that Indian women bring to feminism, notably their commitment to tribal sovereignty as the highest priority for the survival of the Indian peoples. The historical patterns governing Native-American life traditionally have given large roles to women to decide matters of family inheritance and control, and Indian women play a central role in the imagery of spirituality and identification with the land; as Shanley points out, concerns such as challenging the oppression of gender roles in the nuclear family have little relevance in such a context. But rather than suggesting that Indian women should only work in isolation, Shanley argues that the women's movement as a whole will profit from a recognition of diversity as its basis.

Kate Shanley refers to herself as an *academic squaw* because at the time this article was published in 1984 she was working toward a Ph.D. in literature at the University of Michigan. She is part Assiniboine Indian, part Irish, and was born and raised on the Fort Peck reservation in Montana.

Two years ago, after the Ohoyo Conference in Tahlequah, Oklahoma, the Ohoyo Resource Center put together a book titled, *Words of Today's American Indian Women: Ohoyo Makachi.* Among the addresses included is Rayna Green's speech, "Contemporary Indian Humor." A mixture of anecdote and tribute to Indian women, Green's talk addresses with humor the serious problems facing Indian women in America today. Of the relationship of the Indian women's movement to the majority women's movement, however, she writes:

> Many people want to know why the Indian women's movement didn't really join the majority women's movement in this country. I've come up with a new theory of why they have not joined the women's movement. You've all heard that one of the first things people in the movement did was to burn their bras. I've decided why Indian women didn't do that. Being the shape most

Source: Kate Shanley, "Thoughts on Indian Feminism," in *A Gathering of Spirit,* ed. Beth Brant, pp. 213–215. Copyright © 1984 by Beth Brant. Reprinted by permission of Firebrand Books, Ithaca, New York.

of us are in, we were afraid they'd have to bring the fire trucks in from ten
miles around. So you can understand why we were reluctant. We figured we
stopped air pollution in Eastern Oklahoma by not doing that kind of burning.

Aside from the obviously funny reference to the large-chestedness of Indian
women, Green plays off the popular mistaken notion that "the first thing" feminists did to protest women's oppression in this country was to burn their
bras—a weak, if not self-trivializing gesture—and she jokingly cites bra-
burning as the point where Indian and "majority" women depart from each
other. Of course, humor is humor—and what could be worse than taking a joke
seriously? Then again, what could be more foolish than denying the serious
assumptions that underlie most humor, assumptions as commonly-held beliefs.
The American women's movement historically has been and continues to be
more than a weak protest against the notion of woman as sex symbol, but the
questions remain: why do Indian women seem reluctant to join the majority
women's movement? Or do they?

Toward the end of the 1983 Ohoyo Indian Women's Conference on Leadership, I began to notice that the participants were not referring to themselves
as feminists, although the group of women present are as strong and committed as any group of women in America today who are working for change. Why,
then, do Indian women avoid the designation "feminist?" The more I thought
about it, the more that question began proliferating into many questions: how
many other women (of all colors and creeds) have I encountered in my travels
(plenty!) who do not choose to identify as feminists? What do they have in common with Indian women? What is a feminist, anyway?

My thoughts on the questions raised thus far by no means represent a consensus among Indian women; in fact, before I could begin to deal objectively
with the subject of Indian feminism, I had to come to terms with my own de-
fensiveness about representing other women, particularly other Indian women.
On the one hand, I am a woman who refers to herself as a feminist. If most Indian women do not refer to themselves as feminists, does that fact make me
somehow *less* representative, *less* Indian? On the other hand, does the theoretical feminism of the university constitute something different from (though,
perhaps giving it the benefit of the doubt, correlated to) the "grass-roots" feminism Ohoyo represents? To some extent I know that I suffer the conflicts of
an "academic squaw" (to borrow a term from poet and educator Wendy Rose),
a certain distance from the "real world."

Attending the Ohoyo conference in Grand Forks, North Dakota was a returning home for me in a spiritual sense—taking my place beside other Indian
women, and an actual sense—being with my relatives and loved ones after finally finishing my pre-doctoral requirements at the university. Although I have
been a full-time student for the past six years, I brought to the academic experience many years in the workaday world as a mother, registered nurse, volunteer tutor, social worker aide, and high school outreach worker. What I am

offering in this article are my thoughts as an Indian woman on feminism. Mine is a political perspective that seeks to re-view the real-life positions of women in relation to the theories that attempt to address the needs of those women.

Issues such as equal pay for equal work, child health and welfare, and a woman's right to make her own choices regarding contraceptive use, sterilization and abortion—key issues to the majority women's movement—affect Indian women as well; however, equality *per se,* may have a different meaning for Indian women and Indian people. That difference begins with personal and tribal sovereignty—the right to be legally recognized as peoples empowered to determine our own destinies. Thus, the Indian women's movement seeks equality in two ways that do not concern mainstream women: (1) on the individual level, the Indian woman struggles to promote the survival of a social structure whose organizational principles represent notions of family different from those of the mainstream; and (2) on the societal level, the People seek sovereignty as a people in order to maintain a vital legal and spiritual connection to the land, in order to *survive* as a people.

The nuclear family has little relevance to Indian women; in fact, in many ways mainstream feminists now are striving to redefine family and community in a way that Indian women have long known. The American lifestyle from which white middle-class women are fighting to free themselves, has not taken hold in Indian communities. Tribal and communal values have survived after four hundred years of colonial oppression.

It may be that the desire on the part of mainstream feminists to include Indian women, however sincere, represents tokenism just now, because too often Indian people, by being thought of as spiritual "mascots" to the American endeavor, are seen more as artifacts than as real people able to speak for ourselves. Given the public's general ignorance about Indian people, in other words, it is possible that Indian people's real-life concerns are not relevant to the mainstream feminist movement in a way that constitutes anything more than a "representative" facade. Charges against the women's movement of heterosexism and racism abound these days; it is not my intention to add to them except to stress that we must all be vigilant in examining the underlying assumptions that motivate us. Internalization of negative (that is, sexist and racist) attitudes towards ourselves and others can and quite often does result from colonialist (white patriarchal) oppression. It is more useful to attack the systems that keep us ignorant of each other's histories.

The other way in which the Indian women's movement differs in emphasis from the majority women's movement, lies in the importance Indian people place on tribal sovereignty—it is the single most pressing political issue in Indian country today. For Indian people to survive culturally as well as materially, many battles must be fought and won in the courts of law, precisely because it is the legal recognition that enables Indian people to govern ourselves according to our own world view—a world view that is antithetical to the *wasicu* (the Lakota term for "takers of the fat") definition of progress. Equality for Indian women within tribal communities, therefore, holds more significance than equality in terms of the general rubric "American."

Up to now I have been referring to the women's movement as though it were a single, well-defined organization. It is not. Perhaps in many ways socialist feminists hold views similar to the views of many Indian people regarding private property and the nuclear family. Certainly, there are some Indian people who are capitalistic. The point I would like to stress, however, is that rather than seeing differences according to a hierarchy of oppressions (white over Indian, male over female), we must practice a politics that allows for diversity in cultural identity as well as in sexual identity.

The word "feminism" has special meanings to Indian women, including the idea of promoting the continuity of tradition, and consequently, pursuing the recognition of tribal sovereignty. Even so, Indian feminists are united with mainstream feminists in outrage against woman and child battering, sexist employment and educational practices, and in many other social concerns. Just as sovereignty cannot be granted but *must be recognized* as an inherent right to self-determination, so Indian feminism must also be recognized as powerful in its own terms, in its own right.

Feminism becomes an incredibly powerful term when it incorporates diversity—not as a superficial political position, but as a practice. The women's movement and the Indian movement for sovereignty suffer similar trivialization, because narrow factions turn ignorance to their own benefit so that they can exploit human beings and the lands they live on for corporate profit. The time has come for Indian women and Indian people to be known on our own terms. This nuclear age demands new terms of communication for all people. Our survival depends on it. Peace.

Black Feminism

Combahee River Collective

"The concept of the simultaneity of oppression is still the crux of a Black Feminist understanding of political reality and, I believe, one of the most significant ideological contributions of Black Feminist thought." So wrote Barbara Smith, one of the members of Combahee River Collective, a group of black feminists in Boston in the 1970s who drew their name from Harriet Tubman's 1863 guerilla action in the Port Royal region of South Carolina that freed more than 750 slaves. This document, which is dated April 1977, summarizes the major themes of black feminism as it developed in the 1970s. It functions not only as an ideological statement, but also as an attempt to describe "what oppression is comprised of on a day-to-day basis," thus reminding us that oppression is not just some abstraction but a concrete daily experience.

The Combahee River Collective statement refuses to separate the multiple oppressions that shape black women's lives. As it says, "We struggle together with Black men against racism, while we also struggle with Black men about sexism." An overriding commitment to combat racism need not negate the very personal (and political) need to work for women's own liberation within the black community. They name the reason: "because of our need as human persons for autonomy." Like the white women in the women's liberation movement of the late 1960s, for them, the personal is political. The identification of the members as lesbians also reinforces this awareness. But once again, it takes women of color to forcefully point out the unconscious racism that often afflicts the women's movement as a whole.

We are a collective of Black feminists who have been meeting together since 1974. During that time we have been involved in the process of defining and clarifying our politics, while at the same time doing political work within our own group and in coalition with other progressive organizations and movements. The most general statement of our politics at the present time would be that we are actively committed to struggling against racial, sexual, heterosexual, and class oppression and see as our particular task the development of integrated analysis and practice based upon the fact that the major systems of oppression are interlocking. The synthesis of these oppressions creates the conditions of our lives. As Black women we see Black feminism as the logical political movement to combat the manifold and simultaneous oppressions that all women of color face.

We will discuss four major topics in the paper that follows: (1) the genesis of contemporary black feminism; (2) what we believe, i.e., the specific province of our politics; (3) the problems in organizing Black feminists, including a brief herstory of our collective; and (4) Black feminist issues and practice.

1. The Genesis of Contemporary Black Feminism

Before looking at the recent development of Black feminism we would like to affirm that we find our origins in the historical reality of Afro-American women's continuous life-and-death struggle for survival and liberation. Black women's extremely negative relationship to the American political system (a system of white male rule) has always been determined by our membership in two oppressed racial and sexual castes. As Angela Davis points out in "Reflections on the Black Woman's Role in the Community of Slaves," Black women have always embodied, if only in their physical manifestation, an ad-

Source: Combahee River Collective, "A Black Feminist Statement," in *Capitalist Patriarchy and the Case for Socialist Feminism,* ed. Zillah Eisenstein (New York and London: Monthly Review Press, 1979), pp. 362–372. Copyright © 1979 by Zillah Eisenstein. Reprinted by permission of Monthly Review Foundation.

versary stance to white male rule and have actively resisted its inroads upon them and their communities in both dramatic and subtle ways. There have always been Black women activists—some known, like Sojourner Truth, Harriet Tubman, Frances E. W. Harper, Ida B. Wells Barnett, and Mary Church Terrell, and thousands upon thousands unknown—who had a shared awareness of how their sexual identity combined with their racial identity to make their whole life situation and the focus of their political struggles unique. Contemporary Black feminism is the outgrowth of countless generations of personal sacrifice, militancy, and work by our mothers and sisters.

A Black feminist presence has evolved most obviously in connection with the second wave of the American women's movement beginning in the late 1960s. Black, other Third World, and working women have been involved in the feminist movement from its start, but both outside reactionary forces and racism and elitism within the movement itself have served to obscure our participation. In 1973 Black feminists, primarily located in New York, felt the necessity of forming a separate Black feminist group. This became the National Black Feminist Organization (NBFO).

Black feminist politics also have an obvious connection to movements for Black liberation, particularly those of the 1960s and 1970s. Many of us were active in those movements (civil rights, Black nationalism, the Black Panthers), and all of our lives were greatly affected and changed by their ideology, their goals, and the tactics used to achieve their goals. It was our experience and disillusionment within these liberation movements, as well as experience on the periphery of the white male left, that led to the need to develop a politics that was antiracist, unlike those of white women, and antisexist, unlike those of Black and white men.

There is also undeniably a personal genesis for Black feminism, that is, the political realization that comes from the seemingly personal experiences of individual Black women's lives. Black feminists and many more Black women who do not define themselves as feminists have all experienced sexual oppression as a constant factor in our day-to-day existence. As children we realized that we were different from boys and that we were treated differently. For example, we were told in the same breath to be quiet both for the sake of being "ladylike" and to make us less objectionable in the eyes of white people. As we grew older we became aware of the threat of physical and sexual abuse by men. However, we had no way of conceptualizing what was so apparent to us, what we *knew* was really happening.

Black feminists often talk about their feelings of craziness before becoming conscious of the concepts of sexual politics, patriarchal rule, and most importantly, feminism, the political analysis and practice that we women use to struggle against our oppression. The fact that racial politics and indeed racism are pervasive factors in our lives did not allow us, and still does not allow most Black women, to look more deeply into our own experiences and, from that sharing and growing consciousness, to build a politics that will change our lives and inevitably end our oppression. Our development must also be tied to the contemporary economic and political position of Black people. The post World War II generation of Black youth was the first to be able to minimally partake of certain educational and employment options, previously closed completely to Black people. Although our economic position is still at the very bottom of the American capitalistic economy, a handful of us have been able to gain certain tools as a result of tokenism in education and employment which potentially enable us to more effectively fight our oppression.

A combined antiracist and antisexist position drew us together initially, and as we developed politically we addressed ourselves to hetero-sexism and economic oppression under capitalism.

2. What We Believe

Above all else, our politics initially sprang from the shared belief that Black women are inherently valuable, that our liberation is a necessity not as an adjunct to somebody else's but because of our need as human persons for autonomy. This may seem so obvious as to sound simplistic, but it is apparent that no other ostensibly progressive movement has ever considered our specific oppression as a priority or worked seriously for the ending of that oppression. Merely naming the pejorative stereotypes attributed to Black women (e.g., mammy, matriarch, Sapphire, whore, bulldagger), let alone cataloguing the cruel, often murderous, treatment we receive, indicates how little value has been placed upon our lives during four centuries of bondage in the Western hemisphere. We realize that the only people who care enough about us to work consistently for our liberation is us. Our politics evolve from a healthy love for ourselves, our sisters and our community which allows us to continue our struggle and work.

This focusing upon our own oppression is embodied in the concept of identity politics. We believe that the most profound and potentially the most radical politics come directly out of our own identity, as opposed to working to end somebody else's oppression. In the case of Black women this is a particularly repugnant, dangerous, threatening, and therefore revolutionary concept because it is obvious from looking at all the political movements that have preceded us that anyone is more worthy of liberation than ourselves. We reject pedestals, queenhood, and walking ten paces behind. To be recognized as human, levelly human, is enough.

We believe that sexual politics under patriarchy is as pervasive in Black women's lives as are the politics of class and race. We also often find it difficult to separate race from class from sex oppression because in our lives they are most often experienced simultaneously. We know that there is such a thing as racial-sexual oppression which is neither solely racial nor solely sexual, e.g., the history of rape of Black women by white men as a weapon of political repression.

Although we are feminists and lesbians, we feel solidarity with progressive Black men and do not advocate the fractionalization that white women who are separatists demand. Our situation as Black people necessitates that we have solidarity around the fact of race, which white women of course do not need to have with white men, unless it is their negative solidarity as racial oppressors. We struggle together with Black men against racism, while we also struggle with Black men about sexism.

We realize that the liberation of all oppressed peoples necessitates the destruction of the political-economic systems of capitalism and imperialism as well as patriarchy. We are socialists because we believe the work must be organized for the collective benefit of those who do the work and create the products, and not for the profit of the bosses. Material resources must be equally distributed among those who create these resources. We are not convinced, however, that a socialist revolution that is not also a feminist and antiracist revolution will guarantee our liberation. We have arrived at the necessity for developing an understanding of class relationships that takes into account the specific class position of Black women who are generally marginal in the labor force, while at this particular time some of us are temporarily viewed as doubly desirable tokens at white-collar and professional levels. We need to articulate the real class situation of persons who are not merely raceless, sexless workers, but for whom racial and sexual oppression are significant determinants in their working/economic lives. Although we are in essential agreement with Marx's theory as it applied to the very specific economic relationships he analyzed, we know that his analysis must be extended further in order for us to understand our specific economic situation as Black women.

A political contribution which we feel we have already made is the expansion of the feminist principle that the personal is political. In our consciousness-raising sessions, for example, we have in many ways gone beyond white women's revelations because we are dealing with the implications of race and class as well as sex. Even our Black women's style of talking/testifying in Black language about what we have experienced has a resonance that is both cultural and political. We have spent a great deal of energy delving into the cultural and experiential nature of our oppression out of necessity because none of these matters has ever been looked at before. No one before has ever examined the multilayered texture of Black women's lives. An example of this kind of revelation/conceptualization occurred at a meeting as we discussed the ways in which our early intellectual interests had been attacked by our peers, particularly Black males. We discovered that all of us, because we were "smart" had also been considered "ugly", *i.e.,* "smart-ugly." "Smart-ugly" crystallized the way in which most of us had been forced to develop our intellects at great cost to our "social" lives. The sanctions in the Black and white communities against Black women thinkers is comparatively much higher than for white women, particularly ones from the educated middle and upper classes.

As we have already stated, we reject the stance of lesbian separatism because it is not a viable political analysis or strategy for us. It leaves out far too much and far too many people, particularly Black men, women, and children. We have a great deal of criticism and loathing for what men have been socialized to be in this society: what they support, how they act, and how they oppress. But we do not have the misguided notion that it is their maleness, per se—i.e., their biological maleness—that makes them what they are. As Black women we find any type of biological determinism a particularly dangerous and reactionary basis upon which to build a politic. We must also question whether lesbian separatism is an adequate and progressive political analysis and strategy, even for those who practice it, since it so completely denies any but the sexual sources of women's oppression, negating the facts of class and race.

3. Problems in Organizing Black Feminists

During our years together as a Black feminist collective we have experienced success and defeat, joy and pain, victory and failure. We have found that it is very difficult to organize around Black feminist issues, difficult even to announce in certain contexts that we *are* Black feminists. We have tried to think about the reasons for our difficulties, particularly since the white women's movement continues to be strong and to grow in many directions. In this section we will discuss some of the general reasons for the organizing problems we face and also talk specifically about the stages in organizing our own collective.

The major source of difficulty in our political work is that we are not just trying to fight oppression on one front or even two, but instead to address a whole range of oppressions. We do not have racial, sexual, heterosexual, or class privilege to rely upon, nor do we have even the minimal access to resources and power that groups who possess any one of these types of privilege have.

The psychological toll of being a Black woman and the difficulties this presents in reaching political consciousness and doing political work can never be underestimated. There is a very low value placed upon Black women's psyches in this society, which is both racist and sexist. As an early group member once said, "We are all damaged people merely by virtue of being Black women." We are dispossessed psychologically and on every other level, and yet we feel the necessity to struggle to change the condition of all Black women. In "A Black Feminist's Search for Sisterhood," Michele Wallace arrives at this conclusion:

> We exist as women who are Black who are feminists, each stranded for the moment, working independently because there is not yet an environment in this society remotely congenial to our struggle—because, being on the bot-

tom, we would have to do what no one else has done: we would have to fight
the world.

Wallace is pessimistic but realistic in her assessment of Black feminists'
position, particularly in her allusion to the nearly classic isolation most of us
face. We might use our position at the bottom, however, to make a clear leap
into revolutionary action. If Black women were free, it would mean that everyone else would have to be free since our freedom would necessitate the destruction of all the systems of oppression.

Feminism is, nevertheless, very threatening to the majority of Black people because it calls into question some of the most basic assumptions about our
existence, i.e., that sex should be a determinant of power relationships. Here
is the way male and female voices were defined in a Black nationalist pamphlet from the early 1970's.

> We understand that it is and has been traditional that the man is the head of
> the house. He is the leader of the house/nation because his knowledge of
> the world is broader, his awareness is greater, his understanding is fuller
> and his application of this information is wiser . . . After all, it is only rea-
> sonable that the man be the head of the house because he is able to defend
> and protect the development of his home . . . Women cannot do the same
> things as men—they are made by nature to function differently. Equality of
> men and women is something that cannot happen even in the abstract world.
> Men are not equal to other men, i.e., ability, experience or even under-
> standing. The value of men and women can be seen as in the value of gold
> and silver—they are not equal but both have great value. We must realize
> that men and women are a complement to each other because there is no
> house/family without a man and his wife. Both are essential to the devel-
> opment of any life.

The material conditions of most Black women would hardly lead them to
upset both economic and sexual arrangements that seem to represent some stability in their lives. Many Black women have a good understanding of both sexism and racism, but because of the everyday constrictions of their lives cannot
risk struggling against them both.

The reaction of Black men to feminism has been notoriously negative. They
are, of course, even more threatened than Black women by the possibility that
Black feminists might organize around our own needs. They realize that they
might not only lose valuable and hardworking allies in their struggles but that
they might also be forced to change their habitually sexist ways of interacting
with and oppressing Black women. Accusations that Black feminism divides
the Black struggle are powerful deterrents to the growth of an autonomous
Black women's movement.

Still, hundreds of women have been active at different times during the
three-year existence of our group. And every Black woman who came, came

out of a strongly-felt need for some level of possibility that did not previously exist in her life.

When we first started meeting early in 1974 after the NBFO first eastern regional conference, we did not have a strategy for organizing, or even a focus. We just wanted to see what we had. After a period of months of not meeting, we began to meet again late in the year and started doing an intense variety of consciousness-raising. The overwhelming feeling that we had is that after years and years we had finally found each other. Although we were not doing political work as a group, individuals continued their involvement in Lesbian politics, sterilization abuse and abortion rights work, Third World Women's International Women's Day activities, and support activity for the trials of Dr. Kenneth Edelin, Joan Little, and Inéz García. During our first summer, when membership had dropped off considerably, those of us remaining devoted serious discussion to the possibility of opening a refuge for battered women in a Black community. (There was no refuge in Boston at that time.) We also decided around that time to become an independent collective since we had serious disagreements with NBFO's bourgeois-feminist stance and their lack of a clear political focus.

We also were contacted at that time by socialist feminists, with whom we had worked on abortion rights activities, who wanted to encourage us to attend the National Socialist Feminist Conference in Yellow Springs. One of our members did attend and despite the narrowness of the ideology that was promoted at that particular conference, we became more aware of the need for us to understand our own economic situation and to make our own economic analysis.

In the fall, when some members returned, we experienced several months of comparative inactivity and internal disagreements which were first conceptualized as a Lesbian-straight split but which were also the result of class and political differences. During the summer those of us who were still meeting had determined the need to do political work and to move beyond consciousness-raising and serving exclusively as an emotional support group. At the beginning of 1976, when some of the women who had not wanted to do political work and who also had voiced disagreements stopped attending of their own accord, we again looked for a focus. We decided at that time, with the addition of new members, to become a study group. We had always shared our reading with each other, and some of us had written papers on Black feminism for group discussion a few months before this decision was made. We began functioning as a study group and also began discussing the possibility of starting a Black feminist publication. We had a retreat in the late spring which provided a time for both political discussion and working out interpersonal issues. Currently we are planning to gather together a collection of Black feminist writing. We feel that it is absolutely essential to demonstrate the reality of our politics to other Black women and believe that we can do this through writing and distributing our work. The fact that individual Black feminists are living in isolation all over the country, that our own numbers are small, and that we have some skills in writing, printing, and publishing makes us want to carry out these kinds of projects as a means of organizing Black feminists as we continue to do political work in coalition with other groups.

4. Black Feminist Issues and Projects

During our time together we have identified and worked on many issues of particular relevance to Black women. The inclusiveness of our politics makes us concerned with any situation that impinges upon the lives of women, Third World and working people. We are of course particularly committed to working on those struggles in which race, sex and class are simultaneous factors in oppression. We might for example, become involved in workplace organizing at a factory that employs Third World women or picket a hospital that is cutting back on already inadequate health care to a Third World community, or set up a rape crisis center in a Black neighborhood. Organizing around welfare and daycare concerns might also be a focus. The work to be done and the countless issues that this work represents merely reflect the pervasiveness of our oppression.

Issues and projects that collective members have actually worked on are sterilization abuse, abortion rights, battered women, rape and health care. We have also done many workshops and educationals on Black feminism on college campuses, at women's conferences, and most recently for high school women.

One issue that is of major concern to us and that we have begun to publicly address is racism in the white women's movement. As Black feminists we are made constantly and painfully aware of how little effort white women have made to understand and combat their racism, which requires among other things that they have a more than superficial comprehension of race, color, and black history and culture. Eliminating racism in the white women's movement is by definition work for white women to do, but we will continue to speak to and demand accountability on this issue.

In the practice of our politics we do not believe that the end always justifies the means. Many reactionary and destructive acts have been done in the name of achieving "correct" political goals. As feminists we do not want to mess over people in the name of politics. We believe in collective process and a nonhierarchical distribution of power within our own group and in our vision of a revolutionary society. We are committed to a continual examination of our politics as they develop through criticism and self-criticism as an essential aspect of our practice. In her introduction to *Sisterhood Is Powerful* Robin Morgan writes:

> I haven't the faintest notion what possible revolutionary role white heterosexual men could fulfill, since they are the very embodiment of reactionary-vested-interest-power.

As Black feminists and Lesbians we know that we have a very definite revolutionary task to perform and we are ready for the lifetime of work and struggle before us.

A More Personal View
of Black Feminism

Michele Wallace

Writer Michele Wallace's story of her personal route to black feminism contrasts with the primarily intellectual thrust of the Combahee River Collective statement, where it is mentioned in passing. Black women who identify themselves as feminists have been especially insightful about the dangers of claiming that all oppression comes from race, knowing from their own experiences that the element of sexism operates independently of the oppression of racism. Wallace's willingness to criticize black men for their treatment of black women, which she developed in her 1979 book *Black Macho and the Myth of the Superwoman*, was controversial in both the black and white communities. Wallace's identification of this theme was foreshadowed in this 1975 article for *The Village Voice*.

Besides Wallace's perspective on black feminism, her autobiographical piece has resonance for many of the themes of this anthology. She describes the process of growing up female, and growing up black, which at first meant accepting that her dreams were unrealistic, and then after the civil rights and women's movements raised expectations, learning that her early dreams did not have to be abandoned after all. As she grows toward womanhood, she is caught in many of the dilemmas of female adolescence: a weight problem, concern about hair and makeup, worrying if the rain would dampen her Afro haircut, and attempts to meet men. College is a time to test her ideas and link up with the movements for social change then reshaping American society. Her conclusion, that black feminists exist as individuals, not as part of a black women's movement, may be as true today as when she published this article in 1975.

When I was in the third grade I wanted to be president. I can still remember the stricken look on my teacher's face when I announced it in class. By the time I was in the fourth grade I had decided to be the president's wife instead. It never occurred to me that I could be neither because I was Black. Growing up in a dreamy state of mind not uncommon to the offspring of the Black middle

Source: Michele Wallace, "A Black Feminist's Search for Sisterhood," *The Village Voice,* July 28, 1975. Reprinted in Gloria Hull, Patricia Bell Scott, and Barbara Smith, *But Some of Us Are Brave* (New York: The Feminist Press, 1982), pp. 5–12. Reprinted by permission of the author and *The Village Voice.*

class, I was convinced that hatred was an insubstantial emotion and would certainly vanish before it could affect me. I had the world to choose from in planning a life.

On rainy days my sister and I used to tie the short end of a scarf around our scrawny braids and let the rest of its silken mass trail to our waists. We'd pretend it was hair and that we were some lovely heroine we'd seen in the movies. There was a time when I would have called that wanting to be white, yet the real point of the game was being feminine. Being feminine *meant* being white to us.

One day when I was thirteen on my bus ride home from school I caught a brief but enchanting glimpse of a beautiful creature—slender, honey brown, and she wore her hair natural. Very few people did then, which made her that much more striking. *This* was a look I could imitate with some success. The next day I went to school with my hair in an Afro.

On my way out of my building people stared and some complimented me, but others, the older permanent fixtures in the lobby, gaped at me in horror. Walking the streets of Harlem was even more difficult. The men on the corners who had been only moderately attentive before, now began to whoop and holler as I came into view. Becoming exasperated after a while, I asked someone why. "They think you're a whore, sugar." I fixed my hair and was back to normal by the next morning. Letting the world in on the secret of my native naps appealed to my proclivity for rebellion but having people think I was not a "nice girl" was The War already and I was not prepared for it. I pictured myself in a police station trying to explain how I'd been raped. "Come on, baby, you look like you know your way around," sneered an imaginary policeman.

In 1968 when I was sixteen and the term Black consciousness was becoming popular, I started wearing my hair natural again. This time I ignored my "elders." I was too busy reshaping my life. Blackness, I reasoned, meant that I could finally be myself. Besides recognizing my history of slavery and my African roots, I began a general housecleaning. All my old values, gathered from "playing house" in nursery school to *Glamour* Magazine's beauty tips, were discarded.

No more makeup, high heels, stockings, garter belts, girdles. I wore T-shirts and dungarees, or loose African print dresses, sandals on my feet. My dust-covered motto, "Be a nice well-rounded colored girl so that you can get yourself a nice colored doctor husband," I threw out on the grounds that it was another remnant of my once "whitified" self. My mind clear now, I was starting to think about being someone again, not some*thing*—the presidency was still a dark horse but maybe I could be a writer. I dared not even say it aloud: my life was my own again. I thanked Malcolm and LeRoi—wasn't it their prescription that I was following?

It took me three years to fully understand that Stokely was serious when he'd said my position in the movement was "prone," three years to understand that the countless speeches that all began "the Black man . . ." did not include me. I learned. I mingled more and more with a Black crowd, attended the conferences and rallies and parties and talked with some of the most loquacious of my brothers in Blackness, and as I pieced together the ideal that was being presented for me to emulate, I discovered my newfound freedoms being stripped from me, one after another. No I wasn't to wear makeup but yes I had to wear long skirts that I could barely walk in. No I wasn't to go to the beauty parlor but yes I was to spend hours cornrolling my hair. No I wasn't to flirt with or take shit off white men but yes I was to sleep with and take unending shit off Black men. No I wasn't to watch television or read *Vogue* or *Ladies' Home Journal* but yes I should keep my mouth shut. I would still have to iron, sew, cook, and have babies.

Only sixteen, I decided there were a lot of things I didn't know about Black male/female relationships. I made an attempt to fill myself in by reading—*Soul on Ice, Native Son, Black Rage*—and by joining the National Black Theatre. In the theatre's brand of a consciousness-raising session I was told of the awful ways in which Black women, me included, had tried to destroy the Black man's masculinity; how we had castrated him; worked when he didn't work; made money when he made no money; spent our nights and days in church praying to a jive white boy named Jesus while he collapsed into alcoholism, drug addiction, and various forms of despair; how we'd always been too loud and domineering, too outspoken.

We had much to make up for by being gentle in the face of our own humiliation, by being soft-spoken (ideally to the point where our voices could not be heard at all), by being beautiful (whatever that was), by being submissive— how often that word was shoved at me in poems and in songs as something to strive for.

At the same time one of the brothers who was a member of the theatre was also a paraprofessional in the school where my mother then taught. My mother asked him what he liked about the theatre. Not knowing that I was her daughter, he answered without hesitation that you could get all the pussy you wanted. NBT was a central institution in the Black cultural movement. Much time was spent reaching for the "godlike" in one another, the things beyond the "flesh" and beyond all the "white-washing." And what it boiled down to was that now the brother could get more pussy. If that was his revolution, what was mine?

So I was again obsessed with my appearance, worried about the rain again—the Black woman's nightmare—for fear that my huge, full Afro would shrivel up to my head. (Despite Blackness, Black men still didn't like short hair.) My age was one thing I had going for me. "Older Black women are too hard," my brothers informed me as they looked me up and down.

The message of the Black movement was that I was being watched, on probation as a Black woman, that any signs of aggressiveness, intelligence, or independence would mean I'd be denied even the one role still left open to me as "my man's woman," keeper of house, children, and incense burners. I grew increasingly desperate about slipping up—they, Black men, were threatening

me with being deserted, with being *alone.* Like any "normal" woman, I eagerly
grabbed at my own enslavement.

After all, I'd heard the horror stories of educated Black women who had
to marry ditchdiggers and get their behinds kicked every night. I had thought
the Black movement would offer me much better. In 1968 I had wanted to become an intelligent human being. I had wanted to be serious and scholarly for
the first time in my life, to write and perhaps get the chance Stokely and Bald-
win and Imamu Baraka (then LeRoi Jones) had gotten to change the world—
that was how I defined not wanting to be white. But by 1969, I simply wanted
a man.

When I chose to go to Howard University in 1969, it was because it was
all Black. I envisioned a super-Black utopia where for the first time in life I
would be completely surrounded by people who totally understood me. The
problem in New York had been that there were too many white people.

Thirty pounds overweight, my hair in the ultimate Afro—washed and
left to dry without combing—my skin blue-black from a summer in the
sun, Howard's students, the future polite society of NAACP cocktail parties, did not exactly greet me with open arms. I sought out a new clique each
day and found a home in none. Finally I found a place of revelation, if not
of happiness, with other misfits in the girls' dorm on Friday and Saturday
nights.

These misfits, all dark without exception, all with Afros that were too
nappy, chose to stay in and watch television or listen to records rather than take
advantage of the score of one-night stands they could probably achieve before
being taunted into running home to their parents as "fallen women." They came
to Howard to get husbands; if you slept around, or if it got out that you had
slept with someone you weren't practically engaged to, then there would be
very little possibility of a husband for you at Howard.

Such restrictions are not unique in this world, but at Howard, the scene of
student takeovers just the previous year, of riots and much revolutionary talk
about casting aside Western values, archaic, Victorian morals seemed curiously
"unblack." Baffled by my new environment, I did something I've never done
before—I spent most of my time with women, often turning down the inevitable humiliation or, worse, boredom of a date (a growing possibility as I
shed the extra pounds) even when it was offered to me. Most of the women
were from small southern and midwestern communities. They thought me definitely straitjacket material with my well-polished set of "sophisticated" New
York views on premarital sex and atheism. I learned to listen more than I
spoke.

But no one talked about why we stayed in on Friday and Saturday nights
on a campus that was well known for its parties and nightlife. No one talked
about why we drank so much or why our hunger for Big Macs was insatiable.
We talked about men—all kinds. Black and white, Joe Namath, Richard
Roundtree, the class president who earned quite a reputation for driving coeds

out on the highway and offering them a quick screw or a long walk home. "But girl, ain't he fine?" We talked about movie stars and singing groups into the wee hours of the morning. Guzzling gin, cheating at poker, choking on cigarettes that dangled precariously from the corners of our mouths, we'd signify. "If we could only be woman (white) enough" was the general feeling of most of us as we trotted off to bed.

Meanwhile the males on the campus had successfully buried the old standards of light, curly haired young men with straight noses. They sported large, unruly Afros, dashikis, and flaring nostrils. Their coal-black eyes seemed to say, "The nights *and* the days belong to me," as we'd pass one another on the campus green, a fashionable, thin, colorless little creature always on their arm.

Enough was enough. I left Howard for City College after one term, and the significance of all I'd seen there had not entirely escaped me, because I remember becoming a feminist about then. No one had been doing very well when I had left New York but now it seemed even worse—the "new Blackness" was fast becoming the new slavery for sisters.

I discovered my voice and when brothers talked to me, I talked back. This had its hazards. Almost got my eye blackened several times. My social life was like guerilla warfare. Here was the logic behind our grandmothers' old saying, "A nigga man ain't shit." It was shorthand for "The Black man has learned to hate himself and to hate you even more. Be careful. He will hurt you."

I am reminded of a conversation I had with a brother up at City College one mild spring day. We were standing on a corner in front of the South Campus gates and he was telling me what the role of the Black woman was. When a pause came in his monologue, I asked him what the role of the Black man was. He mumbled something about, "Simply to be a man." When I suggested that might not be enough, he went completely ape. He turned purple. He started screaming. "The Black man doesn't have to do anything. He's a man he's a man he's a man!"

Whenever I raised the question of a Black woman's humanity in conversation with a Black man, I got a similar reaction. Black men, at least the ones I knew, seemed totally confounded when it came to treating Black women like people. Trying to be what we were told to be by the brothers of the "nation"— sweet and smiling—a young Black woman I knew had warmly greeted a brother in passing on Riverside Drive. He responded by raping her. When she asked the brothers what she should do, they told her not to go to the police and to have the baby though she was only seventeen.

Young Black female friends of mine were dropping out of school because their boyfriends had convinced them that it was "not correct" and "counterrevolutionary" to strive to do anything but have babies and clean house. "Help the brother get his thing together," they were told. Other Black women submitted to polygamous situations where sometimes they were called upon to sleep with the friends of their "husband." This later duty was explained to me once by a "priest" of the New York Yoruban Temple. "If your brother has to go to the bathroom and there is no toilet in his house then wouldn't you let him use your toilet?" For toilet read Black woman.

The sisters got along by keeping their mouths shut, by refusing to see what was daily growing more difficult to ignore—a lot of brothers were doing double time—uptown with the sisters and downtown with the white woman whom they always vigorously claimed to hate. Some of the bolder brothers were quite frank about it. "The white woman lets me be a man."

The most popular justification Black women had for not becoming feminists was their hatred of white women. They often repeated this for approving Black male ears. (Obviously the brother had an interest in keeping Black and white women apart—"Women will chatter.") But what I figured out was that the same Black man who trembled with hatred for white men found the white woman irresistible because she was not a human being but a possession in his eyes—the higher-priced spread of woman he saw on television. "I know that the white man made the white woman the symbol of freedom and the Black woman the symbol of slavery" (*Soul on Ice,* Eldridge Cleaver).

When I first became a feminist, my Black friends used to cast pitying eyes upon me and say, "That's whitey's thing." I used to laugh it off, thinking, yes there are some slight problems, a few things white women don't completely understand, but we can work them out. In *Ebony, Jet,* and *Encore,* and even in *The New York Times,* various Black writers cautioned Black women to be wary of smiling white feminists. The women's movement enlists the support of Black women only to lend credibility to an essentially middle-class, irrelevant movement, they asserted. Time has shown that there was more truth to these claims than their shrillness indicated. Today when many white feminists think of Black women, they too often think of faceless masses of welfare mothers and rape victims to flesh out their statistical studies of woman's plight.

One unusually awkward moment for me as a Black feminist was when I found out that white feminists often don't view Black men as men but as fellow victims. I've got no pressing quarrel with the notion that white men have been the worst offenders but that isn't very helpful for a Black woman from day to day. White women don't check out a white man's bank account or stockholdings before they accuse him of being sexist—they confront white men with and without jobs, with and without membership in a male consciousness-raising group. Yet when it comes to the Black man, it's hands off.

A Black friend of mine was fired by a Black news service because she was pregnant. When she proposed doing an article on this for *Ms.,* an editor there turned down the proposal with these words: "We've got a special policy for the Black man." For a while I thought that was just the conservative feminist position until I overheard a certified radical feminist explaining why she dated only Black men and other nonwhite men. "They're less of a threat to women; they're less oppressive."

Being a Black woman means frequent spells of impotent, self-consuming rage. Such a spell came upon me when I recently attended a panel discussion at a women artists' conference. One of the panel members, a museum director and a white feminist, had come with a young Black man in a sweatshirt, Pro-Keds, and rag tied around the kind of gigantic Afro you don't see much anymore. When asked about her commitment to Black women artists, she responded with, "Well, what about Puerto Rican women artists, and Mexican women artists, and Indian women artists? . . ." But she doesn't exhibit Hispanic women any more than she does Black women (do I have to say anything about Indian women?), which is seldom indeed, though her museum is located in an area that is predominantly Black and Puerto Rican. Yet she was confident in the position she took because the living proof of her liberalism and good intentions sat in the front row, Black and unsmiling, six foot something and mil-itant-*looking*.

In the spring of 1973, Doris Wright, a Black feminist writer, called a meeting to discuss "Black Women and Their Relationship to the Women's Movement." The result was the National Black Feminist Organization, and I was fully delighted until, true to Women's Movement form, we got bogged down in an array of ideological disputes, the primary one being lesbianism versus heterosexuality. Dominated by the myths and facts of what white feminists had done and not done before us, it was nearly impossible to come to any agreement about our position on anything; and action was unthinkable.

Many of the prime movers in the organization seemed to be representing other interest groups and whatever commitment they might have had to Black women's issues appeared to take a back seat to that. Women who had initiative and spirit usually attended one meeting, were turned off by the hopelessness of ever getting anything accomplished, and never returned again. Each meeting brought almost all new faces. Overhearing an aspiring political candidate say only half-jokingly at NBFO's first conference, "I'm gonna get me some votes out of these niggas," convinced me that Black feminists were not ready to form a movement in which I could, with clear conscience, participate.

It is very possible that NBFO was not meant to happen when it did, that the time was not yet ripe for such an organization.

I started a Black women's consciousness-raising group around the same time. When I heard one of my friends, whom I considered the closest thing to a feminist in the room, saying at one of our sessions, "I feel sorry for any woman who tries to take my husband away from me because she's just going to have a man who has to pay alimony and child support," even though she was not married to the man in question, I felt a great sinking somewhere in the chest area. Here was a woman, who had insisted (at least to me) upon her right to bear a child outside of marriage, trying to convince a few Black women, who were mostly single and very worried about it, that she was really married—unlike them. In fact, one of the first women to leave the group was a recent graduate of Sarah Lawrence, her excuse being, "I want to place myself in situations where I will meet more men." The group eventually disintegrated. We had no strength to give to one another. Is that possible? At any rate, that's the way it seemed, and perhaps it was the same on a larger scale with NBFO.

Despite a sizable number of Black feminists who have contributed much to the leadership of the women's movement, there is still no Black women's movement, and it appears there won't be for some time to come. It is conceivable that the level of consciousness feminism would demand in Black women wouldn't lead to any sort of separatist movement, anyway—despite our very separate problems. Perhaps a multicultural women's movement is somewhere in the future.

But for now, Black feminists, of necessity it seems, exist as individuals—some well known, like Eleanor Holmes Norton, Florynce Kennedy, Faith Ringgold, Shirley Chisholm, Alice Walker, and some unknown, like me. We exist as women who are Black who are feminists, each stranded for the moment, working independently because there is not yet an environment in this society remotely congenial to our struggle—because, being on the bottom, we would have to do what no one else has done: we would have to fight the world.

CHAPTER 11

Women, Work, and Social Change

Demographic changes affecting women's lives had been gathering force over the course of the twentieth century, and these changing social realities were an important precondition for the revival of feminism. Women were living longer, bearing fewer children, and enjoying increased access to education. They were working in far greater numbers outside the home. Marital instability, notably the dramatic rise in divorce, meant that women could no longer assume that the roles of wife and mother would provide the primary identification for their entire lives. All these changes reinforced each other to produce very different life patterns for postwar women than those of their mothers and grandmothers.

There is no dearth of statistics to convey the postwar revolution in women's work. The growth in women's share of the work force between 1950 and 1975 (from 29 percent in 1950 to 40 percent in 1975) surpassed the increase for the entire sixty-year period that preceded it. And the trend continues to accelerate as we approach the twenty-first century. In 1950, 56 percent of the nation's households conformed to the traditional image of male breadwinner and female housewife, but by 1980, the figure had dropped to 27 percent, and by 1992 it was down to only 15 percent. Two-income families or female-headed households are replacing the older pattern of a man serving as the sole means of support for his dependent wife and children.

In the postwar period, paid employment has emerged as a central definition of women's lives. No longer a temporary stint before marriage, more women are becoming, like men, lifelong workers. The kind of women who work has also undergone permanent changes from the turn-of-the-century poor, single, immigrant girl. Between 1940 and 1970, the number of married women in the work force (usually old enough for their children to be in school and increasingly middle-class) surpassed the number of single women. Since the 1970s, the fastest growing group of new female workers has been working

313

mothers with preschool children. In 1982, nearly half of women with preschoolers were working, straining the country's inadequate child care system and causing concern in the media about who was raising the nation's children. Note how working mothers with small children emerged as the focal point of public debate in the 1980s. Just as single women workers had become accepted by 1920, few thought twice by the postwar period about older women entering the work force once their children were in school. But mothers with small children were another matter.

Because of the women's movement and the passage of such legislation as Title VII of the 1964 Civil Rights Act, the media played up women who moved into nontraditional jobs. We hear stories about women bus drivers, construction workers, and electricians; we also read about the elite women who are moving into corporate hierarchies. While a small minority of women have been able to assault traditionally male jobs, the most striking thing about women's occupational structure is how little it has changed since the 1960s. Despite small breakthroughs, women continue to work predominantly in stereotyped female jobs, especially in expanding areas such as clerical and sales work and service jobs. Continuity, rather than revolutionary change, is the story here.

Along with women's jobs continue to go women's wages. In 1984, the median earnings of full-time women workers were $14,479 versus $23,218 for men. A female college graduate still earns less than a male high school dropout, basically 64 cents for every man's dollar. One area where there has been a significant narrowing of the wage gap is between black and white women. As late as 1940, black women earned only 38 percent of white women's median wage, largely because blacks were totally excluded from fields other than agricultural work or domestic service. By 1977, black women earned 88 percent of what white women did, in large part because the civil rights revolution and Title VII opened up higher-paying manufacturing, clerical, and retail work to black women for the first time.

The old pattern of indifference to women has continued in the labor movement in the postwar period, although women have made strides in certain areas of union organizing. In 1980, 15.9 percent of working women belonged to unions (the comparable figure for men was 28.4 percent). In large part, women's low rates of unionization were linked to the general decline in the labor movement since the 1950s, a trend with far-reaching consequences. And yet the situation is not totally bleak. As the manufacturing sector of the economy declines (traditionally the stronghold of the American labor movement), unions have turned to organizing employees in the public sector. Since women hold many of the clerical and service jobs in this area, they have benefited from this upsurge. For example, over 40 percent of the 7.7 million women in public sector jobs in the early 1980s were unionized, more than twice the general level. But these labor breakthroughs came less from attention to organizing women per se, than from targeting certain occupational groups where women happened to predominate.

One of the most disturbing trends related to women's work has been the feminization of poverty. The Census Bureau reported in 1985 that almost half (48 percent) of families living below the poverty level were headed by women, an increase from 30 percent in 1966. Because of the low wages commanded by women (in 1984, at least one quarter of the nation's full-time women workers earned less than $10,000 a year), women can easily slip below the poverty line when they choose or are forced to set up households of their own. The line between welfare and women's wages is often very thin: by 1980, some two thirds of female-headed households received child welfare payments such as AFDC. But because women are denied access to higher paying work, because women continue to come out of divorce in far worse economic shape than men, and because the numbers of births to unwed mothers (both black and white, but especially black) continues to rise, the feminization of poverty will continue to worsen.

The revolution in women's work outside the home, which built throughout the twentieth century, has thus had an ambiguous effect. One historian referred to it as "the radical consequences of incremental change." Work is now accepted as something that most women will do for most of their adult lives. But society has been slower in changing attitudes. While it is no longer a public scandal for women to work, there has been very little concrete attention paid to the problems raised by women working, such as the lack of good day care, inadequate maternity-leave policies, and inflexibility in the workplace. The labor movement has proven an imperfect vehicle for addressing these issues. Most married working women are still stuck with (in the words of one harried worker) "two full-time jobs instead of just one." When, if ever, attitudes and public policy will catch up with changing realities remains uncertain.

Clerical Workers Unite

Cathy Tuley

Many women who work hold jobs like the one Cathy Tuley describes here as a billing clerk in an Alameda County, California, hospital. But not all working women do what Cathy Tuley did: get so involved in starting and running a union of clerks that it dramatically changed her life.

Cathy Tuley was born in 1950 in Kansas City. She dropped out of a local college and got what she described as a "deadening" job as a clerk. She got married and moved to California. She has worked throughout most of her marriage, except for short stretches after the birth of her two children; her husband's periodic unemployment and the need for two incomes to keep the family afloat have kept her in the workplace. The job at the Highland General Hospital billing office she describes in this piece was the longest she ever stayed in one place:

two and a half years. Her commitment to the union, and her responsibilities as a shop steward, kept her there until the birth of her second child. When she returned to work, she landed a better job as a
ward clerk in a county hospital.

Cathy Tuley did not organize her hospital's clerks singlehandedly:
co-worker Kay Eisenhower figures prominently in the story. Eisenhower had been active in civil rights in the South in the 1960s, as well
as in community organizing in Berkeley and the Bay Area. Her involvement in the emerging women's movement and health issues got
her interested in organizing hospital workers. Realizing that "the only
way any real changes were going to be made was through the activities of working people," she joined Tuley in the Alameda County Employees local and with the Coalition of Labor Union Women. Union
activities allowed women to challenge the depersonalized conditions
under which they worked as well as work for broader social change.
For a mother of two like Cathy Tuley, her union work also gave her
the self-confidence to share her story with writer Nancy Seifer for the
book *Nobody Speaks for Me! Self-Portraits of American Working Class
Women* (1976).

I met Kay Eisenhower the first day on my job. We were in the same section.
She came about a month before I did, and she was kind of like the lead clerk.
We have a pretty high turnover! So we just started having lunch together and
talking, and she was interested in organizing a union.

I don't know if she has her master's or what in political science, but she
was really active in student movements and in and out of the women's liberation movement, that type of thing. I think she thought that, rather than teach,
which is what she would have been doing, she wanted to meet people and work
with them and get to know their politics.

Kay was probably the biggest influence on me. She had been involved in
politics for a long time, and at the same time she always worked alongside me,
in the same area and everything. I don't think I would have become as openly
involved in organizing if I didn't have somebody there to push me. I might have,
but I think it would've taken a lot longer and I might have been more afraid. I
just wasn't the type to start doing it on my own, and she made me feel I could
contribute something. Before that, I never really felt I could.

We started off talking about problems in the immediate workplace. Our
supervisor let us organize the work pretty much the way we wanted to. Kay is
very good at that, and I was interested in it, too. So we talked about trying to
get things running smoothly, problems with various other workers, supervisors,
that type of thing. We really just spent a lot of time sitting around analyzing
things.

Then we just felt that we could do more if we were all in one organization—things like getting a contract and having shop stewards, that we never

Source: Reprinted with the permission of Simon & Schuster from *Nobody Speaks for Me!* by Nancy
Seifer, pp. 229–231, 232–233, 235–236. Copyright © 1976 by Nancy Seifer.

had before. In general, just getting better working conditions. The employees' association they had at Highland then was not representing the right people. It was really representing management more and it was more like a social group than a union. They had picnics and this type of thing. And when a clerk would call in to the association for help, they would notify her supervisor that she was calling and she would get jumped on for calling in without going through the channels.

Well, then SEIU—the Service Employees International Union—was organizing hospital workers in the area—maintenance people, LVN's, social workers. Kay knew quite a few other clerks, and SEIU started having organizing dinners, trying to get us to join and help organize the clerks. So Kay invited me and we started going to these dinners and talking about our problems at work, and I started finding out more about unions.

I'd never been a union member before and I felt I had a lot to learn. This was my first association with it all. Before, the word "union" always made me think about blue-collar workers and men. My father was in one. He never talked about it that much. I guess he didn't participate much. But his being a man and a blue-collar worker, I guess that's why I made that association.

In my previous experiences being a clerk, I was never aware of things. I just went and did my job and went home. All of a sudden I was aware of problems between supervisors and workers and the kind of power games people play. In fact, that was the kind of thing that really started us organizing.

We had a supervisor who was an older woman, in her later fifties or early sixties. She wasn't that organized herself, but she was the one who let us do our work the way we wanted to. She never hung over our shoulders or anything. Then a younger woman came in, younger than all of us, and she kind of took over as our lead clerk. Her husband was a supervisor in the same hospital in another department, so she always went to him with her problems, instead of this woman who was her immediate supervisor.

Well, things got very tense in our unit because of her. I think she was envious of some of us. She knew that we had better ideas about doing things than she did, and she resented it. Anyway, our supervisor started being harassed and she really felt like her job was being threatened. She ended up dying very suddenly one day in the office, and just a couple of days before, she had told Kay how she felt.

There was a lot of feeling that she was pushed to her death by this man and this woman. He's my supervisor now and I just can't help but think of this sometimes, especially when he sits there and does his crossword puzzle all day. And I mean, being objective, this woman wasn't the best supervisor I've had. But they purposely tried to get rid of her and it was very evident. That was one thing that really stuck in our minds.

So SEIU was trying to get us to join, and this employees' association was trying to get us to join them, too. For a while we kind of worked on our own. We called ourselves Clerks' County—a name we made up for the clerks in Alameda County—and we put out a newspaper that was our original organizing tool, saying why we were thinking about either joining SEIU or starting our own clerical union. We didn't want to join this association.

We started that in about June of '72, and then one day in February of '73, the association joined with SEIU very secretively. Suddenly, after all this time of us telling people not to join the association it all becomes one union and we were right in the middle of the whole thing. We had to completely reverse what we'd been saying.

I think what happened was the association was in the red. They were going downhill financially, but they had quite a few members. And this was a chance for SEIU to get a lot of people all at one time, without too much effort. So there was something in it for both of them. But we really felt taken. We had been working toward having an open election that was supposed to be held a month after the time that they made this secret affiliation.

So we were all thrown together and now we are in a union with professionals, semi-management-type people. But we have a separate clerical unit where we're able to do things ourselves we couldn't do before, like bargaining. There's about five or six of us who were in it from the original organizing point, and we've added people to our caucus as we went along.

We still have our Clerks' County newspaper that the SEIU organizers helped us start. They had a woman who showed us how to do layout, and we used different locals' mimeograph machines. Then those of us who had never written would team up with someone who had written for some other newspaper or something, and then we just all took turns. We're all responsible for distribution. We set up our own distribution centers throughout the whole county. Most of our caucus members are in the major worksites where most clerks are—the hospitals, welfare centers, libraries.

In our shop Kay and I have gotten almost everybody to join the union. There's about 2,500 clerks in the county and about 40 percent are members of the union now. But in terms of negotiations, that's not enough if you want to show your power. And that's what management relates to, your power. I have people telling me, "Look, I'll join if you get this and that at negotiations. I'm behind you all the way." But I say, "It doesn't help to be behind me, you have to join the union and participate."

It's hard for people to realize that management relates to us in terms of numbers, and they keep very close track of how many members we have. Also, I would just like more people to join so that they can know their rights. And I think the union is the best way to learn them.

I think maybe it's harder to organize clerks than some other kinds of workers, because sometimes they feel that they're halfway into professionalism, like maybe they have one foot in the door. The way it works within the county, you can get a promotion and all of a sudden be management if you know the right people, and that type of thing.

Also, maybe because they're women, they're not as aggressive. They have been taking things the way they are for so long without saying anything, whereas the men . . . Well, like if Tom blew his stack and cussed somebody out at work I think they would accept it more. Sometimes I'd really like to say exactly what I feel when something happens, but I have to kind of control myself more. I feel that if I said what came to my mind, it would probably go on my record. It's more structured, the things that you're allowed to do as a clerk, the things you're allowed to wear. There's the public out there, you know, and all this junk.

I've been a shop steward for a year and a half now. We were the first class, several of our Clerks' County caucus. We all took it together. It wasn't really much training, just four sessions. But we learned union language, and we talked about how to process grievances, becoming familiar with the contract, things like that.

A lot of people come with questions about sick leaves, maternity leave, things which we try to have them look for in the contract themselves. Then there are workload problems and personality clashes between people and their supervisors. I've had quite a few of those. We try to do things informally and not file formal grievances, because this means you have to go through each supervisor, each step. . . .

I think all of this has really helped me to develop myself, my personality. I've become a lot more vocal and aggressive, too, and I'm not as gullible as I used to be. Now, you can tell me something, and I want it proven to me. Sometimes it's kind of rough when you do that to your husband! "Give me the facts," you know. "Prove what you just said."

The first time I had to speak in front of a group I was really shaky and nervous. Maybe glad that I did it, but wondering how I sounded to other people, still worrying about that. That takes a long time, to forget about what they think, you know. It's easier for me now, but I've always had trouble getting up in front of people. I still really get shook. It's better if I do it spontaneously and not have to think about it for a long time. That just makes it even worse.

When I first started going to the organizing meetings, I felt for the first time that maybe I could really do something to change things somehow. Before, I never even thought about trying to. So it was a big change in my whole attitude. Also, I think being recognized as a valuable worker helps, too. I was able to do more than my share of work and do it accurately, and I think they kind of recognized me for that and started listening to my ideas about changing things.

Also, being a shop steward, it helps to be able to keep up your end of it, or else they won't listen to you at all. Some of the supervisors really expect a lot of you. They'll do things like use our ideas, saying that they're their own, and then if we come in late or something, they'll say, "What kind of example is this that you're setting for everybody else?" That happens to me because I'm always late!

I've always wanted to work with people in some way that I could help them. And I think this organizing has kind of given me the attitude that you just can't give up, even more so, and that things don't happen overnight. For me, that's been the hardest thing to learn. I can see people becoming more aware of themselves and their rights. These changes are happening. But sometimes you're just so involved that you don't see how much. And you just cannot change a whole structure of a union overnight, which is what we're trying to do!

The Real "Norma Rae" Tells Her Story

Crystal Lee Sutton

The working lives of southern women, black and white, are often cut from a different cloth than their northern and western sisters. The cloth metaphor is appropriate because of the importance of textile manufacturing to the southern economy. Originally textile factories had been located in places like Lowell, Massachusetts, or Manchester, New Hampshire, but by the early twentieth century, many had moved south, especially to the Piedmont region of North Carolina. The reason was simple: southern towns offered a cheap and plentiful labor supply and a conservative political climate hostile to unions. From the beginning, women and children were crucial to the textile work force in the South, that is, white women and white children. Not until the 1960s did blacks win entry into the mills.

The common denominators of the lives of southern textile workers were poverty, long hours, low pay, isolation, and lack of union protection. The South was noted for its violent and contentious pattern of labor relations, with unionization attempts almost always unsuccessful. This provides the backdrop for Crystal Lee Sutton's story, which is set in Graham, North Carolina.

Married at eighteen and then widowed with a three-year-old child, Sutton remarried, had another child, and began to work at the mills. She was fired in 1973 for the union activity described in this excerpt and was not reinstated until 1978. Even though the union won an election at the plant in 1974 (a necessary step towards representation and collective bargaining under the 1935 Wagner Act), J. P. Stevens managed to delay signing a union contract until 1980.

Sutton's story was later made into the successful Hollywood movie, *Norma Rae,* for which Sally Field won an Oscar. The debt that the movie owed to Crystal Lee Sutton's life story is unmistakable in this excerpt, but she never received a penny from the project.

Nobody really approached me about the union. I had been out on sick leave. I had hurt my foot. My sister worked right down from me and she came up and said, "Lee, somebody was handing out union cards but don't you take one 'cause if you do you'll be fired." I said, "Who's handing them out?" She said,

Source: Victoria Byerly, *Hard Times Cotton Mill Girls: Personal Histories of Womanhood and Poverty in the South,* pp. 205–211. Copyright © 1986 by Cornell University. Used by permission of the publisher, Cornell University Press.

"I don't know but don't you take one." Then she went on back there to her job. So I started asking different ones around and nobody would say nothing. So I asked this older woman, "Do you know anything about this union stuff?" And she said, "Lee, all I know is there's a notice about this meeting on the bulletin board." So I took a piece of paper and wrote down the place, it was going to be at a church, and the time. So I started to talk to different ones about if they were going and nobody said nothing, so I asked my friend Liz. I said, "Liz, how about going with me to that union meeting?" She had three little girls. She said, "Lee, I don't have nobody to keep the kids." I said, "Oh, Cookie [her husband] will keep the children."

I never will forget, I went to Burlington that Saturday on Mother's Day, and Mama got mad with me 'cause I left early to go to that union meeting. She didn't think I ought to go. But I went over to JB Younts, he had been a real close friend, and I knew he knew about unions and all because I remember he tried to get Daddy to join the union at Cone Mills. He told me, "Lee, you do everything you can to try to get that union in." He said, "You get home in time to go to that union meeting." So I did. I never will forget it. Liz and I pulled up at this church—it was a black church—and I had never seen so many blacks in all my life. Liz said, "You sure you want to do this?" and I said, "Well, we're here. We might as well go on in." So we went in and there were maybe four or five other white people there. We went down and sat on the front row 'cause I didn't want to miss out on nothing. After the meeting, I agreed to go into the mill wearing a union button to try to get the union in. We were real strong with the blacks but we were weak with the whites. So I knew a lot of people I was going to talk with.

Eli Zivkovitch was the organizer. He was from Fairfield, Virginia, an ex-coal miner. He and his family were so poor that at one time they lived in a tent. He was a very handsome man, and I really loved my daddy more than anything in this world, but Eli was like what I wish my daddy had 'a been as far as being more modern, like realizing that women had more worth in this world than just being a sex object. That women had brains and that they should use those brains. It was okay for women to do so-called men's work. The men I had met before had always seemed to be more concerned with a woman's outward appearance. Eli was a good man, a fighter and a survivor. Hours meant nothing to him as far as his work went. He was not a nine-to-five person. He was available when you needed him, and that's the way he taught me to work. Eli said we could talk union and hand out literature on our break time in the canteens. So I got people to join the union real quick like.

Then they started calling me into the office. I had never been called into the office to be talked to about anything. But all of a sudden I couldn't do nothing right. Talking too much, standing in the bathroom too much. Nothing had changed, that was just their agitation trying to get me to quit trying to organize. Eli had give us this book called *What the Company Will Do for You*. It was all blank pages. He told us if they called us in the office for us to write down what they said. Because if they had a right to write us up, we had a right to write them up. I always took my pencil and my little book and I would write down things that was happening. This blew the boss men's mind. They couldn't believe I was doing this.

Then what happened was that the company posted a notice on the bulletin board and it was, in effect, trying to scare people. It stated something like it was going to be an all black union. Eli said he needed a copy of it to send to the National Labor Relations Board. So different people said they would copy the letter, you know, but whenever they tried they were told they would be fired. So one day, Eli said, "Crystal, I've got to have a copy of that letter." I said, "Okay." So I went up to the bulletin board and I was trying to copy the letter and the boss man came up and said, "You can't copy that, if you do you'll be fired." I went back to Eli that night and said, "Man, they said they'll fire us." He said, "I'm telling you it's your constitutional right," and he said, "I need a copy of that letter." I said, "I'll get a copy of that letter today." So I went on into work and, lo and behold, they had tables set up with tablecloths on them. They were having a safety dinner for us.

When the company claimed that they had no lost time for accidents they'd give us a little old dinner. But I've actually seen people with an arm in a cast sitting in the office. Prior to the union, we thought they were doing us a favor by letting us come in, sit in the office, and pay us. We didn't know nothing about workmen's compensation.

So I went to the pay phone which the company had conveniently installed to keep us out of the office. They had said we could use it any time we wanted to and I had done so. If there had been a storm, I'd call home to make sure the kids were all right and all. So I called Eli and said, "Look man, I can't copy that letter tonight because we're having a safety supper." 'Course he had to know what that was, so I quickly explained it to him. So I said, "Anyway, Eli, I'm hungry and I want to eat my supper." But he said, "Look, Crystal, you can afford to lose a few pounds and I need that letter." He knew he had made me mad then, so I said, "I'll get that damn letter."

So I started talking around and I came up with this idea. I went over to the ones that were in the union and I said, "Look, Eli needs that letter so I'll tell you what let's do. I'll memorize the first two lines of it and go in the bathroom and write it down. Mary, you memorize the next two" and I told all of them the lines of the paragraph to remember. Well, it got to be a big joke because we were pretending like we were getting water, you know, and trying to read the letter too. But we couldn't remember what we had read by the time we got to the bathroom. So we all got to laughing about it. So I said, "Hell, I got to get that letter." So I said to my sister, she was a service person, I said, "Seretha, I need a clipboard." She said, "What you going to do?" I said, "I'm going to get that letter." We didn't have no set time for a break, they said they would motion for us when it was our turn to go eat. Seretha said, "Oh God," but she gave me a clipboard.

As soon as they motioned for us, I took the clipboard and went immediately to the bulletin board and started to write. Because of the supper, everyone from management was at this dinner. So they took turns coming up to me telling me that I couldn't copy that letter. If I did, I'd be fired. Then the big man come up and he called me Lee. His name was Mason Lee. I said, "Mr. Lee, I didn't know you knew my name." And he said, "Yeah, I know who you are." He told me that if I didn't leave he was going to call the police to come in there and take me out. I said, "Mr. Lee, sir, you do what you want on your break time, you even get to go out for supper, and we can't even sit on the steps. This is my break time and I'm telling you I'm going to copy this letter. It's my constitutional right." So I continued to write and my knees were shaking like I was going to collapse any minute. I said, "If you do call the cops, you're going to have to call the Chief of Police because my husband is a jealous man and he won't let me ride home with just anybody." I thought to myself I'm going to put him to the test. I'm just going to push him and see what he does do.

So I copied the letter and folded it up and stuck it down my bra figuring, well, nobody will get it down there. I went on down there and got me a plate and went to this special canteen that the company had installed within the last month. They no longer let the ones in my department go to the old canteen. As soon as we got into work we had to report to the new canteen. Right there within twenty steps of my job they built this canteen. They went to that much trouble to separate me from the rest of the workers. And I went in there and everybody said, "God, you got more guts, what did they say?" I gave my dinner to some man in there and said, "Well as soon as they blow the whistle, they'll come and get me. Mr. Lee said they were going to fire me and call the police. So y'all can expect anything."

I went back out there when I figured break was about up, put on my lipstick, and was acting real cool, calm and collected, when we all started back to work. Then here they come. Three of them. "Mr. Lee wants to see you in the office." So I said, "Seretha don't you let nobody mess with my pocketbook, I'll be back shortly." "All right," she said. So they took me up to the door of the main office and pushed a button and the door came open and they took me in there where they were all sitting at a big table and Mason Lee was sitting at the head. He started talking to me and I said, "Mr. Lee, sir," I had me a pencil and a piece of paper, I said, "Before you tell me anything you going to have to tell me all your names and how to spell them." So he started to spell his name and then he stopped and said, "I don't have to do that."

Then he started telling me all the things that I had done wrong. Said I had stayed in the bathroom too long, used the pay phone when I wasn't supposed to, and, you know, all different kinds of reasons. He was talking so much I remember putting my hands on my ears and thinking, here is all these people in here that I have served at the restaurant, a couple of them I'd danced with, and my floorlady who had had me call my husband and get him to bring chicken up to the mill for us. All these people knew he was lying but didn't a one of them have the guts to say so. None of them said, "Mr. Lee you're lying, she used that phone on her break time, she was told she could use it." Nobody said nothing. I said, "I don't have anything to say. There is nobody in here on my side. Y'all are all company people and no matter what I say, y'all are going to be right and I'm going to be wrong." So then he said, "You going to have to leave the plant." And I said, "I don't have no way to go home, I didn't drive the car today, I got a ride with my sister." He said, "You call your husband to come and get you." And I said, "My husband's at work." So he said, "You call you a taxi." I said, "I don't have any money. You got to let me go back out there and get my pocketbook." Then he told Tommy Gardner, he said, "You go out there and get her pocketbook." I said, "If anybody touches my pocketbook, I'm going to have a warrant taken out on them for stealing." Finally, he said, "Let her back out there to get her pocketbook."

They went through the door with me and I went on around there and this black woman, Mary Moses, said, "What happened?" I said, "He fired me." Then I said, "Mary, give me your magic marker." So I grabbed it and I took a piece of pasteboard and I wrote the word UNION on it and, for some reason, I don't know why I did it, I climbed on the table and I just slowly turned the sign around. Everybody was in a state of shock and the machines started shutting down and everything got quiet. People started giving me the V sign. Then different ones from management came down there and tried to get me down off the table. Even my sister came down there. She said, "Lee, get down off that table and let me call Cookie to come and get you." Then I said to the boss man, "It's not their break time. Y'all gonna have to fire all of them too." Then sure enough here comes the chief of police. I got off the table and walked over there and he said, "Lee, what's wrong?" I said, "The man fired me and he fired me because I been trying to get the union in." He said, "Come on, let me take you home." I said, "You gonna take me home?" and he said, "Yeah." I said, "I want you to put that in writing." And I handed him a piece of paper and he started to write, and then he balled it up and said, "I don't have to do that." Then he grabbed me and literally forced me out of the gate and I was trying to get back in. I was fighting. It was a damn good thing I didn't know karate or he would have had to shoot me, and would have probably gotten away with it. They forced me in the car and took me to jail and locked me up.

Hard-Hatted Women

Susan Eisenberg

Until the 1970s, occupations like electricians, plumbers, machinists, welders, and carpenters were almost 100 percent male and 100 percent white. But because of the civil rights and women's movements, the barriers began to fall, albeit slowly. Federal action played an important role. For example, a 1978 executive order amended the 1964 Civil Rights Act to set goals and timetables for promoting women's access to jobs in construction. It also made the employer responsible for a harassment-free workplace. Even with such federal mandates, the number of women on construction jobs remains distressingly low—less than 2 percent.

Women wanted jobs in the construction trades for a variety of reasons. Even as young girls, some had wanted the chance to build things or work in non-traditional settings. Many women hated the options for work available to women in the "pink collar ghetto"—wasn't there more to work than typing and filing? But mainly it was the money; work in the building trades often paid two to three times what women could earn in traditional female jobs.

The experience of Boston electrician Susan Eisenberg suggests the rewards and challenges facing hard-hatted women in the 1970s and 1980s. Like most other women in non-traditional jobs, she was the beneficiary of affirmative action guidelines; given the crudeness and hostility that these newcomers often faced on the jobs, it is hard to imagine co-workers voluntarily hiring women. Her story of being pregnant on a blue-collar job gives a new perspective on the challenge of combining childbearing with work. (Another construction worker tells the story of returning to work while still nursing and trying to find semi-private places—like the cab of her loader—to express her breast milk with a pump.) But what comes through most of all is Susan Eisenberg's pride in her work and her young daughter's corresponding pride in her mother who builds things.

Being an electrician has become just another part of who I am—shaping the strengths and weaknesses of my body, the ways I express myself and solve problems, and what I notice. After ten years, both the honeymoon bliss and those first rude shock waves of reality are only strong memories. I find myself both looking back at my decision to become a union electrician without regrets and looking ahead to a life in the trades with a good deal of ambivalence.

Like many of the first women in their locals I've met across the country, I started in 1978, when affirmative action guidelines were mandated. I graduated four years later in the first apprenticeship class of IBEW Local 103 (Boston), to include women. Of the six women who started together, five of us graduated, a higher percentage than the men in our class. We owed that largely to the support, information-sharing and prodding we gave each other. Four of us carpooled together to our two-nights-a-week of school for four years. Our carpool conversations made up somewhat for the isolation of usually being the only woman—of any trade—on our jobs. As more women entered, we formed a group, meeting together for personal support and to identify and address the common problems we faced as women in our union.

Entering construction in the late 1970s was a little like falling in love with

Source: Susan Eisenberg, "Susan Eisenberg—Electrician," in Molly Martin, ed., *Hard-Hatted Women: Stories of Struggle and Success in the Trades* (Seattle: The Seal Press, 1988), pp. 216–224. Reprinted by permission of Susan Eisenberg.

someone you weren't supposed to. The initial honeymoon was powerful. Enormous pride as I gained agility with tools I hadn't even known the names of when I began. Amazement as I watched new muscles pop out in the mirror almost daily. Fierce loyalty toward the older mechanics who took me under their wing and taught me their special techniques. Everywhere I would go—movies, airports, restaurants—immediately, I would notice the wiring: where fixtures were placed and how they were fed; whether receptacles were two-prong or three-; suddenly imagining what was behind ceilings and walls.

I remember, particularly in those first years, the enormous encouragement I felt from women on the outside, as though I represented them as well. Not only friends, but strangers, too. Women driving past my jobsite who would notice me and honk and give me a raised fist. The neighbor who rode to work on the same early morning bus and always cheered me on. The older black woman I met once in the bathroom of a remodel job, who had noticed my tool pouch on the sink and told me about her own unfulfilled ambitions of a job in the skilled trades, and how she had taught herself radio electronics from books. I felt indebted and privileged that I was able to live out a dream of generations of women who had been locked out. This magnified each success and failure, and kept me from following the urge I sometimes had to just walk away.

My initial experience in union construction was my worst. In the first shop that I worked for the journeymen were extremely hostile and unwilling to train me. There was even a foreman I worked under who tried to get me injured. Fortunately, I was laid off, and went to work for another shop where my experience was just the opposite. I was able to work on small jobs with some good mechanics who took me seriously and gave me a chance to learn the trade. They taught me how to mount boxes, pull and connect wires, and lay out the circuitry from a panel in an electric closet to the receptacles and lights in a room. After a lot of insisting, I got a chance to do the bigger and heavier work: wiring motors; cutting, threading and bending pipe; mounting equipment. I learned how to climb and carry ladders, use power tools, and maneuver myself around the debris and dangers on a construction site.

Even though the work and its newness were exhilarating, I also found myself often overcome with anger, depression or the feeling that I was in over my head. Working outside in a New England winter, or even by the water in the fall, is *cold.* And there were a lot of times I just had to grit my teeth and plunge across fear to do what I was asked: climb a crane, walk across a beam, work on scaffolding.

The hardest part of the job for me to get used to, though, was the talk on a construction site. Not the swearing—which guys often apologized for when I hadn't even noticed it—but jokes about beating up wives, racist and anti-Semitic slurs, degrading remarks about each other's girlfriends or some woman who happened to pass by, and comments about each others' personal lives that I found incredibly cruel. Sometimes I was grateful to be an apprentice, the one designated to go for coffee, so I could have the chance to walk outside and cry without being seen. On one remodel job, a residence for elders, one of the electricians joked about pulling the fire alarm and raping all the women residents—mostly in their eighties and nineties, many of whom I had gotten to know in the months working there. When I tried to say why a comment like that wasn't funny, he suggested that I could rape all the men. It was the casualness of the conversation for him, the assumptions underneath, and everyone else's silence that broke right through my armor. Conversations like that would eat away at me for weeks. I had to learn to harden myself, to expect little support from co-workers in group conversations, and to be selective about who and what was worth responding to. It quickly became clear that responding to all the comments I found offensive would guarantee not being heard. It would also mean being set up for entertainment, like anyone on a construction job who is too predictable—that is, things would be said just to get a rise out of you. So, I learned to let most offensive remarks pass by unchallenged, except in one-on-one situations, and often wondered whether or not I had made the right choice.

I had both my children after I became a journeywoman. As the second woman in my local to give birth, I found I had to do a lot of ground-breaking. Our union's disability and health and welfare policies were written only for the pregnancies of a member's wife. A group of women in the local met for several months, doing research and asking a lot of questions, and then wrote a pamphlet explaining how these benefits applied to a pregnant union member. Unfortunately, like many of the changes women have brought to the union, the pamphlet was only in circulation as long as the women members passed it around themselves.

I worked into the sixth month of my first pregnancy without telling anyone except the general foreman and a woman elevator installer that I was pregnant. I told most people on the day I stopped working. Even my foreman and partner only thought I had gained a little weight (thirty pounds!).

To my friends who saw me after work in maternity clothes, it seemed inconceivable that my pregnancy was anything but obvious. But since I wore baggy clothes to work (what I called my maternity overalls) and since no one *expected* to see a pregnant woman on a construction sight—they didn't. I presented myself as I always had—as an electrician there to work and earn a paycheck.

For me, deciding whether, when and whom to tell I was pregnant raised issues of privacy, safety, emotional vulnerability and confidence as a mechanic. I handled the choice differently in two pregnancies that followed, but for my first pregnancy, not telling felt like the right choice for several reasons:

Safety. During the first trimester, when danger to the fetus from chemical hazards is greatest, I was—by good luck—on a job where there were none. It was the finish stage of a new hotel and there were—a pregnant woman's dream!—twenty-eight new bathrooms on each floor. If safety had been an issue, I probably would have made a different choice.

Insecurity as a mechanic. I was a new journeywoman, out of my time (finished with my apprenticeship) only a year. As one of the first women to graduate in our local, my work performance had always been scrutinized closely. I felt I had worked very hard for years, proving I could do the job. I didn't want to call attention to what had become harder and more tiring.

Gaging limits. Pregnancy lasts a while, and it's not something you can untell someone. I wanted to come to my own decisions (from talking with my doctor, reading the little I could find, and listening to my body) about what I could and could not do as a pregnant electrician. I didn't want to have to deal with everyone else's perceptions of my capabilities or their reactions, which I suspected would be overprotecting, followed by resentment.

Gossip, jokes, careless talk. When I am feeling emotionally raw and vulnerable, a construction site is never where I want to be. Pregnant, I felt very raw. Knowing there is a big risk of miscarriage, particularly in the first trimester (one out of five pregnancies ends in miscarriage)—I did not want that to be everybody's business. But even in the second trimester, I found that I wanted the pregnancy to be quietly personal, that I didn't want to risk being the object of crude remarks. Pregnancy was new for me and for the local: I was the second member, the first journeywoman, to be pregnant. It represented big changes in my homelife and in my relationship with my partner. There *were* men on the job who were friends, whom I would have liked to tell, but it was a very big job (fifty electricians), and there were a number of guys who were pretty hostile toward me. It didn't feel possible to tell a few people without everyone knowing fairly quickly.

Not talking about my pregnancy exaggerated the feeling I often have in construction of feeling split in two. At coffee break, I would be intently aware of the kicking in my womb while having a conversation about the Red Sox. It also meant making a clear pact with myself to ask for help when I needed it or refuse to do things I felt I shouldn't do—that I *would* put health and safety ahead of ego.

My second pregnancy—on another job, with another company—began to miscarry on the job. I began bleeding, called my doctor, who told me to come in immediately, and then told my foreman that I was leaving. When he asked why, I just said, "I have to leave." A few days later I did miscarry. When I called to say I would be out another day, the foreman again said he was concerned, did I need help, what was wrong. At that point, I told him what had happened. He said the other guys on the crew were concerned, too, and asked if he could tell them. He said it wouldn't go beyond the electricians (we were a crew of about six). I said that was fine, and I was very impressed and moved to find that that really was what happened. Aside from one bad joke, the crew was incredibly supportive and respectful.

My third pregnancy began a few months later on that same job. This time I decided to tell people once the first trimester was past. I had been out of my time for a few years and felt more confident. It was the same small crew that had been through the miscarriage with me, so I felt a certain level of safety and intimacy. People already saw me as a wife and mother, so this time around, being pregnant again was no big leap in how I was perceived. I had already had a baby and returned to work once. People expected that this is what I would do again (not, as I'd heard so often when I started: why waste this training on women when they'll only have families and quit). And I was more comfortable with being pregnant. I knew what would happen. I could predict what I could and could not do, how I would feel, making it easier to include other people without feeling like I was losing control.

Driving around Boston, I love pointing out to my daughter and son "the jobs we worked together." It brings back the times when I felt like I carried a delicious secret: lying on a plank across an open airshaft on the roof of a building, tying in a fan motor, talking to the baby-in-utero. It gave me a powerful appreciation for the changes we have brought about. "We built that, Susie?" my daughter asks as we drive by a big hotel. "You bet!" I tell her.

For me, one of the biggest rewards of a high-paying construction job has been to feel less trapped by traditional gender roles at home. My husband and I have been able to switch back and forth between being the primary income-earner and being the primary home- and child-care person. He was able to work part-time when I returned to work after our first child, and to take a break from work outside the home when I returned after our second. As I listen to my four-year-old daughter struggle with the differentiations of boys and girls, I am glad that she can try on my workboots as well as my jewelry.

When I'm feeling most positive about construction, it's because I really do enjoy the work, enjoy having a skill that's useful to people around the world, enjoy being able to use tools and think like a mechanic. The work is certainly not always interesting and challenging. Some days it's boring and repetitive: hanging fixtures, putting in receptacles. Some days—if the foreman hasn't ordered the stock or there's been a change and you have to re-do a job for the third time—it's incredibly frustrating. But change is a basic part of the business. Good and bad both pass, and I've been lucky to find enough encouragement around to carry me through the more difficult times.

I have continued to feel a lot of support from other women in the trades. Being a poet, I've had the chance to meet tradeswomen not only locally, but around the country. I've received notes, phone calls or poems from women who read my book* or saw a poem of mine in a magazine. I've met other tradeswomen when I've given poetry readings, and friendships have grown. It's been helpful to discover that women construction workers from different parts of the country share very similar feelings and problems. It has helped me to put my own issues into a larger context. Again and again, I find myself being glad to be part of what feels to me like a community of women who are pretty gutsy, hard-working and straightforward.

Black men were the first group to break through the barriers of the white, male, father/son tradition in the construction unions, with women gaining membership several years later. I've found a camaraderie and pretty consistent support and encouragement from the black men I've met in construction. They were the source of a lot of quick survival tips when I was starting out. My first month, I was carrying a heavy load on my shoulder, trying to get by a bunch of guys who weren't moving, even though I was politely saying, "Excuse me," over and over again. The laborer foreman on the job, a black man,

---

It's a Good Thing I'm Not Macho, Boston: Whetstone Press, 1984.

amused by my predicament, called over to me, "You'll never make it that way. Just yell, 'Coming through!' and keep walking." I took his advice to heart.

During my apprenticeship, I felt very nourished, both by everything I was learning as a mechanic and by the progress I felt the union was making in recognizing its women members. Although I still learn new things at work, it's certainly not at the rate I did when starting out. What's been more difficult, though, has been my growing disillusionment with the union. After ten years, we still have to remind people, "Hey, we're here, too. Please don't send out literature addressed 'Dear Brother,' warning me that if prevailing wage guarantees are defeated, my wife will have to go out and work." Even though there are many more women in the trades now than when I began, the percentages are still ridiculously low (less than two percent). There is no commitment from the unions to change these percentages, nor any pressure on them from the outside that might make a change likely.

Sometimes I think my lows are just battle fatigue. Tiredness. Tired of the same jokes and comments. Tired of being expected to prove myself. Tired of racism, that, unlike sexism, I feel not much better at countering than when I started. I can't as easily challenge it by my example or by one of many acerbic anti-sexist comebacks in my repertoire. I find the constant racist jokes and comments and the difficulty of being heard when you speak against them very draining and discouraging.

The cultural life on jobs—how people talk to and treat each other, picking on someone just to watch them react—has changed little. The insecurities of the construction business, with layoffs a constant threat, make the kind of close relationships that can develop over time in other occupations more difficult. On top of which, friendships between women and men on a job tend to make people nervous.

I feel the pull of demands that offer more passion and intrinsic value. Building luxury hotels does not have built-in satisfaction for me. It's a paycheck. As I've become increasingly committed to developing myself as a writer and added the extra pulls of parenting, I find myself considering alternative work possibilities.

Whenever I have strong thoughts about giving up the work, though, I realize it is more than the high pay that keeps me there. There's something about the work and the culture that has crept into my bones.

Organizing the Farm Workers

Jessie Lopez De La Cruz

Farm work has been a way of life for many Mexican-Americans in the Southwest and California since early in the century. Conditions of life have always been hard: toiling long hours in the fields for incredibly low pay, constantly moving around while families follow the crops, being more susceptible to disease and dying young, being unable to break out of the cycle. Huge corporations such as the Bank of America, Safeway, and the Southern Pacific Company owned much of the land in the West; agribusiness wanted, and usually got, a docile and cheap migrant labor force. That is, until Cesar Chavez and the United Farmworkers began organizing in the fields of the San Joaquin valley in 1962.

Jessie Lopez De La Cruz was very much part of Chavez's organizing drive—what participants called simply *La Causa* (the cause). At the time, De La Cruz was forty-two years old, married and the mother of six children, and had been a farmworker all her life. Breaking out of traditional Mexican-American gender roles to become a union organizer was not easy, but she drew on her personal history: "I'd been trained as a child that the woman just walked behind the husband and kept quiet, no matter what the husband does. But in work I've been equal to men since I was a child, working alongside men, doing the same hard work and earning the same wages." Jessie Lopez De La Cruz put that determination to use as she built support for the farmworkers' union and eventually became a paid union official. Her oral history traces the roots of her union activity and conveys her belief that poor people must stick together to improve their lives. And her story confirms the vital role that women play in this struggle.

The words of Maria Varela, a Latina from the Southwest, suggest the common struggle that unites people of color and women's role in it: "When your race is fighting for survival—to eat, to be clothed, to be housed, to be left in peace—as a woman, you know who you are. You are a principle of life, of survival and endurance. . . . This is even more true when, as a woman, you are involved in battling the forces of oppression against your race."

Growing up, I could see all the injustices and I would think, "If only I could do something about it! If only there was somebody who could do something about it!" That was always in the back of my mind. And after I was married, I cared about what was going on, but I felt I couldn't do anything. So I went to work, and I came home to clean the house, and I fixed the food for the next day, took care of the children and the next day went back to work. The whole thing over and over again. Politics to me was something foreign, something I didn't know about. I didn't even listen to the news. I didn't read the newspapers hardly at all. *True Romance* was my thing!

But then late one night in 1962, there was a knock at the door and there were three men. One of them was Cesar Chavez. And the next thing I knew,

Source: Copyright © 1980 by The Feminist Press. From the book *Moving the Mountain: Women Working for Social Change* by Ellen Cantarow with Susan Gushee O'Malley and Sharon Hartman Strom, pp. 129, 134–137, 145, 151. Reprinted by permission. All rights reserved.

they were sitting around our table talking about a union. I made coffee. Arnold had already told me about a union for the farmworkers. He was attending their meetings in Fresno, but I didn't. I'd either stay home or stay outside in the car. But then Cesar said, "The women have to be involved. They're the ones working out in the fields with their husbands. If you can take the women out to the fields, you can certainly take them to meetings." So I sat up straight and said to myself, *"That's* what I want!"

When I became involved with the union, I felt I had to get other women involved. Women have been behind men all the time, always. Just waiting to see what the men decide to do, and tell us what to do. In my sister-in-law and brother-in-law's families, the women do a lot of shouting and cussing and they get slapped around. But that's not standing up for what you believe in. It's just trying to boss and not knowing how. I'd hear them scolding their kids and fighting their husbands and I'd say, "Gosh! Why don't you go after the people that have you living like this? Why don't you go after the growers that have you tired from working out in the fields at low wages and keep us poor all the time? Let's go after them! *They're* the cause of our misery!" Then I would say we had to take a part in the things going on around us. "Women can no longer be taken for granted—that we're just going to stay home and do the cooking and cleaning. It's way past the time when our husbands could say, 'You stay home! You have to take care of the children! You have to do as I say!' "

Then some women I spoke to started attending the union meetings, and later they were out on the picket lines.

I think I was made an organizer because in the first place I could relate to the farmworkers, being a lifelong farmworker. I was well-known in the small towns around Fresno. Wherever I went to speak to them, they listened. I told them about how we were excluded from the NLRB in 1935, how we had no benefits, no minimum wage, nothing out in the fields—no restrooms, nothing. I would talk about how we were paid what the grower wanted to pay us, and how we couldn't set a price on our work. I explained that we could do something about these things by joining a union, by working together. I'd ask people how they felt about these many years they had been working out in the fields, how they had been treated. And then we'd all talk about it. They would say, "I was working for so-and-so, and when I complained about something that happened there, I was fired." I said, "Well! Do you think we should be putting up with this in this modern age? You know, we're not back in the twenties. We can stand up! We can talk back! It's not like when I was a little kid and my grandmother used to say, 'You have to especially respect the Anglos,' 'Yessir,' 'Yes, Ma'am!' That's over. This country is very rich, and we want a share of the money these growers make of our sweat and our work by exploiting us and our children!" I'd have my sign-up book and I'd say, "If anyone wants to become a member of the union, I can make you a member right now." And they'd agree!

So I found out that I could organize them and make members of them. Then

I offered to help them, like taking them to the doctor's and translating for them, filling out papers that they needed to fill out, writing their letters for those that couldn't write. A lot of people confided in me. Through the letter-writing, I knew a lot of the problems they were having back home, and they knew they could trust me, that I wouldn't tell anyone else about what I had written or read. So that's why they came to me.

There was a migrant camp in Parlier. And these people, the migrants, were being used as strikebreakers. I had something to do with building that camp. By that time, I had been put on the board of the Fresno County Economic Opportunity Commission, and I was supporting migrant housing for farmworkers. But I had no idea it was going to be turned almost into a concentration camp or prison. The houses were just like matchboxes—square, a room for living, a room for cooking, a bathroom that didn't have a door, just a curtain. The houses are so close together that if one catches fire, the next one does, too, and children have burned in them. It happened in Parlier.

So I went to the camp office and said I wanted to go in and visit. By this time, I was well-known as a radical, an educator, and a troublemaker! The man in the office asked what I wanted to talk about. I just wanted to visit, I said.

"Well, you have to sign your name here." I said, "I also would like to know when I can use the hall for a meeting."

"What kind of meeting?"

"An organizing meeting." You see, when it was built, they told us there was supposed to be a hall built for parties and whatever. I felt we could use it for a meeting to talk to the people. But he said, "We can't authorize you to come in here and talk to the people about a union, but you can write Governor Reagan and ask for permission." I left.

I met a nurse who had to go to this camp. She said, "Why don't you come with me as my translator?" Even though she spoke perfect Spanish! So both of us went in, and she said she was from the Health Department and I was her translator. I got in there and talked to the people and told them about our union meetings, and at our next meeting they were there. I had to do things like that in order to organize.

It was very hard being a woman organizer. Many of our people my age and older were raised with the old customs in Mexico: where the husband rules, he is king of his house. The wife obeys, and the children, too. So when we first started it was very, very hard. Men gave us the most trouble—neighbors there in Parlier! They were for the union, but they were not taking orders from women, they said. When they formed the ranch committee at Christian Brothers—that's a big wine company, part of it is in Parlier—the ranch committee was all men. We were working under our first contract in Fresno County. The ranch committee had to enforce the contract. If there are any grievances they meet with us and the supervisors. But there were no women on the first committee.

That year, we'd have a union meeting every week. Men, women, and children would come. Women would ask questions and the men would just stand back. I guess they'd say to themselves, "I'll wait for someone to say something before I do." The women were more aggressive than the men. And I'd get up and say, "Let's go on, let's do it!"

When the first contract was up, we talked about there being no women on the ranch committee. I suggested they be on it, and the men went along with this. And so women were elected.

The women took the lead for picketing, and we would talk to the people. It got to the point that we would have to find them, because the men just wouldn't go and they wouldn't take their wives. So we would say, "We're having our picket line at the Safeway in Fresno, and those that don't show up are going to have to pay a five-dollar fine." We couldn't have four or five come to a picket line and have the rest stay home and watch TV. In the end, we had everybody out there. . . .

Sometimes I'd just stop to think: what if our parents had done what we were doing now? My grandparents were poor. They were humble. They never learned to speak English. They felt God meant them to be poor. It was against their religion to fight. I remember there was a huge policeman named Marcos, when I was a child, who used to go around on a horse. My grandmother would say, "Here comes Marcos," and we just grew up thinking, "He's law and order." But during the strikes I stood up to them. They'd come up to arrest me and I'd say, "O.K., here I come if you want. Arrest me!" . . .

It doesn't take courage. All it takes is standing up for what you believe in, talking about things that you know are true, things that should be happening, instead of what is happening. That's all it takes. The way I see it, there's more poor people than rich people. We're trying to get together, organize, stick together. Say I'm outside, and something is happening inside my house. I need help, and I shout. They'll probably hear me a couple of houses down. But then other people come with me and I say, "Help me shout so they can hear me downtown." It'll take quite a few people. But if we can get a hundred people together and we all shout at the same time, we'll be heard further, and that's what we're talking about!

Women on Welfare

Johnnie Tillmon

What if women want to work and cannot find jobs? What if these women are the sole support of their families? Many women are just one man away from welfare, the saying goes. Women do not always live near available jobs (this is especially true of inner-city residents) and if they have children, long commutes are not feasible; the pay for women's jobs is sometimes so low that working full time still leaves women below the poverty line. So this vicious circle often pushes women onto the welfare rolls.

The problems of women and welfare are especially acute for black Americans, who more often live in households headed by women. In 1950, 17.6 percent of black families were headed by women; by 1980, it had grown to more than 40 percent. The increase in teenage pregnancy in the black community has contributed to this trend, as have the lack of employment opportunities for black men. Many of these families had received help from Aid to Families with Dependent Children (AFDC), the major federal program for welfare in the United States. The dominant pattern, however, is not for families to settle permanently on welfare, but to shift back and forth between welfare and the kinds of low-income employment available as an alternative.

This testimonial by Johnnie Tillmon, published in 1972, forcefully points out that welfare is a women's issue. Tillmon was born in 1928 in Arkansas and started to organize welfare mothers in Los Angeles in 1963 when her health forced her to quit working and go on welfare. She later served as the first chairwoman of the National Welfare Rights Organization (NWRO), an advocacy group founded by George Wiley that lobbied for a guaranteed annual income by arguing that welfare was a basic right of citizenship. Her testimony accentuates the demeaning aspects of going on welfare (the requirement that in order to receive aid, there must not be a man in the house was later modified) and how marginal an existence it provides. She reminds us that the majority of poor families are white, not black, and mocks the idea of "the dignity of work" when the only work available keeps families stuck in poverty. And she punctures the commonly held view that black women have more babies in order to get more welfare money: "Having babies for profit is a lie that only men could make up, and only men could believe." More than anything else, she argues for treating women's work, both paid and unpaid, as worthy of support and respect.

I'm a woman. I'm a black woman. I'm a poor woman. I'm a fat woman. I'm a middle-aged woman. And I'm on welfare.

In this country, if you're any one of those things—poor, black, fat, female, middle-aged, on welfare—you count less as a human being. If you're all those things, you don't count at all. Except as a statistic.

I am a statistic.

I am 45 years old. I have raised six children.

I grew up in Arkansas, and I worked there for fifteen years in a laundry, making about $20 or $30 a week, picking cotton on the side for carfare. I moved

Source: Johnnie Tillmon, "Welfare Is a Women's Issue," *Liberation News Service,* no. 415 (February 26, 1972), in Rosalyn Baxandall, Linda Gordon, and Susan Reverby, *America's Working Women* (New York: Random House/Vintage, 1976), pp. 355–358.

to California in 1959 and worked in a laundry there for nearly four years. In 1963 I got too sick to work anymore. Friends helped me to go on welfare.

They didn't call it welfare. They called it A.F.D.C.—Aid to Families with Dependent Children. Each month I get $363 for my kids and me. I pay $128 a month rent; $30 for utilities, which include gas, electricity, and water; $120 for food and non-edible household essentials; $50 for school lunches for the three children in junior and senior high school who are not eligible for reduced-cost meal programs.

There are millions of statistics like me. Some on welfare. Some not. And some, really poor, who don't even know they're entitled to welfare. Not all of them are black. Not at all. In fact, the majority—about two-thirds—of all the poor families in the country are white.

Welfare's like a traffic accident. It can happen to anybody, but especially it happens to women.

And that is why welfare is a women's issue. For a lot of middle-class women in this country, Women's Liberation is a matter of concern. For women on welfare it's a matter of survival.

Forty-four percent of all poor families are headed by women. That's bad enough. But the *families* on A.F.D.C. aren't really families. Because 99 per cent of them are headed by women. That means there is no man around. In half the states there really can't be men around because A.F.D.C. says if there is an "able-bodied" man around, then you can't be on welfare. If the kids are going to eat, and the man can't get a job, then he's got to go. So his kids can eat.

The truth is that A.F.D.C. is like a supersexist marriage. You trade in *a* man for *the* man. But you can't divorce him if he treats you bad. He can divorce you, of course, cut you off anytime he wants. But in that case, *he* keeps the kids, not you.

The man runs everything. In ordinary marriage, sex is supposed to be for your husband. On A.F.D.C. you're not supposed to have any sex at all. You give up control of your own body. It's a condition of aid. You may even have to agree to get your tubes tied so you can never have more children just to avoid being cut off welfare.

The man, the welfare system, controls your money. He tells you what to buy, what not to buy, where to buy it, and how much things cost. If things— rent, for instance—really cost more than he says they do, it's just too bad for you.

There are other welfare programs, other kinds of people on welfare—the blind, the disabled, the aged. (Many of them are women, too, especially the aged.) Those others make up just over a third of all the welfare caseloads. We A.F.D.C.s are two-thirds.

But when the politicians talk about the "welfare cancer eating at our vitals," they're not talking about the aged, blind, and disabled. Nobody minds them. They're the "deserving poor." Politicians are talking about A.F.D.C. Politicians are talking about us—the women who head up 99 per cent of the

A.F.D.C. families—and our kids. We're the "cancer," the "undeserving poor." Mothers and children.

In this country we believe in something called the "work ethic." That means that your work is what gives you human worth. But the work ethic itself is a double standard. It applies to men and to women on welfare. It doesn't apply to all women. If you're a society lady from Scarsdale and you spend all your time sitting on your prosperity paring your nails, well, that's okay.

The truth is a job doesn't necessarily mean an adequate income. A woman with three kids—not twelve kids, mind you, just three kids—that woman earning the full federal minimum wage of $2.00 an hour, is still stuck in poverty. She is below the Government's own official poverty line. There are some ten million jobs that now pay less than the minimum wage, and if you're a woman, you've got the best chance of getting one.

The President keeps repeating the "dignity of work" idea. What dignity? Wages are the measure of dignity that society puts on a job. Wages and nothing else. There is no dignity in starvation. Nobody denies, least of all poor women, that there is dignity and satisfaction in being able to support your kids through honest labor.

We wish we could do it.

The problem is that our country's economic policies deny the dignity and satisfaction of self-sufficiency to millions of people—the millions who suffer everyday in underpaid dirty jobs—and still don't have enough to survive.

People still believe that old lie that A.F.D.C. mothers keep on having kids just to get a bigger welfare check. On the average, another baby means another $35 a month—barely enough for food and clothing. Having babies for profit is a lie that only men could make up, and only men could believe. Men, who never have to bear the babies or have to raise them and maybe send them to war.

There are a lot of other lies that male society tells about welfare mothers; that A.F.D.C. mothers are immoral, that A.F.D.C. mothers are lazy, misuse their welfare checks, spend it all on booze and are stupid and incompetent.

If people are willing to believe these lies, it's partly because they're just special versions of the lies that society tells about *all* women.

For instance, the notion that all A.F.D.C. mothers are lazy: that's just a negative version of the idea that women don't work and don't want to. It's a way of rationalizing the male policy of keeping women as domestic slaves.

The notion that A.F.D.C. mothers are immoral is another way of saying that all women are likely to become whores unless they're kept under control by men and marriage. Even many of my own sisters on welfare believe these things about themselves.

On TV, a woman learns that human worth means beauty and that beauty means being thin, white, young and rich.

She learns that her body is really disgusting the way it is, and that she needs all kinds of expensive cosmetics to cover it up.

She learns that a "real woman" spends her time worrying about how her bathroom bowl smells; that being important means being middle class, having two cars, a house in the suburbs, and a minidress under your maxicoat. In other words, an A.F.D.C. mother learns that being a "real woman" means being all the things she isn't and having all the things she can't have.

Either it breaks you, and you start hating yourself, or you break it.

There's one good thing about welfare. It kills your illusions about yourself, and about where this society is really at. It's laid out for you straight. You have to learn to fight, to be aggressive, or you just don't make it. If you can survive being on welfare, you can survive anything. It gives you a kind of freedom, a sense of your own power and togetherness with other women.

Maybe it is we poor welfare women who will really liberate women in this country. We've already started on our welfare plan.

Along with other welfare recipients, we have organized together so we can have some voice. Our group is called the National Welfare Rights Organization (N.W.R.O.). We put together our own welfare plan, called Guaranteed Adequate Income (G.A.I.), which would eliminate sexism from welfare.

There would be no "categories"—men, women, children, single, married, kids, no kids—just poor people who need aid. You'd get paid according to need and family size only—$6,500 for a family of four (which is the Department of Labor's estimate of what's adequate), and that would be upped as the cost of living goes up.

If I were president, I would solve this so-called welfare crisis in a minute and go a long way toward liberating every woman. I'd just issue a proclamation that "women's" work is *real* work.

In other words, I'd start paying women a living wage for doing the work we are already doing—child-raising and housekeeping. And the welfare crisis would be over, just like that. Housewives would be getting wages, too—a legally determined percentage of their husband's salary—instead of having to ask for and account for money they've already earned.

For me, Women's Liberation is simple. No woman in this country can feel dignified, no woman can be liberated, until all women get off their knees. That's what N.W.R.O. is all about—women standing together, on their feet.

MUCH IN DEMAND IN 1963

After the publication of *The Feminine Mystique* in 1963, Betty Friedan lectured widely across the country about the controversial findings of her best-selling book. (Note in the picture that she is referred to as Mrs. Friedan; the term *Ms.* had not yet been invented.) But Friedan soon came to believe that the problem of the trapped housewife was being "talked to death," even though she herself had been unable to write her projected next book on the new directions that would allow women to move beyond the feminine mystique. The revival of feminism in the 1960s helped to supply some of the answers, although it also raised new questions. (Credit: Courtesy of the Schlesinger Library, Radcliffe College)

EQUAL RIGHTS DEMONSTRATION AT THE CAPITOL

When the ERA was sent to the states for ratification in 1972, supporters predicted an easy victory. When progress had stalled by 1975, feminists were galvanized into new strategies such as boycotts and mass demonstrations to try to break the stalemate. This 1978 march brought more than 100,000 ERA supporters to Washington to lobby successfully for a three-year extension of the ratification deadline to June 30, 1982. In a conscious evocation of the woman suffrage movement, ERA supporters prominently displayed the suffrage colors of purple, green, and gold in their banners. (Credit: Courtesy of Bettye Lane)

340

A DAY IN THE KITCHEN

Paid employment has more consistently been a part of black
women's lives than whites' because few black families could
survive on the wages paid to black men alone. But until recently
black women faced circumscribed employment opportunities
limited both by racism and by the segmentation of the work force
into dead-end women's jobs. This 1976 photograph introduces
Velma James, head chef of the Roosevelt Hotel in New York
City. (Credit: Coreen Simpson)

WOMEN AND THE LABOR MOVEMENT

Labor unions have only reluctantly recognized the roles that women workers can play in the labor movement. At this Labor Day parade in New York City, the most prominent marchers are Chinese-American garment workers represented by the International Ladies Garment Workers Union (ILGWU). The signs, in English, Chinese, and Spanish, reflect the heterogeneity of the modern labor movement. (Credit: Earl Dotter Archive Pictures Inc.)

PROTESTS IN HIGHER EDUCATION

Women made strides in higher education as a result of the women's movement, but it took demonstrations like the one these Harvard-Radcliffe graduating seniors staged in 1971 to protest Harvard's admission policy that admitted four men for every woman. The women's banners combine the symbols for women and equality, and the middle one incorporates the student protest sign of the clenched fist, along with a dig at Harvard (the richest university in the country) by spelling its motto VERITA$. Harvard soon instituted a sex-blind admissions policy; in the nation as a whole, women now make up a majority of undergraduates. (Credit: Courtesy of Radcliffe College Archives)

HOUSTON, 1977

Betty K. Hamburger, a delegate from Maryland Advocates for
the Aging, captured a lot of attention at the 1977 National
Women's Conference in Houston with her "Pro God, Pro
Family, Pro ERA" hat, which also had "Free Choice" on the
back. Hamburger was seventy-three years old at the time of the
convention and had been active in the Gray Panthers, an
advocacy group for senior citizens. Speaking for older
Americans, Hamburger recalled, "Houston helped us feel that
we were not alone, that younger women had the same feelings
we had. . . . So many of us have so much to give; we have lots of
knowledge and know-how, and we ought to be able to use it."
(Credit: Courtesy of Bettye Lane)

OLYMPIC SUPERSTAR

Florence Griffith Joyner was the dominant American athlete at the 1988 Summer Olympic games in Seoul, Korea, winning three gold medals in track and field. After winning this heat for the 100-meter dash, she took the gold in world-record time. The press lavished attention on "Flo Jo's" appearance, especially her billowing hair, brightly painted fingernails, and the one-legged track suits she wore when she trained. But her obviously muscular body also raised questions of gender transgression, especially whether this well-trained female athlete looked too much like a man. Women athletes continue to struggle to win acceptance as both athletes and women, but stars like Florence Griffith Joyner and her sister-in-law Jackie Joyner-Kersee (who won the heptathlon at the Seoul Olympics) pioneered what sports historian Susan Cahn has called "a style of self-confident, graceful, but muscular athletic womanhood." (Credit: Reuters/Corbis-Bettmann)

ANITA HILL

Accusations by University of Oklahoma professor Anita Hill
that Supreme Court nominee Clarence Thomas had sexually
harrassed her at the Department of Education and Equal
Employment Opportunity Commission in the early 1980s
sparked fierce political debate during his confirmation hearings
in 1991. Many felt that if there had been more women in the
Senate, Professor Hill's charges would have been treated more
seriously. In the wake of the hearings, national polls confirmed
the pervasiveness of sexual harrassment on the job: four of ten
women said they had been the object of unwanted sexual
advances from men at work. Clarence Thomas won his seat on
the Supreme Court, and Anita Hill became a heroine for the
feminist movement. (Credit: Reuters/Corbis-Bettmann)

CHAPTER 12

New Issues of Sex and Sexuality

By the 1960s, American society seemed to be in the grip of a new openness about sexuality, symbolized in many minds by such women's fashions as the miniskirt. Books, movies, and self-help manuals promoted an ethos of casual yet fun sexual relationships. The film industry devised the X rating in 1968 for films that featured nudity, sex, and explicit language, subjects that had been absent from the screen just a few years earlier. When William H. Masters and Virginia Johnson published *Human Sexual Response* (1966), the result of direct laboratory observation of arousal and intercourse, the book became a bestseller. The widespread availability of more effective contraception such as the birth control pill and the intrauterine device (IUD) by the mid-1960s helped to separate sexuality from procreation. Studies of actual sexual practices showed wider experimentation and very few virgins at marriage.

The simultaneous appearance of the so-called sexual revolution and the revival of feminism suggested a link between the two, but in fact they were often at odds. In order for women's sexuality to be freely realized, many of the structures of relationships, such as the double standard, the view of women as sex objects, and the validation of the norms of male dominance and female passivity would have to be changed. Ironically, the wider access to birth control put more pressure on women to engage in sexual relationships with men now that fear of pregnancy was removed. As *Ms.* magazine noted in 1972, "The Sexual Revolution and the Women's Movement are at polar opposites. Women have been liberated only from the right to say 'no.' "

The women's movement did have a significant impact, however, on a variety of issues relating to women's sexuality and health. The 1973 publication of *Our Bodies, Ourselves* by the Boston Women's Health Collective encouraged women to be active participants, not passive patients, in health care issues. Susan Brownmiller's powerful *Against Our Will* (1975) argued that rape was not an issue of sexuality, but of violence and dominance of men over

347

women; feminists organized rape crisis centers that offered counseling and tried to dispel the prevalent tendency to blame the victim for her attack. Women also tried to limit the spread of pornography, which, they argued, encouraged male aggression towards women with its explicitly violent content. Battered-women shelters offered protection to the victims of domestic violence, and the legal system recognized the concept of sexual harassment.

Most of the energy of the women's movement concerned issues of reproductive freedom. The 1965 Supreme Court decision in *Griswold* v. *Connecticut* removed legal restrictions on birth control, but abortion remained illegal in all states, except in extreme cases to save the life of the mother. In the 1960s, as many as one million illegal abortions were taking place each year (as opposed to ten thousand legal abortions performed in hospitals, primarily on elite white women who could convince committees of doctors to terminate their pregnancies on the grounds of mental health). So much money was made in back-alley abortions that only narcotics and gambling surpassed them in criminal revenue. New York was the first state (in 1970) to reform its abortion laws, but abortion still remained restricted throughout most of the country at the time of the 1973 Supreme Court decision in *Roe* v. *Wade,* which legalized abortion.

Reproductive freedom continued to be a central tenet of the women's movement, but the legalization of abortion sparked a powerful Right to Life movement and continued legal challenges to *Roe* v. *Wade.* In 1980 the Supreme Court upheld a congressional amendment denying Medicaid funds for abortions for poor women. The 1989 *Webster* v. *Reproductive Health Services* decision permitted states to restrict abortion, and in 1990 the court upheld a federal regulation that forbade personnel at federally funded health clinics from discussing abortion with their clients. In 1992, a 5–4 decision upheld provisions of a Pennsylvania law mandating a 24-hour waiting period and informed-consent requirements. The Court also reaffirmed what it called the "essential holding" of *Roe* v. *Wade*—that women have a constitutional right to abortion—but that right remains hotly contested.

Not all issues of sexuality raised by the women's movement concerned heterosexual women: to paraphrase a popular slogan, "how dare you presume I am heterosexual?" The concerns of lesbians were part of the new attention to sexual issues in the 1960s and 1970s, intersecting both the rising movement for gay pride and the developing feminist analysis of women's situation. As lesbian writer Jill Johnston stated, "Feminism at heart is a massive complaint. Lesbianism is the solution."

The gay liberation movement is usually dated to the 1969 Stonewall riot in New York City, where male patrons of a gay bar fought back when busted by the police. The movement brought new pride and a collective sense to the nation's homosexual men and women who had been forced to live hidden lives "in the closet" by a society that would not tolerate what it defined as deviance. (Not until 1973 did the American Psychiatric Association agree that homosexuality should no longer be listed as a "mental disorder.") Women as well as men were ennobled by this new movement, but lesbians found it difficult to work with gay men, who seemed often to embody the same chauvinistic values shared by the society as a whole. For the most part, lesbians carried on their struggle separately.

The emerging lesbian consciousness was also closely related to the rise of the feminist movement, which gave both gay and straight women a political context for their personal oppression. But this partnership was also troubled, especially in the early 1970s, when lesbianism was seen as a potential embarrassment to feminism. For example, Betty Friedan and the New York chapter of NOW led a purge of the "lavender menace" in 1970. Too many straight feminists were afraid to let go of what Charlotte Bunch called their "heterosexual privilege" (the "actual or promised benefits for the woman who stays in line") and speak out for the concerns of lesbians. In response, a strand of lesbian separatism celebrated biological differences and women's culture within a nationalist framework. Since the mid-1970s there has been less separation between gay and straight women in the movement, in part because lesbians face many of the same problems in employment, housing, credit, and parenting rights as other women. Civil rights laws, however, have not uniformly been extended to protect gay people from discrimination based on sexual preference.

One issue of sexuality that affects both gay and straight women is Acquired Immune Deficiency Syndrome (AIDS), which was first recognized in 1981. Although its earliest victims were predominantly homosexual men, by mid-decade the epidemic was spreading among heterosexuals, especially intravenous drug addicts and their sexual partners, as well as bisexuals. In the early 1990s, the fastest growing category of new AIDS cases was women. Fears about AIDS and other sexually transmitted diseases made the casual experimentation of the 1960s and 1970s less attractive. Widespread public education about safe-sex methods, such as the use of condoms during every sexual act, cut the spread of the disease, but with no cure or vaccine in sight, sexually active men and women will live under the dark threat of AIDS for the foreseeable future.

Sex and the Single Girl

Helen Gurley Brown

The *Playboy* image of swinging bachelors (who were so secure in their heterosexuality that they could never be confused with homosexuals) took root in the 1950s. Women had to wait until the 1960s for their own version of the swinging single life. Not surprisingly, liberated female sexuality proved a much tamer, paler version than the male variety.

This swinging single of the 1960s was in some ways the spiritual granddaughter of the 1920s flapper. She was economically independent (a job was a good place to meet men, and she needed the income to afford her own apartment), fashion conscious (the women's magazines showed her how to dress, and that too took money), and sexually experimental (the birth control pill helped here). Instead of being pitied as a spinster if she had not married by her twenties, these young women with their sophisticated urban lifestyles were seen as desirable and glamorous. In some ways, they served as a deliberate snub to the child-centered lives of suburban housewives, whose lives were anything but glamorous and sexy.

Cosmopolitan editor Helen Gurley Brown played a large role in creating this new image for single women, or as they were called then, girls. Brown used her own example of waiting until age thirty-seven to marry as proof that women could catch the man of their dreams if they pursued the proper strategies. She breathlessly shared her advice in her bestselling *Sex and the Single Girl* (1962), from which these excerpts are drawn. Helen Gurley Brown unabashedly supports the right of a single woman to have an active sex life and does not condemn affairs with married men: "While they are using you to varnish their egos, you're using them to add spice to your life." She offers personality and beauty tips that define women totally in relation to men, all the while bucking up the single woman's spirits by telling her that she has chosen this life because it is where the action is. But despite her disclaimer that the book is about how to stay single in style, *Sex and the Single Girl* is most definitely about how to get married, for the main goal, indeed reward, held out to women for all their efforts is still a wedding ring.

Theoretically a "nice" single woman has no sex life. What nonsense! She has a better sex life than most of her married friends. She need never be bored with one man per lifetime. Her choice of partners is endless and they seek *her*. They never come to her bed duty-bound. Her married friends refer to her pursuers as wolves, but actually many of them turn out to be lambs—to be shorn and worn by her.

Sex of course is more than the act of coitus. It begins with the delicious feeling of attraction between two people. It may never go further, but sex it is. And a single woman may promote the attraction, bask in the sensation, drink it like wine and pour it over her like blossoms, with never a guilty twinge. She can promise with a look, a touch, a letter or a kiss—and she doesn't have to deliver. She can be maddeningly hypocritical and, after arousing desire, insist that it be shut off by stating she wants to be chaste for the man she marries.

Source: Helen Gurley Brown, *Sex and the Single Girl* (New York: Random House, 1962), pp. 7–11. Reprinted by permission of the author.

Her pursuer may strangle her with his necktie, but he can't *argue* with her. A flirtatious married woman is expected to Go Through With Things.

Since for a female getting there is at *least* half the fun, a single woman has reason to prize the luxury of taking long, gossamer, attenuated, pulsating trips before finally arriving in bed. A married woman and her husband have precious little time and energy for romance after they've put the house, animals and children to bed. A married woman with her lover is on an even tighter schedule.

During and after an affair, a single woman suffers emotional stress. Do you think a married woman can bring one off more blissfully free of strain? (One of my close friends, married, committed suicide over a feckless lover. Another is currently in a state of fingernail-biting hysteria.) And I would rather be the other woman than the woman who watches a man *stray* from her.

Yet, while indulging her libido, which she has plenty of if she is young and healthy, it is still possible for the single woman to be a lady, to be highly respected and even envied if she is successful in her work.

I did it. So have many of my friends.

Perhaps this all sounds like bragging. I do not mean to suggest for a moment that being single is not often hell. But I do mean to suggest that it can also be quite heavenly, whether you choose *it* or it chooses *you.*

There is a catch to achieving single bliss. You have to work like a son of a bitch.

But show me the married woman who can loll about and eat cherry bonbons! Hourly she is told by every magazine she reads what she must do to keep her marriage from bursting at the seams. There is no peace for anybody married *or* single unless you do your chores. Frankly, I wouldn't want to make the choice between a married hell or a single hell. They're both hell.

However, serving time as a single woman can give you the foundation for a better marriage if you finally go that route. Funnily enough it also gives you the choice.

What then does it take for a single woman to lead the rich, full life?

Here is what it *doesn't* take.

Great beauty. A man seems not so much attracted to overwhelming beauty as he is just overwhelmed by it—at first. Then he grows accustomed to the face, fabulous as it is, and starts to explore the personality. Now the hidden assets of an *attractive* girl can be as fascinating as the dark side of the moon. Plumbing the depths of a raving beauty may be like plumbing the depths of Saran Wrap.

What it also doesn't take to collect men is money. Have you ever noticed the birds who circle around rich girls? Strictly for the aviary.

You also don't have to be Auntie Mame and electrify everybody with your high-voltage personality. Do *you* like the girl who always grabs the floor to tell what happened to *her* in the elevator? Well neither does anybody else.

And you don't have to be the fireball who organizes bowling teams, gets out the chain letters and makes certain *somebody* gives a shower for the latest bride.

What you do have to do is work with the raw material you have, namely you, and never let up.

If you would like the good single life—since the married life is not just now forthcoming—you can't afford to leave any facet of you unpolished.

You don't have to do anything brassy or show-offy or against your nature. Your most prodigious work will be on *you*—at home. (When I got married, I moved in with six-pound dumbbells, slant board, an electronic device for erasing wrinkles, several pounds of soy lecithin, powdered calcium and yeast-liver concentrate for Serenity Cocktails and enough high-powered vitamins to generate life in a statue.)

Unlike Madame Bovary you don't chase the glittering life, you lay a trap for it. You tunnel up from the bottom.

You *do* need a quiet, private, personal aggression . . . a refusal to take singleness lying down. A sweetly smiling drop-dead attitude for the marrying Sams, and that means *you too*.

You must develop style. Every girl has one . . . it's just a case of getting it out in the open, caring for it and feeding it like an orchid until it leafs out. (One girl is a long-legged, tennis-playing whiz by day, a serene pool at night for friends to drown their tensions in. Wholesomeness is her trademark. A petite brunette is gamine but serious-minded. A knockout in black jersey, she is forever promoting discussions on Stendhal or diminishing colonialism. An intellectual charmer.)

Brains are an asset but it doesn't take brainy brains like a nuclear physicist's. Whatever it is that keeps you from saying anything unkind and keeps you asking bright questions even when you don't quite understand the answers will do nicely. A lively interest in people and things (even if you aren't *that* interested) is why bosses trust you with new assignments, why men talk to you at parties . . . and sometimes ask you on to dinner.

Fashion is your powerful ally. Let the "secure" married girls eschew shortening their skirts (or lengthening them) and wear their classic cashmeres and tweeds until everybody could throw up. You be the girl other girls look at to see what America has copied from Paris.

Roommates are for sorority girls. You need an apartment alone even if it's over a garage.

Your figure can't harbor an ounce of baby fat. It never looked good on anybody but babies.

You must cook well. It will serve you faithfully.

You must have a job that interests you, at which you work hard.

I say "must" about all these things as though you were under orders. You don't have to do anything. I'm just telling you what worked for me.

I'm sure of this. You're not too fat, too thin, too tall, too small, too dumb, or too myopic to have married women gazing at you wistfully.

This then is not a study on how to get married but how to stay single—in superlative style.

Abortion as a Legal and Feminist Issue

Roe v. Wade

By 1968, women's right to legal abortions had become a central tenet, and one of the most controversial demands, of the developing women's movement. In 1970, New York State became the first to reform its abortion laws, an act followed by fifteen other states and the District of Columbia by 1972. Still, it was estimated that 2,500 illegal abortions were taking place every day, many performed at great risk to women's health.

In 1973, the United States Supreme Court ruled by a 7–2 margin in the cases of *Roe* v. *Wade* and *Doe* v. *Bolton* that the constitutional right of privacy "is broad enough to encompass a woman's decision whether or not to terminate her pregnancy." The "right of privacy" was a legal doctrine developed from the Ninth and Fourteenth Amendments to shield certain areas of private action from state intervention. In this excerpt from Justice Blackmun's majority opinion, the court discusses the historical and legal background of abortion, paying special attention to the interest of the state in protecting the health and welfare of individuals. The court does not agree that women have an absolute right to terminate pregnancies, but rules that in the first trimester (three months of pregnancy) women can legally choose to seek an abortion. After the first trimester, however, it is appropriate for the states to intervene to regulate access and conditions. Note the total absence of feminist rhetoric such as women's right to control their own bodies in the reasoning: the decision turns on the right of privacy, and especially the confidentiality of the doctor-patient relationship. Like birth control, abortion is treated as a medical, not a feminist, issue.

Roe v. *Wade* remains one of the most controversial Supreme Court decisions ever handed down. It provoked a Right to Life movement that seeks to overturn the liberalization of abortion laws either in the states or by constitutional amendment. The issue has become so hotly polarized, both among the public at large and in legal and medical circles, that the future of abortion in the United States remains in doubt.

Source: Roe et al. v. *Wade, District Attorney of Dallas County,* 410 U.S. 113 (1973), pp. 116–117, 147–152, 162–166. Notes have been omitted.

MR. JUSTICE BLACKMUN delivered the opinion of the Court.

This Texas federal appeal and its Georgia companion, *Doe* v. *Bolton, post,* p. 179, present constitutional challenges to state criminal abortion legislation. The Texas statutes under attack here are typical of those that have been in effect in many States for approximately a century. The Georgia statutes, in contrast, have a modern cast and are a legislative product that, to an extent at least, obviously reflects the influences of recent attitudinal change, of advancing medical knowledge and techniques, and of new thinking about an old issue.

We forthwith acknowledge our awareness of the sensitive and emotional nature of the abortion controversy, of the vigorous opposing views, even among physicians, and of the deep and seemingly absolute convictions that the subject inspires. One's philosophy, one's experiences, one's exposure to the raw edges of human existence, one's religious training, one's attitudes toward life and family and their values, and the moral standards one establishes and seeks to observe, are all likely to influence and to color one's thinking and conclusions about abortion.

In addition, population growth, pollution, poverty, and racial overtones tend to complicate and not to simplify the problem.

Our task, of course, is to resolve the issue by constitutional measurement, free of emotion and of predilection. We seek earnestly to do this, and, because we do, we have inquired into, and in this opinion place some emphasis upon, medical and medical-legal history and what that history reveals about man's attitudes toward the abortion procedure over the centuries. We bear in mind, too, Mr. Justice Holmes' admonition in his now-vindicated dissent in *Lochner* v. *New York,* 198 U.S. 45, 76 (1905):

> "[The Constitution] is made for people of fundamentally differing views, and the accident of our finding certain opinions natural and familiar or novel and even shocking ought not to conclude our judgment upon the question whether statutes embodying them conflict with the Constitution of the United States." . . .

Three reasons have been advanced to explain historically the enactment of criminal abortion laws in the 19th century and to justify their continued existence.

It has been argued occasionally that these laws were the product of a Victorian social concern to discourage illicit sexual conduct. Texas, however, does not advance this justification in the present case, and it appears that no court or commentator has taken the argument seriously. The appellants and *amici* contend, moreover, that this is not a proper state purpose at all and suggest that, if it were, the Texas statutes are overbroad in protecting it since the law fails to distinguish between married and unwed mothers.

A second reason is concerned with abortion as a medical procedure. When most criminal abortion laws were first enacted, the procedure was a hazardous one for the woman. This was particularly true prior to the development of antisepsis. Antiseptic techniques, of course, were based on discoveries by Lister,

Pasteur, and others first announced in 1867, but were not generally accepted and employed until about the turn of the century. Abortion mortality was high. Even after 1900, and perhaps until as late as the development of antibiotics in the 1940's, standard modern techniques such as dilation and curettage were not nearly so safe as they are today. Thus, it has been argued that a State's real concern in enacting a criminal abortion law was to protect the pregnant woman, that is, to restrain her from submitting to a procedure that placed her life in serious jeopardy.

Modern medical techniques have altered this situation. Appellants and various *amici* refer to medical data indicating that abortion in early pregnancy, that is, prior to the end of the first trimester, although not without its risk, is now relatively safe. Mortality rates for women undergoing early abortions, where the procedure is legal, appear to be as low as or lower than the rates for normal childbirth. Consequently, any interest of the State in protecting the woman from an inherently hazardous procedure, except when it would be equally dangerous for her to forgo it, has largely disappeared. Of course, important state interests in the area of health and medical standards do remain. The State has a legitimate interest in seeing to it that abortion, like any other medical procedure, is performed under circumstances that insure maximum safety for the patient. This interest obviously extends at least to the performing physician and his staff, to the facilities involved, to the availability of aftercare, and to adequate provision for any complication or emergency that might arise. The prevalence of high mortality rates at illegal "abortion mills" strengthens, rather than weakens, the State's interest in regulating the conditions under which abortions are performed. Moreover, the risk to the woman increases as her pregnancy continues. Thus, the State retains a definite interest in protecting the woman's own health and safety when an abortion is proposed at a late stage of pregnancy.

The third reason is the State's interest—some phrase it in terms of duty—in protecting prenatal life. Some of the argument for this justification rests on the theory that a new human life is present from the moment of conception. The State's interest and general obligation to protect life then extends, it is argued, to prenatal life. Only when the life of the pregnant mother herself is at stake, balanced against the life she carries within her, should the interest of the embryo or fetus not prevail. Logically, of course, a legitimate state interest in this area need not stand or fall on acceptance of the belief that life begins at conception or at some other point prior to live birth. In assessing the State's interest, recognition may be given to the less rigid claim that as long as at least *potential* life is involved, the State may assert interests beyond the protection of the pregnant woman alone.

Parties challenging state abortion laws have sharply disputed in some courts the contention that a purpose of these laws, when enacted, was to protect prenatal life. Pointing to the absence of legislative history to support the contention, they claim that most state laws were designed solely to protect the woman. Because medical advances have lessened this concern, at least with respect to abortion in early pregnancy, they argue that with respect to such abortions the laws can no longer be justified by any state interest. There is some scholarly support for this view of original purpose. The few state courts called upon to interpret their laws in the late 19th and early 20th centuries did focus on the State's interest in protecting the woman's health rather than in preserving the embryo and fetus. Proponents of this view point out that in many States, including Texas, by statute or judicial interpretation, the pregnant woman herself could not be prosecuted for self-abortion or for cooperating in an abortion performed upon her by another. They claim that adoption of the "quickening" distinction through received common law and state statutes tacitly recognizes the greater health hazards inherent in late abortion and impliedly repudiates the theory that life begins at conception.

It is with these interests, and the weight to be attached to them, that this case is concerned. . . .

In view of all this, we do not agree that, by adopting one theory of life, Texas may override the rights of the pregnant woman that are at stake. We repeat, however that the State does have an important and legitimate interest in preserving and protecting the health of the pregnant woman, whether she be a resident of the State or a nonresident who seeks medical consultation and treatment there, and that it has still *another* important and legitimate interest in protecting the potentiality of human life. These interests are separate and distinct. Each grows in substantiality as the woman approaches term and, at a point during pregnancy, each becomes "compelling."

With respect to the State's important and legitimate interest in the health of the mother, the "compelling" point, in the light of present medical knowledge, is at approximately the end of the first trimester. This is so because of the now-established medical fact, referred to above at 149, that until the end of the first trimester mortality in abortion may be less than mortality in normal childbirth. It follows that, from and after this point, a State may regulate the abortion procedure to the extent that the regulation reasonably relates to the preservation and protection of maternal health. Examples of permissible state regulation in this area are requirements as to the qualifications of the person who is to perform the abortion; as to the licensure of that person; as to the facility in which the procedure is to be performed, that is, whether it must be a hospital or may be a clinic or some other place of less-than-hospital status; as to the licensing of the facility; and the like.

This means, on the other hand, that, for the period of pregnancy prior to this "compelling" point, the attending physician, in consultation with his patient, is free to determine, without regulation by the State, that, in his medical judgment, the patient's pregnancy should be terminated. If that decision is reached, the judgment may be effectuated by an abortion free of interference by the State.

With respect to the State's important and legitimate interest in potential life, the "compelling" point is at viability. This is so because the fetus then presumably has the capability of meaningful life outside the mother's womb. State regulation protective of fetal life after viability thus has both logical and biological justifications. If the State is interested in protecting fetal life after viability, it may go so far as to proscribe abortion during that period, except when it is necessary to preserve the life or health of the mother.

Measured against these standards, Art. 1196 of the Texas Penal Code, in restricting legal abortions to those "procured or attempted by medical advice for the purpose of saving the life of the mother," sweeps too broadly. That statute makes no distinction between abortions performed early in pregnancy and those performed later and it limits to a single reason, "saving" the mother's life, the legal justification for the procedure. The statute, therefore, cannot survive the constitutional attack made upon it here. . . .

To summarize and to repeat:

1. A state criminal abortion statute of the current Texas type, that excepts from criminality only a *life-saving* procedure on behalf of the mother, without regard to pregnancy stage and without recognition of the other interests involved, is violative of the Due Process Clause of the Fourteenth Amendment.

(a) For the stage prior to approximately the end of the first trimester, the abortion decision and its effectuation must be left to the medical judgment of the pregnant woman's attending physician.

(b) For the stage subsequent to approximately the end of the first trimester, the State, in promoting its interest in the health of the mother, may, if it chooses, regulate the abortion procedure in ways that are reasonably related to maternal health.

(c) For the stage subsequent to viability, the State in promoting its interest in the potentiality of human life may, if it chooses, regulate, and even proscribe, abortion except where it is necessary, in appropriate medical judgment, for the preservation of the life or health of the mother.

2. The State may define the term "physician," as it has been employed in the preceding numbered paragraphs of this Part XI of this opinion, to mean only a physician currently licensed by the State, and may proscribe any abortion by a person who is not a physician as so defined. . . .

This holding, we feel, is consistent with the relative weights of the respective interests involved, with the lessons and examples of medical and legal history, with the lenity of the common law, and with the demands of the profound problems of the present day. The decision leaves the State free to place increasing restrictions on abortion as the period of pregnancy lengthens, so long as those restrictions are tailored to the recognized state interests. The decision vindicates the right of the physician to administer medical treatment according to his professional judgment up to the points where important state interests provide compelling justifications for intervention. Up to those points, the abortion decision in all its aspects is inherently, and primarily, a medical decision and basic responsibility for it must rest with the physician. If an individual practitioner abuses the privilege of exercising proper medical judgment, the usual remedies, judicial and intraprofessional, are available.

Coming Out

Margaret Cruikshank

Gay liberation developed in the supportive climate of the 1960s and 1970s. Because many gay Americans still find it necessary to conceal their sexual preference, there are no totally reliable figures on the numbers of homosexuals and lesbians in the population at large. Figures from the late 1970s suggested that 13.95 percent of males and 4.25 percent of females had extensive homosexual experience; one out of five women had had some overt lesbian experience since puberty. The Kinsey Institute for Sex Research thus concluded in 1977 that "a significant percentage of the American population is predominantly homosexual in its sexual and affectional preference."

The late 1960s and early 1970s did not create an increase in homosexuality: what the period did was to provide a personal and political climate for many gay men and women to recognize and accept their sexual orientation. This process is known as *coming out*. It encompasses the struggle to tell your friends and parents about your sexual orientation and to challenge the homophobia that discriminates against gays in our society. On a more personal level, it means the end of silence, both personal and political, an acceptance of one's self. As one woman asserted, "Coming out to me is much more than expressing another sexual preference. It is finding and developing a whole self-identity and then becoming comfortable with it."

For women, it made a big difference whether they came out before or after the advent of the women's movement. Women who identified as lesbians before the mid-1960s often conceptualized their sexual preference in terms of women physically loving women; after 1970, lesbianism could be seen in the wider political context of feminist ideology. This autobiographical story by Margaret Cruikshank entitled "Is This the Reward of a Catholic Girlhood?" describes her own growing awareness of her sexual preference. As she reminds us, there is not always a "happy" or simple or even feminist ending to these personal and political journeys.

Source: Margaret Cruikshank, "Is This the Reward of a Catholic Girlhood?" This essay originally appeared in *The Coming Out Stories,* edited by Julia Stanley and Susan Wolfe (Watertown: Persephone Press, 1980), pp. 31–35. Reprinted by permission of Margaret Cruikshank.

My coming out story is unexciting. If I were to fictionalize it, I would make it sexier and funnier, and assign myself a younger age than 26 and a less staid personality. The other woman, Mary, could keep her real age of 23; that's a good age for coming out.

I met her a few months before her 23rd birthday in a literary criticism class at the midwestern Jesuit school where we were both graduate students who had National Defense Education Act grants to get Ph.D.'s. Our educations contributed nothing to the national defense, of course; and it was certainly not the intention of the male bureaucrats at H.E.W. to bring young lesbians out of the provinces and into big cities, where they could meet, fall in love, and oppose the Vietnam war together. Left in the small towns where we grew up and dependent only on private enterprise, Mary and I might never have felt free enough to love each other, or any other woman. From my failures to care deeply about a man, I would have concluded that I was not a caring person or someone who belonged in an intimate relationship.

That at least was my suspicion after an experience with a man in 1965, several months before I met Mary and got her to stop sitting in the front row of lit. crit. class like a pious Catholic schoolgirl and to sit with sloppy indifference next to me in the last row. A male friend from my hometown, whom I had met at the Graduate Record Exam (I hope young lesbians are finding each other these days at the GRE), called to announce that he had that day passed his doctoral comprehensives and could now attend to other business—would I marry him? Confused as I was about love, men, and my future, I saw at once that there was something ludicrous about putting emotional life second to intellectual life. But what to say? I didn't love him, but I knew women were supposed to want marriage. Why didn't I? Awkwardness was the main emotion I felt. As potential mates, John and I had lumbered along in a way that reminded me of the Herbert Spencer-George Eliot romance; and, ironically, his dissertation was to be on Spencer, mine on Eliot. I said on the phone that I would send my answer by mail. I remember going to the library to do the letter, probably because I felt safe in libraries and no doubt also because the letter would be like an assignment. With a directness and honesty I hardly ever attained in those days, I told John that I couldn't marry him because I was not physically attracted to him. Thinking of the letter today I feel frustrated because, although I had correctly diagnosed the problem with that relationship, I was blind to the implications of the letter, which seem so obvious now: 1) no man would be sexually attractive to me, except in a casual/temporary way; and 2) I was attracted to women.

Not understanding these crucial facts about myself in 1965, I had no expectation at all, when I began to spend time with Mary, that I could love her. How could I have been so ignorant of this possibility, I wonder now, when two years before the call from John, one of my roommates had fallen in love with me. I obviously couldn't connect one experience with a woman to another. I was attracted to Karla, the roommate, an Irish Catholic from Iowa with a background much like mine. I remember walking by myself one day and getting a thunderous message from my brain *she loves me* which made me stop suddenly as I was crossing the street. But my attention was focused so much on her dilemma (poor Karla—what a rotten thing to happen to her) that I never asked myself what *my* response might be or thought in any general way about women loving women. Soon I had persuaded myself that I was crazed from studying too much—Karla didn't love me. But one night she came to my room late at night, sat on my floor, and looking very embarrassed she said that Marge, the third woman in our apartment, had been making fun of her for loving me. She hoped I would not be angry with her. I wasn't, but I couldn't have been very sensitive, either. All I remember is that our conversation was short and awkward. In the days that followed, although I did not feel love for Karla, I did want some physical contact with her, but I was too inhibited to touch her. One night we got a little drunk together and sat next to each other on the living room couch with our arms around each other. Marge, who was with us but sober, said: "Goddamned lesbians!" I remember thinking, smugly, No, absurd, if we were goddamned lesbians we would have to be doing this in some secret place; we couldn't be hugging right out here in the living room in the presence of another person. This spectacularly false assumption was one I suppose I had to accept: to question it would have led me to uncomfortable thoughts about the significance of all my attachments to women.

The early weeks of close friendship with Mary gave me no clues about what was to follow. We tossed a football around in the park, hung upside down from the jungle gym, and studied hard. After our long talks late at night, I'd walk her back to her apartment and then she'd walk me back to mine. That pattern should have been a clue. The first Superbowl was also her birthday. We watched together in high spirits and then our friends came for a surprise party. I had never liked a woman well enough to plan a party for her, and no one had ever given a party for Mary. Those clues were lost on us, too. Although she asked me to move in with her when her roommate left, we were so far from knowing what was happening between us that we invited a third woman to share the small apartment with us.

Within a month after the move, I realized I cared for Mary very much, but had no idea that my feelings were the appropriate ones for the beginning of a love relationship. I took my two new roommates to a Clancy brothers' concert on St. Patrick's Day, and during the concert I held Mary's hand in the dark. I had never had that experience before. The raucous Clancy's must have loosened me up. Later that evening as Mary and I were taking off our coats in our big walk-in closet, we stood for a long time with our arms around each other. I felt scared and excited at the same time. Hugging a woman through her winter coat is not very satisfying, I now realize, but for someone like me who had hardly ever been able to touch another woman (or a man or a child), this closet cuddling was a great step forward. One night not long after St. Pat's I was sick in bed. Mary sat for a long time on the edge of my bed and then kissed me on the neck (I think she was aiming for my cheek) and ran out of my bedroom. I was overwhelmed. This was even more exciting than holding her hand or feeling her coat. I wanted to be kissed again but was too shy to say so or to kiss her. But one night when she was reading I sat on the floor at her feet and leaned against the chair she was sitting in. She lifted me into the chair with her and we kissed and laughed for about four hours. That we both liked prolonged physical contact was a great discovery. We must have known vaguely that we were doing a forbidden thing, but whatever guilt we bore did not keep us from doing what felt good. We had both had such repulsively successful careers as Catholic schoolgirls and devout young women that we ought to have been guilt-ridden, but somehow we escaped the tortures of a bad conscience. In all their vivid descriptions of the sinful, secular, atheistical world into which they were reluctantly sending us, those of us not good enough to want to imitate them and become nuns, our teachers never mentioned that feeling sexual attraction for another woman was an abomination. At Mary's college, the "mulier fortis" was much lauded (the valiant woman), and at my school, her counterpart was the "dynamic Christian woman." But we were never told that a mulier fortis must refrain from passionately kissing a dynamic Christian woman. Maybe that's why the *sin* button didn't flash red the night I sat in Mary's lap kissing her and knowing that I loved her.

The rest came only gradually. Once when we were doing our Beowulf lesson together, while sitting on the floor not too close to each other, we began to kiss and somehow got wound around each other on the couch, neither of us sure what to do with our bodies. Mary knew enough the next time to touch me with her hand, and I was amazed by the pleasure she could give me. But I was too frightened and self-conscious to touch her until two weeks later when she came home late one night and demanded that pleasure for herself. I was too surprised to refuse (she was not at all a demanding person). After that, our lovemaking was less inhibited, although often furtive, because of the third woman in our one-bedroom apartment. Luckily she taught an early morning class. As soon as she walked out the door, I would bounce on her bed on my way into Mary's bed. Those were exuberant mornings, and it pleases me to recall that we got the highest grades on the Beowulf exam, too.

We lived together very happily for three years, the last two in our own apartment. During summer vacations we had wonderful times traveling in Mary's Volkswagen. We saw the iron mines in northern Minnesota and walked around on Isle Royale, and watched the Little League world series in Pennsylvania. We got thrown out of a pet cemetery for laughing at the inscriptions on the tombstones, and another time we were stranded in a small town in Scotland and had to sleep in the local jail.

During the school terms we helped each other with teaching (we had the same classes) and with studying. I might not have been able to write a dissertation without Mary's constant reassurances and good suggestions. And for six terrible weeks in 1969 when I was fighting with my department over my dissertation, she plotted my strategy with great cunning, helped me figure out the moves against me, and once when I cracked and decided to go right to the chairman's office and curse him, she literally barred the door and kept me home. She even stood at my side for 2-1/2 hours while I xeroxed the required number of copies of my dissertation for the men who were to sit in judgment of it.

Those days were idyllic. Neither of us pretended to be looking for men to fulfill us. And yet we did not see ourselves as lesbians—the word had vile connotations—as women who had made a conscious choice of a woman to love. I told myself that the person I loved happened to be a woman, and she must have said the same thing to herself. In any case, we had no conversations about lesbians or lesbianism. Perhaps in our happy state we felt no need to reflect on our coming together. As survivors of unhappy families, we must have been relieved and constantly delighted to find ourselves always happy. It would have seemed unnatural, surely, to live together for three years and never mention that we were English teachers or that we loved literature. But a far more basic fact about ourselves (or at least about me), emotional and sexual identity, went unmentioned.

I wish I could end this story on a good lesbian feminist note—perhaps this can't be a *real* coming out story without a good lesbian feminist conclusion. Such as: Peg and Mary discover that they are lesbians, rejoice in the discovery, drive off into the setting sun in the little blue VW, certain to grow more deeply attached to each other, thanks to their raised consciousnesses, and to continue their relationship for many years. Before the discovery and the rejoicing, unfortunately, we separated, without pain, partly because we could not get jobs in the same town and partly because we were ready for a change. But I'm afraid that we separated not really knowing that a female couple could stay together indefinitely, or even that we had in fact been a couple. We had experienced something for which we had no room in our imaginations—an alternative to marriage, a way of living ideally suited to us.

Sex and Sports

Mariah Burton Nelson

Basketball, softball, swimming, tennis, golf—you name the sport, and women love to play it, and play it well. But in very few sports is there gender parity, either on the collegiate or professional level, despite federal laws like the 1972 Title IX of the Civil Rights Act, which forbids gender discrimination in federally funded educational institutions. In 1977 Title IX was extended to cover discrimination in intercollegiate sports. While there have been important breakthroughs for women and girls in organized athletics, they still lag behind men and boys. In

1991 women made up more than half the student population but only one-third of college athletes; women received less than a quarter of athletic budgets and even less for scholarships and recruitment.

Sports may be an American obsession, but once again the focus is on men. One study found that 92 percent of televised sports coverage focused on men, with only 5 percent on women. In newspapers, 81 percent of the coverage was of men's sports and only 3.5 percent of women. Nationwide only 8 percent of sportscasters and broadcasters are female.

One of the most pernicious ways of discouraging women from participating in sports is by implying that there is something unfeminine or sexually deviant about women athletes. Of course, some athletes are gay, but many are not. This stigma of lesbianism is so strong that many female athletes who are gay, especially professionals, remain in the closet for fear of losing sponsors or damaging the image of their sport with the public.

Mariah Burton Nelson's story of being fired from the Women's Pro Basketball League for being a lesbian shows the intersection of sexuality and sports. Unlike male college stars who can plan on careers in professional sports, the former captain of Stanford's women's basketball team had a hard time making a living at the sport she loved. Her openness about her sexual orientation made it even tougher. After her basketball career was summarily ended by homophobia, she wrote several hardhitting books about gender and sports, including *The Stronger Women Get, The More Men Love Football* (1994).

The story of how I got fired from the Women's Pro Basketball League for being a lesbian—which is akin to being fired from the National Basketball League for being black—is the most lucrative and least known story of my athletic career. Lucrative because an earlier version of it was purchased twice: first by what was then called *Women's Sports* magazine, then by *Ms.* magazine. Least known because both magazines "killed" it, citing fears that advertisers would jump ship if the magazines deigned to mention lesbians.

I'll begin the story at the end, or near the end, of my brief stint as a pro basketball player. At San Francisco's Civic Center Plaza, in the summer of 1979, I felt the binocular burn of two eyes staring at me and turned to see who it might be.

There were a lot of possibilities. I was standing among 200,000 other people. The Gay Pride Parade had just marched peacefully through San Francisco, and now we were gathered at Civic Center Plaza to listen to music, hear speeches, and express sorrow and outrage at the recent murder of supervisor Harvey Milk. I was standing to the left of the stage, swaying happily to the

Source: Mariah Burton Nelson, "Paid to Play a Game." © 1994 by Mariah Burton Nelson. Reprinted by permission of the author. First appeared in Susan Fox Rogers, ed., *Sportsdykes: Stories from On and Off the Field* (New York: St. Martin's Press, 1994), pp. 87–94.

music of Linda Tillery. Turning, I scanned the crowd for familiar faces. Finally, I saw on a raised media platform, a television reporter who knew me, and waved weakly. My career as a professional athlete flashed before my eyes.

Just a week or two before, the reporter had interviewed me for a television spot about professional women. In 1979, even female lawyers and bankers were newsworthy, but as a female pro basketball player I was a particular anomaly. During the interview, the reporter posed some antagonistic questions typical of that era (and, unfortunately, still typical of this era): Does playing basketball threaten your femininity? Do you have a boyfriend? Do the men in your life approve of your playing basketball?

"No, basketball doesn't threaten my femininity," I told him, adding pointedly, "but it does seem to threaten some men." I was young (twenty-three), angry, and emboldened by the lesbian and feminist environment in which I had come of age. To the question about male approval I said curtly, "All of my friends approve of my playing basketball or they wouldn't be my friends."

I didn't come out to him because I hadn't come out to my coach on the San Francisco Pioneers, and didn't intend to. The coach had clued me in by telling me our uniforms were made by "a bunch of faggots." He also insisted on calling us girls, though we asked to be called women. "This is a business, not a women's lib thing," he said bluntly. Later in the season, at a home game, a group from Berkeley unfurled a large banner reading "Lesbians Against Police Violence"; the security guards made them take it down. All of the owners and coaches in the Women's Pro Basketball League were men. Evidently it was *not* a women's lib thing.

But Gay Day had become a four-year tradition I was not willing to forego. When, at nineteen, I came out of the closet, I came roaring out, waving banners and carrying torches and making a spectacle of myself. Within months of beginning a relationship with Stephanie, a basketball teammate, I was speaking to high school classes about the joys of being a lesbian. Stephanie founded a Gay Counseling Center on campus. None of this seemed to bother our Stanford coaches, who let us room together on road trips, or our teammates, many of whom, one-by-one and two-by-two, came out themselves.

The gay liberation movement was in its pre-AIDS, giddy, innocent infancy. Anita Bryant had lambasted homosexuals but we lambasted back until the orange juice company dropped her as a spokesperson and she retracted her homophobic comments. The Briggs Initiative proposed firing all of California's gay teachers as well as straight teachers who publicly supported gay colleagues; voters defeated the bill.

I devoured books: *Rubyfruit Jungle, Sappho Was a Right-On Woman.* I discovered, preserved on microfilm at the Stanford library, issues of *The Ladder,* the lesbian newspaper from the fifties, and made it the subject of a paper for a women's history class.

Feminism, even more than the gay movement, validated my life-long observations and my rage. With great glee I read books by Robin Morgan, Toni

Morrison, Marge Piercy, and Susan Brownmiller. I joined a consciousness-raising group. I helped organize a women's film festival and taught a course called Women and Body Image.

On my embroidered jeans jacket one button proclaimed, "A Woman Without a Man Is Like a Fish Without a Bicycle," another said, "Teenage Lesbian," and a third, a small red one, announced: "I'm menstruating."

In these heady days it seemed natural to me that sports teams—groups of strong women who enjoy their own bodies and each other's—would provide an outlet for my feelings of empowerment and love for women. In high school, I had played on a predominantly lesbian basketball team that traveled throughout the southwest. During one car caravan from Phoenix to Gallup, New Mexico, the VW bug I was riding in repeatedly played just one cassette tape: Helen Reddy's "I Am Woman."

For three years at Stanford I was the team captain, and its leading scorer and rebounder. I felt loved and respected, almost revered. In my bedroom I hung a poster that showed women swimming, running, and cycling. "Women in Sports," it said: "We Can."

Yet even before that fateful Gay Pride Day, I had been rudely awakened to the fact that women's sports were not always the lesbian/feminist mecca I wanted them to be. At a summer basketball camp during college I had been the victim of a witch hunt. A group of fourteen-year-old campers accused dozens of counselors of lesbian atrocities, primarily public kissing and fondling. My alleged crime was showering with another counselor. There were details: I had supposedly spread soap suds all over her body. It sounded like fun, but inappropriate, and I didn't do it. I was horrified at having to explain to the camp directors that, though I was gay, I had not committed the crime. To their credit, the directors—themselves closeted lesbians—ultimately gathered all the campers and counselors and lectured them sternly: "If you're going to be in sports, you're going to have to learn to get along with lesbians."

After Stanford I was drafted by the New Jersey Gems of the fledgling (and short-lived) Women's Pro Basketball League, and also by le C.U.C. (pronounced "Le Kook"), a French pro team that traveled throughout Europe. Let's see: France or New Jersey? The decision was not difficult.

But in France I discovered, much to my horror, that I was not the best basketball player in the world. The fall from Stanford star to foreign sub was a steep, miserable descent. Because of a quirk in the French rules, once I was designated backup center I was not even allowed to dress for about half of the games. I'd watch glumly from the bleachers, adding a sad, self-pitying voice to the singsong cheers: *"Allez, les filles."* (Go, girls.) My teammates began to resent my relatively high paycheck, and told me so. I further offended them by not shaving my legs, not eating meat, and not drinking wine. To make matters worse, the woman I fell in love with—the starting center—informed me that she was in love with me too, but Jesus would not approve. She then refused to speak to me.

Eight months later, when I arrived back in the States, the New Jersey Gems still "owned the rights" to me—meaning I could not play for any other pro team until they sold those rights. I agreed to play the last third of the season with them on the condition that I be traded to San Francisco the following year.

In New Jersey I began to recover my athletic self-esteem. Yet my last paycheck—for $1000—bounced. And the gay players would not talk openly. When I asked, two specifically denied their relationship, making me feel slightly crazy as well as angry and isolated.

So it had dawned on me that the "real world" was not going to embrace me as lovingly as idyllic Stanford had. When I saw the television reporter, and saw that he'd seen me, it occurred to me to call him up and ask him not to tell my coach that I'd been at Gay Pride Day. But the contradiction of showing up at Gay Pride Day, then diving into the closet was too great, so I didn't call.

Three weeks into the regular season, I was fired. (They call it being put on waivers, which means that another team is free to buy your contract, but basically you're out of a job.)

"Why?" I asked the coach. I was shocked. I had been playing with confidence, and had expected to start at center.

He looked surprised. "You're not tall enough," he said after a moment's thought.

I stared at him incredulously. "I'm the tallest person on the team!" I protested. Two teammates were exactly my height; no one on the team was taller.

"Oh. Then you're not quick enough," he said lamely.

I learned from a teammate who was close to the coach that the reporter had indeed told the owner of the Pioneers (I never quite got used to calling him "my owner") about my appearance at Gay Pride Day. I had not mentioned the incident to the player, and she had no other way of knowing about it. She responded to me sympathetically but made a mad dash for the closet herself, immediately introducing a "fiancé" to the team.

About half of my teammates, I estimate (including the two tall ones), and at least half of the players in the league were gay. But no others were politically active.

One gay friend was fired along with me; I think they thought we were lovers. When the two of us walked out of the gym that day, into the unusually bright San Francisco sunshine, I was in a stupor. My friend led me to a cafe, where she alternately told chatty, cheerful stories and ranted against the stupidity of our coach. She was already in graduate school, and was to some extent relieved at the prospect of not spending so much time in gyms. She hadn't been enjoying the serious, stifling atmosphere of the professional sports scene. She didn't particularly mind an early departure.

I was devastated. I had thought I'd play in the U.S. pros for at least a year or two, and had given up a shot at the Olympic team with that in mind. I clung to the same dream that led so many naive young women to postpone other careers and to accept bad coaching and bounced checks during that three-year life of the WBL: continuing to play the game we so loved. France had been a disappointment, New Jersey a brief redemption. I wanted more. A Stanford graduate with a psychology degree, I nevertheless had no other career plans.

For three days, I lay in my bed in shock. I was unable to move, unable to feel. I didn't cry. I just lay there. Teammates kindly came by to visit, and for them I lugubriously hauled myself out of bed and into the living room, where I thudded into a beanbag chair. They treated me as if somebody had died.

Two local feminist newspapers learned of the firing but I refused to talk to them, fearing further repercussions. Though I hated the idea of being closeted, my passion for basketball temporarily won out.

Finally my agent called: the California Dreams, of Los Angeles, had invited me to try out. I didn't feel particularly excited. Still depressed, I did not want to move to smoggy L.A. After almost a year in France and New Jersey, I wanted to be home, and because of Stanford, home had become the San Francisco Bay Area. Nevertheless, this opportunity was knocking, and no one else was at the door.

Relinquishing a then-precious symbol of feminism, I bought a razor and shaved my legs. This token attempt at conformity failed when, at the first day of practice with the Dreams, an old friend called across the gym: "I can't believe you shaved your legs!"

Almost immediately, the Dreams sent us to John Robert Powers Charm School. Their intention, of course, was to teach us to portray a feminine (that is, heterosexual) image. Leg-shaving I could do; charm school I could not, so I quietly boycotted, but my teammates reported that they learned such useful skills as how to walk upstairs sideways.

Then, just when I was getting used to the idea of living in L.A., the coach arrived at my door and asked to speak to me alone. I was sharing the apartment with other players, so I invited him into my bedroom. There we sat stiffly on the twin beds, facing each other. "I'm sorry to tell you this," he said kindly, "but we've traded you to the Dallas Diamonds."

"Why?" I asked.

He explained that they needed to let go of one center, and the others had no-cut, no-trade contracts. "I'm sorry," he said again.

I stared at him dumbly. I did not want to go to Dallas. With no warning, all the tears I'd held back in France, and New Jersey, and San Francisco, came pouring out. Great, heaving sobs shook my body, and when I tried to speak, the words were muffled through uncontrollable gasps. Uncomfortable, naturally, the coach stayed with me, not touching me or trying to comfort me, which would have only heightened my embarrassment, but simply sitting on the opposite bed, listening. Thankful for his kindness, I tried to explain that my tears weren't really about these particular California Dreams—they were about a larger dream, and larger losses, and a simple desire to be home. I wanted to tell him more—about the woman I'd loved in France, the Gay Pride Day, the "faggot" remark. This desire to talk to someone—even a man I'd only known for a few weeks—made me realize that I was terribly lonely.

But once I regained my composure, I agreed to go to Dallas. Homesickness and loneliness aside, I still had that dream. "What the heck," I told the coach, drying my face and beginning to laugh at my outburst, "It'll be an adventure."

In Dallas I shared a two-bedroom apartment with Michelle and Valerie, who knitted, watched a lot of television, ate Spaghetti-O's, and carried Bibles in their gym bags. One of them generously offered me what had been her bedroom. "Valerie and I will sleep together until you find your own place," she told me.

I believed that ruse until I woke up in the middle of the first night freezing. It was November in Dallas—cold—and the bed was made with just one thin blanket. Clearly no one had slept in it for months.

The Diamonds wanted me to stay but didn't want to pay my moving expenses. Instead of sending me to San Francisco to get my things, they wanted me to wait until we flew there for a game two months hence. I was still living out of the gym bag I'd brought to Los Angeles nearly a month before. Rather than turn the matter over to my agent, I pointed out to the owner that under the terms of the contract, the Diamonds were obligated to pay the expenses. He then put me on waivers, explaining that I was "too aggressive off the court."

And so it was that my life as a professional athlete ignominiously came to an end. This time there were no tears. I felt as if I had been released from bondage. My agent soon informed me that the New Orleans team was interested, but I told her that I wasn't. I had run out of tolerance for men who called us girls, for ignorant reporters, for gay teammates who hid behind Bibles, for coaches and owners who seemed threatened by outspoken women. Also, after years of jumping, running, and pivoting, my knees were very sore and, as it turns out, permanently damaged. On the flight home to San Francisco from Dallas, I promised my knees I would quit. Then, as I began to imagine life beyond basketball, my spirits began to lift.

For one season I coached the junior varsity at a local high school, a job I enjoyed tremendously, but the varsity coach, herself a lesbian, made it a condition of employment that I not come out to the girls. A college coach—yet another closeted lesbian—invited me to interview with her after that, but I declined.

I turned instead to writing—a lifelong dream predating basketball—where, as in the case of the two "killed" versions of this story, I still sometimes feel stifled by homophobes. But publishers are increasingly making way for the voices of openly lesbian authors, and in my books I've been able to integrate my passions for women's sports, for women's rights, and for women. I was also recently hired to coach high school girls basketball, which makes me one of the first openly lesbian coaches in the country. I hope to write a book about that too. It's become clear to me that sport, with its physical empowerment and lesbian potential, is an inherently feminist act. Another feminist act is telling the truth. I'm doing my best to combine the two.

Women and AIDS

Lisa Tiger

By the turn of the century, half of new AIDS cases will be women. As Mary Fisher, the daughter of a prominent Republican fundraiser who contracted the virus from her former husband, told the Republican National Convention (and a national television audience) in 1992, "If you believe you are safe, you are at risk." While many women who contract the virus will get it from intravenous drug use, the numbers who are affected through heterosexual intercourse are rising. Women are especially vulnerable to heterosexual transmission of the disease, from risky male sex partners and also because it is easier for the virus to enter the body through mucuous tissues such as the vagina. Even when women become HIV-positive, health care providers often fail to spot the early symptoms, assuming, incorrectly, that AIDS still primarily affects men. And as more women become infected, so do children, because the AIDS virus can be passed from mother to child during pregnancy.

In 1988, when she contracted the virus, Lisa Tiger had thought she was not at risk. AIDS was something on the East Coast or West, not in Muskogee, Oklahoma. Over the past seven years, she had had only two relationships, both long-term, and both, she thought, monogamous. But one of her boyfriends was bisexual, and that was how she contracted the virus. After she learned that she was HIV-positive in 1992, she used her own example to give a human face to AIDS, lecturing widely in Oklahoma and the country. Her special concern was AIDS and Native Americans.

Lisa Tiger, a member of the Muscogee Nation and of Creek, Seminole, and Cherokee descent, was born in 1965. Her father, who committed suicide when she was two years old, was Jerome Tiger, a nationally respected Native American artist. In her late teens and early twenties, she worked in the art company her mother founded after her father's death and struggled to overcome an alcohol problem. She had just started college when she learned she was HIV-positive. As this selection describes, her AIDS activism is intimately linked with her identity as a Native American—promoting and preserving this heritage is Lisa Tiger's mission.

Source: Lisa Tiger, "Woman Who Clears the Way," in Barbara Findlen, ed., *Listen Up: Voices from the Next Feminist Generation* (Seattle: The Seal Press, 1995), pp. 192, 199–200, 200–201, 201–203, 204. Reprinted by permission of the publisher.

I have found my purpose. I am living out my dream. I was twenty-nine summers in 1994 and I am doing what I was meant to do.

In the spring of 1992 I was taking college classes. I was feeling a restlessness, an energy that I knew I needed to apply wholeheartedly to some sort of cause. It was driving me crazy. Over and over I asked my professor, an African American man of strong Christian beliefs, "What is my purpose? What am I here to do? I am ready."

"Lisa, you are impatient," he said. "You may not be ready. God will let you know when the time is right."

I argued, "I am ready!"

He said, "You may not even want to know. If you could look into the future and see what you will be doing, it might scare you to death. Just be patient."

A few months later I tested HIV positive and found my purpose. . . .

I am one of an ever-growing number of HIV-positive women. Women with AIDS get sick faster and die sooner than men. Women make up eleven percent of all people with AIDS in the United States, but by the end of this century most new infections will occur in women. Women do infect men, but according to recent studies, a woman is seventeen and a half times more likely to be infected by a man than a man by a woman. Yet many doctors don't associate HIV with women, so women are not encouraged to be tested. In women AIDS has different symptoms, so often women are not diagnosed early enough to benefit from early treatment. Almost all research has been done on men. After a woman tests positive for HIV, she is dealt a second blow when she learns her doctor cannot fight to prolong her life with the same knowledge that is available to treat men.

At the press conference held on July 24, 1992, I stated that I planned to take good care of my health, exercise, eat right and speak out at every opportunity for myself and others living with this virus. Soon I was being asked to speak at schools, colleges, clinics and conferences, first in Oklahoma and later throughout the nation. Now I am given an honorarium for many of my presentations and have turned over my framing and matting business to Donnie Blair, who is now my brother-in-law. Like my father, I feel very lucky to be able to make my living doing something I love to do and would do anyway. It is fortunate that I can't be fired because some of the more conservative people nearly fall out of their seats when I speak—like the administrators at the junior college where I told students that there are other ways to satisfy yourself besides having intercourse. "Try sex toys," I recommended. "A man can't satisfy you the way they can anyway."

When I talk about sex toys, sexually transmitted diseases and condoms, I see the kids sneaking looks at their teachers. Later they tell me they can't believe I talked about penises and genital warts in front of the teachers. My subjects are the same in a junior high as in a college. I get a lot of laughs when I make comments such as "You guys love your penises so much, I'd think you'd want to learn how to protect them." . . .

My message and my goals have changed, strengthened and grown since July 1992. At first I shared my own story as a way to warn others, especially Native Americans and women in general, about HIV/AIDS. Now I learn so much from the people I meet that my presentation changes from day to day and from week to week. I have come to believe it is important for us to stay within the red race when we decide to become parents because we are so few in number we could easily be gone forever. We have gifts that our people must recognize and share. We are a very spiritual people. If our religion had to be described in just one word, the word I would choose is respect, and respect could also be called spirituality. Our respect for all the gifts of the Creator can be seen in our traditional songs, our dances and the sweat lodge as well as in our medicine, which respects and treats the spirit as well as the body. . . .

One of my desires is to shake the hand of every Native American in this country—not an impossible goal, since there are only 1.8 million, and only an estimated 700,000 of us are a quarter blood or more. I share this desire with my audiences and tell them I'd appreciate it if they would help me to accomplish this goal by taking the time to shake my hand at the end of my presentation. I mentioned this to the students at Lodgegrass on the Crow Reservation. They all ran toward me, nearly crushing me against the stage. It was beautiful, especially since I had been told of their reaction before I came to Crow: One student was seen looking at my poster and backing away, saying, "Ooh, scary." . . .

In my story I believe other Native Americans can find hope for their own lives. They too know the pain of losing someone you love. Living on the reservation, they have seen plenty of death. Yet they see me as a happy person with big dreams.

As a Native American woman, I am afraid the AIDS epidemic could wipe our people out. Lots of Native Americans still don't know that AIDS has reached Indian country. But awareness of AIDS won't do any good until we know our lives are worth saving. We suffer disproportionately from murder, suicide, poverty, fatal accidents, fetal alcohol syndrome, alcoholism and drug addiction. Our young people attempt suicide in record numbers and do not fear a virus that may not show symptoms for years. The answer to AIDS will come after we have learned self-esteem. Caring enough to practice safe sex will come when we have our own heroes back.

I am also a feminist, which to me means respecting my sisters' and brothers' dreams. There should be no room for jealousy in a feminist heart. As a Native American feminist I have only to reach back to our traditional ways, before the European influence, to find a feminist culture that flourished for hundreds of years.

I think of myself as Lisa Tiger, a member of the Muscogee (Creek) Nation, and I am most comfortable when I am addressing Native American groups. I went through school without learning about a single Native American hero. I was not taught the Indian way (the Red Road) that says if you contribute and give back to the earth and your people, especially the very old and very young, you will be sustained. After decades of living with the myths made up by white male historians, we, the people of the first nations, have lost confidence in ourselves. I now find the truth and beauty of my Indian people not in books, but in sharing my story on reservations and in Native communities and receiving in return instant, deep and lasting friendships. . . .

I am not yet what I am meant to be, but I am trying. I still have dreams. I dream of reminding my people of just how beautiful they are. Of seeing my niece grow up. Of seeing an end to homophobia. Of all Indian tribes, as proud and sovereign nations, forming an alliance to preserve the health, history and culture of each and every Native American. I dream of living in a world where there is peace and respect among all races. And I dream of growing old and wise. I have a lot to live for, but I do not fear death because when it is time for me to go, I have a lot to go to.

CHAPTER 13

Conflicting Visions and Emerging Voices since the 1970s

Although the women's movement maintained the momentum associated with the sixties longer than any other group, it too had stalled by the mid-1970s. The fate of the Equal Rights Amendment was an early indication of the changing social and political climate.

After passing Congress in 1972, the proposed amendment was expected by most activists to win quick acceptance, and in fact thirty-four states ratified it between 1972 and 1974, just four short of the thirty-eight necessary for ratification. But then the momentum stopped; only one state (Indiana) ratified after 1974. Even with a three-year extension on the ratification deadline, the ERA went down to defeat on June 30, 1982. Although most of the holdouts were in the South, a notable exception was Illinois, where massive organizational efforts by feminists failed to sway the state legislature. While some states have passed their own equal rights amendments, efforts since the 1980s to revive the amendment on the national level have gone nowhere.

Conservative activist Phyllis Schlafly was a major factor in the failure to ratify the ERA. In the 1970s she took on almost singlehandedly, it seemed at times, the fight to stop the amendment, which she portrayed as a threat to women's roles as homemakers. Through such organizations as the Eagle Forum and STOP ERA, she effectively mobilized opposition in state legislatures and stalled progress on ratification. In general, once an amendment becomes controversial, it is very difficult to win ratification, since it takes only a small minority of state legislatures to block adoption. Finally, the very controversial *Roe* v. *Wade* abortion decision in 1973 linked the ERA (inaccurately) with the increasingly polarized abortion debate. As the Right to Life movement gathered momentum, it was able to mobilize sentiment against any more broad changes in women's status.

Although the suffrage amendment was successful (thank goodness) while the ERA was not, there are still many parallels between the two political mobilizations and their aftermaths. After 1982, the women's movement, like suffragists, no longer had a single goal or issue around which to rally, and it now directed its still enormous energy to a variety of issues, such as workplace conditions, sexual harassment, battered women, pay equity, reproductive rights, and pornography. But some of these issues, especially pornography, revealed deep divisions within the women's movement itself about issues of censorship and violence against women.

In another parallel to the 1920s, the political and social climate of the 1980s and 1990s was far less hospitable to social change and reform, and this profoundly affected the fortunes of feminism. The media and popular culture went out of their way to proclaim that feminism was either dead or no longer necessary. (The term *postfeminist* was often accompanied by a smirk or sigh of relief, implying the country was lucky it did not have to deal with that pesky women's movement anymore.) Journalist Susan Faludi documented this backlash in a very influential 1991 book of the same name.

A final parallel to the 1920s was the generational and ideological fault lines that appeared within feminism itself. Many younger women see no need to identify with the feminist movement at all, and those who do (the so-called "third wave feminists") are often at odds with their elders over whether current agendas overemphasize women's oppression and paint women too much as victims (of date rape, pay inequity, the beauty myth, and so forth). Instead some young feminists want to mobilize around issues of empowerment and self-actualization to counter what they see as the passivity of "victim" feminism. Another internal battle concerns those who want to promote equality between men and women versus those who celebrate women's essential differences from men (so-called *cultural feminists,* not to be confused with rightwing followers of Phyllis Schlafly who promote their own version of highly stratified gender roles). Feminism has also struggled mightily in the 1980s and 1990s with the awareness that differences among women, especially by race, class, and sexual orientation, are often as profound as the common bonds that tie women together. How to promote gender consciousness (getting women to say "we") while at the same time acknowledging difference is essential to the continued viability of feminism as a political and ideological movement.

In the 1990s public opinion polls suggest widespread popular acceptance for women's equality with men in the workplace and at home. But as sociologist Alice Rossi pointed out several decades ago, "Many people . . . espouse belief in sex equality but resist its manifestations in their personal lives," an observation that is still true today. And those who profess a commitment to equality still sometimes shun identification with feminism. The many women, young, old, and in between, who say, "I'm not a feminist, but . . ." capture this tension.

Basically, the movement for women's equality has entered a different stage. It is strong testimony to the major changes that have occurred since the 1960s that they have become so quickly accepted as normal. Young women coming of age today have access to sports programs and women's studies courses at school, have the option of being called *Ms.,* and can contemplate careers as doctors, lawyers, engineers, or carpenters. Today's women can build on the political and legislative victories won by previous generations (that is, when they are not defending them from attack from the right) and move on to new concerns. For women of all ages, many of these issues center on the balance between work and family life and relationships, especially how to combine satisfying work with the demands and joys of parenting and still get more than four hours of sleep a night.

While younger women may or may not identify with feminism, their lives, indeed the lives of most Americans, have been profoundly influenced by this far-reaching social movement. More than any other legacy, the revival of feminism in the 1960s and 1970s gave women greater freedom of choice in most aspects of their lives and removed many of the artificial barriers that prevented the realization of women's full capabilities. Even when a powerful conservative backlash stalled further breakthroughs in the 1980s, women's lives were in little danger of reverting to the patterns of the 1950s and early 1960s. Continuing the generational analogy, those of us whose consciousnesses were raised in the 1960s and 1970s are going to be around for a long time, so, to paraphrase Mark Twain, reports of the death of feminism are greatly exaggerated.

Houston, 1977

After a successful conference in Mexico City in 1975 to mark the International Year of the Woman, the United Nations designated the next ten years as the International Decade for Women. In the United States, Congresswomen Bella Abzug and Patsy Mink won a $5 million appropriation from the U.S. Congress for a National Women's Conference to be held in Houston, Texas, in November 1977. (Feminists were pleased, but also pointed out that the appropriation amounted to less than seven cents for every adult woman in the country, not enough even to send them all a postcard.) The two thousand official delegates were chosen at fifty-six state and territorial meetings attended by 130,000 people, making this conference one of the most democratically selected gatherings in American history.

The conference opened with the symbolic lighting of a torch which had been relayed from Seneca Falls, New York, to Houston by volunteer runners. Then the delegates, alongside as many as twenty thousand observers, spent four days of intense discussion and politicking to reach a consensus on the National Plan of Action, of which the preamble is reprinted here. Celebrating the diversity of American womanhood and the changes that are shaping women's lives, the *we* of the preamble call for the equality that is still withheld from women, asking policymakers to join them in forming "a more perfect union."

The rest of the National Plan of Action consisted of twenty-six resolutions adopted by the conference. The various planks addressed the topics that have formed the feminist agenda since the 1960s: violence against women (battered women, child abuse, rape, pornography); issues of credit, employment, and insurance; the rights of homemakers; the special problems of minority women, rural women, older women, and the disabled; education; health; political participation; and welfare and the feminization of poverty. The most controversial plank concerned reproductive freedom, especially support for women's right to abortion. Although not all delegates personally supported abortion, many endorsed the plank in order to present a unified front. While there has been some progress in the decades since Houston, the National Plan of Action will probably continue to serve more as a broad statement of goals rather than concrete achievements.

Declaration of American Women

We are here to move history forward.

We are women from every State and Territory in the Nation.

We are women of different ages, beliefs, and life-styles.

We are women of many economic, social, political, racial, ethnic, cultural, educational, and religious backgrounds.

We are married, single, widowed, and divorced.

We are mothers and daughters.

We are sisters.

We speak in varied accents and languages but we share the common language and experience of American women who throughout our Nation's life have been denied the opportunities, rights, privileges, and responsibilities accorded to men.

For the first time in the more than 200 years of our democracy, we are gathered in a National Women's Conference, charged under Federal law to assess the status of women in our country, to measure the progress we have made, to identify the barriers that prevent us from participating fully and equally in all aspects of national life, and to make recommendations to the President and to the Congress for means by which such barriers can be removed.

We recognize the positive changes that have occurred in the lives of women since the founding of our nation. In more than a century of struggle from Seneca Falls 1848 to Houston 1977, we have progressed from being nonpersons and slaves whose work and achievements were unrecognized, whose needs were ignored, and whose rights were suppressed to being citizens with freedoms and aspirations of which our ancestors could only dream.

Source: "Declaration of American Women," Official report to the President, National Women's Conference, Houston, 1977, reprinted in *What Women Want,* Caroline Bird, ed. (New York: Simon & Schuster, 1979), pp. 85–86.

We can vote and own property. We work in the home, in our communities and in every occupation. We are 40 percent of the labor force. We are in the arts, sciences, professions, and politics. We raise children, govern States, head businesses and institutions, climb mountains, explore the ocean depths, and reach toward the moon.

Our lives no longer end with the childbearing years. Our lifespan has increased to more than 75 years. We have become a majority of the population, 51.3 percent, and by the 21st Century, we shall be an even larger majority.

But despite some gains made in the past 200 years, our dream of equality is still withheld from us and millions of women still face a daily reality of discrimination, limited opportunities, and economic hardship.

Man-made barriers, laws, social customs, and prejudices continue to keep a majority of women in an inferior position without full control of our lives and bodies.

From infancy throughout life, in personal and public relationships, in the family, in the schools, in every occupation and profession, too often we find our individuality, our capabilities, our earning powers diminished by discriminatory practices and outmoded ideas of what a woman is, what a woman can do, and what a woman must be.

Increasingly, we are victims of crimes of violence in a culture that degrades us as sex objects and promotes pornography for profit.

We are poorer than men. And those of us who are minority women—blacks, Hispanic Americans, Native Americans, and Asian Americans—must overcome the double burden of discrimination based on race and sex.

We lack effective political and economic power. We have only minor and insignificant roles in making, interpreting, and enforcing our laws, in running our political parties, businesses, unions, schools, and institutions, in directing the media, in governing our country, in deciding issues of war or peace.

We do not seek special privileges, but we demand as a human right a full voice and role for women in determining the destiny of our world, our nation, our families, and our individual lives.

We seek these rights for all women, whether or not they choose as individuals to use them.

We are part of a worldwide movement of women who believe that only by bringing women into full partnership with men and respecting our rights as half the human race can we hope to achieve a world in which the whole human race—men, women, and children—can live in peace and security.

Based on the views of women who have met in every State and Territory in the past year, the National Plan of Action is presented to the President and the Congress as our recommendations for implementing Public Law 94-167.

We are entitled to and expect serious attention to our proposals.

We demand immediate and continuing action on our National Plan by Federal, State, public, and private institutions so that by 1985, the end of the International Decade for Women proclaimed by the United Nations, everything possible under the law will have been done to provide American women with full equality.

The rest will be up to the hearts, minds, and moral consciences of men and women and what they do to make our society truly democratic and open to all.

We pledge ourselves with all the strength of our dedication to this struggle "to form a more perfect Union."

The Positive Woman

Phyllis Schlafly

The year 1977 marked not only the Houston conference, but the publication of Phyllis Schlafly's *The Power of the Positive Woman*. The incongruity of these two events shows the conflicting visions of women's lives by the 1970s. Phyllis Schlafly's rise to power was intimately connected with conservative Republican politics in the 1950s and 1960s and the rise of the New Right and the Moral Majority in the 1970s. Schlafly first made a splash in right-wing circles in 1963 when she published a best-selling campaign biography of Republican presidential candidate Barry Goldwater. Schlafly's years of political experience made her a superb organizer, and she was able to tap a grassroots movement mainly located in evangelical (or "born-again") protestant churches in support of her conservative views about the centrality of a traditional family life to the future of the United States. In her ability to weave together homilies about women's traditional feminine roles with a concrete political agenda (stop ERA, overturn the constitutional right of abortion, allow prayer in the schools), Schlafly went beyond other conservative writers such as Marabel Morgan, whose *The Total Woman* (1973) offered advice about how women should downplay their own needs to make men happy but failed to connect such traditional gender roles with a wider conservative world vision.

In this selection from *The Power of the Positive Woman*, Schlafly lays out her complaints against the feminist movement. At the core, they come down to Schlafly's acceptance, indeed glorification, of the differences between men and women; she accuses feminists of trying to remove all vestiges of difference in their rush to equality. For her, biological roles are important for a stable and profitable society; the Positive Woman knows that her loyalties should lie in the domestic sphere of home, marriage, and family. Schlafly's message that women had something to lose, instead of something to gain, from women's liberation proved very appealing in the increasingly conservative political climate of the 1970s and 1980s.

The first requirement for the acquisition of power by the Positive Woman is to understand the differences between men and women. Your outlook on life, your faith, your behavior, your potential for fulfillment, all are determined by the parameters of your original premise. The Positive Woman starts with the assumption that the world is her oyster. She rejoices in the creative capability within her body and the power potential of her mind and spirit. She understands that men and women are different, and that those very differences provide the key to her success as a person and fulfillment as a woman.

The women's liberationist, on the other hand, is imprisoned by her own negative view of herself and of her place in the world around her. This view of women was most succinctly expressed in an advertisement designed by the principal women's liberationist organization, the National Organization for Women (NOW), and run in many magazines and newspapers and as spot announcements on many television stations. The advertisement showed a darling curlyheaded girl with the caption: "This healthy, normal baby has a handicap. She was born female."

This is the self-articulated dog-in-the-manger, chip-on-the-shoulder, fundamental dogma of the women's liberation movement. Someone—it is not clear who, perhaps God, perhaps the "Establishment," perhaps a conspiracy of male chauvinist pigs—dealt women a foul blow by making them female. It becomes necessary, therefore, for women to agitate and demonstrate and hurl demands on society in order to wrest from an oppressive male-dominated social structure the status that has been wrongfully denied to women through the centuries.

By its very nature, therefore, the women's liberation movement precipitates a series of conflict situations—in the legislatures, in the courts, in the schools, in industry—with man targeted as the enemy. Confrontation replaces cooperation as the watchword of all relationships. Women and men become adversaries instead of partners.

The second dogma of the women's liberationists is that, of all the injustices perpetrated upon women through the centuries, the most oppressive is the cruel fact that women have babies and men do not. Within the confines of the women's liberationist ideology, therefore, the abolition of this overriding inequality of women becomes the primary goal. This goal must be achieved at any and all costs—to the woman herself, to the baby, to the family, and to society. Women must be made equal to men in their ability *not* to become pregnant and *not* to be expected to care for babies they may bring into the world.

This is why women's liberationists are compulsively involved in the drive to make abortion and child-care centers for all women, regardless of religion or income, both socially acceptable and government-financed. Former Congresswoman Bella Abzug has defined the goal: "to enforce the constitutional right of females to terminate pregnancies that they do not wish to continue."

If man is targeted as the enemy, and the ultimate goal of women's liberation is independence from men and the avoidance of pregnancy and its consequences, then lesbianism is logically the highest form in the ritual of women's liberation. Many, such as Kate Millett, come to this conclusion, although many others do not.

The Positive Woman will never travel that dead-end road. It is self-evident to the Positive Woman that the female body with its baby-producing organs was not designed by a conspiracy of men but by the Divine Architect of the human race. Those who think it is unfair that women have babies, whereas men cannot, will have to take up their complaint with God because no other power is capable of changing that fundamental fact. On some college campuses, I have been assured that other methods of reproduction will be developed. But most of us must deal with the real world rather than with the imagination of dreamers.

Another feature of the woman's natural role is the obvious fact that women can breast-feed babies and men cannot. This functional role was not imposed by conspiratorial males seeking to burden women with confining chores, but must be recognized as part of the plan of the Divine Architect for the survival of the human race through the centuries and in the countries that know no pasteurization of milk or sterilization of bottles.

The Positive Woman looks upon her femaleness and her fertility as part of her purpose, her potential, and her power. She rejoices that she has a capability for creativity that men can never have.

The third basic dogma of the women's liberation movement is that there is no difference between male and female except the sex organs, and that all those physical, cognitive, and emotional differences you *think* are there, are merely the result of centuries of restraints imposed by a male-dominated society and sex-stereotyped schooling. The role imposed on women is, by definition, inferior, according to the women's liberationists.

The Positive Woman knows that, while there are some physical competitions in which women are better (and can command more money) than men, including those that put a premium on grace and beauty, such as figure skating, the superior physical strength of males over females in competitions of strength, speed, and short-term endurance is beyond rational dispute. . . .

The Positive Woman remembers the essential validity of the old prayer: "Lord, give me the strength to change what I can change, the serenity to accept what I cannot change, and the wisdom to discern the difference." The women's liberationists are expending their time and energies erecting a make-believe world in which they hypothesize that *if* schooling were gender-free, and *if* the same money were spent on male and female sports programs, and *if* women were permitted to compete on equal terms, *then* they would prove themselves to be physically equal. Meanwhile, the Positive Woman has put the ineradicable physical differences into her mental computer, programmed her plan of action, and is already on the way to personal achievement. . . .

The Positive Woman recognizes the fact that, when it comes to sex, women are simply not the equal of men. The sexual drive of men is much stronger than that of women. That is how the human race was designed in order that it might perpetuate itself. The other side of the coin is that it is easier for women to control their sexual appetites. A Positive Woman cannot defeat a man in a wrestling or boxing match, but she can motivate him, inspire him, encourage him, teach him, restrain him, reward him, and have power over him that he can never achieve over her with all his muscle. How or whether a Positive Woman uses her power is determined solely by the way she alone defines her goals and develops her skills.

The differences between men and women are also emotional and psychological. Without woman's innate maternal instinct, the human race would have died out centuries ago. There is nothing so helpless in all earthly life as the newborn infant. It will die within hours if not cared for. Even in the most primitive, uneducated societies, women have always cared for their newborn babies. They didn't need any schooling to teach them how. They didn't need any welfare workers to tell them it is their social obligation. Even in societies to whom such concepts as "ought," "social responsibility," and "compassion for the helpless" were unknown, mothers cared for their new babies.

Why? Because caring for a baby serves the natural maternal need of a woman. Although not nearly so total as the baby's need, the woman's need is nonetheless real.

The overriding psychological need of a woman is to love something alive. A baby fulfills this need in the lives of most women. If a baby is not available to fill that need, women search for a baby-substitute. This is the reason why women have traditionally gone into teaching and nursing careers. They are doing what comes naturally to the female psyche. The schoolchild or the patient of any age provides an outlet for a woman to express her natural maternal need.

This maternal need in women is the reason why mothers whose children have grown up and flown from the nest are sometimes cut loose from their psychological moorings. The maternal need in women can show itself in love for grandchildren, nieces, nephews, or even neighbors' children. The maternal need in some women has even manifested itself in an extraordinary affection lavished on a dog, a cat, or a parakeet.

This is not to say that every woman must have a baby in order to be fulfilled. But it is to say that fulfillment for most women involves expressing their natural maternal urge by loving and caring for someone.

The women's liberation movement complains that traditional stereotyped roles assume that women are "passive" and that men are "aggressive." The anomaly is that a woman's most fundamental emotional need is not passive at all, but active. A woman naturally seeks to love affirmatively and to show that love in an active way by caring for the object of her affections.

The Positive Woman finds somebody on whom she can lavish her maternal love so that it doesn't well up inside her and cause psychological frustrations. Surely no woman is so isolated by geography or insulated by spirit that she cannot find someone worthy of her maternal love. All persons, men and women, gain by sharing something of themselves with their fellow humans, but women profit most of all because it is part of their very nature. . . .

Here is a starting checklist of goals that can be restored to America if Positive Women will apply their dedicated efforts:

(1) The right of a woman to be a full-time wife and mother and to have this right recognized by laws that obligate her husband to provide the primary financial support and a home for her and their children.

(2) The responsibility of parents (not the government) for the care of preschool children.

(3) The right of parents to insist that the schools:
   a. permit voluntary prayer,
   b. teach the "fourth R," right and wrong, according to the precepts of Holy Scriptures,
   c. use textbooks that do not offend the religious and moral values of the parents,
   d. use textbooks that honor the family, monogamous marriage, woman's role as wife and mother, and man's role as provider and protector,
   e. teach such basic educational skills as reading and arithmetic before time and money are spent on frills,
   f. permit children to attend school in their own neighborhood, and
   g. separate the sexes for gym classes, athletic practice and competition, and academic and vocational classes, if so desired.

(4) The right of employers to give job preference (where qualifications are equal) to a wage earner supporting dependents.

(5) The right of a woman engaged in physical-labor employment to be protected by laws and regulations that respect the physical differences and different family obligations of men and women.

(6) The right to equal opportunity in employment and education for all persons regardless of race, creed, sex, or national origin.

(7) The right to have local governments prevent the display of printed or pictorial materials that degrade women in a pornographic, perverted, or sadistic manner.

(8) The right to defend the institution of the family by according certain rights to husbands and wives that are not given to those choosing immoral lifestyles.

(9) The right to life of all innocent persons from conception to natural death.

(10) The right of citizens to live in a community where state and local government and judges maintain law and order by a system of justice under due process and punishment that is swift and certain.

(11) The right of society to protect itself by designating different roles for men and women in the armed forces and police and fire departments, where necessary.

(12) The right of citizens to have the federal government adequately provide for the common defense against aggression by any other nation.

The Backlash against Feminism

Susan Faludi

In a widely read 1991 book titled *Backlash: The Undeclared War Against American Women*, Pulitzer Prize-winning journalist Susan Faludi described a powerful counterattack, or backlash, against the gains American women had won in the 1960s and 1970s. In compelling detail, she showed how the media consistently and inaccurately held the women's movement responsible for every ill afflicting modern women—from infertility to eating disorders to rising divorce rates to the "man shortage." For example, Faludi picked apart the statistics put forward by the media showing a drastic decline in the chances for college-educated, unwed women over thirty to marry. (In *Newsweek*'s inflammatory—and inaccurate—headline, women over forty were "more likely to be killed by a terrorist" than make it to the altar.) She also demolished widely reported stories about an "infertility epidemic" among professional women who postpone childbearing or supposed trends of widespread emotional "burnout" among career women. But in a backlash climate, such accusations, even when untrue, seemed plausible.

Faludi proposed a different interpretation. It was a myth that the women's movement and feminism were women's own worst enemy; it was a myth that women were unhappy precisely because they had achieved equality. Instead, many of contemporary women's problems were traceable to the fact that they did not have *enough* equality, not that they had too much. Certainly the current debates about reproductive rights, pay equity, the "glass ceiling," and the "mommy track" suggest that the issues of modern feminism are far from accepted. And very few would argue that women had achieved equality based on how women are portrayed in the media and popular culture, especially in television, film, popular music, and advertising.

As a journalist, Faludi realized the power of the media and popular culture to shape public attitudes and affect public policy. Her agenda was to expose the campaign that was attempting to thwart women's progress in the 1980s and 1990s, to show that women still have many battles to fight before equality would be achieved, and to reaffirm that many women were consciously resisting the backlash message, both individually and collectively. This selection from the introduction, entitled "Blame It on Feminism," shows the passion and conviction which which she argues her case.

To be a woman in America at the close of the 20th century—what good fortune. That's what we keep hearing, anyway. The barricades have fallen, politicians assure us. Women have "made it," Madison Avenue cheers. Women's fight for equality has "largely been won," *Time* magazine announces. Enroll at any university, join any law firm, apply for credit at any bank. Women have so many opportunities now, corporate leaders say, that we don't really need equal opportunity policies. Women are so equal now, lawmakers say, that we no longer need an Equal Rights Amendment. Women have "so much," former President Ronald Reagan says, that the White House no longer needs to appoint them to higher office. Even American Express ads are saluting a woman's freedom to charge it. At last, women have received their full citizenship papers.

And yet . . .

Behind this celebration of the American woman's victory, behind the news, cheerfully and endlessly repeated, that the struggle for women's rights is won, another message flashes. You may be free and equal now, it says to women, but you have never been more miserable.

This bulletin of despair is posted everywhere—at the newsstand, on the TV set, at the movies, in advertisements and doctors' offices and academic journals. Professional women are suffering "burnout" and succumbing to an "infertility epidemic." Single women are grieving from a "man shortage." The *New York Times* reports: Childless women are "depressed and confused" and their ranks are swelling. *Newsweek* says: Unwed women are "hysterical" and crumbling under a "profound crisis of confidence." The health advice manuals inform: High-powered career women are stricken with unprecedented outbreaks of "stress-induced disorders," hair loss, bad nerves, alcoholism, and even heart attacks. The psychology books advise: Independent women's loneliness represents "a major mental health problem today." Even founding feminist Betty Friedan has been spreading the word: she warns that women now suffer from a new identity crisis and "new 'problems that have no name.' "

How can American women be in so much trouble at the same time that they are supposed to be so blessed? If the status of women has never been higher, why is their emotional state so low? If women got what they asked for, what could possibly be the matter now?

The prevailing wisdom of the past decade has supported one, and only one, answer to this riddle: it must be all that equality that's causing all that pain. Women are unhappy precisely *because* they are free. Women are enslaved by their own liberation. They have grabbed at the gold ring of independence, only to miss the one ring that really matters. They have gained control of their fertility, only to destroy it. They have pursued their own professional dreams—and lost out on the greatest female adventure. The women's movement, as we are told time and again, has proved women's own worst enemy.

"In dispensing its spoils, women's liberation has given my generation high incomes, our own cigarette, the option of single parenthood, rape crisis centers, personal lines of credit, free love, and female gynecologists," Mona Charen, a young law student, writes in the *National Review,* in an article titled "The Feminist Mistake." "In return it has effectively robbed us of one thing upon which the happiness of most women rests—men." The *National Review* is a conservative publication, but such charges against the women's movement are not confined to its pages. "Our generation was the human sacrifice" to the women's movement, *Los Angeles Times* feature writer Elizabeth Mehren contends in a *Time* cover story. Baby-boom women like her, she says, have been duped by feminism: "We believed the rhetoric." In *Newsweek*, writer Kay Ebeling dubs feminism "the Great Experiment That Failed" and asserts "women in my generation, its perpetrators, are the casualties." Even the beauty magazines are saying it: *Harper's Bazaar* accuses the women's movement of having "lost us [women] ground instead of gaining it."

The truth is that the last decade has seen a powerful counterassault on women's rights, a backlash, an attempt to retract the handful of small and hard-won victories that the feminist movement did manage to win for women. This counterassault is largely insidious: in a kind of pop-culture version of the Big Lie, it stands the truth boldly on its head and proclaims that the very steps that have elevated women's position have actually led to their downfall.

The backlash is at once sophisticated and banal, deceptively "progressive" and proudly backward. It deploys both the "new" findings of "scientific research" and the dime-store moralism of yesteryear; it turns into media sound bites both the glib pronouncements of pop-psych trend-watchers and the frenzied rhetoric of New Right preachers. The backlash has succeeded in framing virtually the whole issue of women's rights in its own language. Just as Reaganism shifted political discourse far to the right and demonized liberalism, so the backlash convinced the public that women's "liberation" was the true contemporary American scourge—the source of an endless laundry list of personal, social, and economic problems.

But what has made women unhappy in the last decade is not their "equality"—which they don't yet have—but the rising pressure to halt, and even reverse, women's quest for that equality. The "man shortage" and the "infertility epidemic" are not the price of liberation; in fact, they do not even exist. But these chimeras are the chisels of a society-wide backlash. They are part of a relentless whittling-down process—much of it amounting to outright propaganda—that has served to stir women's private anxieties and break their political wills. Identifying feminism as women's enemy only furthers the ends of a backlash against women's equality, simultaneously deflecting attention from the backlash's central role and recruiting women to attack their own cause.

Some social observers may well ask whether the current pressures on women actually constitute a backlash—or just a continuation of American society's long-standing resistance to women's rights. Certainly hostility to female independence has always been with us. But if fear and loathing of feminism is a sort of perpetual viral condition in our culture, it is not always in an acute stage; its symptoms subside and resurface periodically. And it is these episodes of resurgence, such as the one we face now, that can accurately be termed "backlashes" to women's advancement. If we trace these occurrences in Amer-

ican history (as we will do in a later chapter), we find such flare-ups are hardly
random; they have always been triggered by the perception—accurate or not—
that women are making great strides. These outbreaks are backlashes because
they have always arisen in reaction to women's "progress," caused not simply
by a bedrock of misogyny but by the specific efforts of contemporary women
to improve their status, efforts that have been interpreted time and again by
men—especially men grappling with real threats to their economic and social
well-being on other fronts—as spelling their own masculine doom.

The most recent round of backlash first surfaced in the late '70s on the
fringes, among the evangelical right. By the early '80s, the fundamentalist ideology had shouldered its way into the White House. By the mid-'80s, as resistance to women's rights acquired political and social acceptability, it passed
into the popular culture. And in every case, the timing coincided with signs that
women were believed to be on the verge of breakthrough.

Just when women's quest for equal rights seemed closest to achieving its
objectives, the backlash struck it down. Just when a "gender gap" at the voting
booth surfaced in 1980, and women in politics began to talk of capitalizing on
it, the Republican party elevated Ronald Reagan and both political parties began
to shunt women's rights off their platforms. Just when support for feminism and
the Equal Rights Amendment reached a record high in 1981, the amendment
was defeated the following year. Just when women were starting to mobilize
against battering and sexual assaults, the federal government stalled funding for
battered-women's programs, defeated bills to fund shelters, and shut down its
Office of Domestic Violence—only two years after opening it in 1979. Just when
record numbers of younger women were supporting feminist goals in the mid-
'80s (more of them, in fact, than older women) and a majority of all women were
calling themselves feminists, the media declared the advent of a younger "postfeminist generation" that supposedly reviled the women's movement. Just when
women racked up their largest percentage ever supporting the right to abortion,
the U.S. Supreme Court moved toward reconsidering it.

In other words, the antifeminist backlash has been set off not by women's
achievement of full equality but by the increased possibility that they might
win it. It is a preemptive strike that stops women long before they reach the
finish line. "A backlash may be an indication that women really have had an
effect," feminist psychiatrist Dr. Jean Baker Miller has written, "but backlashes
occur when advances have been small, before changes are sufficient to help
many people. . . . It is almost as if the leaders of backlashes use the fear of
change as a threat before major change has occurred." In the last decade, some
women did make substantial advances before the backlash hit, but millions of
others were left behind, stranded. Some women now enjoy the right to legal
abortion—but not the 44 million women, from the indigent to the military work
force, who depend on the federal government for their medical care. Some
women can now walk into high-paying professional careers—but not the more
than 19 million still in the typing pools or behind the department store sales

counters. (Contrary to popular myth about the "have-it-all" baby-boom women, the largest percentage of women in this generation remain typists and clerks.)

As the backlash has gathered force, it has cut off the few from the many—and the few women who have advanced seek to prove, as a social survival tactic, that they aren't so interested in advancement after all. Some of them parade their defection from the women's movement, while their working-class peers founder and cling to the splintered remains of the feminist cause. While a very few affluent and celebrity women who are showcased in news articles boast about having "found my niche as Mrs. Andy Mill" and going home to "bake bread," the many working-class women appeal for their economic rights—flocking to unions in record numbers, striking on their own for pay equity and establishing their own fledgling groups for working women's rights. In 1986, while 41 percent of upper-income women were claiming in the Gallup poll that they were not feminists, only 26 percent of low-income women were making the same claim.

*   *   *   *   *

Women's advances and retreats are generally described in military terms: battles won, battles lost, points and territory gained and surrendered. The metaphor of combat is not without its merits in this context and, clearly, the same sort of martial accounting and vocabulary is already surfacing here. But by imagining the conflict as two battalions neatly arrayed on either side of the line, we miss the entangled nature, the locked embrace, of a "war" between women and the male culture they inhabit. We miss the reactive nature of a backlash, which, by definition, can exist only in response to another force.

In times when feminism is at a low ebb, women assume the reactive role—privately and most often covertly struggling to assert themselves against the dominant cultural tide. But when feminism itself becomes the tide, the opposition doesn't simply go along with the reversal: it digs in its heels, brandishes its fists, builds walls and dams. And its resistance creates countercurrents and treacherous undertows.

The force and furor of the backlash churn beneath the surface, largely invisible to the public eye. On occasion in the last decade, they have burst into view. We have seen New Right politicians condemn women's independence, antiabortion protesters firebomb women's clinics, fundamentalist preachers damn feminists as "whores" and "witches." Other signs of the backlash's wrath, by their sheer brutality, can push their way into public consciousness for a time—the sharp increase in rape, for example, or the rise in pornography that depicts extreme violence against women.

More subtle indicators in popular culture may receive momentary, and often bemused, media notice, then quickly slip from social awareness: A report, for instance, that the image of women on prime-time TV shows has suddenly degenerated. A survey of mystery fiction finding the numbers of female characters tortured and mutilated mysteriously multiplying. The puzzling news that, as one commentator put it, "So many hit songs have the B-word [bitch] to refer to women that some rap music seems to be veering toward rape music." The ascendancy of virulently misogynist comics like Andrew Dice Clay—who called women "pigs" and "sluts" and strutted in films in which women were beaten, tortured, and blown up—or radio hosts like Rush Limbaugh, whose broadsides against "femi-Nazi" feminists made his syndicated program the most popular radio talk show in the nation. Or word that in 1987, the American Women in Radio & Television couldn't award its annual prize for ads that feature women positively: it could find no ad that qualified.

These phenomena are all related, but that doesn't mean they are somehow coordinated. The backlash is not a conspiracy, with a council dispatching agents from some central control room, nor are the people who serve its ends often aware of their role; some even consider themselves feminists. For the most part, its workings are encoded and internalized, diffuse and chameleonic. Not all of the manifestations of the backlash are of equal weight or significance either; some are mere ephemera, generated by a culture machine that is always scrounging for a "fresh" angle. Taken as a whole, however, these codes and cajolings, these whispers and threats and myths, move overwhelmingly in one direction: they try to push women back into their "acceptable" roles—whether as Daddy's girl or fluttery romantic, active nester or passive love object.

Although the backlash is not an organized movement, that doesn't make it any less destructive. In fact, the lack of orchestration, the absence of a single string-puller, only makes it harder to see—and perhaps more effective. A backlash against women's rights succeeds to the degree that it appears *not* to be political, that it appears not to be a struggle at all. It is most powerful when it goes private, when it lodges inside a woman's mind and turns her vision inward, until she imagines the pressure is all in her head, until she begins to enforce the backlash, too—on herself.

In the last decade, the backlash has moved through the culture's secret chambers, traveling through passageways of flattery and fear. Along the way, it has adopted disguises: a mask of mild derision or the painted face of deep "concern." Its lips profess pity for any woman who won't fit the mold, while it tries to clamp the mold around her ears. It pursues a divide-and-conquer strategy: single versus married women, working women versus homemakers, middle- versus working-class. It manipulates a system of rewards and punishments, elevating women who follow its rules, isolating those who don't. The backlash remarkets old myths about women as new facts and ignores all appeals to reason. Cornered, it denies its own existence, points an accusatory finger at feminism, and burrows deeper underground.

Backlash happens to be the title of a 1947 Hollywood movie in which a man frames his wife for a murder he's committed. The backlash against women's rights works in much the same way: its rhetoric charges feminists with all the crimes it perpetrates. The backlash line blames the women's movement for the "feminization of poverty"—while the backlash's own instigators in

Washington pushed through the budget cuts that helped impoverish millions of women, fought pay equity proposals, and undermined equal opportunity laws. The backlash line claims the women's movement cares nothing for children's rights—while its own representatives in the capital and state legislatures have blocked one bill after another to improve child care, slashed billions of dollars in federal aid for children, and relaxed state licensing standards for day care centers. The backlash line accuses the women's movement of creating a generation of unhappy single and childless women—but its purveyors in the media are the ones guilty of making single and childless women feel like circus freaks.

To blame feminism for women's "lesser life" is to miss entirely the point of feminism, which is to win women a wider range of experience. Feminism remains a pretty simple concept, despite repeated—and enormously effective—efforts to dress it up in greasepaint and turn its proponents into gargoyles. As Rebecca West wrote sardonically in 1913, "I myself have never been able to find out precisely what feminism is: I only know that people call me a feminist whenever I express sentiments that differentiate me from a doormat."

The meaning of the word "feminist" has not really changed since it first appeared in a book review in the *Athenaeum* of April 27, 1895, describing a woman who "has in her the capacity of fighting her way back to independence." It is the basic proposition that, as Nora put it in Ibsen's *A Doll's House* a century ago, "Before everything else I'm a human being." It is the simply worded sign hoisted by a little girl in the 1970 Women's Strike for Equality: I AM NOT A BARBIE DOLL. Feminism asks the world to recognize at long last that women aren't decorative ornaments, worthy vessels, members of a "special-interest group." They are half (in fact, now more than half) of the national population, and just as deserving of rights and opportunities, just as capable of participating in the world's events, as the other half. Feminism's agenda is basic: It asks that women not be forced to "choose" between public justice and private happiness. It asks that women be free to define themselves—instead of having their identity defined for them, time and again, by their culture and their men.

The fact that these are still such incendiary notions should tell us that American women have a way to go before they enter the promised land of equality.

A Woman of Conscience

Anita Hill

In 1991, the same year that Susan Faludi published *Backlash,* the confirmation hearings of Supreme Court nominee Clarence Thomas brought the issue of sexual harassment in the workplace forcefully to the nation's attention, with decidedly mixed results. Allegations by University of Oklahoma law professor Anita Hill that she had been sexually harassed by Thomas when he was her boss at the Department of Education and the Equal Employment Opportunity Commission (ironically, the very governmental body delegated to deal with the issue of sexual harassment) almost derailed the confirmation of the conservative African-American Thomas. Hill's forceful and measured accusations, broadcast to a national television audience riveted by this unexpected turn in the hearings, were denied by Thomas himself, who called the event "a high-tech lynching." The Senate narrowly confirmed Thomas by a vote of 52–48.

Opinion polls at the time showed wide divergence in whether people believed Clarence Thomas or Anita Hill. Support did not break down along race or gender lines, with many women (49% in one poll) believing Thomas. In an attempt to discredit the allegations, supporters of the nomination viciously attacked Anita Hill's personal integrity. Feminists rallied around Hill, rebutting the attacks and pointing out that her experience of sexual harassment on the job was unfortunately a far too typical experience for American women. In 1992, Hillary Rodham Clinton stated forcefully, "All women who care about equality of opportunity, about integrity in the workplace, are in Anita Hill's debt."

"They just don't get it," was the refrain of many women as the all-male Senate Judiciary Committee dismissed Hill's charges. The Thomas-Hill hearings spurred the number of women running for political office, with dramatic results in the 1992 elections. When Senator Robert Packwood of Oregon was forced to resign in 1995 after allegations of sexual harassment of staff and campaign workers, it seemed that finally, after all, elected public officials did "get it"—sexual harassment was illegal and devastating to their political careers.

Statement of Professor Anita F. Hill to the Senate Judiciary Committee, October 11, 1991

Mr. Chairman, Senator Thurmond, members of the committee:

My name is Anita F. Hill, and I am a professor of law at the University of Oklahoma. I was born on a farm in Okmulgee County, Oklahoma, in 1956. I am the youngest of thirteen children.

I had my early education in Okmulgee County. My mother's name is Irma Hill. She is also a farmer and a housewife.

My childhood was one of a lot of hard work and not much money, but it was one of solid family affection as represented by my parents. I was reared in a religious atmosphere in the Baptist faith, and I have been a member of the Antioch Baptist church in Tulsa, Oklahoma, since 1983. It is a very warm part of my life at the present time.

Source: "Statement of Professor Anita F. Hill to the Senate Judiciary Committee, October 11, 1991," S. Hrg 102–1084, Part 4 (Washington, D.C.: Government Printing Office, 1993).

For my undergraduate work, I went to Oklahoma State University and graduated from there in 1977. I am attaching to this statement a copy of my resume for further details of my education.

Senator Joseph R. Biden, Jr.: It will be included in the record.

Professor Hill: Thank you.

I graduated from the university with academic honors, and proceeded to the Yale Law School, where I received my J.D. degree in 1980.

Upon graduation from law school, I became a practicing lawyer with the Washington, D.C., firm of Wald, Hardraker & Ross. In 1981 I was introduced to now Judge Thomas by a mutual friend.

Judge Thomas told me that he was anticipating a political appointment, and he asked if I would be interested in working with him.

He was in fact appointed as assistant secretary of education for civil rights. After he was—after he had taken that post, he asked if I would become his assistant, and I accepted that position.

In my early period there, I had two major projects. The first was an article I wrote for Judge Thomas's signature on the education of minority students. The second was the organization of a seminar on high-risk students, which was abandoned because Judge Thomas transferred to the E.E.O.C., where he became the chairman of that office.

During this period at the Department of Education my working relationship with Judge Thomas was positive. I had a good deal of responsibility and independence. I thought he respected my work, and that he trusted my judgment.

After approximately three months of working there, he asked me to go out socially with him. What happened next, and telling the world about it, are the two most difficult things—experiences of my life.

It is only after a great deal of agonizing consideration, and . . . great number of sleepless nights, that I am able to talk of these unpleasant matters to anyone but my close friends.

I declined the invitation to go out socially with him, and explained to him that I thought it would jeopardize at—what at the time I considered to be a very good working relationship. I had a normal social life with other men outside the office. I believe then, as now, that having a social relationship with a person who was supervising my work would be ill advised. I was very uncomfortable with the idea and told him so.

I thought that by saying no and explaining my reasons, my employer would abandon his social suggestions. However, to my regret, in the following few weeks, he continued to ask me out on several occasions.

He pressed me to justify my reasons for saying no to him. These incidents took place in his office, or mine. They were in the form of private conversations, which not—would not have been overheard by anyone else.

My working relationship became even more strained when Judge Thomas began to use work situations to discuss sex. On these occasions he would call me into his office for a course on education issues and projects, or he might suggest that because of the time pressures of his schedule we go to lunch to a government cafeteria.

After a brief discussion of work, he would turn the conversation to a discussion of sexual matters. His conversations were very vivid. He spoke about acts that he had seen in pornographic films involving such matters as women having sex with animals, and films showing group sex or rape scenes.

He talked about pornographic materials depicting individuals with large penises or large breasts involving various sex acts.

On several occasions, Thomas told me graphically of his own sexual prowess.

Because I was extremely uncomfortable talking about sex with him at all, and particularly in such a graphic way, I told him that I did not want to talk about this subject. I would also try to change the subject to education matters or to nonsexual personal matters, such as his background or his beliefs.

My efforts to change the subject were rarely successful.

Throughout the period of these conversations, he also from time to time asked me for social engagements. My reaction to these conversations was to avoid them by eliminating opportunities for us to engage in extended conversations.

This was difficult because, at the time, I was his only assistant at the office of education—or office for civil rights. During the latter part of my time at the Department of Education, the social pressures, and any conversation of his offensive behavior, ended. I began both to believe and hope that our working relationship could be a proper, cordial, and professional one.

When Judge Thomas was made chair of the EEOC, I needed to face the question of whether to go with him. I was asked to do so, and I did.

The work itself was interesting, and at that time it appeared that the sexual overtures which had so troubled me had ended.

I also faced the realistic fact that I had no alternative job. While I might have gone back to private practice, perhaps in my old firm or at another, I was dedicated to civil rights work and my first choice was to be in that field. Moreover, at that time, the Department of Education itself was a dubious venture. President Reagan was seeking to abolish the entire department.

For my first months at the EEOC where I continued to be an assistant to Judge Thomas, there were no sexual conversations or overtures. However, during the fall and winter of 1982 these began again. The comments were random and ranged from pressing me about why I didn't go out with him to remarks about my personal appearance. I remember his saying that some day I would have to tell him the real reason that I wouldn't go out with him.

He began to show displeasure in his tone and voice and his demeanor and his continued pressure for an explanation. He commented on what I was wearing in terms of whether it made me more or less sexually attractive. The incidents occurred in his inner office at the EEOC.

One of the oddest episodes I remember was an occasion in which Thomas was drinking a Coke in his office. He got up from the table at which we were working, went over to his desk to get the Coke, looked at the can and asked, "Who has put pubic hair on my Coke?"

On other occasions, he referred to the size of his own penis as being larger than normal and he also spoke on some occasions of the pleasures he had given to women with oral sex. At this point, late 1982, I began to be concerned that Clarence Thomas might take out his anger with me by degrading me or not giving me important assignments. I also thought that he might find an excuse for dismissing me.

In January of 1983, I began looking for another job. I was handicapped because I feared that if he found out, he might make it difficult for me to find other employment and I might be dismissed from the job I had. Another factor that made my search more difficult was that there was a period—this was during a period—of a hiring freeze in the government. . . .

In the spring of 1983, an opportunity to teach at Oral Roberts University opened up. I participated in a seminar, taught an afternoon session in a seminar at Oral Roberts University. The dean of the university saw me teaching and inquired as to whether I would be interested in further pursuing a career in teaching beginning at Oral Roberts University.

I agreed to take the job, in large part because of my desire to escape the pressures I felt at the EEOC due to Judge Thomas.

When I informed him that I was leaving in July, I recall that his response was that now I would no longer have an excuse for not going out with him. I told him that I still preferred not to do so. At some time after that meeting, he asked if he could take me to dinner at the end of the term. When I declined, he assured me that the dinner was a professional courtesy only and not a social invitation. I reluctantly agreed to accept that invitation but only if it was at the very end of a working day.

On, as I recall, the last day of my employment at the EEOC in the summer of 1983, I did have dinner with Clarence Thomas. We went directly from work to a restaurant near the office. We talked about the work I had done, both at Education and at the EEOC. He told me that he was pleased with all of it except for an article and speech that I had done for him while we were at the Office for Civil Rights. Finally he made a comment that I will vividly remember. He said that if I ever told anyone of his behavior that it would ruin his career. This was not an apology; nor was it an explanation. That was his last remark about the possibility of our going out or reference to his behavior.

In July of 1983 I left the Washington, D.C., area and I've had minimal contacts with Judge Clarence Thomas since. I am of course aware from the press that some questions have been raised about conversations I had with Judge Clarence Thomas after I left the EEOC. From 1983 until today, I have seen Judge Thomas only twice. On one occasion, I needed to get a reference from him and on another he made a public appearance in Tulsa. On one occasion he called me at home and we had an inconsequential conversation. On one occasion he called me without reaching me and I returned the call without reaching him and nothing came of it. . . .

It is only after a great deal of agonizing consideration that I am able to talk of these unpleasant matters to anyone except my closest friends. As I've said before, these last few days have been very trying and very hard for me and it hasn't just been the last few days this week.

It has actually been over a month now that I have been under the strain of this issue.

Telling the world is the most difficult experience of my life, but it is very close to having to live through the experience that occasioned this meeting.

I may have used poor judgment early on in my relationship with this issue. I was aware, however, that telling at any point in my career could adversely affect my future career, and I did not want, early on, to burn all the bridges to the EEOC.

As I said, I may have used poor judgment. Perhaps I should have taken angry or even militant steps, both when I was in the agency or after I left it. But I must confess to the world that the course that I took seemed the better as well as the easier approach.

I declined any comment to newspapers, but later, when Senate staff asked me about these matters, I felt I had a duty to report.

I have no personal vendetta against Clarence Thomas. I seek only to provide the committee with information which it may regard as relevant.

It would have been more comfortable to remain silent. I took no initiative to inform anyone. But when I was asked by a representative of this committee to report my experience, I felt that I had to tell the truth. I could not keep silent.

Women and Disabilities

Nancy Mairs

In understanding recent women's history, phenomena like the Hill-Thomas hearings or the backlash against feminism must be balanced with other developments such as the winning of significant political and social gains for previously overlooked groups or individuals. Until recently, very few people—and even fewer women—talked openly about the issue of disability. But that silence began to change in the 1980s, led in part by groundbreaking anthologies like Marsha Saxton and Florence Howe's edited anthology *With Wings* (1987), which was devoted to literature by and about women living with disabilities or other physical limitations. The disability rights movement, itself a product of the same forces that had spawned the civil rights movement, second-wave feminism, gay rights, and other movements of identity politics since the 1960s, counted a major legislative victory in 1990 with the passage of the Americans with Disabilities Act, which barred discrimination against people with physical or mental disabilities.

All people coping with disabilities suffer widespread discrimination in employment, housing, access, and personal relationships, but women with disabilities face the additional burdens associated with discrimination based on sex. Disabled women earn only 52 percent of what nondisabled women earn, which puts them even further behind able-bodied men. Just like women's contributions in general, disabled women's skills are often minimized or overlooked; disabled women often suffer serious self-esteem problems as they deal with stigma and stereotypes, like the supposed asexuality of all disabled people, despite evidence of those who have been able to maintain relationships and bear and raise children. And yet when many women reflect on their diseases or disabilities, they find that they feel strong, capable, and proud of the lives they are leading. In other words, they don't feel like victims.

In this selection, Nancy Mairs discusses with both insight and humor what it is like to have Multiple Sclerosis (MS), a chronic degenerative disease of the central nervous system for which there is not yet a cure. The title of her essay, "On Being a Cripple," shows how she identifies herself—she enjoys the shock, the slap in the face, that the word conveys, as opposed to more neutral terms like disabled, handicapped, or the hated "differently abled." Her essay conveys both the normality of the life that she leads and the special challenges that she faces every day. Nancy Mairs has taught women's studies and writing at the University of Arizona and UCLA and is the author of *Plaintext* (1986) and *Voice Lessons: Becoming a (Woman) Writer* (1994).

The other day I was thinking of writing an essay on being a cripple. I was thinking hard in one of the stalls of the women's room in my office building, as I was shoving my shirt into my jeans and tugging up my zipper. Preoccupied, I flushed, picked up my book bag, took my cane down from the hook, and unlatched the door. So many movements unbalanced me, and as I pulled the door open I fell over backward, landing fully clothed on the toilet seat with my legs splayed in front of me: the old beetle-on-its-back routine. Saturday afternoon, the building deserted, I was free to laugh aloud as I wriggled back to my feet, my voice bouncing off the yellowish tiles from all directions. Had anyone been there with me, I'd have been still and faint and hot with chagrin.

I decided that it was high time to write the essay.

First, the matter of semantics. I am a cripple. I choose this word to name me. I choose from among several possibilities, the most common of which are *handicapped* and *disabled*. I made the choice a number of years ago, without

Source: Nancy Mairs, "On Being a Cripple," from *Plaintext* by Nancy Mairs, pp. 9–11, 12–13, 16–17, 20. Published by The University of Arizona Press, copyright © 1986. Reprinted by permission of the publisher.

thinking, unaware of my motives for doing so. Even now, I'm not sure what those motives are, but I recognize that they are complex and not entirely flattering. People—crippled or not—wince at the word *cripple,* as they do not at *handicapped* or *disabled.* Perhaps I want them to wince. I want them to see me as a tough customer, one to whom the fates/gods/viruses have not been kind, but who can face the brutal truth of her existence squarely. As a cripple, I swagger.

But, to be fair to myself, a certain amount of honesty underlies my choice. *Cripple* seems to me a clean word, straightforward and precise. It has an honorable history, having made its first appearance in the Lindisfarne Gospel in the tenth century. As a lover of words, I like the accuracy with which it describes my condition: I have lost the full use of my limbs. *Disabled,* by contrast, suggests any incapacity, physical or mental. And I certainly don't like *handicapped,* which implies that I have deliberately been put at a disadvantage, by whom I can't imagine (my God is not a Handicapper General), in order to equalize chances in the great race of life. These words seem to me to be moving away from my condition, to be widening the gap between word and reality. Most remote is the recently coined euphemism *differently abled,* which partakes of the same semantic hopefulness that transformed countries from *undeveloped* to *underdeveloped,* then to *less developed,* and finally to *developing* nations. People have continued to starve in those countries during the shift. Some realities do not obey the dictates of language.

Mine is one of them. Whatever you call me, I remain crippled. But I don't care what I am called, as long as it isn't *differently abled,* which strikes me as pure verbal garbage designed, by its ability to describe anyone, to describe no one. I subscribe to George Orwell's thesis that "the sloppiness of our language makes it easier for us to have foolish thoughts." And I refuse to participate in the degeneration of the language to the extent that I deny that I have lost anything in the course of this calamitous disease; I refuse to pretend that the only differences between you and me are the various ordinary ones that distinguish any one person from another. But call me *disabled* or *handicapped* if you like. I have long since grown accustomed to them; and if they are vague, at least they hint at the truth. Moreover, I use them myself. Society is no readier to accept crippledness than to accept death, war, sex, sweat, or wrinkles. I would never refer to another person as a cripple. It is the word I use to name only myself.

I haven't always been crippled, a fact for which I am soundly grateful. To be whole of limb is, I know from experience, infinitely more pleasant and useful than to be crippled; and if that knowledge leaves me open to bitterness at my loss, the physical soundness I once enjoyed (though I did not enjoy it half enough) is well worth the occasional stab of regret. Though never any good at sports, I was a normally active child and young adult. I climbed trees, played hopscotch, jumped rope, skated, swam, rode my bicycle, sailed. I despised team sports, spending some of the most wretched afternoons of my life, sweaty and humiliated, behind a field-hockey stick and under a basketball hoop. I tramped alone for miles along the bridle paths that webbed the woods behind the house I grew up in. I swayed through countless dim hours in the arms of one man or another under the scattered shot of light from mirrored balls, and gyrated through countless more as Tab Hunter and Johnny Mathis gave way to the Rolling Stones, Creedence Clearwater Revival, Cream. I walked down the aisle. I pushed baby carriages, changed tires in the rain, marched for peace.

When I was twenty-nine, I started to trip and drop things. What at first seemed my natural clumsiness soon became too pronounced to shrug off. I consulted a neurologist, who told me that I had a brain tumor. A battery of tests, increasingly disagreeable, revealed no tumor. About a year and a half later I developed a blurred spot in one eye. I had, at last, the episodes "disseminated in space and time" requisite for a diagnosis: multiple sclerosis. I have never been sorry for the doctor's initial misdiagnosis, however. For almost a week, until the negative results of the tests were in, I thought that I was going to die right away. Every day for the past nearly ten years, then, has been a kind of gift. I accept all gifts. . . .

I lead, on the whole, an ordinary life, probably rather like the one I would have led had I not had MS. I am lucky that my predilections were already solitary, sedentary, and bookish—unlike the world-famous French cellist I have read about, or the young woman I talked with one long afternoon who wanted only to be a jockey. I had just begun graduate school when I found out something was wrong with me, and I have remained—interminably—a graduate student. Perhaps I would not have if I'd thought I had the stamina to return to a full-time job as a technical editor; but I've enjoyed my studies.

In addition to studying, I teach writing courses. I also teach medical students how to give neurological examinations. I pick up free-lance editing jobs here and there. I have raised a foster son and sent him into the world, where he has made me two grandbabies, and I am still escorting my daughter and son through adolescence. I go to mass every Saturday. I am a superb, if messy, cook. I am also an enthusiastic laundress, capable of sorting a hamper full of clothes into five subtly differentiated piles, but a terrible housekeeper. I can do italic writing and, in an emergency, bathe an oil-soaked cat. I play a fiendish game of Scrabble. When I have the time and the money, I like to sit on my front steps with my husband, drinking Amaretto and smoking a cigar, as we imagine our counterparts in Leningrad and make sure that the sun gets down once more behind the sharp childish scrawl of the Tucson mountains.

This lively plenty has its bleak complement, of course, in all the things I can no longer do. I will never run again, except in dreams, and one day I may have to write that I will never walk again. I like to go camping, but I can't follow George and the children along the trails that wander out of a campsite through the desert or into the mountains. In fact, even on the level

I've learned never to check the weather or try to hold a coherent conversation: I need all my attention for my wayward feet. Of late, I have begun to catch myself wondering how people can propel themselves without canes. With only one usable hand, I have to select my clothing with care not so much for style as for ease of ingress and egress, and even so, dressing can be laborious. I can no longer do fine stitchery, pick up babies, play the piano, braid my hair. I am immobilized by acute attacks of depression, which may or may not be physiologically related to MS but are certainly its logical concomitant.

These two elements, the plenty and the privation, are never pure, nor are the delight and wretchedness that accompany them. Almost every pickle that I get into as a result of my weakness and clumsiness—and I get into plenty—is funny as well as maddening and sometimes painful. I recall one May afternoon when a friend and I were going out for a drink after finishing up at school. As we were climbing into opposite sides of my car, chatting, I tripped and fell, flat and hard, onto the asphalt parking lot, my abrupt departure interrupting him in mid-sentence. "Where'd you go?" he called as he came around the back of the car to find me hauling myself up by the door frame. "Are you all right?" Yes, I told him, I was fine, just a bit rattly, and we drove off to find a shady patio and some beer. When I got home an hour or so later, my daughter greeted me with, "What have you done to yourself?" I looked down. One elbow of my white turtleneck with the green froggies, one knee of my white trousers, one white kneesock were blood-soaked. We peeled off the clothes and inspected the damage, which was nasty enough but not alarming. That part wasn't funny: The abrasions took a long time to heal, and one got a little infected. Even so, when I think of my friend talking earnestly, suddenly, to the hot thin air while I dropped from his view as though through a trap door, I find the image as silly as something from a Marx Brothers movie. . . .

Because I hate being crippled, I sometimes hate myself for being a cripple. Over the years I have come to expect—even accept—attacks of violent self-loathing. Luckily, in general our society no longer connects deformity and disease directly with evil (though a charismatic once told me that I have MS because a devil is in me) and so I am allowed to move largely at will, even among small children. But I'm not sure that this revision of attitude has been particularly helpful. Physical imperfection, even freed of moral disapprobation, still defines and violates the ideal, especially for women, whose confinement in their bodies as objects of desire is far from over. Each age, of course, has its ideal, and I doubt that ours is any better or worse than any other. Today's ideal woman, who lives on the glossy pages of dozens of magazines, seems to be between the ages of eighteen and twenty-five; her hair has body, her teeth flash white, her breath smells minty, her underarms are dry; she has a career but is still a fabulous cook, especially of meals that take less than twenty minutes to prepare; she does not ordinarily appear to have a husband or children; she is trim and deeply tanned; she jogs, swims, plays tennis, rides a bicycle, sails, but does not bowl; she travels widely, even to out-of-the-way places like Finland and Samoa, always in the company of the ideal man, who possesses a nearly identical set of characteristics. There are a few exceptions. Though usually white and often blonde, she may be black, Hispanic, oriental, or native American, so long as she is unusually sleek. She may be old, provided she is selling a laxative or is Lauren Bacall. If she is selling a detergent, she may be married and have a flock of strikingly messy children. But she is never a cripple.

Like many women I know, I have always had an uneasy relationship with my body. I was not a popular child, largely, I think now, because I was peculiar; intelligent, intense, moody, shy, given to unexpected actions and inexplicable notions and emotions. But as I entered adolescence, I believed myself unpopular because I was homely: my breasts too flat, my mouth too wide, my hips too narrow, my clothing never quite right in fit or style. I was not, in fact, particularly ugly, old photographs inform me, though I was well off the ideal; but I carried this sense of self-alienation with me into adulthood, where it regenerated in response to the depradations of MS. Even with my brace I walk with a limp so pronounced that, seeing myself on the videotape of a television program on the disabled, I couldn't believe that anything but an inchworm could make progress humping along like that. My shoulders droop and my pelvis thrusts forward as I try to balance myself upright, throwing my frame into a bony S. As a result of contractures, one shoulder is higher than the other and I carry one arm bent in front of me, the fingers curled into a claw. My left arm and leg have wasted into pipe-stems, and I try always to keep them covered. When I think about how my body must look to others, especially to men, to whom I have been trained to display myself, I feel ludicrous, even loathsome.

At my age, however, I don't spend much time thinking about my appearance. The burning egocentricity of adolescence, which assures one that all the world is looking all the time, has passed, thank God, and I'm generally too caught up in what I'm doing to step back, as I used to, and watch myself as though upon a stage. I'm also too old to believe in the accuracy of self-image. I know that I'm not a hideous crone, that in fact, when I'm rested, well dressed, and well made up, I look fine. The self-loathing I feel is neither physically nor intellectually substantial. What I hate is not me but a disease.

I am not a disease. . . .

All the same, if a cure were found, would I take it? In a minute. I may be cripple, but I'm only occasionally a loony and never a saint. Anyway, in my brand of theology God doesn't give bonus points for a limp. I'd take a cure; I just don't need one. A friend who also has MS startled me once by asking, "Do you ever say to yourself, 'Why me, Lord?' " "No, Michael, I don't," I told him, "because whenever I try, the only response I can think of is 'Why not?' " If I could make a cosmic deal, who would I put in my place? What in my life would I give up in exchange for sound limbs and a thrilling rush of energy? No one. Nothing. I might as well do the job myself. Now that I'm getting the hang of it.

The Voice of an Anorexic

Abra Fortune Chernik

In the 1980s and 1990s, excessive dieting and an obsession with thinness seemed so prevalent on college campuses that the media talked about an epidemic of eating disorders and how young American women were literally "at risk." As historian Joan Jacobs Brumberg has shown in *Fasting Girls: The Emergence of Anorexia Nervosa as a Modern Disease* (1988), anorexia had its cultural roots in Victorian America, long before the current cultural obsession with thinness. But broad social pressures, such as widespread dieting and widely dispersed media images of what women are supposed to look like, have made the disease much more prevalent today.

Public awareness of eating disorders, often first called the "starving disease," began to rise in the 1970s; when popular singer Karen Carpenter died of complications from the disease in 1983 at the age of thirty-two, images of her emaciated body were widely disseminated in magazines like *People.* The media often lumped together *anorexia nervosa* (literally "loss of appetite," or self-starving) and *bulimia* (binging on huge amounts of calories, then purging the body through vomiting or laxatives). Like the AIDS epidemic, it is a rare American family that does not know someone who has been touched by an eating disorder.

Abra Fortune Chernik's description of her battle against anorexia confirms the uneasy relationship that many women today have with their bodies. Her whole life was defined by what she ate and how much she weighed, and while she thought that she was gaining control over her body, in fact her eating disorder was taking control of her. Only after three months of hospitalization and two years of out-patient psychotherapy did she learn to accept her body as it was; she now shares her insights with audiences on college campuses, lecture tours, and in a screenplay she has written on the subject. But what about young women who can't afford treatment or don't respond? And what about the rest of us, who while not technically suffering from an eating disorder, still hate our bodies and believe that life would be better if we weighed ten pounds less? Abra Fortune Chernik is one of the lucky ones.

Growing up in New York City, I did not care about the feminist movement. Although I attended an all-girls high school, we read mostly male authors and studied the history of men. Embracing mainstream culture without question, I learned about womanhood from fashion magazines, Madison Avenue and Hol-

Source: Abra Fortune Chernik, "The Body Politic," in Barbara Findlen, ed., *Listen Up: Voices from the Next Feminist Generation* (Seattle: The Seal Press, 1995), pp. 76–81. Reprinted by permission of the publisher.

lywood. I dismissed feminist alternatives as foreign and offensive, swathed as they were in stereotypes that threatened my adolescent need for conformity.

Puberty hit late; I did not complain. I enjoyed living in the lanky body of a tall child and insisted on the title of "girl." If anyone referred to me as a "young woman," I would cry out, horrified, "Do not call me the *W* word!" But at sixteen years old, I could no longer deny my fate. My stomach and breasts rounded. Curly black hair sprouted in the most embarrassing places. Hips swelled from a once-flat plane. Interpreting maturation as an unacceptable lapse into fleshiness, I resolved to eradicate the physical symptoms of my impending womanhood.

Magazine articles, television commercials, lunchroom conversation, gymnastics coaches and write-ups on models had saturated me with diet savvy. Once I decided to lose weight, I quickly turned expert. I dropped hot chocolate from my regular breakfast order at the Skyline Diner. I replaced lunches of peanut butter and Marshmallow Fluff sandwiches with small platters of cottage cheese and cantaloupe. I eliminated dinner altogether and blunted my appetite with Tab, Camel Lights, and Carefree bubble gum. When furious craving overwhelmed my resolve and I swallowed an extra something, I would flee to the nearest bathroom to purge my mistake.

Within three months, I had returned my body to its preadolescent proportions and had manipulated my monthly period into drying up. Over the next five years, I devoted my life to losing my weight. I came to resent the body in which I lived, the body that threatened to develop, the body whose hunger I despised but could not extinguish. If I neglected a workout or added a pound or ate a bite too many, I would stare in the mirror and drown myself in a tidal wave of criticism. Hatred of my body generalized to hatred of myself as a person, and self-referential labels such as "pig," "failure" and "glutton" allowed me to believe that I deserved punishment. My self-hatred became fuel for the self-mutilating behaviors of the eating disorder.

As my body shrank, so did my world. I starved away my power and vision, my energy and inclinations. Obsessed with dieting, I allowed relationships, passions and identity to wither. I pulled back from the world, off of the beach, out of the sand. The waves of my existence ceased to roll beyond the inside of my skin.

And society applauded my shrinking. Pound after pound the applause continued, like the pounding ocean outside the door of my beach house.

The word "anorexia" literally means "loss of appetite." But as an anorexic, I felt hunger thrashing inside my body. I denied my appetite, ignored it, but never lost it. Sometimes the pangs twisted so sharply, I feared they would consume the meat of my heart. On desperate nights I rose in a flannel nightgown and allowed myself to eat an unplanned something.

No matter how much I ate, I could not soothe the pangs. Standing in the kitchen at midnight, spotlighted by the blue-white light of the open refrigerator, I would frantically feed my neglected appetite: the Chinese food I had not touched at dinner; ice cream and whipped cream; microwaved bread; cereal and chocolate milk; doughnuts and bananas. Then, solid sadness inside my gut, swelling agitation, a too-big meal I would not digest. In the bathroom I would rip off my shirt, tie up my hair, and prepare to execute the desperate ritual, again. I would ram the back of my throat with a toothbrush handle, crying, impatient, until the food rushed up. I would vomit until the toilet filled and I emptied, until I forgave myself, until I felt ready to try my life again. Standing up from my position over the toilet, wiping my mouth, I would believe that I was safe. Looking in the mirror through puffy eyes in a tumescent face, I would promise to take care of myself. Kept awake by the fast, confused beating of my heart and the ache in my chest, I would swear I did not miss the world outside. Lost within myself, I almost died.

By the time I entered the hospital, a mess of protruding bones defined my body, and the bones of my emaciated life rattled me crazy. I carried a pillow around because it hurt to sit down, and I shivered with cold in sultry July. Clumps of brittle hair clogged the drain when I showered, and blackened eyes appeared to sink into my head. My vision of reality wrinkled and my disposition turned mercurial as I slipped into starvation psychosis, a condition associated with severe malnutrition. People told me that I resembled a concentration camp prisoner, a chemotherapy patient, a famine victim or a fashion model.

In the hospital, I examined my eating disorder under the lenses of various therapies. I dissected my childhood, my family structure, my intimate relationships, my belief systems. I participated in experiential therapies of movement, art and psychodrama. I learned to use words instead of eating patterns to communicate my feelings. And still I refused to gain more than a minimal amount of weight.

I felt powerful as an anorexic. Controlling my body yielded an illusion of control over my life; I received incessant praise for my figure despite my sickly mien, and my frailty manipulated family and friends into protecting me from conflict. I had reduced my world to a plate of steamed carrots, and over this tiny kingdom I proudly crowned myself queen.

I sat cross-legged on my hospital bed for nearly two months before I earned an afternoon pass to go to the mall with my mother. The privilege came just in time; I felt unbearably large and desperately wanted a new outfit under which to hide gained weight. At the mall, I searched for two hours before finally discovering, in the maternity section at Macy's, a shirt large enough to cover what I perceived as my enormous body.

With an hour left on my pass, I spotted a sign on a shop window: "Body Fat Testing, $3.00." I suggested to my mother that we split up for ten minutes; she headed to Barnes & Noble, and I snuck into the fitness store.

I sat down in front of a machine hooked up to a computer, and a burly young body builder fired questions at me:

"Age?"

"Twenty-one."

"Height?"

"Five nine."

"Weight?"

"Ninety-nine."

The young man punched my statistics into his keyboard and pinched my arm with clippers wired to the testing machine. In a moment, the computer spit out my results. "Only ten percent body fat! Unbelievably healthy. The average for a woman your age is twenty-five percent. Fantastic! You're this week's blue ribbon winner."

I stared at him in disbelief. *Winner? Healthy? Fantastic?* I glanced around at the other customers in the store, some of whom had congregated to watch my testing, and I felt embarrassed by his praise. And then I felt furious. Furious at this man and at the society that programmed him for their ignorant approbation of my illness and my suffering.

"I am dying of anorexia," I whispered. "Don't congratulate me."

I spent my remaining month in the hospital supplementing psychotherapy with an independent examination of eating disorders from a social and political point of view. I needed to understand why society would reward my starvation and encourage my vanishing. In the bathroom, a mirror on the open door behind me reflected my backside in a mirror over the sink. Vertebrae poked at my skin, ribs hung like wings over chiseled hip bones, the two sides of my buttocks did not touch. I had not seen this view of myself before.

In writing, I recorded instances in which my eating disorder had tangled the progress of my life and thwarted my relationships. I filled three and a half Mead marble notebooks. Five years' worth of: *I wouldn't sit with Daddy when he was alone in the hospital because I needed to go jogging; I told Derek not to visit me because I couldn't throw up when he was there; I almost failed my comprehensive exams because I was so hungry; I spent my year at Oxford with my head in the toilet bowl; I wouldn't eat the dinner my friends cooked me for my nineteenth birthday because I knew they had used oil in the recipe; I told my family not to come to my college graduation because I didn't want to miss a day at the gym or have to eat a restaurant meal.* And on and on for hundreds of pages.

This honest account of my life dissolved the illusion of anorexic power. I saw myself naked in the truth of my pain, my loneliness, my obsessions, my craziness, my selfishness, my defeat. I also recognized the social and political implications of consuming myself with the trivialities of calories and weight. At college, I had watched as classmates involved themselves in extracurricular clubs, volunteer work, politics and applications for jobs and graduate schools. Obsessed with exercising and exhausted by starvation, I did not even consider joining in such pursuits. Despite my love of writing and painting and literature, despite ranking at the top of my class, I wanted only to teach aerobics. Despite my adolescent days as a loud-mouthed, rambunctious class leader, I had grown into a silent, hungry young woman.

And society preferred me this way: hungry, fragile, crazy. *Winner! Healthy! Fantastic!* I began reading feminist literature to further understand the disempowerment of women in our culture. I digested the connection between a nation of starving, self-obsessed women and the continued success of the patriarchy. I also cultivated an awareness of alternative models of womanhood. In the stillness of the hospital library, new voices in my life rose from printed pages to echo my rage and provide the conception of my feminist consciousness.

I had been willing to accept self-sabotage, but now I refused to sacrifice myself to a society that profited from my pain. I finally understood that my eating disorder symbolized more than "personal psychodynamic trauma." Gazing in the mirror at my emaciated body, I observed a woman held up by her culture as the physical ideal because she was starving, self-obsessed and powerless, a woman called beautiful because she threatened no one except herself. Despite my intelligence, my education, and my supposed Manhattan sophistication, I had believed all of the lies; I had almost given my life in order to achieve the sickly impotence that this culture aggressively links with female happiness, love and success. And everything I had to offer to the world, every tumbling wave, every thought and every passion, nearly died inside me.

As long as society resists female power, fashion will call healthy women physically flawed. As long as society accepts the physical, sexual and economic abuse of women, popular culture will prefer women who resemble little girls. Sitting in the hospital the summer after my college graduation, I grasped the absurdity of a nation of adult women dying to grow small.

Armed with this insight, I loosened the grip of the starvation disease on my body. I determined to recreate myself based on an image of a woman warrior. I remembered my ocean, and I took my first bite.

Gaining weight and getting my head out of the toilet bowl was the most political act I have ever committed. . . .

The Borderlands

Gloria Anzaldúa

Having opened this anthology with visions of the New Woman at the end of the nineteenth century, it seems appropriate to close it with a piece pointing toward a new consciousness for the twenty-first century. A borderlands consciousness arises wherever two (or more) cultures meet. The most vibrant contemporary examples of this new consciousness come from Latina writers. More than just a combination of English and Spanish, Latina literature reflects the realities of women who live in two cultures, affected by both but often feeling an outsider or alien in each.

Chicana *tejana* lesbian-feminist poet and writer Gloria Anzaldúa is one of the most powerful of these voices. Born and raised along the border between Texas and Mexico, she has been active in the migrant farm workers movement (her father was a sharecropper) as well as teaching Chicano Studies, Feminist Studies, and creative writing at various universities. Anzaldua was a coeditor of *This Bridge Called My Back: Writing by Radical Women of Color* (1981), an enormously influential anthology that brought together prose, poetry, personal narrative, and analysis from African-American, Asian-American, Latina, and Native American women. Her memoir, *Borderlands/La Frontera: The New Mestiza,* from which the final selection was excerpted, was published in 1987. In 1990 she edited *Making Faces, Making Soul/Haciendo Caras: Creative and Critical Perspectives by Women of Color* (1990).

The term *mestizo/mestiza* refers to a person of mixed Indian and Spanish blood. The new consciousness that Anzaldúa is talking about is very much women's consciouness, *una conciencia de mujer,* as well as a consciousness of ambiguity, constant flux, multiple identities, and divided loyalties. Most fundamentally it is a highly political consciousness, deeply aware of past injustices and looking to a future where we see reality and ourselves within a collective struggle that, as Anzaldúa hopes, could "bring us to the end of rape, of violence, of war."

Una lucha de fronteras / A Struggle of Borders

Because I, a *mestiza,*
    continually walk out of one culture
and into another,
    because I am in all cultures at the same time,
alma entre dos mundos, tres, cuatro,
    me zumba la cabeza con lo contradictorio.
Estoy norteada por todas las voces que me hablan
    simultáneamente.

The ambivalence from the clash of voices results in mental and emotional states of perplexity. Internal strife results in insecurity and indecisiveness. The mestiza's dual or multiple personality is plagued by psychic restlessness.

In a constant state of mental nepantilism, an Aztec word meaning torn between ways, *la mestiza* is a product of the transfer of the cultural and spiritual values of one group to another. Being tricultural, monolingual, bilingual, or multilingual, speaking a patois, and in a state of perpetual transition, the *mes-*

Source: Gloria Anzaldúa, *Borderlands/La Frontera: The New Mestiza,* © 1987 by Gloria Anzaldúa, pp. 77–81, 83–86, 87–88. Reprinted with permission from Aunt Lute Books. Notes have been deleted.

tiza faces the dilemma of the mixed breed: which collectivity does the daughter of a darkskinned mother listen to?

El choque de un alma atrapado entre el mundo del espíritu y el mundo de la técnica a veces la deja entullada. Cradled in one culture, sandwiched between two cultures, straddling all three cultures and their value systems, *la mestiza* undergoes a struggle of flesh, a struggle of borders, an inner war. Like all people, we perceive the version of reality that our culture communicates. Like others having or living in more than one culture, we get multiple, often opposing messages. The coming together of two self-consistent but habitually incompatible frames of reference causes *un choque,* a cultural collision.

Within us and within *la cultura chicana,* commonly held beliefs of the white culture attack commonly held beliefs of the Mexican culture, and both attack commonly held beliefs of the indigenous culture. Subconsciously, we see an attack on ourselves and our beliefs as a threat and we attempt to block with a counterstance.

But it is not enough to stand on the opposite river bank, shouting questions, challenging patriarchal, white conventions. A counterstance locks one into a duel of oppressor and oppressed; locked in mortal combat, like the cop and the criminal, both are reduced to a common denominator of violence. The counterstance refutes the dominant culture's views and beliefs, and, for this, it is proudly defiant. All reaction is limited by, and dependent on, what it is reacting against. Because the counterstance stems from a problem with authority—outer as well as inner—it's a step towards liberation from cultural domination. But it is not a way of life. At some point, on our way to a new consciousness, we will have to leave the opposite bank, the split between the two mortal combatants somehow healed so that we are on both shores at once and, at once, see through serpent and eagle eyes. Or perhaps we will decide to disengage from the dominant culture, write it off altogether as a lost cause, and cross the border into a wholly new and separate territory. Or we might go another route. The possibilities are numerous once we decide to act and not react.

A Tolerance for Ambiguity

These numerous possibilities leave *la mestiza* floundering in uncharted seas. In perceiving conflicting information and points of view, she is subjected to a swamping of her psychological borders. She has discovered that she can't hold concepts or ideas in rigid boundaries. The borders and walls that are supposed to keep the undesirable ideas out are entrenched habits and patterns of behavior; these habits and patterns are the enemy within. Rigidity means death. Only by remaining flexible is she able to stretch the psyche horizontally and vertically. *La mestiza* constantly has to shift out of habitual formations; from convergent thinking, analytical reasoning that tends to use rationality to move toward a single goal (a Western mode), to divergent thinking, characterized by movement away from set patterns and goals and toward a more whole perspective, one that includes rather than excludes.

The new *mestiza* copes by developing a tolerance for contradictions, a tolerance for ambiguity. She learns to be an Indian in Mexican culture, to be Mexican from an Anglo point of view. She learns to juggle cultures. She has a plural personality, she operates in a pluralistic mode—nothing is thrust out, the good the bad and the ugly, nothing rejected, nothing abandoned. Not only does she sustain contradictions, she turns the ambivalence into something else.

She can be jarred out of ambivalence by an intense, and often painful, emotional event which inverts or resolves the ambivalence. I'm not sure exactly how. The work takes place underground—subconsciously. It is work that the soul performs. That focal point or fulcrum, that juncture where the mestiza stands, is where phenomena tend to collide. It is where the possibility of uniting all that is separate occurs. This assembly is not one where severed or separated pieces merely come together. Nor is it a balancing of opposing powers. In attempting to work out a synthesis, the self has added a third element which is greater than the sum of its severed parts. That third element is a new consciousness—a mestiza consciousness—and though it is a source of intense pain, its energy comes from continual creative motion that keeps breaking down the unitary aspect of each new paradigm.

En unas pocas centurias, the future will belong to the mestiza. Because the future depends on the breaking down of paradigms, it depends on the straddling of two or more cultures. By creating a new mythos—that is, a change in the way we perceive reality, the way we see ourselves, and the ways we behave—*la mestiza* creates a new consciousness.

The work of *mestiza* consciousness is to break down the subject-object duality that keeps her a prisoner and to show in the flesh and through the images in her work how duality is transcended. The answer to the problem between the white race and the colored, between males and females, lies in healing the split that originates in the very foundation of our lives, our culture, our languages, our thoughts. A massive uprooting of dualistic thinking in the individual and collective consciousness is the beginning of a long struggle, but one that could, in our best hopes, bring us to the end of rape, of violence, of war.

La encrucijada / The Crossroads

> A chicken is being sacrificed
> > at a crossroads, a simple mound of earth
> a mud shrine for *Eshu,*
> > *Yoruba* god of indeterminacy,
> who blesses her choice of path.
> > She begins her journey.

Su cuerpo es una bocacalle. La mestiza has gone from being the sacrificial goat to becoming the officiating priestess at the crossroads.

As a *mestiza* I have no country, my homeland cast me out; yet all countries are mine because I am every woman's sister or potential lover. (As a lesbian I have no race, my own people disclaim me; but I am all races because there is the queer of me in all races.) I am cultureless because, as a feminist, I challenge the collective cultural/religious male-derived beliefs of Indo-Hispanics and Anglos; yet I am cultured because I am participating in the creation of yet another culture, a new story to explain the world and our participation in it, a new value system with images and symbols that connect us to each other and to the planet. *Soy un amasamiento,* I am an act of kneading, of uniting and joining that not only has produced both a creature of darkness and a creature of light, but also a creature that questions the definitions of light and dark and gives them new meanings.

We are the people who leap in the dark, we are the people on the knees of the gods. In our very flesh, (r)evolution works out the clash of cultures. It makes us crazy constantly, but if the center holds, we've made some kind of evolutionary step forward. *Neustra alma el trabajo,* the opus, the great alchemical work; spiritual *mestizaje,* a "morphogenesis," an inevitable unfolding. We have become the quickening serpent movement.

Indigenous like corn, like corn, the *mestiza* is a product of crossbreeding, designed for preservation under a variety of conditions. Like an ear of corn— a female seed-bearing organ—the *mestiza* is tenacious, tightly wrapped in the husks of her culture. Like kernels she clings to the cob; with thick stalks and strong brace roots, she holds tight to the earth—she will survive the crossroads. . . .

Que no se nos olvide los hombres

> *"Tú no sirves pa' nada—*
> you're good for nothing.
> *Eres pura vieja."*

"You're nothing but a woman" means you are defective. Its opposite is to be *un macho.* The modern meaning of the word "machismo," as well as the concept, is actually an Anglo invention. For men like my father, being "macho" meant being strong enough to protect and support my mother and us, yet being able to show love. Today's macho has doubts about his ability to feed and protect his family. His "machismo" is an adaptation to oppression and poverty and low self-esteem. It is the result of hierarchical male dominance. The Anglo, feeling inadequate and inferior and powerless, displaces or transfers these feelings to the Chicano by shaming him. In the Gringo world, the Chicano suffers from excessive humility and self-effacement, shame of self and self-deprecation. Around Latinos he suffers from a sense of language inadequacy and its accompanying discomfort; with Native Americans he suffers from a racial amnesia which ignores our common blood, and from guilt because the Spanish part of him took their land and oppressed them. He has an excessive compensatory hubris when around Mexicans from the other side. It overlays a deep sense of racial shame.

The loss of a sense of dignity and respect in the macho breeds a false machismo which leads him to put down women and even to brutalize them. Coexisting with his sexist behavior is a love for the mother which takes precedence over that of all others. Devoted son, macho pig. To wash down the shame of his acts, of his very being, and to handle the brute in the mirror, he takes to the bottle, the snort, the needle, and the fist.

Though we "understand" the root causes of male hatred and fear, and the subsequent wounding of women, we do not excuse, we do not condone, and we will no longer put up with it. From the men of our race, we demand the admission/acknowledgment/disclosure/testimony that they wound us, violate us, are afraid of us and of our power. We need them to say they will begin to eliminate their hurtful put-down ways. But more than the words, we demand acts. We say to them: We will develop equal power with you and those who have shamed us.

It is imperative that mestizas support each other in changing the sexist elements in the Mexican-Indian culture. As long as woman is put down, the Indian and the Black in all of us is put down. The struggle of the mestiza is above all a feminist one. As long as *los hombres* think they have to *chingar mujeres* and each other to be men, as long as men are taught that they are superior and therefore culturally favored over *la mujer,* as long as to be a *vieja* is a thing of derision, there can be no real healing of our psyches. We're halfway there—we have such love of the Mother, the good mother. The first step is to unlearn the *puta/virgen* dichotomy and to see *Coatlapopeuh-Coatlicue* in the Mother, *Guadalupe.*

Tenderness, a sign of vulnerability, is so feared that it is showered on women with verbal abuse and blows. Men, even more than women, are fettered to gender roles. Women at least have had the guts to break out of bondage. Only gay men have had the courage to expose themselves to the woman inside them and to challenge the current masculinity. I've encountered a few scattered and isolated gentle straight men, the beginnings of a new breed, but they are confused, and entangled with sexist behaviors that they have not been able to eradicate. We need a new masculinity and the new man needs a movement.

Lumping the males who deviate from the general norm with man, the oppressor, is a gross injustice. *Asombra pensar que nos hemos quedado en ese pozo oscuro donde el mundo encierra a las lesbianas. Asombra pensar que hemos, como femenistas y lesbianas, cerrado neustros corazónes a los hombres, a nuestros hermanos los jotos, desheredados y marginales como nosotros.* Being the supreme crossers of cultures, homosexuals have strong bonds with the queer white, Black, Asian, Native American, Latino, and with the queer in Italy, Australia and the rest of the planet. We come from all colors, all classes, all races, all time periods. Our role is to link people with each other—the Blacks with Jews with Indians with Asians with whites with extraterrestrials. It is to transfer ideas and information from one culture to another. Colored homosexuals have more knowledge of other cultures; have always been at the forefront (although sometimes in the closet) of all liberation struggles in this country; have suffered more injustices and have survived them despite all odds. Chicanos need to acknowledge the political and artistic contributions of their queer. People, listen to what your *jotería* is saying.

The mestizo and the queer exist at this time and point on the evolutionary continuum for a purpose. We are a blending that proves that all blood is intricately woven together, and that we are spawned out of similar souls.

Somos una gente

> *Hay tantísimas fronteras*
> *que dividen a la gente,*
> *pero por cada frontera*
> *existe también un puente.*
>   —Gina Valdés

Divided Loyalties. Many women and men of color do not want to have any dealings with white people. It takes too much time and energy to explain to the downwardly mobile, white middle-class women that it's okay for us to want to own "possessions," never having had any nice furniture on our dirt floors or "luxuries" like washing machines. Many feel that whites should help their own people rid themselves of race hatred and fear first. I, for one, choose to use some of my energy to serve as mediator. I think we need to allow whites to be our allies. Through our literature, art, *corridos,* and folktales we must share our history with them so when they set up committees to help Big Mountain Navajos or the Chicano farmworkers or *los Nicaragüenses* they won't turn people away because of their racial fears and ignorances. They will come to see that they are not helping us but following our lead.

Individually, but also as a racial entity, we need to voice our needs. We need to say to white society: We need you to accept the fact that Chicanos are different, to acknowledge your rejection and negation of us. We need you to own the fact that you looked upon us as less than human, that you stole our lands, our personhood, our self-respect. We need you to make public restitution: to say that, to compensate for your own sense of defectiveness, you strive for power over us, you erase our history and our experience because it makes you feel guilty—you'd rather forget your brutish acts. To say you've split yourself from minority groups, that you disown us, that your dual consciousness splits off parts of yourself, transferring the "negative" parts onto us. (Where there is persecution of minorities, there is shadow projection. Where there is violence and war, there is repression of shadow.) To say that you are afraid of us, that to put distance between us, you wear the mask of contempt. Admit that Mexico is your double, that she exists in the shadow of this country, that we are irrevocably tied to her. Gringo, accept the doppelganger in your psyche. By taking back your collective shadow the intracultural split will heal. And finally, tell us what you need from us. . . .

El día de la Chicana

> I will not be shamed again
> Nor will I shame myself.

I am possessed by a vision: that we Chicanas and Chicanos have taken back or uncovered our true faces, our dignity and self-respect. It's a validation vision.

Seeing the Chicana anew in light of her history. I seek an exoneration, a seeing through the fictions of white supremacy, a seeing of ourselves in our true guises and not as the false racial personality that has been given to us and that we have given to ourselves. I seek our woman's face, our true features, the positive and the negative seen clearly, free of the tainted biases of male dominance. I seek new images of identity, new beliefs about ourselves, our humanity and worth no longer in question.

Estamos viviendo en la noche de la Raza, un tiempo cuando el trabajo se hace a lo quieto, en el oscuro. El día cuando aceptamos tal y como somos y para en donde vamos y porque—ese día será el día de la Raza. Yo tengo el conpromiso de expresar mi visión, mi sensibilidad, mi percepción de la revalidación de la gente mexicana, su mérito, estimación, honra, aprecio, y validez.

On December 2nd when my sun goes into my first house, I celebrate *el día de la Chicana y el Chicano.* On that day I clean my altars, light my *Coatlalopeuh* candle, burn sage and copal, take *el baño para espantar basura,* sweep my house. On that day I bare my soul, make myself vulnerable to friends and family by expressing my feelings. On that day I affirm who we are.

On that day I look inside our conflicts and our basic introverted racial temperament. I identify our needs, voice them. I acknowledge that the self and the race have been wounded. I recognize the need to take care of our personhood, of our racial self. On that day I gather the splintered and disowned parts of *la gente mexicana* and hold them in my arms. *Todas las partes de nosotros valen.*

On that day I say, "Yes, all you people wound us when you reject us. Rejection strips us of self-worth; our vulnerability exposes us to shame. It is our innate identity you find wanting. We are ashamed that we need your good opinion, that we need your acceptance. We can no longer camouflage our needs, can no longer let defenses and fences sprout around us. We can no longer withdraw. To rage and look upon you with contempt is to rage and be contemptuous of ourselves. We can no longer blame you, nor disown the white parts, the male parts, the pathological parts, the queer parts, the vulnerable parts. Here we are weaponless with open arms, with only our magic. Let's try it our way, the mestiza way, the Chicana way, the woman way.

On that day, I search for our essential dignity as a people, a people with a sense of purpose—to belong and contribute to something greater than our *pueblo*. On that day I seek to recover and reshape my spiritual identity. *¡Aní-mate! Raza, a celebrar el día 'de la Chicana.*

SUGGESTIONS FOR FURTHER READING

Acosta-Belen, Edna, ed. *The Puerto Rican Woman.* New York, 1986.

Bataille, Gretchen M. and Kathleen Mullen Sands. *American Indian Women: Telling Their Lives.* Lincoln, NE, 1984.

Brownmiller, Susan. *Against Our Will: Men, Women, and Rape.* New York, 1975.

Cade, Toni, ed. *The Black Woman: An Anthology.* New York, 1970.

Cahn, Susan K. *Coming on Strong: Gender and Sexuality in Twentieth-Century Women's Sport.* New York, 1994.

Castillo-Speed, Lillian, ed. *Latina: Women's Voices from the Borderlands.* New York, 1995.

Chafe, William H. *Women and Equality: Changing Patterns in American Culture.* New York, 1977.

Cohen, Marcia. *The Sisterhood: The True Story of the Women Who Changed the World.* New York, 1988.

Collins, Patricia. *Black Feminist Thought: Knowledge, Consciousness, and the Politics of Empowerment.* Boston, 1990.

Crow Dog, Mary, and Richard Erdoes. *Lakota Woman.* New York, 1990.

Davis, Angela Y. *Women, Race, and Class.* New York, 1983.

D'Emilio, John, and Estelle Freedman. *Intimate Matters: A History of Sexuality in America.* New York, 1988.

Douglas, Susan J. *Where the Girls Are: Growing Up Female with the Mass Media.* New York, 1994.

Echols, Alice. *Daring to Be Bad: Radical Feminism in America, 1967–1975.* Minneapolis, 1989.

Eisenstein, Hester. *Contemporary Feminist Thought.* Boston, 1983.

Evans, Sara. *Personal Politics: The Roots of Women's Liberation in the Civil Rights Movement and the New Left.* New York, 1979.

——— and Barbara Nelson. *Wage Justice: Comparable Worth and the Paradox of Technocratic Reform.* Chicago, 1989.

Faderman, Lillian. *Odd Girls and Twilight Lovers: A History of Lesbian Life in 20th Century America.* New York, 1991.

Faludi, Susan. *Backlash: The Undeclared War Against American Women.* New York, 1991.

Findlen, Barbara, ed. *Listen Up: Voices from the Next Feminist Generation.* Seattle, 1995.

Fisher, Dexter, ed. *The Third Woman: Minority Women Writers of the United States.* Boston, 1980.

Freeman, Jo. *The Politics of Women's Liberation.* New York, 1975.

Friedan, Betty. *It Changed My Life.* New York, 1977.

Gabin, Nancy. *Feminism in the Labor Movement: Women and the United Auto Workers, 1935–1975.* Ithaca, 1990.

Garrow, David. *Liberty and Sexuality: The Right to Privacy and the Making of Roe v. Wade.* New York, 1994.

Gilligan, Carol. *In a Different Voice: Psychological Theory and Women's Development.* Cambridge, 1982.

Ginsburg, Faye. *Contested Lives: The Abortion Debate in an American Community.* Berkeley, 1989.

Harrison, Cynthia. *On Account of Sex: The Politics of Women's Issues, 1945–1968.* Berkeley, 1988.

Hartmann, Susan M. *From Margin to Mainstream: American Women and Politics Since 1960.* New York, 1989.

Hochschild, Arlie. *The Second Shift: Working Parents and the Revolution at Home.* New York, 1989.

Hoff-Wilson, Joan, ed. *Rites of Passage: The Past and Future of the ERA.* Bloomington, 1986.

hooks, bell. *Ain't I a Woman: Black Women and Feminism.* Boston, 1981.

———. *Feminist Theory: From Margin to Center.* Boston, 1984.

———. *Talking Back: Thinking Feminist, Thinking Black.* Boston, 1989.

Howe, Louise Kapp. *Pink Collar Workers: Inside the World of Women's Work.* New York, 1977.

Hull, Gloria, Patricia Bell Scott, and Barbara Smith. *But Some of Us Are Brave: Black Women's Studies.* Old Westbury, 1982.

Kennedy, Elizabeth Lapovsky, and Madeline D. Davis. *Boots of Leather, Slippers of Gold: The History of a Lesbian Community.* New York, 1993.

Klatch, Rebecca E. *Women of the New Right.* Philadelphia, 1987.

Linden-Ward, Blanche, and Carol Hurd Green. *American Women in the 1960s: Changing the Future.* New York, 1993.

Mandel, Ruth. *In the Running: The New Woman Candidate.* Boston, 1981.

Mansbridge, Jane J. *Why We Lost the ERA.* Chicago, 1986.

Mathews, Donald G., and Jane Sherron DeHart. *Sex, Gender, and the Politics of the ERA: A State and the Nation.* New York, 1990.

Mitchell, Juliet, and Ann Oakley. *What Is Feminism: A Reexamination.* New York, 1986.

Mora, Magdalena, and Adelaida Del Castillo. *Mexican-American Women in the United States: Struggles Past and Present.* Los Angeles, 1980.

Moraga, Cherrie, and Gloria Anzaldúa. *This Bridge Called My Back: Writings by Radical Women of Color.* Watertown, MA, 1981.

Morrison, Toni, ed. *Race-ing Justice, En-gendering Power: Essays on Anita Hill, Clarence Thomas, and the Construction of Social Reality.* New York, 1992.

Rosenberg, Rosalind. *Divided Lives: American Women in the Twentieth Century.* New York, 1992.

Rubin, Lillian. *Worlds of Pain: Life in the Working-Class Family.* New York, 1976.

Seifer, Nancy. *Nobody Speaks for Me! Self-Portraits of American Working Class Women.* New York, 1976.

Smith, Barbara, ed. *Home Girls: A Black Feminist Anthology.* New York, 1983.

Solinger, Rickie. *Wake Up Little Susie: Single Pregnancy and Race Before Roe v. Wade.* New York, 1992.

Stack, Carol B. *All Our Kin: Strategies for Survival in a Black Community.* New York, 1974.

Steinem, Gloria. *Outrageous Acts and Everyday Rebellions.* New York, 1983.

Wallace, Michele. *Black Macho and the Myth of the Superwoman.* New York, 1979.

Wandersee, Winifred. *On the Move: American Women in the 1970s.* Boston, 1988.

Williams, Patricia J. *The Alchemy of Race and Rights.* Cambridge, 1991.

Wolf, Naomi. *The Beauty Myth.* New York, 1991.

Zavella, Patricia. *Women's Work and Chicano Families: Cannery Workers of the Santa Clara Valley.* Ithaca, 1987.